A Critical Introduction

to Coaching & Mentoring

SAGE was founded in 1965 by Sara Miller McCune to support the dissemination of usable knowledge by publishing innovative and high-quality research and teaching content. Today, we publish over 900 journals, including those of more than 400 learned societies, more than 800 new books per year, and a growing range of library products including archives, data, case studies, reports, and video. SAGE remains majority-owned by our founder, and after Sara's lifetime will become owned by a charitable trust that secures our continued independence.

Los Angeles | London | New Delhi | Singapore | Washington DC | Melbourne

A Critical Introduction to Coaching & Mentoring

Debates, Dialogues & Discourses

David E Gray
Bob Garvey
David A Lane

Los Angeles | London | New Delhi
Singapore | Washington DC | Melbourne

SAGE

Los Angeles | London | New Delhi
Singapore | Washington DC | Melbourne

SAGE Publications Ltd
1 Oliver's Yard
55 City Road
London EC1Y 1SP

SAGE Publications Inc.
2455 Teller Road
Thousand Oaks, California 91320

SAGE Publications India Pvt Ltd
B 1/I 1 Mohan Cooperative Industrial Area
Mathura Road
New Delhi 110 044

SAGE Publications Asia-Pacific Pte Ltd
3 Church Street
#10-04 Samsung Hub
Singapore 049483

Editor: Susannah Trefgarne
Editorial assistant: Edward Coats
Production editor: Rachel Burrows
Marketing manager: Tamara Navaratnam
Cover design: Lisa Harper-Wells
Typeset by: C&M Digitals (P) Ltd, Chennai, India
Printed and bound in Great Britain by Ashford
Colour Press Ltd

Library of Congress Control Number: 2015951597

British Library Cataloguing in Publication data

A catalogue record for this book is available from
the British Library

MIX
Paper from
responsible sources
FSC® C011748
www.fsc.org

ISBN 978-1-4462-7227-5
ISBN 978-1-4462-7228-2 (pbk)

At SAGE we take sustainability seriously. Most of our products are printed in the UK using FSC papers and boards.
When we print overseas we ensure sustainable papers are used as measured by the PREPS grading system.
We undertake an annual audit to monitor our sustainability.

Contents

List of Figures and Tables

Figures

Tables

About the Authors

David E. Gray (BSc Econ., MA Ed., MSc, Cert Ed., PhD, FRSA) is Professor of Leadership and Organisational Behaviour at the University of Greenwich. His research interests, and publication record, include research methods, management learning (particularly coaching and mentoring), professional identity, action learning, reflective learning, management learning in small and medium-sized enterprises (SMEs) and the factors that contribute to SME success. He has published books (e.g., *Doing Research in the Real World*, 3rd edn, 2014) and articles on research methods, work-based learning, and coaching and mentoring. David has led a number of EU-funded research programmes, including one examining the impact of coaching on the resilience of unemployed managers in their job-searching behaviours and another on how action learning can sustain unemployed managers in starting their own business. He is currently completing a global survey into the professional identity of coaches.

Bob Garvey holds the Chair in Business Education at York St John Business School. He is a Fellow of the Higher Education Academy and of the Royal Society of Arts and is one of Europe's leading academic practitioners of mentoring and coaching. Bob has extensive experience in working across many sectors of social and economic activity. This includes both large and small business and the public and voluntary sectors. He has developed many training films, delivered international Webinars and developed interactive training materials on a variety of coaching and mentoring topics. He is a member of the European Mentoring and Coaching Council (EMCC) and the International Mentoring Association (IMA). He regularly contributes to the professional journal *Coaching at Work*, and in 2014 the journal presented him with a lifetime achievement award for contributions to mentoring. Also in 2014, Bob received the EMCC's Mentor of the Year award.

David A. Lane has coached in a wide range of organisations, including major consultancies, multinationals, and public sector and government bodies, and has contributed to research and the professional development of coaching. He also pioneered the international development of work-based Masters degrees for experienced coaches. He was

Chair of the British Psychological Society (BPS) Register of Psychologists Specialising in Psychotherapy and convened the European Federation of Psychologists Associations group on Psychotherapy. He has served on committees of the BPS, Chartered Institute of Personnel and Development (CIPD), Worldwide Association of Business Coaches (WABC) and EMCC, and is a founder member of the Global Coaching Community. His contributions to counselling psychology led to his being presented with the Senior Award of the BPS for 'Outstanding Scientific Contribution'. In 2009, he was honoured by the British Psychological Society for his Distinguished Contribution to Professional Psychology.

Preface

Mentoring activity is embedded in organisational and social life, and coaching has now come of age. Over the last decade both have developed from esoteric activity on the fringes of mainstream learning and development, to central elements of workplace learning in a huge range of organisations. Coaching and mentoring are now the norm in a majority of corporate organisations, and are widespread in the public and voluntary sectors. From being almost exclusively a phenomenon of the English-speaking Anglo-Saxon world, the use of coaching and mentoring has spread around the globe into a vast number of countries, cultures and language communities. Today, a burgeoning literature, both 'popular' and scholarly, bears testimony not only to the diffusion of coaching and mentoring throughout organisational life, but also to the level of interest in these important developmental activities.

The relationship between coaching and mentoring

The relationship between coaching and mentoring, long contentious, remains problematic, because the two are at the same time distinct yet closely related. Some have gone so far as to suggest that the behaviours of coaching and mentoring are so close to being identical that it no longer makes sense to speak of them as separate phenomena, and are using the term coach-mentoring. While there are great similarities between coaching and mentoring in terms of skills, techniques and processes, there are also differences. The differences relate mainly to the context in which the activity is performed and the perceived or actual purpose of the activity. Mentoring is often, but not always, a voluntary role within an organisational, social or voluntary sector context. It performs a psychosocial function and provides ongoing support within an educative or learning and development framework. Coaching is more often a paid, professional activity with the coach acting as a facilitator of learning and development within an organisational context.

While much professional literature is adamant that coaches do not perform a mentoring role, in practice they might, depending on the coachee's needs, and the mentoring literature clearly suggests that coaching may be part of the mentor's role.

The mentoring literature strongly recommends that the mentoring function works best outside of the line relationship due to the inherent power dynamics, but practices vary in different organisations. The topic of 'line manager' as coach has been on the organisational agenda since the late 1970s and, like mentoring, power dynamics can create difficulties for the coachee and coach alike. In our view, this issue is not tackled sufficiently and we seek to address the issue of 'power' in this book.

A further issue in which there is considerable debate around the similarities and differences is the question of 'whose agenda is it?' There is no easy answer to this question although both mentoring and coaching literature have contradictory views. These are often addressed by either the coaching literature making negative comments about mentoring or vice versa.

What makes this book different?

This book questions simplistic and prescriptive accounts of coaching and mentoring by holding up all featured models and frameworks to equal, dispassionate and research-informed scrutiny. It is important to strip away some of the unnecessary mystique and hype surrounding coaching and mentoring, but also to pinpoint the genuine contribution that these activities can make with the active informed commitment of all parties and stakeholders. For example, much is spoken and written of the importance of 'a coaching culture' or the 'mentoring organisation' and their contribution to organisational success. However, comparatively little attention is given to identifying genuinely critical factors in implementing and maintaining a culture of coaching and dealing with some of the inevitable tensions and conflicts that may ensue along the way.

The apparently simple exhortation to 'foster a coaching culture' or 'develop a mentoring organisation' masks a deep and far-reaching challenge to entrenched models and behaviours of leadership and management in all our organisations. Logically it implies that a coaching-mentoring style (person-centred, listening, driven by the individual, and non-directive) becomes the default management style to be modelled by senior management and emulated throughout all levels of the organisation. Yet the dominant discourse of rational, pragmatic management remains resistant to change and the power dynamics that this implies persist. The implications of a break-down of this discourse are revolutionary, and yet much that is written on the topic seems to underplay the seismic nature of this revolution within organisations. The seismic nature is often portrayed as superficial at best, and window-dressing at worst within much of the literature.

Most of the literature on coaching that has burgeoned over the last decade has a very promotional, almost proselytizing tone to it. This may have been appropriate during the period when coaching was finding a place in organizational life. Now, coaching activity, according to the evidence, has become accepted and established, and as such requires questioning and critique as well as explanation and promotion. Much of the current literature on coaching relentlessly ignores or lightly acknowledges the contribution of mentoring. Given the tendencies of both sets of literature to criticise each other, it is now time for longer-established research-based literature on mentoring to contribute to the coaching world, particularly in the area of culture development. This enables coaching to start from a more advanced place and together with the combined knowledge of research and practice in both fields, create new insights for practitioners.

This book also has many practical features built into it and these are presented in the 'coaching and mentoring way'. These include:

- Case studies
- Activities for individual and group learning extension
- Summaries at the end of each chapter
- Topics for discussion
- 'Questions that remain' at the end of each chapter
- Suggestions for further reading

We are passionate about coaching and mentoring but that passion does not exclude critique. Critical thinking is the lifeblood of development, for without it we are condemned to go around the same loops over and over again. We hope you enjoy the challenges within these pages.

Acknowledgements

David E. Gray

I would like to thank the many members of the professional coaching associations for their collaboration over many years. A group of practitioners dedicated to their own professional development in order to help others.

Bob Garvey

Thanks to Margaret for her support in this project and in life! Thanks also to my colleagues, David Gray and David Lane, for the spirit of cooperation and collaboration we found in writing this book.

David A. Lane

I would like to thank all my students and clients who have over the years kept me focused on practicalities, and to colleagues who have constantly challenged my thinking to keep me unbalanced and therefore growing as an academic and practitioner.

Part I

Introducing Coaching and Mentoring: Where do I start?

1

Why Coaching and Mentoring? Why Now?

Keywords

Discourse, social context, history

Chapter objectives

After reading this chapter, you will be able to:

- Understand and appreciate the complex history of mentoring and coaching
- Appreciate that they are both social constructions
- Understand that a single definition is not possible
- Elucidate some arguments for the development of mentoring and coaching in modern society
- Engage in critical debate about coaching and mentoring

Introduction

In this chapter, we explore the historical basis of both coaching and mentoring through an analysis of their historical discourses and contexts. We consider the implications of these discourses on modern constructions of coaching and mentoring. The chapter goes on to consider the reasons behind the exponential growth of coaching and mentoring in recent times, and compares and contrasts current practice in a range of contexts. Finally, we present arguments for the integration of the traditions of coaching and mentoring while maintaining their distinctiveness.

The notion of discourse

The notion of 'discourse' is important in the study of people and society. Discourses are basically how people talk about things, and they are ways of supporting and transmitting meaning through social contexts. Bruner (1996) suggests that people have two main ways of developing a sense of meaning and organising their thoughts:

> One seems more specialized for treating of physical 'things' the other for treating of people and their plights. They are conventionally thought of as logical-scientific thinking and narrative thinking. (Bruner, 1996: 39)

To build on Bruner, narratives involve language, and language, as a vehicle for communicating meaning, plays an important part in human sense-making: 'Language is the primary motor of a culture,' and: 'Language is culture in action' (Webster, 1980: 206). It is also important to understand that:

> language is never 'innocent'; it is not a neutral medium of expression. Discourses are expressions of power relation and reflect the practices and the positions that are tied to them. (Layder, 1994: 97)

So, we need to proceed with caution. While discourses may contain 'truths', they may also contain 'lies' and deceptions (Gabriel, 2004). This apparent paradox is important. At the heart of discourse is interpretation, and it is very clear that one person's interpretation is not the same as another's. Any interpretation, therefore, has to be made by taking into account the social context in which it is employed. Within coaching and mentoring, as dialogic-learning activities, the notions of discourse and meaning are of critical importance. Discourse, as employed in the range of social contexts in which coaching and mentoring take place, is a major theme in this book – a volunteer mentor in a scheme for young offenders, for example, may take a very different view on mentoring to a paid executive coach working in a large corporation and vice versa!

Tracking the discourse in mentoring

Case Study 1.1 is an abbreviated version of the original Ancient Greek poem the *Odyssey*. Written by Homer as an epic poem, it tells the tale of King Odysseus, the King of Ithaca. Within the main poem is a subplot which explores the implications of Odysseus' absence for his son, Telemachus. The poem starts this chapter to explore the ancient roots of mentoring and their meaning and to illustrate the impact of the social context on the interpretation of the narrative.

Case study 1.1

The original story

King Odysseus is believed to be killed in the Trojan Wars. During his ten-year absence many unsuitable suitors visit his wife in the hope of gaining her hand and more importantly acquiring Odysseus' fortune. Telemachus, Odysseus' son mixes with these ill-bred visitors and learns uncouth ways.

Athene, the goddess of civil administration, war and wisdom wants to protect the stability and wealth of Ithaca. She sees Telemachus as key to the achievement of this aim. Telemachus, however, has his problems in that he is young, immature, lacking in experience and has modelled himself on the wasters who have been visiting his mother. Athene, realising that she must offer some Godly assistance to the young man, agrees with Zeus, her father, that she will go to help Telemachus to enhance his reputation.

Telemachus has a dilemma: he doesn't know if his father is alive or dead and this creates inaction. Athene appears in the male form to Telemachus as first Mentes (a stranger – an honoured title in Ancient Greece) and then as Mentor, his father's main assistant. Athene sets the young man some challenges. As Mentes, she comes to the palace as a beggar to test Telemachus' character. Greek custom has it that a stranger should be welcomed into the household and given sustenance. Contrary to Ancient Greek etiquette, the suitors keep Mentes waiting at the door. When Telemachus discovers this error, he is horrified and immediately makes amends. This incident enables Telemachus to recognise his true role and responsibility as a potential king and he immediately distances himself from his mother's suitors. Telemachus and Mentes discuss the political implications of his dilemma about his father.

Athene also tests the young man's political acumen and his courage. She finds him wanting. As Mentes, she tries to inspire him with some advice by suggesting he 'grows up' and behaves in a way that befits his large frame and status. Mentes helps

(Continued)

(Continued)

Telemachus to deal with the suitors and suggests he undertakes a voyage to learn the truth about his father. This, Athene hopes, will develop his leadership potential and develop his courage so that he will be an aide to his father when he returns.

As Mentes, Athene has established Telemachus' potential and provided the vehicle for him to develop it. In her next guise as Mentor, she builds on this and provides him with some specific leadership development opportunities and political support. Mentor helps Telemachus persuade the Ithacans to rise up against their enemies and to support his quest for news of Odysseus. The young man notices the lack of self-interest in Mentor and sees that his only motive is to protect the absent king's interests. Mentor enables the voyage to happen by a series of interventions. In one, he (she) takes the form of Telemachus in order to recruit the sailors needed for the voyage. In another, he (she) puts enemies to sleep so as to protect him from ambush.

Mentor introduces Telemachus to King Nestor and facilitates the relationship and later delegates his (her) responsibility for Telemachus to Nestor. King Nestor is favoured by the Gods and it is a great honour for Telemachus to be placed in his care. King Nestor, together with his son, takes on the guiding role from Mentor.

Eventually, Odysseus returns and joins with his son to fight off and violently punish the suitors and various other traitors. Athene, her task completed, turns herself into a swallow and flies into the rafters taking no part in the final battle.

Questions

1. What do you see as the key elements of the story?
2. What elements of the Ancient Greek context influence events in the story?
3. How far does our modern context influence the interpretation of this story?

The Middle Ages and on …

The first recorded use of the term 'mentoring' in the English language was in 1750 in a letter from Lord Chesterfield to his son. There are no direct references to mentoring in any literature that we can discover until the Middle Ages and here the references are associative rather than direct. However, some (Darwin, 2000; Murray, 2001) link mentoring to the practice of apprenticeships or knight and squire relationships. Nevertheless, accounts of the period show that these relationships were not called 'mentoring' but they were often one-to-one and they could be exploitative and manipulative. Often, the master craftsman would use the apprentice as a source of cheap labour with the promise of teaching the particular trade. The master craftsman would often pass the apprentice's work off as his own or keep them under tight controls by restricting food and payment. The apprentice's options were clearly limited under these circumstances.

This behaviour could be viewed as 'discourses of exploitation' or 'discourses of power' and given the above discussion on discourse, this may be one source of some modern-day negative perceptions of mentoring (see, for example, Rosinski, 2004; Nielsen and Nørreklit, 2009). Clearly, this is not an 'innocent' discourse! Of course, there were also positive accounts associated with apprenticeships of this period and craft guilds played a role in attempting to regulate bad practice. However, it is interesting that modern accounts of mentoring which make the association to apprenticeships tend to take a positive perspective. Perhaps this is because they are hoping to add historical credibility to the concept of modern mentoring and thus create a positive discourse.

Moving on, Eby et al. (2007: 7) suggest that 'the concept of mentoring' (but not the word itself) is discussed in Shakespeare's *Much Ado about Nothing*. This is a curious association and perhaps another attempt to establish an illustrious and time-honoured background to mentoring. Perhaps it is part of the discourse that mentoring is nothing new and not a passing fad due to its historical roots – a 'mentoring is as old as the hills discourse'. The play itself is about the interplay of the sexes. It turns the tables on the traditional female sex-role stereotyping of the period. It is also about infidelity, deception, mistaken identity, and the title itself suggests that the society of the day made a great fuss about things that are insignificant – the battle of the sexes.

Whether or not there is a potential interpretation that the mentoring concept features here, Shakespeare does not use the term 'mentor' in any of his plays. In fact, no writers of the Elizabethan period use the term. That is not to say that they were unfamiliar with the concept. The basis of education, for those fortunate enough to receive it, was Latin and Greek and, therefore, the potential for such ideas to influence writings was present. According to Ben Johnson, Shakespeare's contemporary, he had little Latin and less Greek! However, it is not until the eighteenth century that the mentoring concept really took hold in Europe.

The eighteenth-century development of mentoring

In Europe during the eighteenth-century, mentoring as an educational process started to develop. This may have been due to the development of an education system with a continuance of the Latin and Greek focus. The first to write about mentoring was Fénelon, Archbishop of Cambrai and later tutor to Louis XIV's heir. He developed the mentoring theme of the *Odyssey* in *Les Aventures de Télémaque*. This work had a major impact on France and England in the understanding of mentoring, its role in learning, leadership development and education. However, at the time, the royal court viewed Fénelon's work as a political manifesto for the establishment of a monarchy-led republic in France. Fénelon dared to suggest that leadership could be developed and was not a divine right. Louis XIV was unhappy about this suggestion and Fénelon was sacked. However, Fénelon may well have been at the source of the idea that leadership is something which people can learn. His work is probably the start of the notion of one-to-one developmental conversations with experiential learning at its heart. Evidence for this claim may be found in other eighteenth-century writings on mentoring and learning by Rousseau (1762) in his book *Emile*, Caraccioli (1760) in *The True Mentor, or, An Essay on the Education of Young People in Fashion* and Honoria's (1793; 1796) *The Female Mentor*. These all refer directly to Fénelon's mentoring model of reflective questioning, listening, challenge and support. Fénelon's work was translated into English the year after its publication in French and became a European bestseller and, according to Clarke, 'pedagogues of every sort found the book a god-send' (1984: 202).

In other writings, Rousseau claimed that the perfect class size for education was one-to-one and both Caraccioli and Honoria thanked Fénelon in their introductions for 'showing them the way'. As a precursor to the discourse of holistic development within mentoring, Caraccioli suggests that mentoring was about both the 'heart' and the 'mind'. In the main, these authors were discussing one-to-one male relationships but Honoria introduced group mentoring for women. Her books are accounts of educational conversations with the mentor, Amanda. Topics included comparative religion, great women from history and philosophical arguments about 'truth'.

Lord Byron made use of the term 'mentor' in three poems describing the mentor as 'stern' and 'flexible', and Lord Chesterfield in his letters to his son referred to the mentor as 'friendly', suggesting that a mentor may have different personas.

The eighteenth century seems to be the modern source of the mentoring that we know about today and these works seem to have established a discourse about mentoring which locates it in an educational setting. This confirms Clarke's assertion that:

> by the early eighteenth century and unlike Télémaque, who remained his strictly fictive status, Mentor had entered both French and English as a common noun. (1984: 202)

More modern developments in mentoring

In 1976, in *Passages: Predictable Crises of Adult Life*, Gail Sheehy discusses adult development from a female perspective. She noted that mentoring relationships were not as common among women as they were for men. In her revised edition, *New Passages: Mapping your Life across Time* (1996), she adds developmental maps on both male and female development and notes that mentoring had become more common among women.

In Levinson et al. (1978) *The Seasons of a Man's Life*, a longitudinal study, there are multiple references to mentoring in relation to male development. Levinson describes 'mentor' as someone, often half a generation older, who helps accelerate the development of another. He also refers to mentoring as a 'love' relationship. This may be suggesting that the learning relationship requires certain human attributes, for example trust, respect and honesty, for it to develop and become productive. Levinson claimed that mentoring could accelerate maturation and his work was probably the catalyst for a rapid growth of career-progression-based mentoring in the USA during the late 1970s and early 1980s.

David Clutterbuck brought this modern concept of mentoring to the UK in 1985 with the publication of his book *Everyone Needs a Mentor*. This was a case study book inspired by David's experience in America. It is still in print and is an all-time best-selling business book. Many publications and a substantial body of research followed these milestones on both sides of the Atlantic and mentoring became established in developed economies.

In 1983 in the USA, Kathy Kram emerged as the first substantial mentoring researcher. Her main contribution is that mentoring activity performs a 'psychosocial function' (ibid.: 616); the mentee is socialised into a specific social context and develops self-insight and psychological well-being. Kram (ibid.) also articulated developmental phases in mentoring relationships.

With reference to the affective side of learning, Zaleznik (1977: 78) argues that leadership ability is developed through intense and often intuitive mentoring relationships which contribute to the development of a deep insight into the effective 'emotional relationships' of leaders.

Further support for emotional and psychological development through mentoring is found among many writers. For example, Berman and West (2008), Clawson (1996), Mullen (1994), Smith (1990) and Zey (1984), all discuss the link between mentoring and emotional development. Others, like Levinson et al. (1978), link the motivation to mentor with Erikson's (1978) psychological concept of 'generativity' – the desire to bring on the next generation. McAuley (2003) employs the psychological concepts of transference and counter-transference in order to provide deeper insight into the power dynamics that may be at play between mentor and mentee relationships. Garvey (2006b) argues that the intention or mentoring is not 'therapy' but its affect can be 'therapeutic' and he links the development of the mentees to Levinson et al.'s (1978) framework of age-related transition and Jung's (1958) psychological concept of individuation.

Clutterbuck and Lane (2004) suggest that there are two models of mentoring. In the USA, the emphasis is on 'career sponsorship', whereas in Europe it is 'developmental'. There is evidence (Kram and Chandler, 2005) that mentoring in the USA is shifting to include a more holistic perspective on development. Research in America shows that the 'sponsorship' perspective brings with it many advantages for mentee, mentor and their host organisation. Carden (1990) and Allen et al. (2004) note that on the positive side, sponsorship mentoring activity can enhance knowledge, emotional stability, problem-solving, decision-making, creativity, opportunity, leadership abilities in individuals, and organisational morale and productivity. However, Ragins (1989, 1994), Carden (1990), Ragins and Cotton (1991), and Ragins and Scandura (1999) show through their research that career sponsorship mentoring can also be exclusive and divisive, encourage conformity among those with power, maintain the status quo and reproduce exploitative and hierarchical structures. This can lead to relationships becoming abusive or simply breaking down.

By contrast, research into the developmental model of mentoring in the UK (Clutterbuck and Lane, 2004; Garvey, 1995; Rix and Gold, 2000) shows that similar benefits are derived from mentoring as in the sponsorship model but with less examples of abuse or relationship breakdown. However, there are inevitably problems with some of these discourses.

Problematic discourses in mentoring .

There are curiously uncontested problems of the mentoring model in Homer as well as many negative connotations with mentoring in later writings. It is possible that some of these negative perceptions persist today. One is the sexism of Ancient Greece! Athene could not have appeared as herself because women were viewed as second-class citizens at that time. Interestingly, some modern writings on mentoring, particularly from the USA, present male-dominated models of mentoring. Another issue is the brutal violence in the ancient story, particularly the treatment of Telemachus' enemies, for example, the final act of bloody vengeance is taken on the suiters and the women of the court is described in graphic detail. Telemachus and Ódyssess cut off their body parts and feed them to the dogs whilst they are still alive and then they string up the women on a line.

Not quite the model of human resources development practice today! However, themes of revenge and violence were commonplace in Ancient Greek writings. Further, Roberts (1999) argues that the interpretations in modern writings of the link to Homer's Mentor are incorrect and misleading. He suggests that it is in Fénelon that we find the true base of the character of mentor. Caraccioli (1760) provides a model of mentoring that involves 'reprimand' and 'correction'. These words have an authoritarian ring to them but, again, the context of the period made these acceptable and made the meaning different to today.

A nineteenth-century association with mentoring is found in George du Maurier's 1894 novel *Trilby*. Svengali is the name of his fictional character: a stereotype of an evil hypnotist. The novel was a sensation in its day and the image of Svengali still persists in, for example, the early twentieth century in many silent film versions of the story and in later talking pictures. The word 'Svengali' has entered the language to mean a person who, with sinister intent, manipulates another into doing what is desired. It is frequently used for any kind of coach or mentor who seems to want to dominate a performer.

In recent history, mentoring within the community or societal contexts has had a dominant discourse of 'non-judgemental', 'voluntary', 'support' and 'encourage' as key qualities and behaviours within the relationship. However, governments on both sides of the Atlantic were the main drivers of mentoring policy and therefore the holders of the power and the finance! In the UK in 2001, for example, Gordon Brown, the then Chancellor of the Exchequer, invested £13 million in youth mentoring schemes across the country. This funding was matched by the fast-food chain McDonald's. Governments and private sector companies do not invest money without an expectation of a return.

Freedman (1999) suggested that the US Government started its 'Big Brothers and Big Sisters' youth mentoring scheme in a 'fervor without infra-structure'. His argument was that government-funded youth mentoring was politically motivated and tapped into the US middle-class fears of the 'underclass', providing a 'quick fix' to social problems. He argued that it produced a 'heroic conception of social policy' (ibid.: 21). Other studies (Grossman and Tierney, 1998) suggest that youth mentoring in the USA made a positive difference to the mentee. However, they also found that mentors who focused on the prescribed goals of the funders rather than those of the mentee had much less success. Colley (2003a) found the same in her studies in the UK.

The question of whose agenda is being played out in government-sponsored schemes is part of the discourse of power. Their arguments are not necessarily based on any form of 'truth' position but, as Garmezy suggests, on a 'false sense of security in erecting prevention models that are founded more on values than on facts' (1982: xix).

Activity 1.1   Four case examples of mentoring

This activity section is designed to help the reader consider some key elements of modern-day mentoring activity. These are drawn from an organisation where mentoring is actively taking place. Mentoring was established to assist with the business growth strategy. This involved growth by acquisition. Mentoring is employed to help integrate newly hired employees and to support leadership development for the future. The following four case vignettes of two mentees and two mentors illustrate what can happen in mentoring, the potential gains, and the special character of the mentoring relationship.

(Continued)

(Continued)

Case 1 Jackie (mentee, lead analyst, private sector)

I've been working with my mentor for well over a month now, and I really can't put into words how much I've benefited from the experience. I am so new to the management role, and he has so much experience to draw on. He doesn't tell me what to do, but he listens and gets me to challenge my own preconceived ideas and biases. It's been fantastic having that sounding board. He is truly objective and his work is separate enough from mine that it just feels safe and like my own mini version of management training. He's very positive and has a great attitude about work, people and life in general, and that's been an example for me. I really am the biggest advocate of the programme and I think it's great that it is available in our business. I would strongly encourage everyone to join the programme, no matter what their role is.

Questions

1. What is the purpose of mentoring in Jackie's case?
2. What are the key skills of mentoring as described by Jackie?
3. What are the key characteristics of Jackie's mentor?

Note: some possible answers to these and the following questions are given at the end of this chapter.

Case 2 John (mentee, international manager, private sector)

For me, having a mentor is like a big support system within the company, and the feeling of someone there to hear all your concerns and to provide constructive advice that adds more value to that process. We share different time zones, and it's always challenging when the person is not just in front of you. However, in spite of that, my mentor has made sure we speak at least once in a month, and I have started appreciating the process, which probably keeps me motivated day after day. Overall, we have built a good relationship where I share my thoughts about the work and the company. I feel mentoring helps me to keep my head cool and not take hasty decisions during those tough times.

Questions

1. What is the main purpose of mentoring for John?
2. What are the main outcomes of mentoring for John?

Case 3 Fatima (mentor, scientific consultant, private sector)

As a mentor, I see the primary benefit is for my mentee but I am happy to support this as I believe this is generally a good thing to do … which is to build a strong community within the business and develop company advocates for those that do move on. What has worked well for me is the regular contact and open dialogue. If I had a mentee again, I would try to meet them earlier, if that's not practical, then I will use our video conference facility. I have benefited by better understanding how different people view life and the business.

Questions

1. What does Fatima see as her function as a mentor?
2. What is Fatima's main skill as a mentor?
3. What purpose does she feel mentoring plays in the business?

Case 4 Bob (mentor, country manager, private sector)

Working with someone and being a support and help in their development has been personally very rewarding. It is also challenging, as my mentee will often ask questions about issues and situations that I have not considered before. Thinking about these can be a help to my own role. As a manager, it is helpful to see the perspective of someone being managed. Our relationship has been fairly informal, which has been good. However, this level of informality may not always work best; it depends on the two individuals involved. Both should be aware of the type of relationship they are trying to develop. Overall, I have found this a very positive experience.

Questions

1. What does Bob gain by being a mentor?
2. What does Bob see as a central feature of mentoring?

To conclude the section on the history of mentoring and its development, the following is a summary of key discourse themes:

- Mentoring's roots are educational
- Mentoring supports psychosocial development
- Learning is fundamentally based on critical reflections of experience
- Leadership is learnable and involves challenges and opportunities to practice and reflect
- Leadership development is more than a function of the individual – there are wider societal and political interests to be served
- Human relationships built on trust and mutual respect offer important contexts for learning
- Power dynamics play a role in shaping meaning and can be both helpful and destructive
- There are three types of mentor – stern, friendly and flexible
- Motivation to mentor may be linked to the concept of 'generativity'
- Skills include listening, questioning, challenge and support
- Mentoring has been adopted with zealotry fervour, particularly in the public sector, to tackle social problems

Tracking the discourses of coaching

There is much speculation in the coaching literature about its origins. Coaching activity is derived from a similar but not so ancient a tradition as mentoring. In modern practice, it has many more variations than mentoring. However, some claim (McDermott and Jago, 2005; Zeus and Skiffington, 2000) that coaching is derived from prehistory on the basis that prehistoric peoples 'must have' helped each other to improve their hunting and stone-throwing skills! This argument resonates with Erikson's (1978) 'generativity' concept mentioned above in the mentoring section but these are speculative arguments with clear associations with 'performative' learning.

Some coaching writers (Brock, 2014; Brunner, 1998; de Haan, 2008; Hughes, 2003) link coaching to Socratic teachings and the Socratic method. This is an Ancient Greek association. Essentially, the purpose of Socratic dialogue was the pursuit of self-knowledge and truth. It was a stylised dialectic process involving a debate and inquiry between people of opposing viewpoints. The Socratic method takes, for example, a generic 'truth' and dissects it with questions to test consistency and coherence. The process makes it necessary to take a 'devil's advocate' position to defend one point of view against another. The Socratic method was also a competitive process where one participant sought to weaken the position of the other in order to strengthen their own.

Others (Brock, 2014; Starr, 2002; Wilson, 2007) claim that coaching is derived from sport and historical references from the nineteenth century cited below support this idea. Brock (2014) also argues that coaching has many other antecedents which lead back to the nineteenth century. These include: philosophy, biology (neuroscience), anthropology, linguistics, psychology, sociology, education and economics. She further links coaching to both East Asian and Western philosophies in a highly complex web of relationships of ideas.

Wildflower (2013) argues that the notion behind coaching started with the nineteenth-century author and political reformer, Samuel Smiles. In a speech made in 1845, Smiles stated that:

> Every human being has a great mission to perform, noble faculties to cultivate, a vast destiny to accomplish. He should have the means of education, and of exerting freely all the powers of his godlike nature. (Smiles, 1956: 71)

His famous book *Self-Help* set the tone for a kind of individualistic economic reform that placed learning and development at its centre and, despite its radical reforming theme, Smiles became, perhaps unfairly, a favoured symbol of the right of the UK Conservative Party (Jarvis, 1997) for his advocacy of individual responsibility and criticism of excessive government interventions. Arguably, coaching today could be viewed, with its performative leanings, to be heavily influenced by an economic success discourse based on individualism.

Wildflower's (2013) book convincingly tracks and argues links between 'success' in a capitalist world and ideas found in the self-help notion (Smiles, Carnegie); human potential movement (Esalen Institute); person centeredness (Rogers); personal responsibility (Erhard); sports psychology (Gallwey); various branches of psychology (Freud, Jung, Reich, Olalla, Perls, Erikson, Berne); psychometrics; sociology and identity – a complex historical web, indeed.

However, the first recorded use of the word 'coaching' in relation to a 'helping' activity in the English language was in 1849 in Thackeray's novel *Pendennis*. Here, coaching is used in connection with helping to improve academic attainment at Oxford University.

Unlike the use of the word 'mentoring' in the eighteenth century which was found in educational treatise, the word 'coaching' was used in the popular press. It is found in newspaper, magazine and journal articles throughout the nineteenth century – for example, Smedley (1866); *London Evening Standard* (1867); *Grantham Journal* (1885); and *Cambridge Daily News* (1889). This suggests that coaching was a much more popularist activity, defined by the varied social contexts in which it was found. For example, coaching is referred to in the press as something associated with improved performance in boating and rowing, learning scientific procedures and craft skills, improving parenting skills, improving academic attainment, teaching the defence of wicket in cricket – the main discourse of the period being: 'performance improvement in a skilled activity'. Its process seemed to broadly involve observation, questions, demonstration, performance and feedback. In the main, it was the coach who held the agenda as the person who 'knows'. There do not appear to be any works which directly use the term 'coaching' as a 'helping activity' that predate the nineteenth century.

More modern developments in coaching

A central discourse of more modern developments in coaching continues to be 'performance improvement'. Despite the historical associations with coaching, others also link the beginning of modern business coaching to Timothy Gallwey's (1974) book *The Inner Game of Tennis*. Located in the sports context, Gallwey focuses on the mental state of the sportsperson and not on the skills of the sport. His emphasis is on the player reaching a state of 'relaxed concentration'. The thesis of 'the inner game' is to enable players to discover their true potential. Psychological discourse threads run through the book, involving notions such as visualisation, non-judgemental observation and trust. The 'inner game' offers insight into the psychology of human performance and resonates with various approaches to therapy.

In 1979, Megginson and Boydell published the manual *A Manager's Guide to Coaching*. They define coaching as: 'a process in which a manager, through direct discussion and guided activity, helps a colleague to solve a problem, or to do a task better than would otherwise have been the case' (ibid.: 5). In this manual, coaching is located in the workplace as a management activity focused on performance improvement.

In 1992, John Whitmore first published *Coaching for Performance*. This work is now in its third edition.This featured the GROW (Goals, Reality, Options and Wrap up) model of coaching. In this work, performance is again a strong driver of coaching and the discourse of 'goals' as a driver of performance is central. Arguably, it is *Coaching for Performance* that was the vanguard of much of what we understand coaching to be today and whilst there are many variations of practice, this book is probably the most influential.

We conclude from this brief historical analysis that coaching has emerged from a variety of social contexts and spread by social means. It is therefore a strongly social activity, drawing on broad intellectual frameworks. Modern coaching practices are dynamic and contextual, with coaching appearing as an alternative approach to thinking about performance. Its roots are in education, sport, psychology and psychotherapy.

The research base of coaching, however, is thin to date. The earliest account seems to be in the research of Coleman Griffith from 1918. He later headed a research unit at the University of Illinois from 1926, which included the aim 'towards increasing the effectiveness of coaching methods'. He published *Psychology of Coaching* in 1926. In 1937, research by Gorby was looking at coaching for performance improvement with a focus on waste reduction and profit enhancement. According to Grant and Cavanagh (2004), in a period of more than 50 years from 1937 onwards, there were only 50 papers or PhD dissertations cited in the PsychInfo and DAI databases. The period 1995 to 1999 saw an increase in output, with 29 papers or PhD dissertations published, and between 2000 and 2003 there were 49 citations.

The British Library theses database of PhDs in UK universities cites a total of 69 works on non-sports-connected coaching between 2003 and 2015.

Problematic discourses in coaching

During the nineteenth century, the use of coaching in, for example, rowing, was viewed as unsporting because it provided direct help to the rowers in the form of instructions being shouted from the towpath. This form of directive coaching in sport is still evident. For example, Jones and Wallace (2005) suggest that: 'Despite its complex nature, associated literature has traditionally viewed coaching from a rationalistic perspective a "knowable sequence" over which coaches are presumed to have command.' (ibid.: 121). They call for ways in which a coachee in sports can develop his or her own 'agency' rather than compliance to the whims of the coach. Potrac et al. (2002) also highlight some negative discourse in the sports coaching model. These included 'controlling', 'directive' and 'imposition of the coach's agenda on the coachee' – perhaps this is an association with the 'Svengali' character.

It is interesting to note that many former sports people are engaged in coach training in the business context and this raises the question of which model of coaching they promote. Arguably, this may be a goals-oriented framework derived from sports coaching. The goals discourse in business coaching is a very dominant one and it is possible that this is a direct influence from sport. It may also come from the traditions of 'management by objectives' – a dominant discourse in management today.

However, Kayes (2006) and Spreier et al. (2006) suggest that goals 'blind you to danger'. Johnson and Bröms (2000) indicate that target-chasing does not improve anything and can lead to disappointment and frustration, and this is dealt with in various articles and book chapters (see, for example, Clutterbuck and Megginson, 2005b; Garvey et al., 2009; and Megginson, 2007). Megginson (2007) has many issues with the goals discourse in coaching. These are condensed here as follows:

- Conflict in goals between sponsor, coach and client diffuses motivation
- Goals narrow the focus of discussion too soon
- Goals can encourage collusion in not addressing painful areas
- Meandering can be useful exploration
- If I am in transition, I can't commit to a goal and it is an unknowable world
- Goals are often a compliance to the dominant discourse and divert people from what they really want to work on
- Goal-setting can be profoundly destructive of coaching process
- The coachee may not be ready to discuss goals and they may resist and slow the process
- Why set goals for over-targeted managers anyway?
- Goals can create avoidance

The association with the Socratic method is another problematic discourse. Again, like mentoring, this association may be an exercise in establishing historical credibility, longevity and a rebuff to the 'something new and untried' accusation. Socratic dialogue is a reductionist and stylised process. Socratic dialogue is also a competitive methodology aimed at winning a 'truth' argument. It has, therefore, the potential to develop cynicism and scepticism (this is its purpose) and perhaps more dangerously, the notion that there is only one truth – the essence of reductionism. Socrates, as de Bono (2006) reminds us, was trained as a sophist and that pattern of argument reduces the opportunity for creative ways of seeing and finding new directions.

While this position may appeal to the managerial discourse of 'one best way', some (Goldman, 1984; Kimball, 1986; Stone, 1988) view the process as corrosive rather than confirming. This is at odds with both the modern coaching and mentoring discourse of autonomy of choice and the creative process. Moreover, the philosopher Nietzsche (1974) suggested that Socrates was responsible for the destruction of artistry which he argued was driven out by rationality and reductionism. Clearly, the rational pragmatic discourse of management is found in the Socratic method and this may help explain why so many coaches adopt the Socratic approach or at least claim that it is a fundamental element in coaching. Neenan (2009), for example, asserts that it is essential in coaching practice.

A further issue is the question of motivation and intent of the coach. Downey (2003: 57) questions the motivations of novice coaches suggesting that they may be driven by the 'need to solve, to fix, to heal, to be right or to be in control'. Perhaps, with the advent of the professionalisation of coaching (or at least attempts in this direction – see Chapter 11), this becomes a bigger issue. A paid coach, within a business setting, is under pressure to demonstrate cost-effectiveness of their intervention. This will inevitably influence the motivation and intent behind the process. Linked to this are the expectations of coachees, for example a novice coachee may have expectations of improved personal or team performance or that they will be recipients of expert advice. These are also contrary to the dominant coaching discourse of non-directiveness by following the coachee's agenda.

With the case of a line-manager coach, Nielsen and Nørreklit (2009: 208) suggest that the description of line-manager coaching as presented in Hunt and Weintraub (2002: 101) is actually a 'fake dialogue' that anticipates given responses and, therefore, the power position of the line-manager coach distorts and controls the dialogue. The 'line manager as coach' discourse is again an example of a discourse which ignores the potential conflict of power inherent between the coach and the coached.

Activity 1.2   Four case examples of coaching

The following four case vignettes of two coachees and two coaches illustrate what can happen in coaching, the potential gains, and the special character of the coaching relationship.

Case 1 Jane (coachee, operations manager, manufacturing)

My coach is a manager in another part of the business. We have met monthly for about six months now. I have found the coaching session immensely satisfying and helpful in giving me time to reflect and consider my options carefully rather than rushing into things because of the general busyness of my section. It helps me to think about the challenges ahead and encourages deeper thinking about work and my performance and this impacts on the performance of my team.

Questions

1. What is Jane's purpose for coaching?
2. How does she benefit?

Case 2 Scott (coachee, accountant in finance department)

I welcomed the idea of having a coach, although some of my colleagues did ask what it was that I had done wrongly! I have learned quite a lot about myself and how I think about my work and performance – my manager said that she noticed the difference in me after three or four sessions! I think that I have become more confident and not scared about making wrong decisions. My coach doesn't judge me, if you know what I mean, but helps me think things through. I feel that I have also become more accountable for my decisions and able to justify them.

Questions

1. How do Scott's colleagues position coaching?
2. What do Scott's comments suggest about the coaching he receives?

Case 3 Rhona (internal coach, team leader, manufacturing business)

I think that by being a coach I have developed some key people skills which can be used on a daily basis in formal and informal settings and providing insights into how to be a better manager. I have been surprised by how much I have learned and understood aspects of the business by simply listening, hearing, helping and guiding my coachees into new ways of looking at their work. It gives me a lot of satisfaction seeing people grow, develop and improve their performance knowing that I helped it happen!

Questions

1. How does being a coach contribute to Rhona's development?
2. What is Rhona's motivation to coach?

Case 4 Sushant (external coach)

I work as a consultant but often find myself coaching people as part of my work. Learning coaching has developed my skills and widened my perspective on how people are in business. I think that

(Continued)

(Continued)

coaching has been good for people in business because it helps people think for themselves and it challenges the status quo somewhat! Coaching can improve relationships as well as performance. It does matter who I coach because not everyone gets on and this can make or break the coaching relationship. Coaching has challenged me to think differently about my relationships and my role as a consultant. I think I work very differently because of it, in my work and life, I now ask questions rather than tell people what to do.

Questions

1. How does Sushant view coaching?
2. How has coaching impacted on Sushant's behaviour as a consultant?

To conclude this section on coaching's history and development, we summarise some key discourse themes:

- Coaching's roots are educational
- It broadly has a performative agenda
- From education, coaching practice migrated to sport
- Its development continued with a focus on skills improvement, task achievement and parenting skills development
- Power dynamics play a role in shaping meaning and can be both helpful and destructive
- Motivation to coach may be linked to the concept of 'generativity'
- Skills include listening, questioning, challenge and support
- Coaching has a positive, fluid social and popular history
- Mental processes play a strong role in improved performance
- Goals play a part in performance improvement
- There are directive branches and non-directive branches of coaching and both have the potential to develop performance

The existence of these contested discourses matters. When we think about the *purpose* of coaching and mentoring as an activity and even more so as a profession, we cannot simply assume that it is a good thing or politically neutral. We are taking a position in a discourse when we define coaching and mentoring, and the definition we choose carries with it connotations from the discourse. Similarly, when we meet with a client and agree on the purpose of the piece of work we will undertake together, we are taking a position within a discourse. This has implications for what we do, how we do it and why we consider it a worthwhile activity.

The rise and rise of coaching and mentoring

Mentoring activity is embedded in organisational and social life, and coaching has now come of age. Over the last decade, both have developed from esoteric activities on the fringes of mainstream learning and development, to central elements of workplace learning in a huge range of organisations. In the UK, for example, coaching and mentoring are widespread throughout all types of organisation – public, private, large, small and not-for-profit. In recent years, the UK Home Office has spent £10 million per annum on mentoring for young offenders; the Department for Education and Science (DfES) spent £25 million on young people's schemes; and in the NHS, approximately 250,000 people – or 20 per cent of all staff – are engaged in mentoring activity. More recently, in 2012, the UK Government provided £1.9 million for the 'Get Mentoring Project'. Here 15,000 business mentors were trained to support entrepreneurs. They committed one hour each month for two years. The then Business Minister said: 'We have invested in mentoring because we know that good mentors can provide the practical advice and support that an entrepreneur needs to take their business idea to the next level' (www.gov.uk/government/news/business-mentors-are-ready-and-waiting-to-support-smes, accessed 16 April 2015).

The Penna Survey (2014) on talent management states that 70 per cent of Fortune 500 companies have mentoring arrangements and Youth Business (www.youthbusiness.org/18949-youth-led-businesses-supported-by-ybi-last-year/) helped 18,949 young entrepreneurs to start businesses in 40 different countries with the help of trained volunteer mentors during 2014.

According to two studies, the Bresser *Global Coaching Survey* (2009) and the Bresser *European Coaching Survey* (2008), there are an estimated 43,000–45,000 business coaches currently operating worldwide. While many countries in the world engage in business coaching, there are some quite strong clusters of coaching activity. Europe accounts for 20 per cent of coaches and the combination of North America and Australia have an estimated 80 per cent of all business coaches. Within Europe, the UK and Germany have over 70 per cent of EU coaches. In the UK and Ireland, there is about one business coach for every 8,000 inhabitants.

The Chartered Institute of Personnel and Development's (CIPD) *Resourcing and Planning* report (2015a) shows a steady increase from 2008 in both coaching and mentoring support within the surveyed organisations. The CIPD's *Learning and Development* report (2015b) finds that 75 per cent of all organisations surveyed employ some form of coaching and mentoring to support learning and development, with a further 13 per cent planning to introduce coaching or mentoring the following year.

The *Ridler Report* (Ridler & Co., 2013) indicates a steady growth in team coaching and an increase from 2011 in the use of coaching for senior people and a high rating of coaching as an intervention for senior leadership development.

A 2013 small-scale study conducted for the International Coach Federation shows that, despite the very small sample size, coaching appears to be covered in at least seven different classifications of business sectors: Health, Pharma and Science; IT and Social Media; Manufacturing, Engineering and Defence; Retail and Consumer; Public Sector and Non-Profit; Consulting and Financial Services and Transport; and at least six different geographic locations on the globe (PwC, 2013).

These surveys indicate that business coaching and mentoring are still in the growth phase around the globe.

A notable development from approximately 2000 onwards has been the growing interest in coaching among psychologists and therapists. Here, there is a debate about the role of psychology and therapeutic practice within executive coaching (Brunning, 2006; Hart et al., 2007; Kilburg, 2004a). This debate, which is rather similar to the debate about similarities and differences between coaching and mentoring, is about the distinction between psychotherapy and coaching. Grant and O'Hara (2006), for example, suggest that: 'some individuals seek coaching as a socially-acceptable form of therapy'; and in a rather barbed comment, Williams and Irving (2001: 3–7) state that: 'Coaching looks like counselling in disguise – without the stigma, but also without the ethics.' To create even more debate on ethics in the psychotherapeutic coaching arena, Bono et al. (2009) show that qualified psychologists have higher fees for coaching than for therapy and they charge more than non-psychologist coaches for their services – elitism perhaps? Suggesting strong commercial interest, this group also derives 50 per cent of its income from coaching.

The rise of different brands of coaching contrasts with the rather limited brands of mentoring. Here, there is a different social phenomenon at play as coaching is more associated with performance and increasingly a professional activity, whereas mentoring is often linked to voluntarism. However, Garvey et al. (2009) also argue that both coaching and mentoring are increasingly subject to commodification as 'products'. This is particularly prevalent in the coaching world, as evidenced by the increase in 'return on investment' research (Feldman and Lankau, 2005; Jarvis et al., 2006; Joo, 2005; Smither et al., 2003; Tucker, 2005) but also in the emergence of an overwhelming number of 'brands' of coaching. So what accounts for this rise and rise of coaching and mentoring in both developed and developing countries?

Mentoring, as a phenomenon which gained increasing momentum from the late 1980s in both the UK and USA, may be linked to the reconceptualisation of organisations, such as the 'knowledge-creating company' (Nonaka, 1991). It can be located within the wider concept of the learning society, which 'needs to celebrate the qualities of being open to new ideas, listening to as well as expressing perspectives, reflecting on and enquiring into solutions to new dilemmas, co-operating in the practice of change and critically reviewing it' (Ranson, 1992: 75).

In such a society, learning is not confined to formal learning institutions, but permeates and enriches the lives of all people at work and by implication, enhances the host organisation's performance, which, consequently, enriches the wider social context.

The reasons for this increasing interest in learning at work are varied and complex. The business world in the late eighties and early nineties saw 'the quality boom'. This was primarily aimed at organisations achieving competitive advantage through the superior quality of their products or services. This, combined with a drive to cut costs, saw great developments in technology and changes in working practices. Manufacturing industries saw the introduction of sophisticated automation and consequently the demand for a technically skilled workforce able to be flexible and adaptable increased. Paradoxically, some skilled workers started to become deskilled as a result of technology. Within a short period, competing organisations found that much less divided them in terms of differences in the quality of their products or services, pricing and processes. High-quality products with high-quality service at reduced cost became the entry point at which organisations could do business (Hamel and Prahalad, 1989, 1991).

Competitive advantage based on quality alone became more difficult to sustain. Business started to develop new customer-led strategies that required quality products, value for money, quality service and after-sales care. Slogans began to appear in organisational documents such as 'people mean business', 'we're in it for the long haul', 'people are our most important asset', and the concepts of strategic human resource development and teamworking evolved.

UK Government action to support this idea created the 'Investors in People' initiative (a Conservative Government initiative aimed at improving organisations through training and development). This brought real benefits in the form of improved training systems, improved skills and motivation, a better identification of training and development needs and enhanced financial performance (HMSO, 1995: 82, para. 7.10; and Hillage and Moralee, 1996). More generally, 'intangible sources' such as personal and organisational networking were identified as a source of 'sustainable competitive advantage' (Hall, 1994; Nonaka, 1991; Hamel and Prahalad, 1991).

Some saw these events as managerial attempts to 'gloss' over the flaws in 'disorganised capitalism' (Lash and Urry, 1987), but others took a more generous view. Later, as Kessels (1996: 4) put it:

> a far more cogent argument would be that organisations have a direct stake in the personal enrichment of employees because excellence on the job requires employees who are comfortable with their work and who have strong and stable personalities. Personal enrichment is thus less an employee privilege than a condition for good performance.

In this period, many organisations were attempting to develop into 'learning companies' (Pedler et al., 1991) in order to achieve a competitive edge.

The UK public sector during the Thatcher Government, similar to today's Conservative Government, saw many changes. In the main, these were driven by the rhetoric of the reduction of public expenditure but at the same time there was an attempt to improve the quality of service. Many public sector organisations became subject to 'market principles' and the notion of 'public service' diminished. The public sector started to become more 'managerial' in its approach with the support and encouragement of a right-wing, free market political agenda. The public sector saw compulsory competitive tendering and a 'commercialisation' of its activities. Within the Health Service, Trusts were established and locally the long tradition of cooperation within the Service was put under strain as some started to view one another as competitors.

Arguably, the free market economic philosophy coming out of the USA and the UK generated a social sense of urgency and competitiveness, a desire to do things differently. The implications of this fast-changing and competitive climate on individuals were considerable. The need increased for people able to adapt to change rapidly, be innovative and creative, be flexible and adaptive, to learn quickly and apply their knowledge to a range of situations. The whole nature of work changed and the notion of having a career for life was transformed (Beck, 1992; Handy, 1990; Nonaka, 1991). Clearly, this climate also had implications on individuals and the need for employees to have 'strong and stable personalities' (Kessels, 1996) as individualism became increasingly important. In association with this fast-changing climate, there was a tendency in both the public and private sectors towards 'objectivity' in all work activities. Newtonian scientific method applied to organisational life became a dominant preoccupation of managers. The exponential growth in performance league tables for organisations and performance objectives for individuals offered evidence of this (Caulkin, 1995, 1997). The pressure for improved performance accelerated.

Both coaching and mentoring activity developed in practice in a range of contexts around this period, perhaps to address the relational and supportive needs of people in change, holistic learning and development and performance improvement. Both seemed to have emerged as offering an alternative discourse to the rational, pragmatic and performance-driven world of organisations but, at the same time, curiously part of this discourse. This is illustrated in Figure 1.1.

By examining publications on coaching and mentoring over time, it is possible to get some sense of the developing or changing discourses. Figure 1.1 shows that publications in peer-reviewed journals (the gold standard of research) on both coaching and mentoring between 1983 and 2000 were approximately the same in number. It also shows that peer-reviewed articles focused on learning and development during this period rather than on performance.

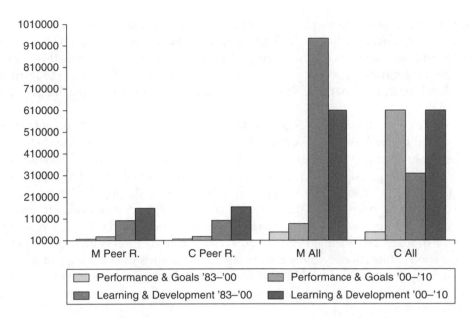

Figure 1.1   Numbers of published articles which link learning and development and performance to coaching and mentoring (Garvey, 2011)

There is an increase in articles linking coaching and mentoring to the learning and development agenda between the years 2000 and 2010, with a slight increase in articles linking coaching and mentoring and performance.

What is particularly striking are the figures for mentoring and the links to learning and development between 1983 and 2000 with over 910,000 publications, but declining quite dramatically between 2000 and 2010 as the coaching agenda started in organisations. There is also a low number of articles linking mentoring and performance in the whole period of 1983–2010.

For coaching literature, there is a marked difference. Between 1983 and 2000, there are few articles linking coaching and performance, with a huge increase between 2000 and 2010. Between 1983 and 2000, coaching was moderately linked to learning and development, but between 2000 and 2010 the link between coaching and learning and development increased considerably.

This demonstrates a shift in the discourses in both coaching and mentoring in the last ten years.

In 1990, a major publication was launched – *The Fifth Discipline* by Peter M. Senge. According to the 1997 *Harvard Business Review*, this was one of the seminal works of the last 75 years! There is little doubt that it was a bestseller and had a huge impact on both sides of the Atlantic. This publication also coincided with a whole raft of 'learning organisation' literature. This literature argued that the route to enhanced performance in business was to develop a learning environment. During this period, the mentoring movement was growing in the UK, and it linked itself to the learning and development discourse of this period, with the coaching discourse linking up to this later.

Coaching and mentoring are now the norm in a majority of corporate organisations, and are widespread in the public and voluntary sectors. From being almost exclusively a phenomenon of the English-speaking Anglo-Saxon world, the use of coaching and mentoring has spread around the globe into a vast number of countries, cultures and language communities. Today, a burgeoning literature, both 'popular' and scholarly, bears testimony not only to the diffusion of coaching and mentoring throughout organisational life, but also to the level of interest in them. In the UK ten years ago, Oxford Brookes and Sheffield Hallam universities and the Professional Development Foundation internationally pioneered postgraduate awards in coaching and mentoring, and by 2015 at least 25 UK higher education institutions are either delivering directly, or accrediting, undergraduate- and Masters-level programmes in coaching and/or mentoring.

Towards integration and distinctiveness

All the above highlights that both coaching and mentoring share similar skills and process and that the results are often similar! However, in Activity 1.1 and 1.2, all the case examples are based on organisational schemes and, therefore, an internal coach may have a very similar function to an internal mentor. Both involve voluntary effort, both impact on the participants and the business. In broad terms, these examples suggest that mentoring mainly supports learning and development with some performance orientation and coaching supports performance improvement with some learning and development.

Clutterbuck and Megginson (2005b) observe that in a range of books on both coaching and mentoring, some authors seem to position coaching and mentoring as different and distinctive from each other, criticising one and elevating the other. One of the areas of difference is in the experience of the coach or the mentor. Mentoring is often associated with passing on experience and, at times, this is described as 'handing out gratuitous advice'. Coaching is often described as non-directive and experience-free. Neither position is wholly accurate. Experience for both a mentor and a coach can be valuable but it is the way that it is used that counts!

Activity 1.3

An experienced mentor from a mentee's point of view

My mentor has a lot of experience and he uses it as examples to illustrate. He sometimes shares his experience as a 'story'. This gives him a kind of human feel. He never says: 'do it like this because I got success this way'. He never dishes out advice either. I wouldn't take it anyway! What he says is: 'this is my experience now let's unpick it and discuss it to see if there is anything to learn here'. I find this helpful as it gives a sense of reality to our discussions. I wouldn't want it any other way.

- How is the mentor using experience in this case?

An experienced coach from a coachee's point of view

I have a coach who comes from outside of my business. He has lot of business experience. I think this gives him some credibility. I think he uses his experience to inform his questions sometimes and at other times he shares his experience. I don't copy him, if you know what I mean, but I do get ideas for action from his stories and I find them interesting. If he spent all his time just listening and asking me what I think all the time, I'd question his value. I mean, what would be the point of that?

- How is the coach using experience in this case?

Distinctiveness?

Despite the obvious similarities between coaching and mentoring in terms of skills and processes, there are some models of coaching and mentoring that are clearly distinctive. In the world of mentoring, there are five basic models:

- Developmental mentoring to support the mentee's learning and development as he or she experiences some sort of change. This is often part of an organisational scheme within the private, public or social sectors
- Sponsorship mentoring to fast-tracking the mentee's career. This is predominantly a US model (Clutterbuck and Lane, 2004), but versions of this approach may be found in 'Talent' programmes in the UK and Europe
- Executive mentoring is for executives who may be working on their performance, leadership skills and longer-term strategic thinking

- Reverse mentoring is a relatively new innovation to the mentoring model. Here a younger, junior person may be a mentor to a more senior or older person. This approach focuses on the differences of experience or understanding and attitudes as mentor and mentee learn about each other's worlds. An example of this is found in the US with the company Time Warner. Younger, technically expert people mentor senior executives and in the UK Health Sector, patients may mentor health care professionals on the self-management of long-term health conditions
- Peer mentoring where colleagues are mutually supportive

There is another form of mentoring developing with Marsha Carr (www.selfmentoring. net, accessed 9 October 2015) in the US known as 'self-mentoring'. Currently, this is in its infancy. It has developed in order to counter the sometimes destructive power elements found in mentoring. It is based on a reflective and reflexive model of learning and values and respects an individual's resourcefulness.

Within the coaching world, Garvey et al. (2009: 81) suggest that, there are five basic forms of coaching:

- Sports coaching derived from the sports world in line with the historical roots as outlined above
- Life coaching derived from person-centred counselling (there is one eighteenth-century reference to developing parenting skills as a form of life coaching)
- Executive coaching which is a commercial- and business-oriented form of coaching with its roots in sponsorship mentoring and psychotherapy
- Team coaching associated with sports coaching and probably developed from the tradition of action learning
- Brief coaching/solution-focused coaching developed from therapy, goal-oriented and time-limited intervention – an increasingly developing business model focused on the time-limited executive

Whilst it is clear that many of these forms share processes, skills and techniques, some key differences may be found in what people think that coaching and mentoring might be for, whether or not it is a paid or voluntary activity and, of course, the main driver of this book, the contexts in which they happen.

A starting point as a coach or mentor is to consider the *purpose* of the field, as we perceive it and the way it is defined in our work with clients. As is clear from the various discourses within the field, defining that purpose for persons (as clients) or peoples (as a profession) involves taking a position. These positions include:

- The intent of the work – what is it designed to accomplish?
- The values it represents – what informs it?

- The philosophical stance taken – what evidence base is called upon to justify the activity?
- The context in which it is defined as worthwhile – what makes it a meaningful activity?

As coaches and mentors we need to take responsibility to have considered our position, the discourse that underpins the stance we take and to justify the *purpose* of the activity as we practice it.

These issues will be explored as the book progresses. We invite you to reflect on these positions as preparation for the journey through the chapters ahead.

Summary

- The notion and importance of 'discourse' is highlighted as key element of this book
- Both coaching and mentoring have a long history
- There is a dominant positive narrative about coaching and mentoring in the literature but there are also some negative narratives
- Both coaching and mentoring have educational roots
- The history of coaching has a performative aspect, whereas mentoring has a more developmental aspect
- Coaching and mentoring are similar and yet distinctive

Topics for discussion

1. What do you see as the main similarities or differences between coaching and mentoring?
2. Do these matter?
3. What impact might the different contexts of coaching and mentoring in practice have on their operation?
4. How far does our past shape our present?

Questions that remain

1. How does the stated purpose of coaching or mentoring influence its practice?
2. Are coaching and mentoring about skills and techniques or something else? If something else, what else?
3. What difference does the model of coaching or mentoring make to practice?

Further reading

Daloz, L.A. (1999) *Mentor: Guiding the Journey of Adult Learners*. San Fransisco, CA: Jossey-Bass. An excellently and artistically written account of mentoring in the education system. The chapter on learning theories and mentoring is particularly impressive.

Dutton, J.E. and Ragins, B.R. (2007) *Exploring Positive Relationships at Work*. Mahwah, NJ: Lawrence Erlbaum Associates. A good interdisciplinary account about developmental relationships in the workplace.

Western, S. (2012) *Coaching and Mentoring: A Critical Text*. London: Sage. An interesting and critical account of coaching and mentoring. 'Scoping the Field: Definitions and Divergence of Practice' is a particularly helpful chapter.

What next?

In Chapter 2, the notion of discourse continues. Here we highlight the psychological discourses. These include the discourse associated with the rational pragmatic, which revolve around the practical applications of various brands of psychology to coaching and mentoring for practitioners – the 'how to' discourse. We raise the discourse of the theorists and these include the discourses of the behavioural and cognitive approaches, the psychoanalytic and therapeutic and the humanistic. We also raise the academic discourse of 'critique' and argue that more needs to be done in the way of critical writing on coaching and mentoring. Critique is important, for without it there is blind compliance! Continuing on the academic theme, 'evidence' is another discourse. However, it is clear that one person's evidence is another person's subjective opinion, therefore we raise the discourse of 'what is truth'?

Possible answers to questions on pp. 14–15

1. Support in a new job role
2. Listening and challenge
3. Positive role model and sounding board
4. Exploring ideas, motivational support
5. Helping with decision-making and thinking things through
6. Building a strong community of support
7. Her reflective ability and awareness of her own need to learn
8. Social integration and understanding diversity
9. He develops himself by being challenged by his mentee

10. Sensitive awareness about relationship dynamics
11. It develops strategic thinking
12. It provides space for her to think future challenges through
13. They may see it as remedial or that he has performance issues?
14. His coach is non-directive and non-judgemental and it develops autonomy
15. Coaching has enabled Rhona to develop important people skills
16. She is motivated by performance improvement she sees in others
17. Coaching is changing the organisational culture and empowering people
18. He has become less directive and more facilitative
19. The mentor is offering his experience to develop ideas and demonstrate empathy
20. The coach is establishing credibility and the questions are informed by experience

Psychology as a Perspective to Inform our Work in Coaching and Mentoring

Chapter outline

- Using psychology theory to inform our practice
- Using evidence to inform our practice
- Critiques of psychology as a model of practice
- Examples of coaching and mentoring from different perspectives

Keywords

Personal, interpersonal, systemic, science practitioner, constructionist, dominant discourse

Chapter objectives

After reading this chapter, you will be able to:

- Identify the main psychological approaches used in coaching and mentoring
- Distinguish between approaches in terms of their value, what they offer and the disadvantages they bring
- Understand how psychology informs practice and use this to justify the choices you make
- Critically evaluate the role of the psychology as an enabling and disabling force

Introduction

In Chapter 1, we argued that it is central to an effective framework for coaching and mentoring that the purpose of the activity is clearly defined but that definition sits within specific discourses on coaching and mentoring. Practitioners need to understand what underpins the offer they are making and be open with clients on the stance taken so that they can feel comfortable that the needs they explore can be met by the offer made. Once a purpose is defined, it is possible to consider which perspectives can be used to inform the coaching and mentoring journey on which they are engaged.

Historically, as we argued in Chapter 1, coaching and mentoring theory has been drawn from many backgrounds, depending on the area in which it was practised. For example, in organisations, coaching was an activity conducted by psychologists and organisational development consultants (AMA, 2008: 3; Kilburg and Diedrich, 2007), thus perspectives from organisation psychology were dominant. More recently, as it has been applied to life coaching, and as a result other fields of psychological theory such as counselling and psychotherapy, coaching and mentoring have been more influential (Passmore et al., 2013; Peltier, 2001). Other key influences have been from adult learning theory (Lane et al., 2016), neuroscience and sports science (Ringleb and Rock, 2010; Rock and Page, 2009; Stout Rostron, 2009, 2014).

How visible are those perspectives to the client? When a client approaches a psychologist for help, the first task (Corrie and Lane, 2010) is to be an appreciative audience for the story they tell. However, the teller is also seeking assistance to help them unravel whatever puzzle concerns them. Presumably, they have approached a psychologist because they are assuming that a psychological perspective will be helpful to them. To the extent that coaches and mentors use psychology to inform their practice, what *can* the client assume? Psychology is one underpinning perspective in the coaching and mentoring process – what does it bring or not bring to our understanding? How transparent is the psychology in the offer? How dominant and how much of the critique of the field is visible to the client? To the extent that coaches and mentors feel that psychology has something to offer their practice, how informed are they about the dilemmas facing the perspectives on which they draw?

The impact of psychology as a perspective in coaching and mentoring can feel pervasive. As the Chartered Institute of Personnel and Development (CIPD) argues, the influence of psychology is so strong sometimes that it is difficult to distinguish between coaching and counselling because so many theories from the latter have influenced the former (CIPD, 2012; Gold et al., 2010). As Kahn (2014) has pointed out, this impact has been formalised by the advent of the field of coaching psychology. He points to the role of the British and Australian Psychological Societies, the establishment of journals in the field (*International Coaching Psychology Review*;

Palmer and Cavanagh, 2006) and the growing size of bodies such as the British Psychological Society (BPS) Special Group which has over 2,000 members. (Palmer and Whybrow, 2006: 5). Several psychological associations have now joined with the International Society for Coaching Psychology to create a body to promote the role of psychology and psychologists in this field. So how are these influential psychological perspectives acquired by coaches?

Using psychology theory to inform our practice

The role of underlying perspectives in coaching and mentoring is to inform the journey which the practitioner and client make together. They provide ways to understand what emerges and guidance on the process itself. Each party to the encounter will be bringing their own perspectives to the journey. The client will have a view on what is happening and why it is happening. The sponsors will have their own view. The practitioner brings a further set of views. A difference is that, in assuming the role of guide, expert, facilitator (or whatever definition the practitioner chooses), they are designated as holding relevant knowledge to inform the work. This knowledge will have many origins but will include content drawn from particular epistemologies. The practitioner is expected to know stuff!

If we look at any number of well-regarded texts on coaching (for example, Cox et al., 2010; Palmer and Whybrow, 2007; Wildflower and Brennan, 2011) that identify a range of psychological models as a knowledge base for practice, we can see a familiar pattern. A psychological model (for example, cognitive behavioural therapy (CBT), Gestalt, and Neurolinguistic Programming (NLP)) is described and then its application to coaching outlined and the benefits of the approach are noted. Rarely are the dilemmas, disputes or contradictions in that perspective outlined or discussed. Hence, coaches, unless they do a great deal of looking, will not know what view is taken by its detractors, its limitations and the existing evidential lacunae as well as the benefits.

Of course, this does not just apply to the use of psychology. Many coaches draw on adult learning theory in one of many forms, yet it is often a limited version that is considered. This includes the concept of andragogy in contrast to pedagogy first proposed by Kapp but developed by Knowles et al. (1984). Perhaps Kolb's (1984) work serves as a good example of this (see Chapter 6). His Learning Cycle is often presented devoid of the detailed framework that sits underneath. Hence, the debates about his work are bypassed in favour of a simple chart.

Not all coaching books take this stance. There are exceptions where the authors try to grapple with the complexities of the concepts used, for example Chapman (2010) and Stelter (2014) who present fuller accounts of the ideas developed. These authors assume that coaches will welcome the philosophical discourse involved rather than just look for helpful tools. Clearly, the books referenced are merely examples of a pattern (ironically chosen because they are very useful texts which have much to recommend them). However, if we really want to draw on psychology to inform our practice as coaches and mentors, it may be that we have to be prepared to engage with the critiques of the field.

So what in psychology informs the practice of coaches and mentors? There are a number of ways to explore this. We could look at the chapters in edited texts that serve as handbooks as these tend to identity favoured approaches. We could ask training courses what models inform their programmes. We could ask practitioners what they use. What would this reveal?

Texts

Coaching and mentoring are burgeoning areas and therefore it is not possible to say which are definitive texts. However, the pattern across a range of books is similar. There are those which present a given approach and they are intended to provide specific tools for practitioners. Examples in coaching would include Whitmore's work and the GROW model (2002), solution-focused approaches (Greene and Grant, 2006), positive psychology (Corrie, 2010) and deep structure models (Oxtoby, 2009). Examples in mentoring would include 'the three-stage process' (Alred and Garvey, 2010), practical case examples on mentoring in action in Megginson et al. (2006), and a practical philosophy, principles and practice of mentoring in Pegg (1999). These provide coaches and mentors with a clear guide but not any way to understand the critiques of those approaches. Critique is important, for without it there is blind compliance!

There are those which look at particular contexts for coaching. Examples would include coaching in family business (Shams and Lane, 2011), coaching in education (van Nieuwerburgh, 2012) and internal coaching (St John-Brooks, 2014). In mentoring, examples include mentoring in adult education (Daloz, 1999), mentoring in the health sector (Gopee, 2011) and mentoring in schools (Garvey and Langridge, 2006). These provide a detailed understanding of that context to assist the practitioner, but again the theoretical underpinnings chosen are those seen as helpful to the field, however the critique is more limited.

The core books on many courses include those which attempt an overview. Examples would be many of the 'handbooks' in the field (Allen and Eby, 2007; Cox et al., 2010; Palmer and Whybrow, 2007; Wildflower and Brennan, 2011). These usually invite practitioners and, to some extent, academics within particular theoretical traditions to describe and give examples of practice from within a theoretical stance.

(They do other things but at the theoretical level this is the primary approach.) Those accounts are virtually devoid of critique. For example, someone reading about cognitive behavioural approaches would be unaware of the disputes within that field between cognitive and behavioural traditions or from outside that field (House and Loewenthal, 2008).

However, we see a wide range of theoretical positions as influencing coaching and mentoring practice: Palmer and Whybrow (2007) list 11 approaches; Cox et al. (2010) list 13; and Wildflower and Brennan (2011) list 8. There is considerable overlap between them. Hence, the first (behavioural/cognitive), second (psychoanalytic) and third (humanistic) wave of approaches from counselling and psychotherapy are always represented. Developments from within these traditions such as *transactional analysis*, *existential theory* and Gestalt are commonly explored. Newer approaches such as NLP, *narrative*, *solutions focused* and *positive psychology* are again commonly featured. Others are less rarely featured but are central to some practitioners – examples being *social constructionist* and *ontological* approaches. In any very recent text, approaches from neuroscience will appear (Passmore, 2014). Each book explores multiple other areas of influence such as developmental theory, appreciative inquiry and spiritual traditions in Wildflower and Brennan (2011). Cox et al. (2010) add a detailed consideration of contexts and Palmer and Whybrow (2007) add areas such as sustainable practice.

So the books do not present a picture of the field as dominated by particular single-theory models but they do leave the models largely un-critiqued. It could be argued that by presenting the different approaches side by side, the readers will be able to do their own critique, although without a framework for doing so this is made quite difficult. Perhaps one of the key areas requiring more critique is how ideas developed within one context (say, psychotherapy) can be transported across to another (say, executive coaching) without significant new research to support it.

Perhaps the critique comes from the way coaches and mentors are trained and developed? In this respect, within the mentoring literature, Giebelhaus and Bowman (2002), Orly (2008) and Pfund et al. (2006) compare mentors with training with those without and rather unsurprisingly, these studies show that 'trained' mentors seem able to achieve better outcomes in their mentoring activity. Some literature on mentoring training (Alred et al., 1998; Johnson et al., 1999; Moberg and Velasquez, 2004) shows that mentor training draws on developmental psychology whereas others – for example, Aryree and Chay (1994), Beech and Brockbank (1999), Colley (2002), Erdem and Aytemur (2008), McAuley (2003), Morgan and Davidson (2008), Turban and Dougherty (1994) and van Emmerik (2008) – employ various psychodynamic, personality type, and emotional frameworks drawn from psychology to underpin their work. Several writers – for example, Johnson et al. (1999), Levinson et al. (1978), Moberg and Velasquez (2004) and Ragins and Scandura (1994) – link mentoring activity to the psychological concept of 'generativity' (Erikson, 1978) and Garvey and Westlander (2012) advocate an andragogic perspective (Knowles, 1984) to mentor development. However, there is a paucity of literature on the use of other psychological concepts in the education of mentors.

In the coaching literature, there appears to be a split position on the employment of psychological concepts. Berglas (2002) and Dean and Meyer (2002), for example, believe that psychological education and understanding is essential for a coach. Filipczak (1998), on the other hand, believes that it is potentially harmful for coaches to have psychological training, stating that the lack of business awareness and understanding in a coaching psychologist may give them a tendency to see a business 'as another dys-functional family that needs to be fixed' (ibid.: 34). Lee (2003) argues that it is better to have coaches who have 'psychological mindedness', and Bluckert (2006: 87) argues that it is 'people's capacity to reflect on themselves, others, and the relationship in between' that is important for a coach.

There are, then, differences of opinion in the coaching literature and within the men-toring literature psychological constructs are employed more to help build theory than to inform practice.

Courses

For this chapter, 20 postgraduate programmes offering training in coaching and/or men-toring (in the UK) were approached to discover what psychological and other theory informs their courses. Of the 12 who responded, it is clear that a very wide range of theories are in use. All of the approaches identified above are covered across the courses, although certainly not within them. There are a few which feature in some courses that are absent from the main texts (reverse theory, for example). It is apparent that for many courses it is not just about introducing psychological theories but rather the theory is used to inform the way candidates are trained. Even though multiple approaches are taught within courses and while some programmes favour certain approaches, most require the student to develop their own model of practice. Thus, although most of the psychological theory originated in counselling or therapy contexts, unlike those fields, students are not trained within one preferred frame.

Coaching, therefore, is unlike the fields from which it is drawn. Most programmes are asking candidates to understand and critically reflect on the ideas and build a per-sonally relevant model of practice. Some explicitly use the theory itself (for example, integrative theory) to ask the student to look at themselves and create an integrative model of practice which fits with their own sense of self. The directions for that explo-ration vary between courses, with some placed within certain linked theories and others adopting a wider range of exploration. Beyond psychology there is significant use of adult learning theory, particularly the theories put forward by Kagan, Kolb and Meizrow (see Chapter 6).

In looking at the implication of this, we could argue that coaching and mentoring are broadly based and critically reflective. Alternatively, we could argue that they are lacking in the rigour and depth of knowledge that focusing on a particular approach would bring. No therapy or counselling training attempts the breadth that is apparent is some coaching and mentoring programmes.

There are implications for how we see the field as an evidence-based profession. We might ask what a legitimate evidence base for our work is (see Chapter 7 on evaluation and Chapter 14 on research). Psychology since the late 1940s has been predicated on the notion of the 'scientist-practitioner'. It is, according to the British Psychological Society, fundamental to the work of the psychologist. It assumes that practice is informed by research and research by practice. As Lane and Corrie (2006) argue, the field has evolved since that period and there are now many ways of being a scientist and multiple approaches to validating knowledge exist. However, centrally there is still the assumption that whatever form the science takes, practice is still informed by it. In coaching, and even less so in mentoring, few courses identify a 'scientific-practitioner' foundation to the practice of the coaching and mentoring profession.

There are exceptions such as Cavanagh and Grant (2006) who regard it as a fundamental building block, but while many courses share with psychology a commitment to reflective practice, the concept of evidence-based approaches is less clear. Given that most trainees are asked to build their own model of practice, this is perhaps an important shortcoming in embedding rigour into practice. What is the evidence base that supports a personal model of practice? This is an important debate and we have to ask – what is the discourse of the scientific and what is the discourse of the practitioner? How are those discourses related, complementary or contradictory, and how do they emerge in practitioner accounts? What might a practitioner say that they use to inform their work?

Practitioners

Since 2003 in the UK, the Special Group in Coaching Psychology has surveyed coaching psychologists asking what models they use. More than 28 approaches were mentioned in the surveys, and solution-focused, goal-focused and cognitive and behavioural methods have consistently proved to be the most popular (Palmer and Whybrow, 2007). Again, this is indicative of a very wide range of ideas influencing coaching practice.

Similarly, an earlier review for the Global Coaching Convention (Dublin Declaration, 2008) identified a wide range of perspectives; however, it made the point that for coaches, they see the knowledge base upon which they draw as emergent from the process of coaching and mentoring. It includes the knowledge that coach and client bring to the session; the emergent knowledge that is borne out of the process; and the dynamic of the relationship. The knowledge base is largely driven by client needs; it is organic and continually evolving. Domains of knowledge can include psychology, education and continuing development, family and organisational systems, history, language, culture, industry specific knowledge, business knowledge, ethics and values, transpersonal work and mindfulness practice. A few examples of the influential perspectives include:

- Learning theory (Kolb, Bloom, Bandura, Boud, Mumford)
- Change (Hudson, Batson, Kotter, Scott and Jaffee)
- Developmental (Kegan, Dubrowsky, Kohlberg)
- Ego (Loevinger, Cook)
- Communication (Witgenstein, Watzlavick)
- Systemic thinking (Lewin, Senge)
- Social psychology (Izen)
- Organisational development (Ulrich, Smallwood, Schein, Beckhard, Burke)
- Process work (Mindell)
- Action learning (Revans, Board, Weinstock)
- Culture (Schein)
- Self-directed learning (Boyatzis)
- Leadership (Bennis, Jaques, Blanchard, Greenleaf)
- Existential (Yalom, Spinelli)
- Chaos theory (Poncaré, Wheatley)
- Cognitive behavioural psychology (Beck, Ellis, Bandura, Skinner, Thorndike, Seligman)
- Emotional intelligence (Pert, Goleman)
- Spiritual intelligence (Zohar)
  (Dublin Declaration, 2008)

What is apparent from this list from the Dublin Declaration is that the perspectives used cover a wide set of assumptions about the nature of behaviour, learning and the process of change. Some (such as CBT) assume change to be a personal process, involving the need for challenging existing ways to thinking in order to create new ways that impact more positively on feeling and behaviour. Thus change comes from within.

Others, such as some forms of learning theory and action learning, see this as an interpersonal process in which the learning is happening between the participants in the action; whereas approaches based on chaos theory assume that change is a whole system process. The practitioner basing their perspectives on chaos theory will understand the process of change for the client very differently from a cognitive-oriented coach. The process of working with the client will be very different, as will the definition of the purpose of the work.

Given this breadth, it raises important questions about what theory is relevant and how the decision to use an approach is made. It perhaps also raises a question about what constitutes a 'theory' in the mind of a coach or mentor and what is considered useful to guide practice.

Activity 2.1

Consider your own practice as a coach or mentor:

- What explicit theory or theories guide your practice?
- Does your approach to theory include: listening skills, any tool, or other method applied – what theory underpins them?
- Are there any implicit theories underpinning your practice?

Having reflected on the above, ask yourself:

- What is the client entitled to know about the underpinning knowledge that I bring?
- How do I make that knowledge explicit to my client and when do I do so?

The issue of what coaches and mentors are taught and how they learn their practice also becomes relevant if they are building their own models. Are courses expected to teach a range of models, provide guided practice in their use, ask trainees to coach and mentor people in those models and be supervised? Or, given the personal nature of the model built, do they receive direction on where to look and then go away and find it for themselves?

If courses are allowing them to do their own integration of ideas from reading, practice, role-play, coaching and supervision, does this really provide a rigorous way to conceptualise a professional activity? Critics of the field from other professions will point to the absence of a defined knowledge base as evidence that this is not a professional field of activity. A discourse of 'one best way' does emerge (which is often what professional bodies declare), whereas the reality of professional practice is more tenuous. Garvey et al. (2014: 259) provide a framework which indicates that both coaching and mentoring activities are drawn from different bodies of theory, as shown in Table 2.1.

This is probably because both coaching and mentoring are social constructs and have spread by social means in practical usage rather than through an academic subject discipline. This offers both challenge and potential as the notion of coaching and mentoring as professions, as they are currently conceived, are becoming more fragile and the knowledge base on which they draw is in dispute (for an exploration of the changing nature of the professions and the idea that maybe new forms are emerging, see: Cavanagh and Lane, 2012; Gray, 2011; Lane and Corrie, 2006; Lane et al., 2010 and Lo, 2006).

Let's look at this from the perspective of some sample courses.

Table 2.1 Coaching and mentoring theory source framework

Antecedents	Mediating concepts	Practical applications
Sport	Goals and targets Measurement Competitiveness Performance	GROW Model Mental rehearsal Visioning Goal focus The inner game
Developmental psychology	Education theory Conversational learning theory Motivations Sense-making Theories of knowledge Mindset Role of language Narrative theory Situated learning Adult development theories Age transitions	Levels of dialogue Holistic learning Knowledge productivity Johari's window
Psychotherapy	Emotional disturbance Stress and well-being Blindspots and resistance to change Transference Generativity Narrative theory Age transitions	7-eyed model of supervision CBT techniques Psychometrics Challenge Devil's advocacy Visioning Solution focus The dream The inner game Johari's window
Sociology	Organisational theory relationships Change, power and emancipation Language, culture and context Dominant discourse Strategy Mindset Narrative theory	360° feedback SWOT and PESTS Performance management Human Resource management practice Return on investment (ROI) Discourse analysis
Philosophy	Power, morality and mindset Dominant discourses and meaning Notion of expert	Evidence-based coaching Existential coaching Ethical frameworks and standards

Source: Garvey et al. (2014: 249)

Activity 2.2

Consider these five statements by different training providers. Then reflect upon the questions below (Part 1 and Part 2).

Oxford Brookes

Our philosophy is to promote professional competency in coaching and mentoring by understanding and development of the self in a context of one-to-one professional engagements. We aim to develop coaches and mentors as critical and independent learners capable of becoming learning companions for their coaching and mentoring clients. An essential part of postgraduate study therefore is engaging with a range of concepts, theories, tools and techniques and subjecting these to rigorous critical scrutiny and debate … we create the opportunities to develop personal styles and approaches to coaching and mentoring underpinned by robust theoretical and intellectual foundations.

Metanoia

Our preference is for an approach based on integrative theory and students are encouraged to develop their own model of practice based on integrating theory and practitioner experience. They have to be able to articulate a model that is coherent in theory and in use. Principles of integration help them to surface assumptions underpinning their practice, understand them and critique them. They have to show how their theories are compatible or, if in tension, how that tension is held. Integration offers a process theory for looking at how change happens in coaching relationships as well as providing a meta theory for integrating different psychological theoretical strands into a model of coaching.

York St John Business School

Coaching and mentoring are underpinned by two important philosophies. First, 'people are experts in their own life and work', and second, 'the solution lies within'. In practice, this means that coaching and mentoring are processes which enable and facilitate independent thinking, autonomy and self-efficacy. This programme creates an environment in which participants work collaboratively to share information and insights and to develop knowledge and skills in the tradition of the 'coaching and mentoring way'. Through these modules, you will be able to demonstrate:

- The effective practice of coaching and mentoring in a variety of settings
- A critical understanding of the roles and functions of coaching and mentoring in a variety of settings
- Critical awareness of current issues in coaching and mentoring

- The effective practice of coaching and mentoring to develop leadership and enhance performance
- Decision-making in unpredictable situations
- Self-direction and autonomous skill in tackling problems, planning and implementing solutions
- Personal responsibility for continuing to develop your own knowledge and skill

Professional Development Foundation

We seek to create confident, professionally skilled and competent coach/mentors who can identity their Purpose as coach or mentor, bring a coherent set of Perspectives to inform their journey with the client and co-create a viable Process to enable the journey. They continue to develop their personal model of practice through a commitment to an evidence informed practice, continuing professional development (CPD) and reflective practice on supervision and client work. We believe that professional practice is becoming more complex and this applies in particular to the competent practice of coaching. It follows therefore that coaches must be able to operate with a range of modes from the simple goal-oriented to the complex process-based models. In order to operate competently with this level of diversity, practitioners will need to draw upon cross-disciplinary fields of knowledge as well as their own personal values beliefs and self knowledge. The demands on practitioners are changing rapidly and to operate competently requires awareness of major ethical, social, cultural and political controversies concerning coaching and mentoring. Hence, coaches and mentors need more than competent practice in one theoretical frame.

PB Coaching

Our intention is to develop delegates' awareness of and capability to work with clients' thinking and feeling and do so primarily through awareness-raising, and do this through fundamental coaching skills like listening, paraphrasing, summarising, empathy, open questions and holding clients' attention on their experience in the here-and-now. We encourage them to engage with the personal development challenge involved here, such as noticing their usual reactions to other peoples' emotions – which is often one of discomfort and thus closing down the space.

  We focus on generic skills that enable people to engage at the psychological level – 'psychological dimension' – rather than having a strong attachment to a particular model or approach.

Part 1

- What is the essential theory in play for each of these statements?
- What form does the journey with the client take when working with a coach/mentor trained here?
- How are the multiple ideas in play brought together into a coherent framework for coaching and mentoring?

(Continued)

(Continued)

Part 2

- Now write a statement about your practice of similar detail to those above.
- What is the essential theory in play?
- What form does the journey with the client take when working with a coach/mentor trained here?
- How are the multiple ideas in play brought together into a coherent framework for coaching and mentoring?

Using evidence to inform our practice

It is clear that psychological theory is a key influence on coaching and mentoring texts, courses and practice. It is also apparent in a number of core handbooks in the field that reference to research informing practice is attempted (Garvey et al., 2014; Palmer and Whybrow, 2007) but it is not common. Yet, there is a burgeoning research literature in coaching and mentoring, and Masters-level courses require some from of project. If we use psychological evidence to inform our practice – what questions does it raise and exclude?

What evidence exists for the underlying coherence or 'utility' of the perspective? Is there evidence for effectiveness in the original context in which the perspective was developed? If not, what are the justifications for use in a new context such as coaching or mentoring? Even if there is evidence that using an approach to coaching or mentoring works, it does not provide evidence that the underlying perspective is sound. Their function is often pragmatic in order to aid, predict and guide action.

This is a challenging conundrum! Darwin (2010) argues that the 'truth' of 'evidence' is dependent on a philosophical position or belief system as to what constitutes 'truth'. The concept of 'alethic pluralism' is used to illustrate this. Based on an analysis of the philosophies of Kuhn, Popper, Feyerabend and Lakatos, Darwin (2010) argues that there are four possible ways in which something can be 'true'. Stokes (2010), in an unpublished essay, expresses these as follows:

- Correspondence – what is said about a phenomenon must be true if it corresponds with what can be seen in the 'real' world
- Coherence – what is said about a phenomenon must be true if the claims made seem plausible and internally consistent
- Consensus – what is said about a phenomenon must be true if there is consensus between people about what it does
- Pragmatism – what is said about a phenomenon must be true if it works/is practically adequate

To relate these ideas to the practice of mentoring and coaching, for example, the 'correspondence' view would seem to be legitimate in the light of the historical evidence presented in Chapter 1. The 'coherence' view in relation to mentoring and coaching is clearly contestable because of the sheer variety and the lack of internally consistent plausibility. Despite there being much 'consensus' in the literature that both coaching and mentoring are 'good things', this position is also compromised due to the sheer variety of practice, particularly in coaching. The 'pragmatism' perspective, while contestable, offers a stronger position as those who write about both coaching and mentoring tend to agree that it works! This would clearly satisfy the rational pragmatic manager and may help to account for the rise of coaching and mentoring practice.

Evidence-based practice within psychology seeks to build up a reliable and common stock of stories (i.e., theories and models – perspectives) that can be used (at least at a functional level) as exemplars of the individual and unique client stories we encounter in the world (Corrie and Lane, 2010). This accords with the psychologist Jerome Bruner's view of discourses in psychology. He states that:

> there appear to be two broad ways in which human beings organize and manage their knowledge of the world, indeed structure even their immediate experience: one seems more specialized for treating of physical 'things' the other for treating of people and their plights. They are conventionally thought of as logical-scientific thinking and narrative thinking. (Bruner, 1996: 39)

Bruner (1990) goes further, however, and states that 'meaning' is a central notion within human psychology and suggests that:

> we shall be able to interpret meanings and meaning-making in a principled manner only in the degree to which we are able to specify the structure and coherence of the larger contexts in which specific meanings are created and transmitted. (ibid.: 64)

In other words, contexts are very important!

Case study 2.1

Trevor approaches a coach complaining of anxiety over presenting to members of the Board of his company. The cognitive behavioural approach has a model of social anxiety that can be used to explain and make sense of Trevor's experience. This understanding, in turn, guides both the coach and Trevor in selecting some actions or interventions and rejecting others.

(Continued)

(Continued)

The intervention selected is evidence-based to the extent that the exemplar story, and the indicated intervention, have been subject to validation via empirical testing with many other clients who also demonstrate presentation anxiety. To the extent that an individual client's story conforms to this empirically validated story, it is useful. To the extent that the client story is not captured by this common or stock exemplar, it can be misleading, or even unhelpful.

This is the basis of an evidence-informed approach. A fundamental unstated assumption in the above approach to practice, and in most psychological theories, is a chain of cause and effect that is relatively stable, can be known and can be used to predict and control outcomes. This position is challenged by many from both social constructionist (Gergen and Gergen, 2004; Shotter, 1993; Stelter, 2014), complexity (Cavanagh and Lane, 2012) and decision theory (Lane and Corrie, 2012) perspectives. Filipczak (1998) goes much further, suggesting that psychological training for coaches is **potentially harmful**. The argument here is that a psychologist may not have any understanding of the business environment or context and they may have a tendency to see a business **'as another dysfunctional family that needs to be fixed'** (Filipczak, 1998: 34). Or, in the case of Trevor, outlined above, the word 'anxiety' may trigger many things in a coaching psychologist's mind, different things in a business coach's mind and something else in the mind of a mentor!

There are also major critiques from outside psychology on the way it categorises and institutionalises discrimination. These critiques of psychology as a model would apply equally to its use in coaching and mentoring.

Critiques of psychology as a model of practice

Psychology in general has an uneasy relationship with its critics and in particular over its lack of attention to diversity (Gould, 1981). Its place as an agent of social control (Corrie and Lane, 2010) has been a matter of contention in the literature certainly since the 1970s. McClelland (2014) recently referred to its role as an ideological dimension in how we think about illness or deviant behaviour. To the extent that we place our understanding of coaching as a way of working within the internal dialogues of the client, we deny the role of cultural diversity and the oppressive effects of inadequate services to minority groups and the marginalisation of professionals from these communities (Hobson, 2012; Jackson, 1977). The core failure, according to some, lies in a focus on cultural difference and inferiority rather than on diversity and value (Keise et al., 1993):

> The dominant paradigm provides a seeming explanation … it permits intervention, especially intervention for a target person's own good … one may feel virtuously while acting tyrannically. (Ullman, 1977, quoted in Miller and Lane, 1993: 194)

There is an increasing focus around alternative theories in psychology. For example, within the CBT field, Radical Black Behaviourism (Hayes, 1991) was a call to behaviourists to engage in approaches that challenged the status quo and changed life opportunities. Kelly (2006) has noted the collaborative and non-judgemental nature of CBT as offering value to marginalised groups. Its value as an anti-oppressive framework (to challenge oppressive internal dialogues) has been explored by Ross et al. (2008). Orford (2008) has called for practice that is based in core values of liberation, empowerment and social justice; to which we can add liberation psychologies (Watkins and Shulman, 2008), critical theory (Kagan et al., 2011), critical race and postcolonial theories (Dalal, 2002; Fernando, 2010; Hook, 2011), feminist theories (Boyle, 1997; Gillis et al., 2007; Wilkinson, 1986) and therapy linked to political action (Waldgrave and Tamasese, 1993). Some of these debates are carried out within a limited amount of literature; for example, in mentoring, Colley (2003a, 2003b) discusses social mentoring through the lens of feminist Marxism. Nielsen and Nørreklit (2009) employ a critical discourse analysis approach to explore power relations in management coaching and Garvey (2014) employs a critical theory perspective to supervision in coaching and mentoring. Many more are needed!

Examples of coaching and mentoring from different perspectives

One way to consider perspectives in coaching and mentoring would be to take a single example and look at how the coach or mentor works from different stances and consider the questions raised by the approach.

Case study 2.2

Jo is a middle-level manager who has just been promoted to a senior role in a reorganised department. This requires Jo to encourage the staff to sign up to a new strategy (it precedes Jo's appointment) and run a series of 'town hall' events to promote it to staff. Jo has never done presentations to large groups of people and is highly fearful

(Continued)

(Continued)

of doing so because, previously, a sense of being frozen occurred in front of groups when making presentations. The preferred approach for Jo is small meetings with key people and a gradual process of engaging people in the strategy. There has been a lot of success with this strategy in the past. However, a series of large meetings was announced by the company. In response to Jo's anxiety about these presentations, you have been asked to offer coaching or mentoring to support in the build-up to these events – six weeks away – and in the aftermath.

How might the practitioner informed by a cognitive orientation approach this client?

Here are some options.

A cognitive coach will work with the basic assumption that how we view ourselves, the world and the future, shapes the expression of emotions and behaviour. Hence, a practitioner is concerned to explore the patterns of thinking for Jo in relation to the situation with a view to devising alternative thinking patterns that can lead to new feelings and behaviours (we draw on Dudley and Kuyken, 2014; Palmer and Szymanska, 2007; and Williams et al., 2014).

A starting point will be to explore the concerns that Jo has in relation to the presentation and obtain a statement of Jo's emotions, thoughts and behaviours in as specific a way as possible. Some practitioners will explore background factors – when did this concern first occur, relevant educational, family or occupational histories, and the personal and social resources that Jo is able to draw on. A series of short-, medium- and long-term goals will be agreed – with an emphasis on 'strategic and specific, measurable, attainable, results-based and time-bound' (SMART) goals (Williams, Edgerton and Palmer, 2014). *These are considered to be presenting issues.*

The practitioner is likely to begin to explore the proximal, external and internal factors that trigger Jo's thoughts about the presentation. So, when in a situation involving presenting what thoughts occur to Jo, what feelings are aroused and what behaviours follow on that? ('I start to think that I am going to make a mess of this, my stomach tenses and I feel sick, I keep my head down do not look at the audience and try to focus on my script for the session.') A series of other descriptions from areas of Jo's recent experience will also be explored to identify common trigger factors, common thoughts (appraisals) and common reactions. *These are considered to be the precipitating issues.*

Once a pattern has been clarified between practitioner and client, the factors which maintain that pattern will be explored. In cognitive approaches, it is assumed that repeated patterns are reinforced through cognitive or behavioural factors to create a maintenance or vicious cycle which ensures the continuation of the concern. The evidence-based nature of cognitive approaches tends towards the idea that there are specific patterns for various disorders. So, the practitioner (drawing on that literature) might look for evidence that Jo presents a pattern typical of, say, an anxiety disorder. This would guide potential interventions. However, common patterns such as avoidance or worry are also explored. For example, where avoidance occurs, it prevents the person from experiencing the actual event, so the imagined consequences are never challenged by actual experience and become magnified in the individual's thought process. Problematic beliefs are never disconfirmed. Exploring with the client the factors which perpetuate the concern helps to devise intervention strategies. *These are considered to the perpetuating issues.*

Of course, Jo will also bring various strengths to her situation – there has just been a promotion, so she is clearly valued by the employer. Exploring strengths and areas of resilience provides a good path to intervention – building on strengths may enable solutions to be found. For example, how the strengths in working with smaller groups might be applied to this situation, what might be set up in advance to create smaller group processes even within a larger meeting. *These are considered to the protective issues.*

The coaching or mentoring is likely to build on this exploration with the practitioner and client in a collaborative research project together observing, collecting data, testing out the data to arrive at an intervention that makes sense and which is further tested in behavioural experiments back to the working context for Jo. Sometimes, practitioners working in this area will explore factors that make it more likely that Jo had difficulties in this area. Prior and particularly early experiences that lead to anxieties in group situations might be present. Core beliefs about sense of worth (worthlessness) may be evident. Jo might be operating with a set of rules or conditional beliefs about self or the world ('if I show weakness, others will exploit me'). Jo might be using compensatory strategies which enable feelings to be masked (drinking too much, not showing emotions at all). Or images of traumatic events in the past (abuse, bullying, etc.) may be triggered by the current situation. Where these are long-standing, a practitioner may well consider a referral. However, there is much that can be accomplished even here with the intervention (Tehrani et al., 2012). *These are considered to the predisposing issues.* For example, in the support phase of this contract once the initial presentation has been completed these issues might be explored.

Where the issues that emerge as the presenting issues are explored and seem to be straightforward, a simplified problem-solving and solution-seeking framework might be applied (e.g., PRACTICE, ABCDEF; see Palmer and Szymanska, 2007).

The totality of this understanding will be used for Jo and the practitioner to devise the approach to bringing about a change in the thinking patterns that trigger the feelings and behaviours. A whole range of interventions become possible – targeting particular goals, disputing beliefs and challenging thinking errors.

How might a practitioner informed by a psychodynamic orientation approach this client?

Here are some options.

A psychodynamic practitioner will work with the basic assumption that unconscious and past experiences shape present ways of relating to self and others. By providing a safe relationship to explore, name and integrate difficult feelings, thoughts and memories, the client is enabled to approach new challenges with greater clarity and authenticity. As a result of early experiences, primarily with caregivers, we develop unconscious strategies for regulating our emotions. Defence mechanisms (denial, repression and projection) from those experiences are triggered in current situations that are experienced as unpleasant or too difficult. By becoming aware of these, they can be looked at and understood. The range of emotional expression of the client can be extended so that they have other options available to them (we draw on Lee, 2010; Leiper, 2014; Roberts and Brunning, 2007).

The practitioner will likely (as for the cognitive behavioural coaching (CBC) approach above) use some generic framework to contract the scope of the work, assess and gather information, and, through understanding patterns, help develop the client to move forward, implement new learning, and review and realign the approach as needed. A primary difference here is the focus on the role of the unconscious agenda.

With Jo, the initial scope of the work is an important consideration. The practitioner may very well agree a scope for the initial stage focusing on the skills and performance aspects while looking to the support phase to do more developmental work. For example, Lee (2010) looks at integrated patterns of 'actions, cognitions and emotions' when providing skills or performance coaching. So, with Jo, the exploration of that sense of freezing might be explored. Once the sense of it is detailed, previous experiences of that same feeling might be examined. When in the past had Jo sensed that same feeling, what were the circumstances for that? It is assumed that some past key relationship had laid down the potential for this sense and uncovering that would enable Jo to recognise where the fear originated. For example, Lee uses the case of someone whose father's look of disapproval was unconsciously projected onto an audience during a presentation. If a similar issue applied to Jo becoming aware of this, it would help to shift the approach to the presentation. The exploration is designed to uncover such past experiences.

Beyond this initial performance-oriented approach, work might continue developmentally with Jo to look at the core passions and convictions that have driven both life and work. Thus, a broader exploration of patterns in the current situation is undertaken to uncover the possible impact of unconscious choices in the past that may have shaped these. Working with a client like Jo who is facing leadership challenges of a new type does place a premium on the past patterns of attachment which may generate particular styles of leadership. For example, an approach in which self-doubts or vulnerabilities are denied may result in a dominant style of leadership which evokes resistance in others. Awareness of the attachment patterns opens up the possibility of examining a range of other responses.

A psychodynamic approach is about the agendas below the surface of which the individual may be unaware.

How might a practitioner informed by a narrative orientation approach this client?

Here are some options.

A narrative practitioner will work with the basic assumption that problems in living occur when the stories that people have available about themselves do not accord with their lived experience. This links to the social constructionist view of questioning taken-for-granted assumptions and seeing them as historically and socially specific. Often, people have come to see their lives in a limited and limiting story rather than one which is multiple and multi-texted. The practitioner works with the clients to find those alternative stories and construct new possibilities through new or modified stories about themselves and their lives (we draw on Drake, 2010; Harper and Spellman, 2014; Law, 2007). As for the approaches above, a generic framework might be used (this frame is offered by Drake, 2010):

1. An issue or goal is presented by the client
2. An invitation is made to tell a story about it and other related elements or stories are elicited
3. Any themes or patterns are tracked
4. A guiding image or metaphor is identified that seems to be at the heart of the issue
5. This image is worked within the conversation
6. A resolution occurs – often in ways that transcend the original polarity of the issue

Thus, working with Jo, a narrative practitioner would explore the narrative about problems with presenting to large groups. Alternatives to that dominant 'problem' narrative would be explored, focusing on Jo's purpose for this new role, the beliefs Jo brings to it, the hopes, dreams, vision and commitments Jo has for it. Jo would be encouraged to stand back from seeing these as internal states or as strengths and weaknesses, but rather ask if the stories Jo was using enriched or limited the possibilities available. Jo would be asked to explore options and choices and examine stories about the situation and self which had been previously marginalised or subordinated.

Drake (2010) identifies four essential processes and dynamics:

1. Identity is situated – rather than explore past or future, the focus becomes what is, the present. This honours the way people use stories to situate themselves in an ongoing dialogue with others and their environments. So, with Jo, the stories about self in relation to others and the key environments would generate core themes. Jo has a number of stories about communicating with others in large groups, in smaller groups, as ways to generate engagement both successfully and otherwise. The themes that underpin the stories about these can give Jo ways to think about self in relation to other. How is identity defined in the stories?

2. Growth is liminal – practitioners use employment strategies to make sense of their experience. Practitioners help their clients to identify the plots in the stories. Thus, Jo might explore what events are included, what characters are seen as significant, whose voices are privileged. Equally, who is left out, what gaps exist in the stories, where are the boundaries drawn when explored creates the potential for alternatives narratives. People form stories where their world breaks down, expectations are not met. Bruner (1990) calls these 'breeches of the commonplace'. It is in the liminal (threshold) spaces between what is and what might be where growth is assumed to be most likely. This may be such a moment for Jo – the excitement of the new role, and the fear of the first public performance in that role, create a threshold. What is the narrative plot with all its twist and turns?

3. Discourse is powerful – it helps clients to examine deeply their assumptions about reality. The preconscious schemas and conceptual frames which shape their lives are revealed, so we work with coachee's stories to help address internalised restraints that prevent noticing exceptions to their to current self-descriptions. These provide potential scaffold to a new way of being in the world (Drake, 2010). So, for Jo, what is traditionally available as behaviours – ways to be – in that narrative and what latent potential stories might exist?

4. Re-storying is possible – it creates a new alignment between one's identity, narratives and behaviours in order to be and behave in different ways. What really matters to the client, what key value is at stake? This is where Jo has to face the hardest challenge and answer the most essential question. Jo might be asked what really matters – what in this role is key to the vision of self? How might a story be preferenced in which it is possible to talk to a whole range of groups, small and large. What would that look like?

Activity 2.3

In relation to your own approach, consider the following questions:

1. What would you see as your purpose in working with Jo?
2. What perspectives would inform your approach with Jo?
3. What process would you use to manage the work with Jo?
4. How might your approach differ from the three outlined above?

5. What areas did each approach explore that you might not have considered?
6. What areas did you consider which were not included in the approaches above?
7. What questions would be generated in your practice by adopting one of the approaches above that you do not currently employ?
8. How might your clients benefit from broadening your approach?

Summary

- Psychology is a key influence at the very top of the agenda in coaching practice and less so in mentoring practice
- Psychological theory includes models developed for use elsewhere such as CBT, Gestalt and narrative theory which have been imported into both coaching and mentoring
- Other core influences derive from multiple sources but adult learning theory predominates
- There is a question over how practitioners develop a coherent approach to practice since most programmes require them to build their own model – unlike the disciplines from which it is drawn which teach a model
- The issue of evidence-informed practice is not a major feature of many texts in the field and the scientist-practitioner model which informs psychological practice is in limited use in coaching and mentoring training
- If we build our own model of practice from multiple sources, we need to show how it is coherent and rigorous
- Different practitioners using varied models will approach the same client issue from very different perspectives. We need to understand the implication of this for our developing field

Topics for discussion

1. Should psychology be the dominant frame for the training of coaches and mentors?
2. Should the critics of psychology be a core part of our training as coaches and mentors?
3. Should we understand only one approach or several in our training?
4. Are we working as agents of social control when we accept the sponsor's definition of need?
5. Are coaching and mentoring part of the problem or a solution, if so for what?

Questions that remain

1. How will the use of psychological theory in coaching and mentoring develop?
2. How will we balance our internal sense that we have a coherent model with an external evidence base to understand how coaching and mentoring happen in practice?

(Continued)

(Continued)

3. Can someone really build a personal model of practice yet claim to be part of a psychological tradition?
4. How standardised might coach/mentor training need to become if professional bodies start to impose approaches?
5. Might each personal model being drawn from diverse traditions require its own set of ethical standards?

Further reading

Colley, H. (2003b) *Mentoring for Social Inclusion: A Critical Approach to Nurturing Relationships*. London: RoutledgeFalmer. A feminist Marxist critique of social mentoring.

Hay, J. (2007) *Reflective Practice and Supervision for Coaches*. Maidenhead: Oxford University Press. Helps coaches to review their practice through reflection and by using the services of a supervisor in order to raise self-awareness and improve professional competence.

What next?

In Chapter 3, we raise the idea of the contexts in which coaching and mentoring take place. Here, we consider the discourses of *purpose*, *perspective* and *process*. The *purpose* discourse relates to four main elements:

1. Understanding the questions we each wish to explore
2. Understanding the expectations of key stakeholders who will have a view on our journey
3. Clarifying the role that each party wishes to play, given the enablers and constraints the context imposes on our work together
4. Appreciating the wider context that gives meaning to the *purpose* and the way in which it has come to be defined

The *perspective* discourse relates to the position a coach or mentor may take on a particular theory, where a coach or mentor will perform the theory irrespective of the client. Alternatively, there is a repertoire discourse, where the coach or mentor will first hear the client's story and work with what seems to fit in terms of a theory. Both are *power* discourses. In the case of the theory-led approach, the practitioner will dominate the client interaction with their preferred underpinning theory of practice – despite the rhetoric to the contrary. In the second discourse, the practitioner will decide on what seems to be the most appropriate for the client but this still has the effect of placing the client in a weaker position.

The *process* discourse is about the particular model employed by the practitioner to facilitate the dialogue between the two parties:

> We construct, deconstruct and reconstruct the narrative as we proceed and our clients do the same. We, just like our clients, may retrace our steps, stop, start, restart, give up, re-commit and arrive somewhere, before starting all over again. (Lane and Corrie, 2006: 54)

Part II

Coaching and Mentoring Skills and Process: What do I actually do and why?

3

Coaching and Mentoring Process

Chapter outline

- Context as an influencing factor
- Considering *purpose*, *perspective* and *process* in coaching and mentoring
- The coaching and mentoring process: Some concluding comments

Keywords

Context, self-narrative, relational narrative, purpose, perspectives, process, architecture

Chapter objectives

After reading this chapter, you will be able to:

- Identify the main impact of the context for the work on the process of coaching and mentoring
- Distinguish between the purpose of coaching and mentoring, the perspectives that inform the work and the process used to assist clients
- Consider the architecture that governs your work – steps in your process
- Reflect upon the difference between a personal (self-)narrative of your process and a relational narrative emerging in the process of working

Introduction

In the previous chapter, we reviewed some of the psychological frameworks that influence our field. So, how might we build a clear model that addresses core issues, regardless of the theoretical perspective taken?

Clearly, for some practitioners, a theoretical model (as outlined in the previous chapter) does shape the way they work, which creates the possibility of depth of knowledge of that approach but may limit breadth to work in diverse contexts. Yet, even within core models there is considerable diversity in approach. For example, Corrie and Lane (2016), in discussing cognitive behavioural approaches, point to ongoing debates within that family. They argue that both practitioners and supervisors need to 'situate' themselves within the range of approaches available.

If we ask any sample of coaching and mentoring practitioners what it is that they do when face-to-face with a client, we will get a very diverse picture of our field. This is part of the strength we bring; we are diverse and the work we do is equally so. Yet, this makes it difficult for our clients and the buyers of our services to know what it is they are getting when they employ us. Yes, they may ask about our experience, qualifications or even our competence (the subject of Chapter 4), but will they understand what happens in the room – the process they are going to experience? Even if we point them to some examples in the literature, they will find very different processes described (Stout Rostron, 2014), some of which look like a list of standard questions. Thus, some practitioners may be experimenting with ideas and others may be using a fixed logic and process (Cox et al., 2014). As Garvey (2013) reminds us, if only life were simple, we could apply standard rules. It is difficult to know what understanding or epistemologies sit behind those questions and therefore how we choose to evaluate them (for discussion of the evaluation issues, see Gray, 2004). This can generate confusion (Cox et al., 2014).

We hope that the ideas and activities in this chapter will help you reflect, consider and locate yourself within a conceptual landscape that makes sense for the context in which you act as coach or mentor. What informs the process we use?

Context as an influencing factor

We refer to the influence of the context in Chapter 1. When considering the context of the coach's or mentor's work this leads to many questions being raised. If, for example, we coach or mentor in very different circumstances (say, coaching someone recovering from a road accident or someone facing a critical Board meeting), does not the context greatly influence the way the work will unfold? Can a standard set of questions meet those differing needs?

How does the context for our work underpin all we do – generating meaning for our clients and ourselves? We need to agree a purpose for our practice that is informed by our values, ethics and evidence base, and expectations of clients, sponsors and ourselves. How do we define our role as coach and mentor? What perspectives – ways of seeing the world – influence how we coach and mentor? How do our perspectives distort and illuminate the journey with the client? These and many other questions will need to be explored to build a process for our practice, informed by the context for the work. In this chapter, we will explore some of these questions and help you to think through a clear working model that is informed and viable to sustain ethical practice.

The journey with the client assists them to move from where they are now to where they want to be. Primarily in coaching and mentoring, it is often but not always (see David et al., 2013) based on a process of negotiating appropriate goals. However, the more complex the context we face, the more difficult it is to identify clear goals early in the encounter. So, the journey may start as an exploration, with goals emerging later in the process. Our framework might need to encompass this variance in process. We propose (along with Lane, 2002 and drawing on Lane and Corrie, 2006) that this shared framework centres around the three core themes of **purpose**, **perspective** and **process** as follows:

1. What *purpose* is our coaching or mentoring designed to serve? For example, is the purpose to help the client construct a meaningful narrative that enables them to make sense of their situation? Or is it to ease communication with colleagues? Is the aim to meet an external agenda for change imposed following an assessment centre or 360° feedback process or precede a referral for disciplinary action? Each of these tasks has been asked of us as practitioners but they require very different responses. As we argued in Chapter 1, this is contested ground – we need to clarify which coaching and mentoring discourse influences our purpose
2. What *perspectives* will inform the journey we undertake together? Are we drawing on specific psychological perspectives as outlined in the previous chapter? Or are we adapting frameworks to meet the needs of the client in front of us? The agreement we make on that will influence its direction. We also have to take into account the intentions of different stakeholders, including their beliefs and views on human experience. If the journey we undertake together is collaborative, then multiple perspectives will be present in the room, including views leaking in from beyond the walls. The choice of perspective is not a neutral one – each is situated in different discourses of power
3. Taking into account the agreed purpose for the work and the perspectives each party brings to the encounter, what *process* is needed to create a useful journey together that is coherent with the perspectives and meets the purpose? We must remain alert to the implications of the embedded discourse in our process – it enables some narratives and disables others

A slightly different emphasis is given to this by Cox et al. (2014). They suggest that a personal model of coaching must contain three elements:

- A philosophy that underpins coaching practice: How do practitioners see human nature and the world? What is important for them?
- The main purpose of coaching: What is it for? What is the coach trying to achieve?
- A coherent process: What tools, methods and procedures are needed and are appropriate for working towards this purpose and are congruent with this philosophy?

Commenting from the perspective of psychoanalytic supervision, Lesser wrote that: 'It is important to be aware that the supervisory room is crowded with all sorts of "persons" who create anxieties for both the supervisor and the supervisee' (1983: 126). We would argue that the coaching or mentoring room is equally crowded, and hence bringing together hopes, fears and expectations of the crowd makes this a fascinating, complex, challenging but rewarding field of practice.

Activity 3.1

Consider the frameworks that underpin your own approach to coaching and mentoring. In particular:

- How do you decide that coaching or mentoring is likely to be of benefit to a client? When and how do you approach the task of thinking through a process for this?
- What framework/s or model/s do you tend to use? Are they generally similar whatever the context or do they vary greatly by context? How do you decide what works best for the client?
- How do you ensure that the client's perspectives are respected and other stakeholders considered? How do you design a process for the work based on your framework or model? What specific steps do you take and what Processes do you favour to meet client needs?

Case study 3.1

You have been asked to coach a middle manager in a financial institution. This somewhat traditional body had taken pride in building long-term relationships with clients and offering services structured to meet their needs. There were no sales targets. This suited the manager well and he had thrived in this environment. More recently, following a consultancy report, the Head Office had decided that managers needed to be much more sales-oriented and in particular sell the in-house products that were being developed. Specific sales targets were set. In approaching you to work with this person, you have been told that this manager had struggled under this new regime and was failing to meet targets. When asked about this by his manager, he had raised concerns about an approach in which he was required to sell to his clients rather than advise them.

You have been asked to coach him in sales skills and help him to meet his targets:

- Keeping in mind the questions above, how would you approach this client?
- What discourses of coaching and mentoring are in play?

Considering *purpose*, *perspective* and *process* in coaching and mentoring

In a study looking at coaching as a profession, Lane, Stelter and Stout-Rostron (2010) have considered the development of our field and considered some of the issues facing professions in general and coaching in particular. (Mentoring sits in a somewhat different place, as it tends not to seek professional status.) It is increasingly recognised that all professions are becoming fragile (Lo, 2006). Impacts of market commoditisation and wider information access through the Internet and social media have challenged the traditional hegemony held by professions. Newer groupings such as coaches and mentors cannot rely on the traditional status they have to demonstrate through the value offered to clients that the service is worth the price paid. This has implications for how we define the purpose of our work so that clients feel it is a service that in a crowded marketplace they would choose to purchase. So, we start here by – defining our purpose.

1. Our purpose as a coach or mentor (Where we are going and why?)

We have argued that we need to understand our purpose as a practitioner. The approach adopted in training programmes (that adopt the model-building approach) is to invite the practitioner to build a personal model of practice – a story they can tell. This draws on the questions that Cox et al. (2014) define as necessary to create a personal model of coaching. Drake (2008) refers to coaches seeking a new identity reflecting part of the confusion around who we are and what we do, hence what personal models we seek to build.

However, if we take a view from a postmodern perspective (Gergen and Gergen, 1988), we have to see the process of defining purpose as having two elements. One part of this is the self-narrative we create that defines 'I the coach or mentor'. This has been termed a 'reflexive identity'. Others may be involved in shaping it but it is a personal narrative. However, as soon as we enter the room with the client, and indeed before we do so, other narratives are in play. In the work we do together, an agreed narrative has to be facilitated. This has been termed a 'relational identity' (for discussions of the types of identity, see Chappell et al., 2003). So, part of the definition of purpose emerges from this relational process. Hence, we can start by defining our *purpose* but that purpose and our identity within it are quickly shaped into an adapted version. The personal model 'reflexive narrative' becomes a co-constructed model 'relational narrative'. We do not just author our own tale, we are co-authors in an emerging story. Critical questions in this regard include:

- What is our *purpose* in working together?
- Where are we going and how do others view this journey? What do they want us to achieve?
- Where do we want to go in our overall journey – how might I as coach/mentor act as your guide?

Defining the *purpose* of the work comprises four essential elements:

1. Understanding the questions we each wish to explore
2. Understanding the expectations of key stakeholders who will have a view on our journey
3. Clarifying the role that each party wishes to play, given the enablers and constraints the context imposes on our work together
4. Appreciating the wider context that gives meaning to the *purpose* and the way in which it has come to be defined

---

Activity 3.2

Go back to Case Study 3.1 and consider how these four elements might emerge in your first coaching conversation with that client.

During the process of clarifying the question to be explored, the expectations of key stakeholders and the role that each party wishes to play, the coach/mentor and the client have to make an initial decision – does it make sense for us to work together? However, this is not a final decision, for it leads to a further set of questions:

- How can we ensure that our process for working makes it possible for other stories to be heard? Can we meet that need?
- What boundaries do we place on the *purpose* of the work so that we can clarify what is and what is not legitimate in our discussions?
- Among the stakeholders, who might be beneficiaries and who might be the victims of the work we do together? (Checkland, 1989)

2. Our *perspective* as a coach or mentor (What will inform our journey?)

The *perspective* component of the *purpose*, *perspective* and *process* model is concerned with trying to understand those factors that influence the journey.

Corrie and Lane (2010) have argued that traditionally psychologists have tended to work from one of two starting points:

1. As the professional, they know the key to the puzzle that the client presents and that this lies in a single theory or model – that is, a particular *perspective.*
2. As a professional, I cannot know the key to the puzzle, so I have to hear the story first and then jointly seek the *perspective* which best fits.

If we read any number of coaching texts, we can see the first approach – thus, here lies 'personal-centred coaching', 'solution-focused coaching', 'cognitive coaching', 'ontological coaching', 'GROW', etc. – which assume that the professional knows the key to the client's puzzle in the form of a particular approach to questioning and exploring. Stout Rostron (2014) has identified some of the dangers in this approach.

This is an issue, which confronts us in our field as we draw heavily on psychology. It is not a necessary position, as Kahn (2014) demonstrates in his analysis of a coaching axis between individual and organisational perspectives. However, it is a common one. Even approaches such as narrative coaching which start with the client story and place considerable emphasis on enabling its telling are still predicated on a single view. Thus, the client's story provides (as Chappell et al., 2003, define it) a reflexive identity. Narrative practitioners (Drake, 2014) see an intimate connection between the way people narrate and enact their lives. Coaches help the person to identify and tell more enabling stories, which open new possibilities. It has its own essential processes and dynamics, which shape the way in which the emerging stories are told.

The criticism of such single-theory approaches is that they will cause practitioners to look at specific aspects of the client's concerns (that fit the model) rather than at the client as a whole. The understanding which emerges will be filtered through the lens of a specific theoretical or conceptual worldview. Such a view limits the number of key events considered critical to bringing about change. Alternatively, we may adopt a multi-theory approach. This generates the possibility of a wider range of narratives becoming available. The criticism of a process based on multiple perspectives is that, while it may take varied forms with key events woven into a story, it lacks rigour. It may be convincing to those involved but it cannot be tested against an evidence base for practice.

Corrie and Lane (2010, 2015) define the first approach as a tale – the practitioner favours a particular explanation for the puzzles that the client presents. For example, in cognitive behavioural coaching (CBC) (Williams et al., 2014), use is made of the concept from therapy of a cycle of situation–emotion–thought–behaviour (Bieling and Kuyken, 2003). The assumption is that the interpretation of an event leads to emotional distress (Grant et al., 2008). Each single tale has its own set of assumptions that guide the practice from within whichever theoretical foundation upon which it relies. Hence, while listening, the coach gives preference to material from the client's interpretations of events that best fits the practitioner's foundational assumptions.

The second approach they term a 'story'. Multiple tales from different players are woven together and a central theme, protagonist and plot emerges. The understanding becomes specific to that client and their story. It is proposed that in working collaboratively it is for the practitioner and client to work to deconstruct the various tales and out of these identify those they need to address so that they can create a new story that has implications for change (Corrie and Lane, 2010). The difficulty is that the decisions made and the choices justified are less clear than in a single tale.

While linear decision-making approaches (implied in single-theory models) seem clear-cut, they are more limited; and while multiple, especially non-linear, approaches offer more complexity, both are faced with the dilemma: is accuracy or utility the most important consideration (Lane and Corrie, 2012)?

Activity 3.3

Go back to the example in Case Study 3.1 above and consider:

- What tales might be in play in this case?
- What perspectives are implied in the way the assignment has been presented to you?
- What implied role have you been assigned?
- What is implied by the description of this manager as told to you?
- How might these considerations emerge in your first coaching conversation with that client?

Whichever approach (or variant on these themes) we adopt, we are shaping the way the work unfolds. We are not somehow objective observers impartially guiding a process. We are actors who either follow a script or improvise as we go along. We need to be able to address such questions as:

- What *perspectives* ('tales') are informing your approach to work with the client?
- What *perspectives* ('tales') are informing the client's approach to the work you undertake together?
- What do you do to ensure that the client is able to explore their tale?
- What do you need to do to ensure that other tales are heard?
- How can you enable a coherent process to explore the various tales?

So, how we define the purpose and the perspectives we bring to the encounter will inform the process we use, enabling some narratives and disabling others. This is considered next.

3. Process for coaching and mentoring (How will we get there?)

Having briefly considered *purpose* and *perspective*, we now turn to the *process* we use.

There are a number of different ways to think about process.

One is to think of it as what happens as you work. In behavioural terms, it refers to what an outsider, the client or the sponsor could observe. This approach has a long history in other disciplines (Lane, 1990; Lane and Corrie, 2015), but also underpins a number of coaching approaches where there is an emphasis on measurable change – the focus is on the observable process (Goldsmith, 2014). The other view is for those who see process as an underlying set of influences that are not necessarily evident as surface events. Probably the best known of these arise from the process consultation models of Schein (1997) but are also present in fields such as Gestalt process models in coaching – the focus is on the implied process (Bluckert, 2014).

Our sister professions have focused heavily on this aspect and a number of concepts have filtered through from there to influence our field. Some of the more important include:

1. The concept of the client as the expert (Anderson and Goolishian, 1992), where the coach/mentor adopts a not-knowing approach to the process of exploring the client story
2. Parallel process (Bloom, 2011; Doehrman, 1976), where issues outside of the room are represented by processes happening in the room
3. The relational nature of the process (Gergen, 2001; Hersted and Gergen, 2012), where we have to think of this as a dialogic, systemic and hence emergent process rather than simply a contracted transaction. (See Safran and Muran, 2000, for an alternative approach to the relational nature of the alliance)
4. The role of countertransference (Prasko and Vyskocilova, 2010), where we have to take account of the coach's own material influencing the relationship with the client

These are just some of the influences on the process as it unfolds. Approaches to coaching or mentoring which imply a linear step-by-step transaction fail to recognise these latent elements according to the assumptions behind these process concepts. However, confusion can arise when coaches or mentors talk about their 'model', but what they describe is a process used in a session – steps or phases but ones that do not include the underpinning knowledge which is implied by the activity. Process is not of itself a model, although often wrongly described as such and thus a process for working is confused with the perspectives, which underpin it.

In the field of coaching, Stout Rostron (2009, 2014) has usefully distinguished between coaching frameworks (architecture for the process) and models (analogies about the world). We can see in the range of architectures that she describes, approaches based on both the observable and the implied process. Let's consider some of the process architectures.

Two-stage frameworks

Stout Rostron uses behavioural concepts (e.g., functional analysis; Peltier, 2001) and action learning (Revans, 2011) within this grouping.

Three-stage frameworks

Examples include Egan's (1975) system of exploration, understanding and action (discussed in the mentoring literature by Alred and Garvey, 2010, as the 'three-stage process'). They are designed to assist the 'helper' to appreciate the power of asking questions as opposed to instructing the client and to instil a preference for active listening. Examples of questions within a three-stage framework might include: What is working? What is not working? What (if anything) can you do differently?

Four-stage framework

The GROW (Goals, Reality, Options and Wrap up) model is the best example of this. Popularised by Whitmore (2002), this sets out a framework for developing a process for questioning and exploring between coach and coachee. Although the book places the question framework within a philosophical stance, very often just the question framework is used as the point of reference, which rather undermines what Whitmore is trying to achieve.

Six-stage framework

An example of a six-stage framework is Kline's (2003) thinking frameworks. Kline provides a thinking environment sequence, where the aim is to select and replace one central limiting assumption with a more empowering worldview, through drawing on six stages of questioning: exploration, further goal development, assumptions, incisive questions, recording and appreciation. Examples of applications of this include team effectiveness, where achievement is seen as directly related to the quality of thinking that the team can achieve.

Ten-stage framework

Finally, an example of a ten-stage framework is one based in 'moment of change transformations' (Ditzler, 1994). The coach assists the individual or team to establish goals and to devise a new vision, where the main focus is on the transformation from a disempowering to an empowering paradigm. The ten-stage question framework helps the coach focus on the past 12 months initially before shifting to a new vision for the next 12 months. Key questions include: What were your accomplishments over the last 12 months? What were your biggest disappointments and frustrations in the last 12 months? In what way do you stop yourself from achieving your best, and how can you change? What is it that gets you up in the morning, motivated and ready to go?

Stout Rostron (2014) also describes various models for coaching (including the one we have used here: purpose, perspective and process) which provide a metaphor for the journey the coach and client undertake and act as a guide to the territory.

She argues that each coaching session must synchronise with the overall journey on which coach and client have embarked, irrespective of the allegiance to a specific model (perspective). That is, she concludes, as do we, that each stage of the process must be consistent with the purpose. However, she clearly sees all models as analogies and not representations of a truth. They are useful or not and the justification for them lies in their utility.

To this point, we have focused largely on coaching processes. We now turn to mentoring.

Mentoring processes

In the mentoring literature, Garvey and Alred (2000) suggest that there is a 'mentoring way'. This represents an orientation towards the client reminiscent of Rogers' (1969) 'core conditions of learning'. Megginson et al. (2006: 4) offer a contextual framework presented as 'levels of mentoring' with which to help understand the process of mentoring. This is particularly relevant to this book because the model takes into account:

- The variants in the mentoring culture
- The mentoring scheme design
- The nature of the mentoring relationship
- The mentoring episode
- The mentoring techniques employed
- The mentoring moment

This onion-like framework offers various units of analysis of the mentoring process and clearly indicates that what goes on in the room is part of a complex process of influences.

Gibb and Megginson (1993) and Clutterbuck and Lane (2004) offer further insight as they identify two main models of mentoring in current usage: the career sponsorship model in the USA and, in the UK, the developmental model. Garvey (2012) identifies a hybrid of these two models which is emerging through talent-management programmes.

However, thinking about the process we use and the questions to which they give rise assists coaches and mentors to structure more effective conversations. It enables the creation of coherence between what happens in an individual session and the overall purpose of the work.

Activity 3.4

Go back to Case Study 3.1 above and choose two frameworks (other than those outlined by Stout Rostron) with which you are familiar and consider:

- What issues raised by the client might elicit interest from the coach/mentor?
- What questions might the coach/mentor ask to elicit information from the client to support the process?
- What is implied in each framework about the role that the coach/mentor might play?
- How might these different frameworks influence your first coaching/mentoring conversation with that client?

These frameworks and the models that sit behind them are a small selection from the multitude of coaching and mentoring approaches available. We have yet to reach the nightmare scenario that our sister professionals in psychotherapy face, where it is reputed that there are more than 450 approaches, with new frameworks being frequently added. We are beginning to suffer from the tendency in other fields whereby coaches want to name a model for themselves rather than build a coherent body of knowledge from within a frame. Krasner and Ullman (1973) described the process of creating new approaches, the development of schools and thereby trainings, the splitting of adherents, new schools and new trainings and conflicting claims for accreditations and respectability. There are perhaps parallels in coaching.

The positive take here is that the strength offered by this variety is that each framework (and the models on which they are based) can add value to our field. The limitations occur when we treat the architecture as a shortcut to a process of working using the questions they generate. Yet, those questions become devoid of the perspective that sits behind it and perhaps even more so the *purpose* that it is designed to serve.

The coaching and mentoring process: Some concluding comments

There are many approaches to thinking about the process we use in coaching and mentoring to assist our client's journeys. Some are based in single theories, while others attempt an integration of multiple perspectives. There is no exemplar to which we can direct the reader and say – this is the way to go. We have to consider if it is to be an open emergent process or one in which direction is set (but not immovable) by the architectural process delineated in the model? Any approach has to help the client to get from where they

Coaching and Mentoring Process

are to where they want to be, although we have to be open to the thought that we may decide to go somewhere entirely different from our initial goal:

> We construct, deconstruct and reconstruct the narrative as we proceed and our clients do the same. We, just like our clients, may retrace our steps, stop, start, restart, give up, re-commit and arrive somewhere, before starting all over again. (Lane and Corrie, 2006: 54)

Activity 3.5

For this exercise, select a coaching or mentoring case that you have recently completed. Describe the encounter from initial referral to closure. Then consider the following points.

Purpose

Did you have an idea of the purpose from the initial referral? How did it change on meeting the client? How did it change or not over the course of the work? Who influenced the development of your purpose? Was the purpose met in its initial or final form? Using the questions from earlier in the chapter:

- What was the question you and the client set out to explore?
- Who were the key stakeholders in the enquiry (that is, those with a significant investment in the work) and what were the expectations of each party?
- What was the role that each party was prepared to play?
- What was the wider context that gave meaning to the purpose of the work you did together?

If the purpose changed in the course of the work, what in the client's story caused you to take a different approach – how was that change communicated to other stakeholders?

In light of your answers to the above questions, would you, with hindsight, have defined the purpose of the work with this client any differently?

Perspective

Consider the perspective that influenced your approach to this work. Was it influenced by a single theory or an integrated approach? If a single theory, how did you ensure that the client's perspective on the world was fully incorporated? If an integrated approach, how did you make the choices as to what to include or leave out?

(Continued)

(Continued)

- What perspectives ('tales') informed your approach?
- What perspectives ('tales') informed the client's approach?
- To what extent was there coherence between your client's perspective and your own?
- How did you ensure that the client was able to explore their beliefs, knowledge and competencies within the encounter?

In light of your answers to the above questions, would you, with hindsight, have used the same or a different perspective to guide your work?

Process

Based on the purpose and perspective as you defined them, what did you actually 'do' with the client? You may wish to consider the following questions:

- What process (including any method or tool) did you use to ensure that the purpose was met within the constraints of the perspectives available to you and your client?
- How did you structure the process for the work?
- Was this process similar to, or different from, the approach you usually take? What were the factors that mediated your choice?

Now consider how you might have altered the process and reflect on how that would have changed the experience for you or your client.

Finally, consider the implications of your answers to all of the above questions for your model of practice.

Summary

- We need to consider the purpose of our work and the perspectives that underpin it and build a process for our work that is coherent
- We need to consider if a self-narrated model of our work (reflexive identity) is sufficient or do we need to consider a relational narrative (relational identity)?
- There are many different approaches to the concept of process, including behavioural and implied process. We draw heavily on sister professions for ideas in both approaches to process
- A useful distinction is between the way we structure our approach (what Stout Rostron, 2014, calls its 'architecture') and the models that underpin them. This distinction gives rise to different frameworks and steps in our process of working

- There is a question over how coaches develop a coherent approach to practice since most programmes require them to build their own model – unlike the disciplines from which it is drawn which teach a model
- If we build our own model of practice from multiple sources, we need to show how it is coherent and rigorous
- Different coaches using varied models will approach the same client issue from very different perspectives. We need to understand the implication of this for our developing field

Topics for discussion

1. Is it appropriate for coaching to offer standardised models for practice?
2. Should we understand only one approach or several in our training?
3. How do we decide what is an appropriate approach for our clients?
4. Are we working as agents of social control when we accept the sponsor's definition of need?

Questions that remain

1. What are the contexts and issues for which coaching is uniquely suited?
2. What are the contexts and issues for which mentoring is uniquely suited?
3. There is a considerable lack of evidence on what works for whom, when and where in our field as a practitioner – how might you begin to contribute possible answers?
4. Some approaches clearly teach one model, while others argue for a personal model – can they both be right?

Further reading

Corrie, S, and Lane, D.A. (2010) *Constructing Stories Telling Tales: A Guide to Formulation in Applied Psychology*. London: Karnac, chapter 2. An account of using 'stories' to affect change.

Garvey, B., Stokes, P. and Megginson, D. (2014) *Coaching and Mentoring: Theory and Practice* (2nd edn). London: Sage, chapter 5. A fairly comprehensive account of different models and processes found in a range of coaching and mentoring settings.

What next?

In Chapter 4, we consider the discourses associated with the skills and the competencies for coaching and mentoring. Whilst there are many examples of competence models being adopted in many different parts of society, particularly within human resource management, leadership and management, the discourse of competence has its problems. Again, the underpinning discourse is that of the rational pragmatic and this leads to the creation of reductionist linear models of skill development which ignore complexity. The rational pragmatic discourse is, however, satisfied through the development of the associated performance criteria used to manage and measure organisational and individual performance.

It is also clear that the competency discourse influences pedagogy in education and training and offers the prospect of the control of professional practice. It is also clear that another discourse associated with competency is the notion of 'predictability', which we argue is at odds with the discourse of 'change' found in some many walks of life in that competence frameworks represent a view of past performance rather than act as a predictor of future behaviour.

Competence and Performance for Coaching and Mentoring: A contested discourse

Keywords

Skill, competence, performance, standards, adult development, expertise

Chapter objectives

After reading this chapter, you will be able to:

- Identify the difference between competence and performance
- Distinguish between different approaches to defining competence
- Consider the standards of different bodies and relate them to your own practice
- Reflect upon the difference between a personal model of competence and a national/international standard

Introduction

To engage in any art, craft or occupation requires the development of a range of skills necessary to carry out the activity involved. As coaches or mentors, we all need to develop a skill base for the work. We might need to be skilled listeners, able to hear the needs the client is struggling to express and help them define those needs in the form of goals to be achieved. Many different skills may be called upon to achieve this core matter of defining client needs.

Often, when we watch someone engage in skilful practice, we can recognise it. We can see that the client and coach or mentor have arrived at a way of working together that meets the client's needs. However, we do not also have to judge the level of skill we observed. We can admire it, be impressed with the skill displayed in the execution of the craft, but we are not required to say that they are competent to perform the task.

As professionals, the matter is different as we may be required to assess the person's skilled practice and say 'yes' they are competent to perform the skills and, more than that, they are fit to practice in our discipline. Yet, when we do so, we say more than that they show the necessary skill when judging fitness to practice. We also require that they are familiar with the knowledge base, which we have codified as marking the underpinning to our practice. They have to know 'what', not just 'how'. We also require that they know why they should act in particular ways – to grasp a values and ethical basis for practice. The concept of competence therefore goes beyond the demonstration of skill: it implies a judgement – competent or not to be admitted into our ranks. For how these ideas inform the debate about the professionalisation of coaching, see Chapter 12.

The competence movement has become all-encompassing in the UK, with groups from all occupations and professions finding themselves subject to national vocational standards. Coaching and mentoring have followed other occupational groups in adopting competence models. Yet, as Bates (1997) argues, the development of competence models outstrips understanding of its effectiveness and social significance. Some go further and argue that competence models are depriving students of access to the ability to define the meanings underpinning the knowledge base necessary for professional practice (Wheelahan, 2007). Competence models promoted by all coaching and mentoring bodies have therefore been endorsed without serious debate of the consequences of adopting this approach to selecting, training and assessing fitness to practice.

A key feature of the competence debate has been to establish generic competencies across occupational groups. Thus, in the USA, the Office of Personnel Management has promoted generic competence models (Rodriguez et al., 2002) and, in the UK, the Health and Care Professions Council has created cross-occupational competencies shared by its many different professional members. Coaching has gone down a different route, with each of the many bodies in the field developing its own competencies, although there are many similarities between them (Stout Rostron, 2014).

They have each adopted different methodologies to define them, but what all occupational models share is a focus on the minimum standard needed to practice rather than achievement of excellence in practice. Our sister professions share similar issues when confronting the competence debate. Hence, counselling psychologists are asked to share some part of a core competence framework with dieticians and radiographers because they are regulated by the same body. There are models for defining competence which focus on defining conditions for excellence – for example, comparing top practitioners with average ones, or asking practitioners to look at factors underpinning their best work. However, the tendency is towards minimal standards necessary for practice rather than highest levels possible. There are a few exceptions. The model used by the European Federation of Psychologists' Associations (EFPA) for psychotherapy was based on aspirational standards which recognised that, for many, they would be currently beyond reach (Lane and Althaus, 2011). Much of the debate has also ignored the difference between competence to practice and conditions related to actual performance in the work context.

Discourses

Given the range of discourses on the role of competencies and skills in the field and the largely absent debate on their effectiveness and social significance, this gives rise to a number of the dialogues which will be addressed. We also consider the possibility for other approaches to defining competence.

Five discourses – 'there and back again'

Discourse 1

Developing competence models is now important to define our profession, but if it lacks critical thinking and critique, we will be ill-served

So what is *competence*?

Grant et al. (1979) used the following definition of competence as a basis for their research into American developments:

> Competence-based education tends to be a form of education that derives a curriculum from an analysis of prospective or actual role in modern society and that attempts to certify student progress on the basis of demonstrated performance in some or all aspects of that role. Theoretically, such demonstrations of competence are independent of time-served in formal educational settings (Grant et al., 1979, quoted in Magnusson and Osborne, 1990).

There are three key features highlighted in the competence debate: the derivation of the goals of training from the analysis of occupational roles; the translation of these goals into training 'outputs' in the form of performance criteria rather than the more traditional teaching parameters of training 'inputs' such as syllabi; and the freeing up of possibilities for individuals to progress at their own speed on the basis of readily available opportunities for performance assessment rather than coverage of course content. The primary tool used to create competences is a process called 'functional analyses' of occupations. It consists of the specification of what is to be learned in terms of performance criteria. To this is added the idea of self-paced learning, whereby rather than setting defined hours for training, learners pace themselves and can be tested to see if they are competent when they are ready. These have come to be regarded as the defining characteristics of competence-based education and training (CBET) in the UK.

Although the discussion above looked at a broad definition of competence to include, for example, values, some within the competence movement focus just on skills. This has been a core issue for the critics of the field. Another core feature of the competence debate largely ignored by bodies in most fields – but including coaching and to some extent, mentoring – is the argument that competence models free up opportunities for individuals to develop at their own speed. They can have available to them multiple opportunities for their performance to be assessed. They are not measured by covering over time a defined course content. Thus, we do not necessarily need to take courses of defined lengths or complete a certain number of practice hours to be judged competent. Yet, all bodies in the field require set training and certain defined practice hours to be admitted to the ranks of the competent. Thus, we constrain ourselves with a CBET model but do not use the freedom it encompasses to enable those with existing expertise to practice. The competence movement has become all-encompassing in the UK, USA, Australia and South Africa – to mention just a few. Groups from all occupations and professions are finding themselves subject to national vocational standards.

Coaching, mentoring and coaching psychology have followed other occupational groups in adopting competence models. We have models from the Australian Psychological Society (APS), the Association for Coaching (AC), CIPD, British Association for Counselling and Psychotherapy (BACP), European Mentoring and Coaching Council (EMCC), International Coach Federation (ICF), Special Group in Coaching Psychology (SGCP), International Society for Coaching Psychology (ISCP) and onward and onward (the Global Convention on Coaching (GCC) identified more than 300 bodies in the field). Each body builds its model (sometimes with reference to others or not). There are calls for collaboration. The GCC in the Dublin Declaration (Mooney, 2008) brought more than sixty international delegates from within more than 40 separate bodies and called for attempts to draw core competencies across the various areas of practice while respecting that some areas will need to build from these in specialist areas. More recently, Kilberg (2015), commenting on a project to develop a competence model for coaching psychology in the USA, stated that rather than have separate professional bodies go their different ways, a more productive approach would be to have one international body (for executive coaching) that encompassed all professionals working in the field.

Given so many different models supposedly defining the same (or at least parallel) activity, can we really argue that we know what competence defines fitness to practice as coaches or mentors? If we cannot define it, how can we make judgements on what is or is not contained within the field and what training is necessary to practice? Our critics would argue that attempts to define a profession on the basis of competence ignore the co-constructed nature of the activity and the fact that our identity as practitioners is built in specific sites of social action (Lo, 2006). To understand what is happening in a coaching or mentoring engagement from this perspective requires that we focus on the multiple contexts in which the activity happens. (Ways to do this will be explored later in the chapter.)

Bates (1997) has outlined the core elements of the approach to competence adopted in the UK and the cultural impact of this movement. In the UK, by the mid-1980s, the government adopted competence-based vocational qualifications (DfES, 1986). The National Council for Vocational Qualifications (NCVQ) was established to specify and implement standards of occupational competence across a range of activities. Bates (1997) makes the point that one person, Gilbert Jessup, played a prominent role and therefore we need to look at key actors, economic, political and social factors.

To be recognised, qualifications had to be based on statements of competence and these were the responsibility of industry, operating through Industry Lead Bodies (ILBs). An attempt was made to establish a body for coaching and it produced a competence model for coaching but it excluded all the key professional bodies in the field, notably for example, the AC, EMCC, ICF, Association for Professional Executive Coaching and Supervision (APECS), BPS and CIPD. As a result of an intervention by these bodies, the work was redirected but it makes the point that establishing who is credible in our field was problematic. The process used (as Bates points out) is to employ consultants to analyse jobs using a process of *functional analysis* to break down the 'key purpose (of the industry) into smaller components' and ultimately into performance criteria (Ellis, 1992: 202). These, in turn, are grouped in 'elements of competence' and then into 'modules'. This stands in stark contrast to the approach in professions more traditionally (e.g., medicine, psychology) where the core knowledge base is established in the form of content-based syllabi.

The nature of what it means to be a professional has been changed by the competence movement. However, critics such as Bates (1997) and Wheelahan (2007) argue that this represents a cultural shift affecting the world of work. Drawing on their analysis, we can point to a number of key implications:

1. There is a growing interest in competence as a means of human resource management (see, for example, Lawler, 1994; Prahalad and Hamel, 1990). Thus, it extends the impact of the competence movement further into leadership and management.

Employers have introduced competencies as part of a clear strategy of business planning and also of assessment of internal skill requirements. Thus, the way we think about business becomes restricted to reductionist linear models of skill development that ignore complexity. However, the rational pragmatic discourse of management becomes satisfied.

2. The competence movement has included the use of performance criteria to manage and measure organisational and individual performance. Hence, all aspects of personal performance become linked in the chain

3. The arrival of competence-based pedagogy promotes deeper changes in structures and processes of social control over work, education and training. Thus, the competence movement enables closer and all-encompassing control of professional practice by organs of the state and they create a limited and mechanistic approach to learning (Brundrett, 2000)

4. Barnett (1994: 73) argues that 'the notion of competence is concerned with predictable behaviours in predicable situations' – a position surely at odds with the discourse of change found in so many work organisations

5. Competence frameworks represent a view of past performance rather than act as a predictor of future behaviour (Cullen, 1992; Lester, 1994)

Apart from Garvey (2011), in discussions around the development of competencies in coaching and mentoring, these criticisms are absent. We have simply and almost uncritically accepted a specific worldview and therefore are complicit in this probably unhelpful cultural shift.

Case study 4.1

You have been asked to coach a school counsellor who has accepted a part-time appointment in the evening to work for a crisis walk-in centre for adolescents. In his other role as a counsellor he is based in one school. He trained as a school counsellor and met the competence standards defined for this. He has a clear referral policy that defines what issues can and cannot be dealt with. His service is backed up by pastoral roles in the school, clear support policies, supervision from an outside agency and established child protection procedures. In the crisis centre, he has no idea what issues will cross the threshold, he is not supervised and has no pastoral system to back him. There are some minimal child protection policies in place but essentially he has to work with whatever is presented at times of the day when limited alternatives are available for referral.

Activity 4.1

Take Barnett's argument in point 5 above. What discourse around competence is implied in his role as school counsellor? What discourse on competence is implied in his new role? How might you support him to negotiate these different discourses? What competences against which you were assessed while in training best assist you in understanding each of these discourses?

Discourse 2

It is not only our critics we ignore, we sometimes ignore the implications for our own practice

These critics point to competence approaches as a relentless social trend that will grow rather than decline. What is learned is not to be determined by subject experts but, rather, trainers become deliverers and assessors of pre-determined learning outcomes. Wheelahan (2007) describes this as the ultimate teacher-proof model.

Wheelahan (ibid.) further argues that existing criticisms are ignored. Quoting Marshall (1991) and Stuart and Hamlyn (1992), she points out that functional analysis, the tool of choice for competence-builders, depends on functionalist traditions in sociology. Yet, the various sociological critiques of functionalism are not addressed, and an example of this is where employers use a single model of employer and employee interests rather than recognising the possibility of conflicting perspectives on the nature of work priorities. She quotes Barnett (1994: 73):

> What counts as good practice in social work, the law, medicine and so on are contested goods … the identification of the occupational standards is not something that can be settled, and competences read off in any absolute fashion.

The research by her group suggests that disputes about the way to do a job is widespread in skilled, semi-skilled and unskilled occupations, as well as in the professions (Wheelahan, 2007).

In the field of coaching and mentoring, we are either ignorant of these debates or choose to ignore them. If we take on these criticisms, then a number of questions need to be examined:

1. What do we mean by skills and competence?
2. Are they the same?

3. How does competence relate to performance?
4. Does one ensure the other?
5. Are coaching and mentoring competency frameworks different somehow?
6. Is there a shared core of competences we each hold?
7. Where might different approaches to coaching and mentoring require extended competences?
8. How are standards evolving in coaching and mentoring, where are we now, where might we be heading?
9. What do we share with sister professions, what is common to all practitioners providing service to others?
10. Does the coach/mentor need to be more skilful than the client, or can the one guide the other?
11. Developing our skills – what does it take, what might models of adult development and learning teach us?

All these become important areas of contestation.

If we look at the relationship between competence models and approaches to training coaches in Chapter 3, the contested nature of this area becomes clear. As stated, training in coaching tends to operate in a number of ways and different programmes are committed to these entirely contradictory routes:

1. You learn a model. Thus, you are encouraged to develop skills in one way of looking at client issues and in working with them. The upside is that you can become very skilful in applying that perspective. You become competent and are assessed against your understanding of a set perspective on the world. Your ability to operate that model is the basis of the judgement made about your competence
2. You adapt models. Thus, you are encouraged to work from parallel perspectives such as cognitive behavioural, positive psychology, solution-focused models and find a way to integrate them coherently in your practice. The choice of models matters, since integrating models which take starkly contrasting perspectives on the world is more difficult. The upside is that you can draw upon a range (even if limited) of ways to help your clients. You become competent and are assessed against your understanding of a group of perspectives on the world. Your ability to operate coherently with those perspectives is the basis of the judgement made about your competence
3. You build your own model. Thus, you are encouraged to look at your own view of the world and find ways to bring alternative perspectives into your orbit of understanding. You build a model unique to yourself which may have much in common with other perspectives but which is owned by you. The upside is that it that you can authentically operate the model because it reflects your own values. You become competent and are assessed against your ability to present a personally authentic framework. Your ability to operate that framework is the basis of the judgement made about your competence

These are contested views about the nature of coaching and to some extent, mentoring, yet, as discussed in Chapter 3, the dialogue about them does not seem to appear in any of the key texts in the field, where the perspectives are simply presented as alternatives for a free choice rather than fundamental differences in the way the world is seen and which have important implications for the service offered to clients.

The evidence base for justifying these three approaches to building models does not feature. No other profession trains its practitioners in these ways. This may be a positive and, as Cavanagh and Lane (2012) argue, maybe the nature of our views on professionalism need to change and coaching can lead the way. But the key is that it is contested space and we are not contesting it, rather, we tolerate diversity on the basis that 'everybody has won and all must have prizes'. Like the psychotherapy debate, we assume that all approaches, regardless of their components, produce equivalent outcomes. (Originally coined as the Dodo Bird verdict on psychotherapy by Rosenzweig in a 1936 drawing on Lewis Carroll's 1865 *Alice's Adventures in Wonderland*; see Duncan, 2002.)

Case study 4.2

You meet a client for the first time. They have had previous experience of coaching and very much prefer a clear set of goals defined early, then a plan to meet them. They lay out what they think is the issue that they need to address but this is at odds with the 360° feedback from their appraisal that has been shared with you. You raise this point and they respond by asking for guidance on the goals that could be defined to change the perceptions in the feedback. Do you assist with this or explore further? Given the model you use in your work, what competencies would you draw upon to make the decisions on which route to take?

Activity 4.2

We meet a client for the first time and seek to understand their needs/wishes/goals. If we take defining client needs generic competencies, we might draw upon the following from the EMCC framework and include:

(22) assists client to clarify and review their desired outcomes and to set appropriate goals

(62) assists clients to effectively plan their actions, including appropriate: support, resourcing and contingencies

(24) explores a range of options for achieving the goals

(Continued)

(Continued)

(66) describes and applies at least one method of building commitment to outcomes, goals and actions

(23) ensures congruence between client's goals and their context

(63) helps client to develop and identify actions that best suit their personal preferences

Questions

1. What assumptions are built into this competency frame about client needs?
2. Once you have considered and stated these assumptions, look at how they might play their role in different models
3. If we train in a specific approach, say as a cognitive behavioural coach (CBC), how might those competencies be manifest? What areas might you explore?
4. Let's say you have an adapted model to include cognitive behavioural, positive psychology and solution-focused approaches, how might those competencies be manifest? What areas might you explore?
5. If as a coach you have built your own model, what might it include?
6. How would the generic competences look different based on these three approaches?

Discourse 3

If the world is more complex, can linear competence models hold?

The standard definition of competence (above), as well as being goal-based also assumes that the world is linear – we can define cause and effect. Yet, the context for coaching is now often:

A world that is increasingly V (volatile) U (uncertain) C (complex) and A (ambiguous).

The idea of a VUCA world arises, as Bennett and Lemoine (2014) have argued, from the adaption of a military analogy to the world of business and in particular strategy. It is sometimes stated that if the world is becoming increasingly volatile, uncertain, complex and ambiguous, how can you plan a strategy since you cannot know what will happen? This, Bennett and Lemoine argue (https://hbr.org/2014/09/a-framework-for-understanding-vuca), is wrong in part because you have to understand and act on each element of V.U.C.A. rather than lump them together as one thing (VUCA). However, the arguments about (VUCA) have highlighted that the linear rational world of simple or even complicated cause-and-effect relationships depends on approaches to planning and strategy-building, which are inappropriate in complex contexts.

What do we know about working in these contexts? One thing is clear, we cannot work in non-linear contexts using coaching models which assume a linear cause–effect relationship. There are a surprising range of perspectives that can help us consider this. These include research in Leadership, Trauma and Decision Sciences.

Leadership research

A number of authors are now exploring both leadership and management in complex spaces (Down and Lane, 2015). Cavanagh and O'Conner (2012), for example, in their research into leadership in high-stress environments have shown through network analysis the complexity of the relationships and multiple ways in which influence has a role. In Garvey (2012), a case study on an executive mentoring programme conducted in the banking sector during the banking crisis, the mentoring programme (established before the crisis) was expected to develop leadership abilities in relation to the competency framework. However, the bank in question was a failing bank and the executives were under huge pressure in the complex crisis and, as suggested by Garvey et al. (2009: 191): 'when professionals are highly anxious … under strong resource pressure, then the delivery of competencies can degrade'.

In leadership development, the competency approach offers to address the rational pragmatic mindset and assumes the possibility of accountability, measurement and quality control to determine value for money and achievement. However, the required leadership behaviours in modern organisations are more complex than competencies alone. For example, the widely agreed (Barnett, 1994; Bolden and Gosling, 2006; Buckingham, 2001; Laloux, 2014; Sosik and Megerian, 1999) behaviours of flexibility, innovation, creativity and improvisation cannot be delivered through a competency framework.

We can coach or mentor leaders to work more effectively in these complex environments and the evidence from this research suggests that they add lasting value. However, the current discourse of competencies in coaching and mentoring do not appear to be addressing skill development of coaches or mentors from these perspectives.

Trauma research

Research in the field of trauma (Agaibi and Wilson, 2005; Joseph, 2012; Tehrani, 2011) has changed considerably in recent years. Originally it focused on pathology and factors that lead to difficulties and resulting post-traumatic stress. More recently, it has looked at:

- Resilience across a range of events – here we are concerned with indications that resilience is a factor in a range of areas; organisations can be more or less resilient in dealing with rapidly changing environments. Individuals can similarly be more or less resilient to traumatic impacts
- Common features across areas for resilience – here, the concern is where we can identify common features which underpin features of resilience
- Post-trauma growth – what is it and what affects it – here, we are concerned with conceptualising post-trauma growth
- We are interested in the existence of pre-existing levels of vulnerably and resilience – here, we are concerned with the idea that post-trauma growth can make us stronger – what does not kill you …

Thus, we have an area of study concerned with rapidly changing complex environments and factors which enable organisations and individuals to manage them as well as an approach to help practitioners to assist them. There have been a few attempts (Tehrani et al., 2012) to apply this to understanding the skills that coaches might bring but they are few in number. Yet, if we are to coach or mentor in a VUCA world, competence in these areas will be necessary.

Decision sciences

The decision sciences are a vast area of research that includes making decisions under varying conditions of uncertainly (Kahane, 2004; Kahneman, 2011; Kayes, 2006; Lane and Corrie, 2012; Sterman, 1994). Understanding from these fields creates the possibility, not of goal-orientated linear coaching or mentoring, but of enabling a process of 'emergence'.

What gives that emergence a sense of meaning is purpose, and this seems to benefit from the ways in which people can reconstruct their stories about self and events. This is perhaps where coaching and mentoring has made strides in encompassing narrative approaches (Drake, 2007; Garvey, 2006b; Stelter, 2014).

Both the leadership and trauma research shows that when faced with high-stress contexts, there is a tendency to close down and seek certainty. A more sustainable approach is to open up to possibilities of co-authoring a new story. Many approaches offer these possibilities to us as coaches and mentors, so how might we incorporate understanding of them to build our competency to deal with a VUCA environment?

Approaches that involve a broad base of ideas include:

- Deep Democracy
- Open Space
- World Café
- Appreciative Enquiry

- Socio-Drama Topography
- Participant-Directed Facilitation (PDF)

Decision science teaches us that we need approaches that encourage us to think:

- Differently, wider, deeper, complexly
  - Think differently – experiment with ideas and behaviours so that new possibilities emerge
  - Think wider – see the world through a wider-angled lens that goes beyond personal models and into interpersonal and systems thinking
  - Think deeper – go within self to the implicational level
  - Think with more complexity – see the world as interconnected and non-linear

Yet, as outlined in Chapter 3, these broader perspectives hardly feature in the coaching and mentoring literature. Some, such as mindfulness, are clearly present, but decision sciences and others discussed above are notably absent.

Case study 4.3

You have been asked to coach a team that is facing a complete reorganisation of its approach. The team have spent several months trying to design a way to move from the annual and five-year planning cycle which previously governed their work, to a system that seeks, receives and is responsive to client feedback in real time. They have failed to create a plan to achieve this. How might you help them to think differently, wider, deeper and with more complexity?

What ideas from your model of practice would help you to assist them to achieve this?

Discourse 4

There are other ways to build on core competence – going beyond standards towards excellence

To recap, *functional analysis* based on analysis of jobs is the preferred foundation for building competence models. The resulting generic competences are both occupation-specific and cross-groups. The advantage is that it covers a wide range of practitioners, but the disadvantage is that it is context free and excludes excellence and factors impacting on performance. It is important because it defines minimum standards for admission into the field and is part of creating a professional identity (see Chapter 12). As Garvey et al. (2104: 222) state:

> No one wants to be operated upon by a brain surgeon who got 1 per cent over the pass/fail boundary, but lots of patients are operated on by just such people and the same principle follows for qualified coaches.

But we can go further ... Excellence in coaching or mentoring might be an alternative way to think about competencies based on comparing best performers with average performers. This would result in context-specific definitions that can include excellence but still exclude performance factors. Context analysis, comparing what factors are present when we do our best work, covers context, excellence and factors impacting on performance. Studies of competence built using these types of models result in approaches to competence that focus on our best work while taking account of factors which impinge upon it. Thus, there are multiple ways that we might approach the competence debate in coaching and mentoring that can fit the contexts in which we work, including complex environments.

However, there is one important omission to much of the skills and competence debate in coaching and mentoring. We have largely ignored the burgeoning research over the past few decades that has looked at expertise. The development from novice to expert has been studied across multiple professions, sports, chess and other activities. The results are remarkably similar whatever the field of expertise. Outstanding performance is not due to any innate talent but is based upon many years of deliberate practice, coaching and mentoring. It seems that if you want to be great, you need a good coach or mentor. You need to push yourself and find a coach or mentor who will do so beyond your comfort zone to new and unimagined levels of skills.

Ericsson et al. (2006) have looked at data gathered by more than 100 scientists who looked at elite surgeons, chess players, writers, athletes, pianists and other experts and specialists. The key they found was in engaging in 'deliberate' practice, which they described as a sustained focus on tasks that they couldn't do before. They argued that experts 'continually analyzed what they did wrong, adjusted their techniques, and worked arduously to correct their errors'. In common with other findings, they suggested that it took at least ten years (the 10,000 hours concept) and needs the help of an expert teacher/coach or mentor to provide difficult and often painful feedback. Eventually, experts come to guide their own behaviour through developing their inner coach or self-mentor (Carr, 2011) thus supporting the old adage that practice makes perfect or to rephrase this, practice makes things easier.

If we used the expertise research or some of the other existing approaches to developing competence for coaching and mentoring, we would have a different list to that produced by functional analysis. The research also points to the level of practice necessary to be great and this is not in the number of hours alone, it is also in practice of critical reflection and the development of reflexivity. If you want to be great, get a good coach or mentor and practice, practice, practice! Another way of exploring what a good coach or mentor looks like might be to explore the nature of the conversations they have with their clients.

Stein (2009) has done significant relevant work in this area. Through interviewing coaches and analysing session transcripts, she identified 16 'conversational identities'. The typology is designed for the coaches' own self-reflection and learning, rather than to be used by the coachee. Stein usefully categorises the identities into three frames, a Process Frame, a Content Frame and a Relationship Frame. Discursive Identities in the Process Frame include Agenda Facilitator, Business Administrator, Learner and Orchestrator. Eight discursive identities in the Content Frame are divided into three categories: the 'Coach Elicits' category includes Exploration Facilitator, Action Facilitator and Narrative Listener; the 'Coach Informs' category includes Expert, Guide and Reflector; and the 'Coach and Client Co-contribute' category includes Practice Player and Problem-Solver. The four discursive identities in the Relationship Frame are Supporter, Challenger, Believer and Colleague/Friend.

Running such analyses on the coaches of great performers might be an interesting place to start our analysis of the competencies necessary for both coaching and mentoring.

Case study 4.4

You have been asked to facilitate a residential workshop over three days for a group of teachers, psychologists, head teachers, support teachers and parents who are concerned to create effective systems for ensuring pro-social behaviour in schools. They work in very different contexts, but this group have been brought together because each one has been involved in projects which are regarded by peers as great examples of getting it right in both devising ways to work with children having difficulties and in promoting positive behaviour in schools. How might you help them to define what underpins their excellence and find a way to draw from this some guidance or maybe the key competences for others seeking to follow their path? As the facilitator, you have no knowledge of the field in which your role has to find a way to help them understand excellence and to communicate.

Coaching and mentoring skills and competencies: Some concluding comments

Coaching and mentoring is no longer about fixing problems (if it ever was) – we tell a wide variety of stories about our work. Yet, one of the discourses to which we adhere is the concept of a generic competence model to underpin practice. That model varies by stint of the professional body to which we belong, yet we all claim to be members of a shared field of endeavour. We have also adopted the competence route fairly uncritically, ignoring the different discourses on competence that exist in the literature. In particular, we have ignored the need to go beyond the idea of core competence. Perhaps we need to pay more attention to the idea of excellence in practice that underpins it and how we can develop it. Excellence is always context-dependent – we need to think about competency for uncertainty and increasingly equip our field to address messy complex issues.

If there are many approaches to thinking about the competence we use in coaching and mentoring to assist our client's journeys, perhaps our approaches to defining competence need to reflect this. The approach taken by most professional bodies is to use a process based on functional analysis to define minimal competences for practice. These are generically defined and apply to all. This is based on the assumption from other professions that there is a core framework of knowledge and skills, which define the profession. Its purpose is agreed. Yet, the way we practice in coaching and mentoring is very different. Some practices are based on single theories, others attempt integration of multiple perspectives, and yet others build their own model of practice. Can a generic competence model encompass this variety? There is no exemplar in other professions to which we can direct the reader and say: this is the way to go. We have to consider if we need an open emergent process to defining our skills set or one in which direction is set by the architecture of functional analysis? Any approach we use has to help the client to get from where they are to where they want to be. Perhaps it is time for us to be open to the thought that we may decide to go somewhere entirely different to our initial goal of defining competencies for our field:

> We construct, deconstruct and reconstruct the narrative as we proceed and our clients do the same. We, just like our clients, may retrace our steps, stop, start, restart, give up, re-commit and arrive somewhere, before starting all over again. (Lane and Corrie, 2006: 54)

Summary

- The discourse on competence has become dominant in our field
- It is, however, a limited discourse, which is built from a functional approach to understanding what we do, which is based on minimum standards for practice
- This discourse ignores the many critiques of the field of competence-based education and training
- We need to consider if the varied contexts for our work render competence frameworks as necessary or sufficient to reflect our practice

- There are many different approaches to the building of competence models, some of which are based on excellence rather than minimum standards. They become aspirations to which we journey rather than fixed points
- To the extent that we work in increasingly diverse and unpredictable contexts, it raises the question of the value of competence models to support our work
- There is a question over how coaches/mentors can develop a coherent approach to practice based on competences if programmes alternatively require them to build their own model, use multiple sources or use single sources

Topics for discussion

1. Is it appropriate for coaching and mentoring bodies to offer standardised models of competence?
2. If our field is becoming increasingly diverse and is dealing with complex situations, what competencies might be relevant for future trainees?
3. When you are doing your best work, what competence do you feel has underpinned it?
4. What does excellence in coaching or mentoring look like – how would we know?
5. Does leadership, trauma or decision sciences have most to contribute to the knowledge base of our field – why?

Questions that remain

1. What would an excellence-based model of professional practice contribute to our field?
2. What other discourses, currently underrepresented in our field, need to be part of our development as a profession?
3. What does the way we currently approach competence-building in our field add as well as detract from the profession?

Further reading

Barnett, R. (1994) *The Limits of Competence*. London: Open University Press and Society for Research into Higher Education. An intelligent critique of the idea of competence.

Wheelahan, L. (2007) 'How competency-based training locks the working class out of powerful knowledge: A modified Bernsteinian analysis', *British Journal of Sociology of Education*, 28(5): 637–51. An intelligent critique of competency frameworks.

What next?

In Chapter 5, we consider the discourses associated with learning. We look at a combination of many theories into three main discourses:

- Phase theory
- Stage theory
- Journey theory

Coaching and mentoring could feature in all three of these discourses. In Chapter 5, we offer another discourse 'conversational learning'. Here, context, situation and experience become important.

5

Coaching and Mentoring in the Learning Mix

Chapter outline

- Learning theories linked to coaching and mentoring
- Conversational learning
- How is learning achieved?
- What makes coaching and mentoring affective and distinctive?

Keywords

Learning, conversational learning, benefits and outcomes, the emotions and the cognitive

Chapter objectives

After reading this chapter, you will be able to:

- Not feel the need for pre-specified objectives!
- Develop critical insights into the importance of meaning-making in human learning and progress
- Develop insights and critical perspectives into learning theories and how they relate to coaching and mentoring
- Understand the potential benefits and outcomes of coaching and mentoring conversations
- Develop critical insight into how these benefits are achieved
- Appreciate that contexts influence the perceptions of the benefits of coaching and mentoring

Introduction

Coaching and mentoring are rooted in the idea of conversational learning within a dyadic relationship. In this chapter we consider this idea of 'conversational learning', which is, arguably at least, a backbone to coaching and mentoring theory. Here, context, situation and experience become important. To aid the discussion, we consider a combination of many theories into three main discourses:

- Phase theory
- Stage theory
- Journey theory

The phase theory discourse is a major underpinning philosophy to education systems around the world. It is based on the idea of 'what happens to people psychologically as they grow older?' Phase theory is based on age-related discourse.

Stage theories also contribute to the design of education systems. This is based on a discourse of stages of development – the assumption is that people learn in stages and we climb up these to progress.

The journey theory discourse is based on life as the great educator where people learn through and with and by experiences.

Coaching and mentoring could feature in all three of these discourses. In this chapter we offer an alternative discourse to the competency and skills discourse.

Learning theories linked to coaching and mentoring

Some (Brunner, 1998; Carmin, 1988; Caruso, 1996; Garvey 2011) argue that both coaching and mentoring are radically under-theorised. For the rational pragmatic manager working in an organisation, this may not present too much of a problem! However, there is little doubt that research influences practice and 'there is nothing as practical as a good theory' (Lewin, 1951: 169). While there is no theory that is unique to either coaching or mentoring, it is possible to examine a range of learning theories and find resonances with both coaching and mentoring practice. In this case, we are adopting a set of 'proxy theories' to inform this chapter, and this indicates that coaching and mentoring have the potential at least to be a very powerful learning processes.

Daloz (1999) provides a useful summary of three main learning theories as follows:

- Phase theory (Jung, Levinson, Buhler, Neugarten)
- Stage theory (Kegan, Piaget, Gilligan, Kohlbergh)
- Journey theory (Perry, Daloz)

Phase theories

Phase theory is based on the idea that people go through phases of learning and development. Phase theory is driven by the question: 'What happens to people psychologically as they grow older?' Therefore, phase theories are, in the main, chronologically determined. However, phase theories also recognise the influence of cultural attitudes on the ageing process and, therefore, are also culturally determined – i.e., people in one culture may have a different view of older people to those in another. The best known example of age related phase theory is found in a diagram in Levinson et al. (1978: 57).

The basic idea is that life is full of age-related transitions. These transitions coalesce around the decades. As a person approaches a significant birthday, they start to consider the implications of what it means to be 20 or 30, for example. It then takes a further period once this birthday has passed to develop into being, for example, a 30-year-old. Levinson's original work on males suggested that the average time it takes to make a transition is seven years, whereas those with mentors to assist the process reduced the transition period to an average of three years. The ideas expressed in the above age-transition model were probably the birth of organised mentoring for career progression in the USA in the early 1980s. This was an attempt to replicate the positive benefits of natural mentoring. It could be argued that coaching activity, which shares the same skills and process as mentoring, has the potential to offer similar benefits to those in transition.

Stage theories

Stage theories, unlike phase theories, are based on the idea that there are stages of development for people. These were identified mainly in educational settings with, Piaget (1970) being the main force behind this notion. In general terms, Daloz (1999) suggests that these theories can be summarised as having three main stages:

- Pre-conventional stage, in which one's own survival is important ...
- through to ...
- Conventional stage, in which we wish to fit and belong ...
- through to ...
- Post-conventional stage, in which broader issues than survival or fit are considered

While Piaget's work has been subject to criticism in that his stages of development are not rigidly defined, a view with which we would agree with, and, more importantly, his research methodology was unrepresentative and therefore not generalisable, his model of development dominates the landscape of curricula in the education systems around the world. The relationship between this set of theories and coaching and mentoring is similar to that of the phase theories. A coach or mentor may enable a shift from the plateau affect implied by stage theory to enable progression to the next stage.

Journey theories

Journey theories, according to Daloz (1999), are based on a movement from naïve, simplistic thinking to complex and relativistic reasoning. Life is positioned as a journey in which choices are made and adventures are to be experienced, or not!

The idea of a journey of learning is the basis of the *Odyssey* and *Les Aventures de Télémaque* (see Chapter 1), and the metaphor of 'journey' is often used in practice in relation to both coaching and mentoring activity – a coach or mentor could be positioned as a guide for the journey or a catalyst for the journey or one who enables choice at particular milestones in the journey.

In Case Study 5.1, an attempt is made to link the three theories of learning and development to lived experience.

Case study 5.1

Fred is 36 years old. He is a highflier. He is an insurance expert and has developed his expertise in three different companies. Fred, in his own words, is regarded as an 'industry expert'. He had recently joined his current organisation having left a senior post in a large recently privatised utility. He was recruited on the basis of his specialist knowledge and Fred now holds the most senior position in the Insurance Department in his new organisation. The coach was asked to work with him on his written communication skills.

Fred's concerns were miles away from report-writing skills! He kept trying to talk about reports and had examples of his work but he really wanted to talk about how he felt as a new recruit in this organisation. He felt that his 'cultural orientation is strained' in the new business. He commented that: 'the language is different, politics are different, there are different skill requirements on me. These are in terms of changing from just giving the Board information upon which to make a decision, to me having to be persuasive and influence them.'

He repeatedly expressed his lack of confidence, insecurity and sense of guilt about his salary: 'They pay me shedloads of money, but I'm not worth it.' He talked of resigning and the alternatives. He played in a jazz band, and he was keen to explore the possibility of doing this for a living. He commented: 'All my life I have been climbing the corporate ladder and now I realise that I have been leaning the ladder on the wrong wall!' He felt trapped by his position and salary, his family obligations, the mortgage, the school fees, holidays and his lifestyle and had become used to living with 'shedloads of money'.

As the coaching progressed, Fred talked more about report-writing and the challenge of communication in the new organisation. He returned to the issue of 'cultural orientation'. He realised that he was using a different language to the readers of his reports and he knew that he needed to change it if he wanted to remain with this organisation. He also knew that he needed to develop a new network of relationships and allies to break his isolation. Fred's attitude shifted as he became more engaged in the communication process and less concerned with his feeling of inadequacy and guilt. At the penultimate meeting, Fred said: 'I am worth the money, I'm good at what I do, I just forgot that for a while as I tried to fit into a new organisation.' During the last session, he said: 'I think I've cracked it now, I can still play in my jazz band and do this job, it's not either/or, it's both, I've got things in perspective – I just needed to learn the ropes, that's all.' Fred, had with him his latest report. This was very much in the style of the organisation. He was using the language of the Board and he was structuring the report in a succinct but persuasive manner. He was making decisions and persuading others that his views were sustainable.

(Based on Garvey, 2006b.)

Discussion of Case Study 5.1

Fred was extracting meaning from the conversations and 'meaning is ambiguous because it arises out of a process of interaction between people' (Riessman, 1993: 15). 'Meaning is fluid and contextual, not fixed and universal' (ibid.). The meaning made here was dynamic and shifted over time – it takes time to learn but, arguably, the time taken in this transition was reduced for Fred as a result of the conversations.

We now discuss the above case in relation to the learning theories previously presented above.

Phase theory and Case Study 5.1

Fred was in transition. On one level, this was clearly about his new job in the new organisation but in terms of his age, at 36 Fred was on the cusp of the settling-down and midlife transition. He was therefore in a reappraisal phase, where neglected aspects of his life, his music perhaps, were calling out to him. Levinson et al. (1978) suggest that the settling-down/midlife transition is when men in particular address the polarities of their lives and seek balance or equilibrium. Here, he was still defining himself and he needed a coach or mentor to help him with this transition. Whilst the relationship was short, it was significant to Fred.

(Continued)

(Continued)

Stage theory and Case Study 5.1

Similar to phase theories, Fred had been pushed from his previous Stage 2 conventional thinking back into Stage 1 pre-conventional thinking, where he was struggling again. Fred had separated himself from one culture by leaving his old job and had joined a new one. Jung (1958) calls this 'individuation'. This transition process is where we learn to differentiate ourselves from our culture, while at the same time this differentiation enables a re-engagement with the culture, resulting in a greater sense of belonging. In a sense, it was a critical and reflected choice to re-engage rather than a driving desire to belong. So, issues of survival were important to him and the jazz band offered escape. However, into Stage 3, where Fred emerged, he was considering issues beyond survival and fit which involved his family, his career and a new sense of his own identity.

Journey theory and Case Study 5.1

Fred's story is a common one and it is a story about a development journey in change. Fred had left one situation and was in a new role in a new company and he needed to understand the culture. This meant understanding the language of the new organisation. He also seemed to have a confidence crisis in the transition and he needed to remind himself of who he was and what he could do and how he could be – he had temporarily forgotten! So his learning was about reframing the situation and creating a new frame to which he could relate his life's narrative. As this happened, his knowledge and skills, which were temporarily forgotten, were adapted and transferred into the new situation. Fred had no real intention of becoming a full-time jazz musician but this had become a temporary but comforting distraction during a difficult transition. He had moved from naïve thinking in which he sought escape to relativistic complex reasoning – he could have it all and he could learn to adapt and he was skilled and competent. He was supported in this journey by someone who listened to him and reflected this back to him. This enabled the reframing to take place.

However, a risk of all three theoretical positions is that 'outcome', moving through a phase, shifting a stage or the destination, may become the sole driver. This is the idea behind learning objectives in training and educational programmes and the notion of goals in coaching and mentoring. As raised in Chapter 1, there is a growing tendency in both the public and private sectors towards 'objectivity' in work activity. Clearly, this approach is driven by notions of accountability and quality control but the emphasis on outcomes alone may push to one side more 'process' and relational elements of learning. The outcome approach may get us where we supposedly want to go but says little about alternative destinations or that in travelling, we may be enriched. It also sets the ground for the idea that we might accelerate the travelling or view learning in economic terms as offering a 'quick return' (Garvey, 2006b).

Barnett (1994: 32–7) goes further when he states that: 'Society is more rational, but it is a rationality of a limited kind' and 'genuinely interactive and collaborative forms of reasoning' are in danger of being driven out from this discourse. So, rationality is self-limiting and drives out interaction and collaboration, rather like Socrates in Chapter 1. Coaching and mentoring are arguably 'genuinely interactive and collaborative form of reasoning' (Barnett, 1994: 37), and this may go some way towards explaining the rise of coaching and mentoring in all sectors of society across the developed and developing worlds. Perhaps the rational pragmatic context of modern society, which attempts to minimise emotional support, is smart enough to recognise that emotional support and trust are necessary (Levinson et al., 1978; Pegg, 1999; van Emmerik, 2008) for good quality learning to take place in intimate dialogic settings like coaching and mentoring and are thus supporting the activity. This provides another explanation for their exponential growth. Coaching and mentoring offer a humanising antidote to the driving culture of the rational pragmatic.

Activity 5.1

Consider Joe …

Joe is 48 years old. He worked with his 'old' company for many years and had climbed the corporate ladder to be head of a division. He had spent most of his working life in sales and had a strong network of people both internally and externally. Joe is very sociable with very well-developed interpersonal abilities. His 'old' company had recently 'merged', or as Joe described it, was 'hijacked by the bigger outfit'. Joe had, in his own words, 'survived the mugging' and 'had come out of it quite well'. However, his networks had changed and he 'no longer felt in charge and safe in his ability'.

Joe was having difficulties with report-writing. His bosses weren't happy with his reports and he felt 'under the microscope, in a different world'. Joe felt angry: 'I can write, I've been writing stuff for years but this lot have changed the rules. Now, it's not "write as you speak", it's "put a case", "make an argument", "persuade and influence, not present and tell"'. Despite this, Joe was keen to learn and understand: 'after all, if that's what they want, I'd better learn it or get another job, and at my age that's not so easy'. But in the coaching sessions, Joe wanted to talk about other things – personal life, and family, finance, health and future plans. He did this by asking the coach to talk about these things. Joe was good at getting people to talk – it was one of his main skills in life! Eventually, once

(Continued)

(Continued)

he had got this from his coach, he talked about his family, his large house, private education for his three children and the cost of it. He wondered if it was worth it. He was contemplating selling off part of his garden to finance a new lifestyle for himself, 'to get out of the rat race and relax a bit, have a life'. The coach and Joe then explored his options and choices.

Joe's recurring metaphor was a variation on: 'stuck on the treadmill', 'hamster in a wheel', 'slave to the corporation' and 'poor little rich man'. He discussed these feelings and explored their meanings. He concluded that the merger had contributed to him 'losing my self-belief', and that the new environment is 'challenging my competence and making me feel exposed'.

Joe did know how to write and adapt to people but he had temporarily forgotten this fact. The sessions helped him to re-establish his confidence and self-belief. Joe understood that he needed to establish a new network, adapt his language and apply previously held knowledge into a new context. Joe was going to 'sell' himself into the new organisation. Joe emailed the coach: 'No problem now, getting there, thanks for the reminders of my abilities and the reorientation!'

(Based on Garvey, 2006b.)

Questions

1. Analyse Joe by making use of the three theoretical positions outlined above
2. What are the similarities and differences between Joe and Fred?
3. What are your thoughts about the influence of the context of the workplace on Joe?

These theoretical positions are all associated with the next section of this chapter – the concept of 'conversational learning'.

Conversational learning

As discussed in Chapter 1, coaching and mentoring are, in essence, dialogic learning processes. This section of the chapter explores this idea.

Bruner (1990: 33) states that: 'The central concept of human psychology is meaning and the process and transactions involved with the construction of meaning.' In essence, this chapter is about learning, and learning is about meaning, and central to meaning is narrative. The narrative or story by which each one of us lives our lives influences our actions and thoughts, and shapes who and what we are and what we might become. Coaches and mentors also know that people often position themselves and others within a narrative as characters. In this sense, 'telling stories and being "told" by stories, becomes therefore the basis for personal identity' (Edwards and Usher, 2000: 45). It is, however, also important to remember, as discussed in

Chapter 1, that individual narratives are in addition shaped by the social context. As Fairclough (1992: 23) suggests, 'whenever people speak or listen or write or read, they do so in ways which are determined socially and have social affects'. Coaching and mentoring activity deals in narratives and the stories brought into the coaching and mentoring room are often relentlessly affective – they deal in emotions, which means that the 'observer' or coach or mentor cannot be dispassionate or detached because understanding and insight are arrived at by 'getting on the inside'. Coaches and mentors know this and know that objectivity in relation to human affairs is 'a figment of our minds; it does not exist in nature' (Skolimowski, 1992: 42), and, here, taking all points made above, sits the power of the kind of conversational learning found in coaching and mentoring conversations. Some have gone further and have built a conversational science for psychology, arguing for the central importance of the learning conversation (Thomas and Harri-Augstein, 1985). Their work has a particular interest for coaches and mentors in that they provide a detailed framework for investigating and working with conversations applicable to coaching and mentoring.

A model which is often employed to illustrate the coaching and mentoring process is Kolb's (1984) notion of 'experiential learning'. Often, employing this model is instinctive – there is nothing as practical as a good theory! Kolb's (ibid.) work, developed from the work of Dewey (1958), Lewin (1951) and Piaget (1970), clearly argues that learning from experience is a process and not a product or outcome. Kolb viewed the process as cyclic, as shown in Figure 5.1.

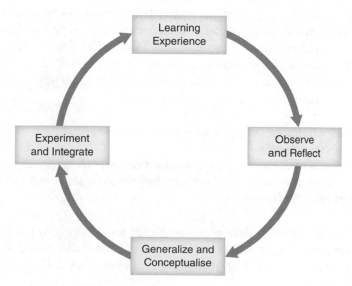

Figure 5.1   Kolb's Learning Cycle

As well as the four points in the cycle, there are also two dimensions set in opposition to each other:

1. Concrete experience set against abstract conceptualisation
2. Active experimentation set against reflective observation

Both dimensions have the potential to contribute to learning in two main ways: gaining experience through action; and gaining experience through reflection. Action-based experience leads to apprehension; whereas reflective experience leads to comprehension. Kolb (1984) suggests that experience gained during action or testing is 'concrete experience'. Experience which is gained through apprehension, may involve feelings of the 'heat' of the situation, the mood, the ambience. The concrete experience will include a whole range of events, some of which will be tangible and others, intangible. The resultant knowledge is 'accommodative knowledge'.

At the other end of the vertical axis, generalisations are the result of the concrete experience being comprehended in the form of a model or theory. This introduces an element of predictability into the knowledge. Experience which is grasped through comprehension and transformed through intention is known as 'assimilative knowledge'. The testing element on the horizontal axis is not part of an experiential stage but one that transforms the abstract into concrete experience through experimental activity. Separating active experimentation and concrete experience may be difficult because they may occur simultaneously. However, they do represent different dimensions. A task may be performed identically by two separate individuals but the resultant concrete experience may be completely different. Reflection on the other horizontal axis occurs after a concrete experience. Reflection or observation is part of the documentation process. No interpretation takes place, only description. From reflection, abstract theories or concepts may be generated. These may be further tested.

Kolb was keen to emphasise that four conditions need to be in place for people to learn from experience:

1. Voluntary, willing and active involvement in the experience
2. Opportunities for reflection
3. The learner needs to have and be able to use analytical skills to conceptualise the experience
4. The learner needs decision-making and problem-solving skills to make use of the new ideas gained from the experience

Kolb's work has been further developed specifically for coaching by Chapman (2010), who also integrates the work of Wilber (2000). Kolb is not without his critics, although he seeks to answer them in the latest edition of his works (see Kolb, 2015 and also see Lane et al., 2016).

These four elements seem important in relation to coaching and mentoring activity. For example, Megginson et al. (2006) suggest that voluntary participation in mentoring schemes is a core condition of success, and Neilson and Eisenbach (2003) show that ongoing reviews or reflection by the mentoring pair about the nature of their relationship is key to its successful outcome. Reflection is positioned by many (Dembkowski and Elridge, 2003; Kilburg, 2004b; Merrick and Stokes, 2008) as a central ingredient of coaching and mentoring. However, Boud et al. (1985) argue that Kolb's model does not develop the notion of reflection sufficiently. This is important in the context of coaching and mentoring because part of their function is to support reflection through focused conversation. Additionally, coaching and mentoring work with people's experience and their story, and in this sense Kolb's model has relevance. To take points 3 and 4 in the list above, these are also central to coaching and mentoring practice and may be found in the competency list for coaches and mentors in, for example, the European Mentoring and Coaching Council's (EMCC) competency framework.

Kolb and Fry (1975) also brought us the notion of learning styles and this offers the acknowledgement that people are different and learn in different ways. Coaches and mentors know this, but Jarvis (1987) and Tennant (1997) argue that, despite the neat logic and integration of Kolb's model, the very neatness and logic do not necessarily make them legitimate. The main issue for Jarvis and Tennant is that this model does not apply in all contexts and does not deal with, for example, information assimilation or memorisation. Additionally, the very idea that the complexity of human learning can be reduced to four styles does seem to stretch credulity!

A further criticism of Kolb is that the underpinning research did not allow for cultural variation (Anderson, 1988). This is not a criticism all would accept since Kolb did see experiential learning as a developmental process – a product of both personal and social knowledge influenced by the culture in which the individual operates (see Lane et al., 2016, for a discussion of this). Coaching and mentoring practices are influenced by the social and cultural context, as discussed throughout this book, and so, too, are peoples' approaches to learning. This needs to be taken into account when engaging in conversational learning between peoples with, not only different learning styles but also with their communication and cognitive styles that are influenced by their cultural roots. It is here that coaches and mentors need to take into account the individual's sense of 'self' in relation to their cultural heritage, and the underpinning 'Western' assumptions in Kolb and Fry (1975) simply may not apply. Kolb and Fry are also influenced by the dominant rational pragmatic discourse which dominates Western thinking. However, in the final chapter of Kolb's original text, there is a discussion of higher levels of learning and the integrative knowledge which includes consideration of Eastern and Western thinking – a theme further developed in the recent edition. Despite these problems, Kolb and Fry offer a helpful framework for the coaching and mentoring practitioner wanting to develop their practice.

Jarvis (1992) goes further and argues that, while Kolb's model has a neat simplicity about it, in reality learning is likely to be far more complex. He offers a typology of learning, developed from Kolb. He suggests that a learner may experience any combination of the three forms at any one time and he presents this as movements from one position to another (see Table 5.1).

Table 5.1 Typography of learning

Category of response to experience	Type of learning/non-learning
1. Non-learning	Presumption
2. Non-consideration	
3. Rejection	
4. Non-reflective	Preconscious learning
5. Skills learning	
6. Memorisation	
7. Reflective learning	Contemplation*
8. Reflective skills learning*	
9. Experimental learning*	

Note: *Each of the reflective forms of learning can have two possible outcomes – conformity or change
Source: After Jarvis (1992: 72)

With regard to the idea of a 'non-learning' experience, Jarvis (1992: 72) suggests that 'people do not always learn from their experiences'. The 'presumptive' aspect is 'a response to everyday experience. It involves a sense of trust that the world will not change and therefore that successful acts can be repeated.' Jarvis argues that this is the basis of 'social living' for many and it would be 'quite intolerable for people to have to consider every word and every act in every social situation before they performed it' (ibid.: 73). In Table 5.1, taken from Jarvis, he suggests that 'presumption' in 'non-learning' follows the route of 1 – 'non-learning', 'presumption' through to 4 – 'non-reflective', 'preconscious learning'. As for the 'non-consideration' aspect, Jarvis (1992) points out that people have a variety of reasons for not considering a learning experience. In terms of the routes taken in Table 5.1, 'non-consideration' also moves from 1 to 4. In coaching and mentoring, this may offer an explanation for a lack of activity following a session. The lack of action may simply be because what was discussed gets rejected by the coachee or mentee. This is not always a deliberate act.

However, where the 'rejection' aspect of 'non-learning' is employed following a coaching or mentoring conversation, an individual may experience or consider something but decide to reject the idea and confirm the present state. Sociologists may argue that an individual may not have much real freedom to reject experiences because, to some extent, we are products of our social conditioning and therefore respond to many experiences in an almost predetermined way. Jarvis believes that those who experience life in a 'presumptive' way, experience considerable freedom and little anxiety because they expect life to unfurl in a prescribed way. Those who operate in this way will not feel pressured to perform to comply, despite social pressures. Using Table 5.1, rejection takes a route of 1 to 3 to 7 to either 4 or 9.

Jarvis (1992) also discusses the notion of 'non-reflective' learning. He subdivides this into the elements of 'preconscious learning', 'skills learning' and 'memorisation'. He (ibid.: 75) argues that 'preconscious learning' is difficult to isolate, describing it as a person being 'vaguely aware'. Arguably, both coaching and mentoring could enable greater awareness if appropriate. Using Table 5.1, 'preconscious learning' moves from 1 to 3 to 6 to 4.

'Skills learning' is linked to training for manual activities. Jarvis (ibid.) qualifies this as learning 'simple, short procedures', and he argues that skills – in this learning mode – are acquired through imitation and role-modelling. This relates to the model of coaching outlined in Megginson and Boydell (1979: 5) as: 'a process in which a manager, through direct discussion and guided activity, helps a colleague to solve a problem, or to do a task better than would otherwise have been the case', and role-modelling is something associated with mentoring activity (Erikson, 1978; also see Chapters 1 and 7). However, Jarvis (1992: 75) suggests that 'skills learning' happens in an 'action mode of experience rather than in communicative interaction', and therefore this may not relate to a discursive form of coaching and mentoring but more to a demonstrating approach. 'Skills learning' moves through Table 5.1 from 1 to 3 to 5 to 8 to 6 and to either 4 or 9.

The final element of the 'non-reflective' category is 'memorisation'. This is a commonly understood aspect of learning. It is often associated with formal education. Children memorise when they learn and revise for school exams and adults believe that this is what is expected of them when they attend higher education courses. 'Memorisation' works in both interactive communication and the action mode. Jarvis (1992) points out that 'memorisation' moves through Table 5.1 from 1 to 3 to 6 then possibly 8 to 6 and then either to 4 or 9.

These three modes of 'non-reflective learning' – 'preconscious learning', 'skills learning' and 'memorisation' – are processes of social reproduction where essential social structures and processes are not questioned or challenged and compliance to social norms is the main outcome. Arguably, for professional bodies in coaching and mentoring, these forms or modes of learning when it comes to their rules and codes are quite applicable.

The third element of Jarvis' typography is 'reflective learning'. Many (Argyris, 1982; Freire, 1972a, 1972b; Kolb, 1984; Schön, 1983, 1987) have explored the importance of reflection in the learning process. Reflection is also heralded as a key aspect of both coaching and mentoring. Jarvis (1992) argues, however, that 'reflective learning' is not always innovative. Nevertheless, he does concede that the pace of change in modern life is such that the 'change, then, is one of the conditions of the modern world' (ibid.: 84). There is a tension here for people, in that their internal systems of thought and the external feedback from their social context may be at odds with each other, creating a paradox of imbalance. It is this tension which seems to be at the very centre of innovative learning. 'Reflection' plays a crucial role in progressing understanding in paradoxical situations. Both coaching and mentoring often work in these tensions in order to help people resolve, reframe or develop strategies for the paradox of change.

From Table 5.1, 'contemplation' is an element of 'reflective learning'. The word itself has a religious significance, because it is through 'pure thought' (which may involve meditation, philosophical reasoning and other deep-thought process) that a learner reaches a conclusion. This may also happen in a coaching or mentoring situation. The process of 'contemplation' moves through Table 5.1 from 1 to 3 to 7 to 8 to 6 to 9, with a possible two-way process operating in the later stages.

Schön (1983) indicates that 'reflective skills learning' is where professionals tend to 'think on their feet'. It is learning which occurs spontaneously and in the heat of a situation and as Jarvis (1992: 77) suggests, it is 'a more sophisticated approach to learning practical subjects. It involves not only learning a skill but also learning the concepts that undergird the practice.' This is what others (see Smith, 1997) refer to as practical judgement. In relation to the Jarvis (1992) model (Table 5.1), reflective skills learning moves from 1 to 3 to 5, 7 and 8 and loops many times around in both directions from 5 to 8 to 6 to 9 (see also, Gray, 2007).

Experimental learning is 'theory tried out in practice and as a result is a new form of knowledge that captures social reality' (Jarvis, 1992: 78). Using Table 5.1, this starts at 1 goes through 3 to 7, 5 and 8 and loops many times around in both directions from 7 to 8 to 6 to 9. Coaching and mentoring practitioners work with experience.

How is learning achieved?

The ideas presented above are all dependent on activity and action and this provides a strong link to the underpinning practice of coaching and mentoring, and marks a clear distinction between therapeutic intervention and coaching and mentoring. Both coaching and mentoring tend towards a future orientation with the assumption of action and activity. This is built into the main process models of both coaching and mentoring – GROW (Whitmore, 2002) and Three Stage Process (Alred and Garvey, 2010). However, there is a sequencing problem with both of these theories – in life, many things happen at once! The Jarvis model limits itself by an assumption of stage theory and the Kolb model is diminished by the limited experimental base from which it is derived.

So the learning context is important. Vygotsky (1978: 86) suggested that the 'zone of proximal development' plays an important role in the learning process. He described this as 'the distance between the actual development level as determined by independent problem-solving and the level of potential development as determined through problem-solving under adult guidance or in collaboration with more capable peers'. The implication here is that a greater potential for enhanced understanding and learning is unlocked if there is guidance or collaboration – dialogue as in coaching and mentoring. This notion, first formulated by Vygotsky around 1930, has major implications on how we organise for learning, particularly with reference to coaching and mentoring. The influence and power of the social context in the learning process is not in doubt. The practical implications of this important understanding of learning are that in Kolb's (1984) or in Jarvis's (1992) terms, the models of experiential learning are essential for the learner to develop higher order and critical thinking abilities. In Vygotskian terms, it is a 'unity of perception, speech and action, which ultimately produces internalization' (Vygotsky, 1978: 26) and both coaching and mentoring have the potential to assist in the internalising of understanding. In other words, detailed discussion of experience is essential to make sense of that experience.

So, in terms of coaching and mentoring, it is process that matters – 'how' people learn rather than 'what' people learn is a key driver of practice. There is a clear distinction between the two. The 'what' approach is Barnett's (1994) 'technical rationality' and 'how' is more to do with 'reflective skills learning', as expressed by Jarvis (1992) and Schön (1983) or Barnett's 'genuinely interactive and collaborative forms of reasoning' or 'practical judgement' (Smith, 1997). Practical judgement has its roots in Aristotle's ideas:

> Aristotle gives a picture of what he calls phronesis that seems fruitful for this purpose … Phronesis can be translated in a number of ways: as practical judgement, practical reasoning or practical wisdom. (Smith, 1997: 3)

Aristotle presents two notions, one he refers to as 'phronesis' and the other as 'techne'. Techne is akin to the modern world's understanding of scientific thinking and behaviour. It is the domain of the practical craftsperson and involves preplanned organisation and leads to a contentment in the learner at having achieved the planned outcome by following a set of procedures or protocols.

Phronesis is linked to the idea of 'noticing' or by attentiveness to a specific situation. It involves flexibility of thought and interpretation. Dunne (1993) calls this 'situational appreciation' or 'alertness'. This is different to the concept of 'mastery' which is often a characteristic of instrumental or technical reasoning. Phronesis leads learners to be open to further experience and challenge.

Practical judgement has an ethical dimension which is based on an assumption that people express good citizenship, demonstrate integrity and are open to and honest in their dealings rather than corrupt. Jarvis (1992) would agree. Learning is fundamentally an ethical activity.

Practical judgement also has an emotional dimension. It combines many elements of 'character' and therefore contributes greatly to the learning process:

> In practical judgement knowledge, wisdom and feeling hold together and inform each other. Practical judgement and learning are intrinsically and essentially linked. The point cannot be emphasised too strongly. (Smith, 1997: 4)

Boisot (1995) suggests that tacit, uncodified knowledge is that which is internal to an individual but this is only of any value if it has become explicit. Tacit knowledge becomes explicit through social interaction. The environment in which the social discourse takes place is a significant influence on the ability of the participants to exchange and develop their mutual understanding. The participants 'make sense' of their worlds through social engagement. Therefore, it is through listening and interacting in dialogue that perspectives are modified and developed and sense is made. The participants engage in 'an intersubjective world, common to all of us' (Schutz, 1945: 534).

For coaching and mentoring, the dialogue point is crucial. As Bruner (1985: 23) says, 'language is a way of sorting out one's thoughts about things'. Coaching and mentoring practice is about this very thing with reference to the context in which the thoughts are generated. The notion of 'situated learning' (Lave and Wenger, 1991: 29) can offer some help here. Situated learning involves an act of active participation within a community of practice:

> A person's intentions to learn are engaged and the meaning of learning is configured through the process of becoming a full participant in a sociocultural practice. This social process includes, indeed it subsumes, the learning of knowledgeable skills. (Ibid.)

What makes coaching and mentoring affective and distinctive?

So, there are strong resonances here with coaching and mentoring relationships. Arguably, these are at the heart of situated learning. This is supported by Bruner's (1978: 25) writings on Vygotsky, 'since learning for him involved entry into a culture via induction by more skilled members'. For mentoring, this is Kram's (1983) psychosocial function in action and for coaching this could be what is meant by 'relational coaching' (de Haan, 2008). In the cases of both Fred and Joe, discussed above, the coach may have not been 'more skilled' but perhaps 'differently skilled'. Vygotsky (1981: 162) stated:

> Any higher mental function necessarily goes through an external stage in its development because it is initially a social function … Any higher mental function was external because it was social at some point before becoming an internal, truly mental function.

What is clear is that the human relationship and the conversational learning between coach and coachee, mentor and mentee is essentially about learning in a social context and the learning which takes place, because it is social, externalised and internalised, is of a higher order. Coaching and mentoring then reach the parts that other forms of learning just cannot reach and it is this that makes them special and different.

Summary

- This chapter examined three main categories of learning theory and these are related to coaching and mentoring practice
- Kolb and Fry's model of experiential learning is frequently associated with coaching and mentoring practice and this is subjected to critical examination
- Jarvis' typography of learning is explored in relation to coaching and mentoring
- Neither framework offers a complete picture
- Both offer insights into the dynamic and situational nature of learning
- Situational learning and practical judgement are considered as alternative philosophies
- A combination of all these elements is found within coaching and mentoring practice and, therefore, these practices offer huge potential for authentic, deep and powerful learning

Topics for discussion

1. How are you able to integrate these different ideas into your practice?
2. If coaching and mentoring are so powerful, why do these as learning interventions sometimes go wrong?

Questions that remain

1. How much of a problem is the incompleteness of knowledge about learning for coaching and mentoring?
2. How relevant are all these models and processes of learning to the practice of coaching and mentoring?

Further reading

Jarvis, P. (1987) *Adult Learning in the Social Context*. London: Croom Helm. Develops the ideas presented in this chapter further.

Lave, J. and Wenger, E. (1991) *Situated Learning: Legitimate Peripheral Participation*. Cambridge: Cambridge University Press. A fuller insight into this idea which is introduced in this chapter.

Vygotsky, L.S. Anything by Vygotsky! Always interesting and stimulating in relation to language, discourse and learning.

What next?

In Chapter 6, we look at the evaluation of coaching and mentoring. In research in general, there are different (and often conflicting) philosophies and discourses as to the purpose of research, what counts as evidence and the kinds of conclusions that can be drawn from it. In Chapter 6, we raise the assumptions that underpin evaluative research and highlight how these assumptions influence practice. The two main discourses of quantitative and qualitative evaluation are explored and critiqued and it is acknowledged that evaluation still has a way to go to satisfy all voices in coaching and mentoring.

Evaluating Coaching and Mentoring

Keywords

Evaluation, formative evaluation, summative evaluation, return on investment (ROI), World Café, Open Space

Chapter objectives

After reading this chapter, you will be able to:

- Define what is meant by 'evaluation'
- Specify the focus of evaluation
- Identify the aspects of coaching that need evaluating
- Select the stakeholders that should be involved in evaluation
- Choose the timescales for evaluation
- Choose appropriate tools with which to conduct an evaluation
- Plan and conduct a personal and organisational evaluation process

Introduction

'Evaluation' involves the systematic collection of data about the characteristics of a programme or learning intervention (Gray, 2014). As part of this process, evaluation explores what it is about a programme that needs to be changed, the procedures that are likely to bring about this change, and what kinds of evidence can be accrued to show that change has actually occurred (Warr et al., 1970). Unfortunately, as Campbell (1997) suggests, the process of evaluation often suffers from a lack of accuracy, incomplete information, wrong information or untimely information. However, there is now growing pressure for evaluation to be taken much more seriously in relation to training and professional development interventions – coaching and mentoring being no exceptions – in part, because of tightening economic resources and the pressure to show 'value for money'. Indeed, while this situation is slowly changing, there has been a lack of evidence-based research into the efficacy of coaching and mentoring interventions both at the individual and the organisational level (see Chapter 13), so measuring the impact of coaching and mentoring is now a matter of urgency.

In this chapter, we will explore evaluation from a number of perspectives. In research in general, there are different (and often conflicting) philosophies and discourses as to the purpose of research, what counts as evidence and the kinds of conclusions that can be drawn from it. The world of evaluation, including the evaluation of training and development – which encapsulates coaching and mentoring – is no stranger to these controversies. As we shall see in this chapter, there are those who adapt what is termed an objectivist philosophy of research, which links inquiry to 'scientific' observation through which generalisations can be produced. Such a philosophy tends to favour the use of 'scientific' research designs and the use of quantitative forms of measurement (see the section on 'Quantitative designs in evaluations'). In contrast, constructivist researchers assert that natural reality (and the laws of science) and social reality are different and require different types of method. So, while the natural sciences are looking to create 'laws', for constructivists the focus tends to be on 'those aspects that are "unique, individual and qualitative"'(Crotty, 1998: 68). The section on 'Qualitative designs in evaluations' provides an evaluation strategy which is typical of this approach.

Why evaluate coaching and mentoring?

Coaching and mentoring need to be evaluated because people seek to check on whether the resources they have invested have been worthwhile. For individuals, evaluation will provide a guide as to whether they need:

- More coaching and mentoring (with the same coach/mentor)
- More coaching and mentoring (but with a different coach/mentor)
- A change in the balance between coaching and mentoring (for example, less career mentoring and more performance coaching)
- No more coaching or mentoring, for the time being

For organisations they may need to consider:

- If coaching and mentoring are doing what the organisation wants it to do
- If there is anything that may be learned that might need to be changed or developed
- If any training is needed or adaptations to the design of the 'scheme'

Evaluation might even reveal that the person being coached or mentored is now ready (and motivated) to take on some coaching or mentoring responsibilities themselves.

Most training and development processes are evaluated in some way or another. But coaching and mentoring, in particular, need evaluation because they are practised by people with such a diverse range of skills, experience, qualifications and knowledge. Unlike, say, medicine, where, in most countries, entry to the profession requires many years of study, formal examination, adherence to a specific code of conduct and statutory regulation by a professional body, coaching and mentoring, as yet, have no single, unified professional structure.

This is not to call into question the competence of many practising coaches and mentors. But a number of stakeholders have much to gain from the evaluation process. Evaluation offers coaches and mentors an opportunity to analyse and receive feedback on their professional practice – their competence (recall Chapter 5). If the evaluation takes place at a formative stage (during the coaching or mentoring programme), then there is still an opportunity to make changes if there are any emerging problems. Evaluation is of value to those organisations using coaching and mentoring services because it allows them an opportunity to identify the strengths (and weaknesses) of individual coaches and mentors. It can also provide data on the organisational and financial benefits of coaching and mentoring in comparison, say, to other more traditional training and development initiatives. Evaluation may include, then, a cost–benefit analysis of the coaching and/or mentoring intervention.

The call for more evaluation of initiatives has been growing. In a study for the Chartered Institute of Personnel and Development (CIPD) the importance of evaluation was stressed and practical tools that could be applied by HR were outlined together with a plea to do it (Jarvis et al., 2006). Yet, by 2010, the CIPD found that only 36 per cent of survey participants were practicing evaluation. A study for the Chartered Management Institute (by McBain, Ghobadian, Switzer, Wilton, Woodman and Pearson in CIPD, 2012) found that higher-performing organisations evaluate their learning more than poorer performing ones. More recently, St John-Brooks (2014) provided a number of case studies of organisations assessing their coaching and included some core questions that could be answered in internal coaching studies within organisations. So, it can be done and is being done.

We will examine some approaches to cost–benefit analysis in the section on 'Quantitative designs in evaluations'. Case Study 6.1 illustrates how the views and interests of different organisational stakeholders come into play.

Case study 6.1

Evaluating early

Teenage Crisis is a voluntary agency which supports young people identified as being at risk of drug abuse and crime. Over the last six months, all 20 managers of the Teenage Crisis centres across the country have been receiving one-to-one coaching to help them cope with stress caused by the increasing demands of their jobs. At this point, the trustees of the agency have decided to commission an evaluation of the programme to see if it has had the hoped for positive outcomes. With another six months of the programme still to run, the trustees hope that the evaluation will determine whether the managers feel that they are benefiting from the programme, whether they have chosen the coaches that are right for them, and what changes, if any, should be made. The evaluation, conducted by 30-minute telephone interviews, shows that the coaching is going very well, in that performance targets are now being achieved and evaluative feedback from colleagues has been positive. However, some managers are worried about what will happen after the 12-month coaching programme is complete. Will they still have access to a coach? In particular, can they retain their current coach? It seems that a level of 'coach dependency' is already emerging. By recognising this problem at an early stage, the trustees have been able to take remedial steps by finishing the formal coaching, but introducing instead a system of peer mentoring between managers. All managers attend a two-day internal programme designed to improve their mentoring skills.

(Adapted from Gray, 2014.)

Activity 6.1

In Case Study 6.1, the trustees have chosen peer mentoring as the most appropriate replacement for coaching. What do you think about this recommendation?

Models of evaluation

Interest in the process of evaluation can be traced back to the 1970s, influenced strongly by the seminal work of Kirkpatrick, who focused particularly on the evaluation of training programmes – hence, the significance of Kirkpatrick's (1959) model to the evaluation of coaching and mentoring. He suggests that the evaluation of training programmes is important because it helps to:

- Justify training department budgets because it shows how they contribute to organisational goals and objectives
- Decide on whether the programme should continue, be modified or axed
- Gather data on how a programme should be improved

Kirkpatrick (ibid.) argues that, in essence, the evaluation of training programmes should concentrate on four levels:

- *Level 1, Reaction*: evaluating the responses of participants to the programme, often through eliciting responses using a questionnaire. This helps to determine general levels of satisfaction with a programme
- *Level 2, Learning*: measuring the knowledge, skills and attitudes that result from the programme, often against a set of training objectives specified at the commencement of the programme. The extent of learning can be tested through assessment
- *Level 3, Behaviour*: measuring how resulting changes in behaviour lead to improved job performance
- *Level 4, Results*: relating the results of the training to organisational objectives and other criteria of effectiveness

Unfortunately, as Bramley and Kitson (1994) comment, in the UK and USA, over 80 per cent of training is only evaluated at Level 1, with participants completing 'happiness sheets' to indicate the extent to which they enjoyed a programme. In many cases, the organisational evaluation of coaching and mentoring programmes is often at this level. However, on the positive side, even if evaluation is at Level 1, negative responses might at least prompt training designers to improve a programme (Pershing and Pershing, 2001).

Looking at the four levels, and with coaching and mentoring in mind, it is probably Levels 3 and 4 that are most important. At Level 1, participants can enjoy their coaching and mentoring programme but their performance may remain the same. At Level 2, they may be able to show an increase in knowledge and understanding but maintain the same behaviours. For measuring at Level 3, improved job performance and behaviour, Kirkpatrick (2005) suggests that, if possible, a control group should be used against which the performance of the trained (coached and mentored) group can be compared (see the section on 'Quantitative designs in evaluations'). Evaluation takes place both before and after the intervention (pre- and post-design), and ideally there should be a time gap before the post-programme group is measured to give time for new attitudes and behaviours to 'bed in'. As many stakeholders as possible should be involved in the evaluation process: course participants, their line managers, their subordinates and other relevant parties.

Table 6.1 Cost–benefit analysis of a coaching and mentoring programme

Behaviours expected of, and benefits to, coachees and mentees	Outcomes
Improved and new skills leading to:	
• Improved job prospects	High job mobility both internally and externally
• Higher earnings	Higher average earnings, including bonuses
• Improved job satisfaction	Higher job-satisfaction levels as measured by organisational surveys
Behaviours expected of, and benefits to, supervisors and line managers	
Improved and new skills leading to:	
• Increased output	Higher output (as long as this can be operationally defined)
• Higher value of output	Increased output x selling price. But best if costs are also taken into account
• Greater flexibility and innovativeness	Needs to be operationally defined: e.g., more labour mobility; new products/services; new working practices
• Likelihood of staying longer	Longer records of employment
• Less likelihood of sickness/stress	Reduced sickness rates
• Less likelihood of absence	Lower absence rates
• Less need to supervise	Reduced number of supervisors; flatter management structures
• Increased safety	Lower accident rates
Benefits to customers:	
• Better quality of work	Fewer customer complaints; greater customer satisfaction
• Less need to return work	Less inconvenience
• More 'on-time' deliveries	Reduced time between customer order and shipping

Source: Adapted from Bramley and Kitson (1994)

Evaluating a coaching and mentoring programme at Level 4 means showing how the intervention has impacted on organisational performance. Bramley and Kitson (1994) caution that the problems of evaluating at Levels 3 and 4 are not well understood. Measuring changes in job performance, for example, is problematic, partly because of the amount of work involved in designing measurement criteria. They proceed, however, to offer some solutions. As Table 6.1 shows, cost–benefit analysis is one way of measuring the benefits emerging from a programme, described as a list of performance indicators.

The Kirkpatrick model has been modified by Kaufman and Keller (1994), who argue that the original four-level model fails to take into account the broader impact of interventions on society. They add a Level 5, which requires organisations to measure this. At the same time, they also modify some of the other Kirkpatrick levels. Hence, at Level 1, instead of just participant reaction to an intervention, they include an evaluation of the value and worth of the resources put into the programme. Level 3 becomes application, that is, whether participants are able to apply what they have learned on the job. So, say an organisation wants to introduce a new coaching programme aimed at increasing diversity awareness, using the Kaufman and Keller (ibid.) approach it would: evaluate the programme in terms of whether people considered it used an appropriate amount of resources (Level 1); whether it was conducted according to its design and objectives (Level 2); and whether it succeeded in reducing or eliminating sexist or racist behaviour (Level 3). It would then evaluate what payoffs the programme achieved for the organisation (Level 4) and society (Level 5).

Table 6.2 Five levels of evaluation

Level	Kirkpatrick	Kaufman & Keller	Kaufman & Keller focus
5		Societal contribution	Societal and client responsiveness, consequences and payoffs
4	Results	Organisational payoff	Organisational contributions and payoffs
3	Behaviour	Individual or small-group payoff	Individual and small-group (products) utilisation within the organisation
2	Learning	Individual or small-group payoff	Individual and small-group mastery and competence
1	Reaction	Process acceptability and efficiency	Methods, means and processes acceptability and efficiency
		Resource availability and quality	Availability and quality of human, financial and physical resources inputs

Source: Gray (2014)

While the Kirkpatrick approach (and modified versions of Kirkpatrick) has been used extensively to evaluate programmes, there are alternatives. Brinkerhoff (2006) advises a five-step approach. Step 1 is to plan the evaluation, which can comprise of either a formative or summative evaluation, or both. Step 2 involves identifying the critical success factors that the programme is meant to achieve, such as how the training intervention is going to improve staff satisfaction. At Step 3, a survey is administered with an inbuilt scoring system to identify those employees who have achieved the greatest success and those who have achieved the least success. Step 4 then involves interviewing successful and least successful employees, and asking some basic questions, such as: (a) What, if anything, has changed as a result of the training intervention? (b) How has the intervention changed your job-specific behaviour? (c) Did the intervention result in any worthwhile outcomes? At Step 5, conclusions are reached as to the impact of the programme in terms of its overall achievements, whether some elements of the programme were more successful than others, and the value of outcomes generated. This helps to generate some answers to the fundamental question: Did the benefits of the programme outweigh the costs?

Case study 6.2

Steps in the evaluation process

Greengauge is a small consultancy business whose mission is to advise organisations on how to reduce their environmental footprint, particularly the heat and insulation efficiency of buildings. The Greengauge consultants are also trained business coaches.

Having won a new contract to coach the senior facilities directors of an international bank, they decide to build evaluation into the coaching process. Using the Brinkerhoff (2006) approach, at Step 1 they plan to evaluate at the three-month stage and at the end (six months). For Step 2, they work with the clients to identify a set of critical success factors, which in this case are going to be to lower aggregate carbon footprint scores by 20 per cent across the bank's buildings infrastructure, globally, within 12 months of the coaching programme's completion. At Step 3, at the end of the programme, all ten directors (one from each of the bank's regional headquarters) are asked to submit their plans for carbon-footprint reduction for the coming 12 months. This shows that the most ambitious plan gives a reduction of 30 per cent, whilst the most cautious predicts only 8 per cent. Both directors are interviewed to ascertain the factors (often organisational or societal) that make the gap so large. Finally, at Step 5, a calculation is preformed to give the financial benefits of the changes (if they are fully implemented) but evaluations reduce these by 25 per cent because this is the risk calculated as the possibility of non-implementation.

Activity 6.2

Taking Case Study 6.2, plan an evaluation using the Kirkpatrick model. How would it differ from the Brinkerfhoff approach? Which do you think is more effective?

Who should evaluate?

If the coach or mentor has been hired by an individual for their own personal benefit, then these are the main parties involved in evaluating the coaching. In these circumstances, an approach such as 'Appreciative Inquiry' (AI) (see 'Qualitative designs in evaluation: Appreciate Inquiry', below) might work well for both parties. However, if the coaching and mentoring have been planned and delivered by an organisation, then there may be various stakeholders involved in the coaching or mentoring relationship, and, in principle, all of them could play a part in the evaluation process. Hay (1995), discussing coaching, says that it is a four-way process involving the coachee, the coach, the organisation (especially the HR department) and the coachee's line manager. All, potentially, have a contribution to make, and each can add a different perspective. One of the dangers of coaching or mentoring only being evaluated by the direct beneficiary, is that they will tend to focus only on their direct experience – which might be somewhat subjective and lacking in broader perspectives. A more effective way is to also elicit the feedback of line managers, peers and team members who are in a better position to notice if performance or attitude changes in the beneficiaries have taken place.

The difference stakeholders, then, may evaluate in different ways:

- *Coachees and mentees.* They will tend to focus on the personal gains (knowledge, skills, confidence, etc.) and balance these against the time and effort they have expended on the learning process. Were the objectives of the coaching/mentoring relationship achieved? Has the process left any lasting and useful knowledge, or understanding?
- *The HR department* (if involved in organising the intervention). They will be interested in measuring tangible outcomes against programme objectives. HR departments are increasingly interested in 'return on investment' (ROI). Few, however, have managed to measure the direct impact of coaching and mentoring
- *Line managers.* Has the coaching and mentoring led to benefits in terms of the performance of individuals. Since coaching and mentoring are increasingly delivered to teams, has the intervention improved team performance?
- *Coaches and mentors.* As professional practitioners, coaches and mentors will want to evaluate their own practice. This may involve seeking feedback from the coachee/mentee, and perhaps their line managers. Table 6.3 is typical of the kinds of checklists for evaluating the performance of the coach or mentor, often completed by the coachee

or mentee. But evaluation should also involve coaches and mentors engaging in a process of self-evaluation. This is why all coaches who value best practice (and some mentors) make use of a supervisor with whom they can discuss their own performance and receive feedback.

Table 6.3 Checklist for evaluating the performance of the coach or mentor

Competency	Strongly agree	Agree	Neither agree nor disagree	Disagree	Strongly disagree
Establishes rapport	○	○	○	○	○
Creates trust and respect	○	○	○	○	○
Demonstrates effective communication skills	○	○	○	○	○
Promotes self-awareness and self-knowledge	○	○	○	○	○
Uses active listening and questioning techniques	○	○	○	○	○
Assists goal-development and goal-setting	○	○	○	○	○
Motivates	○	○	○	○	○
Encourages alternative perspectives	○	○	○	○	○
Assists in making sense of a situation	○	○	○	○	○
Identifies significant patterns of thinking and behaving	○	○	○	○	○
Provides an appropriate mix of challenge and support	○	○	○	○	○
Facilitates depth of understanding	○	○	○	○	○
Shows compassion	○	○	○	○	○
Acts ethically	○	○	○	○	○
Inspires curiosity	○	○	○	○	○
Acts as a role model	○	○	○	○	○
Values diversity and difference	○	○	○	○	○
Promotes action and reflection	○	○	○	○	○
Comments:					

Source: Adapted from Jarvis (2004)

Activity 6.3

Using Table 6.3 as a guide, construct your own performance evaluation form.

Another key issue is whether the evaluation process should be conducted by internal or external evaluators. Table 6.4 outlines some of the potential benefits and drawbacks of each. Although internal evaluators will be more familiar with the culture and needs of an organisation, they may not always possess the independence required by a thorough and systematic evaluation programme. External evaluators, however, bring independence to the evaluation process and can use their experience of evaluating in other organisations as a comparative benchmark.

Table 6.4   The advantages and disadvantages of using internal or external evaluators

Advantages

Internal evaluators will be:

- Familiar with the history, policies, issues and culture of the organisation
- Likely to focus on the central concerns of management

External evaluators have:

- An independent stance and offer a fresh perspective
- An overview of numerous organisations to serve as a comparison
- Knowledge and experience of a wide range of evaluation techniques

Disadvantages

Internal evaluators may:

- Have a vested interest in a particular outcome
- Sometimes be over-influenced by the views of management
- Find it difficult to persuade stakeholders to participate in the evaluation process

External evaluators may be:

- Unaware of who the key players are in a particular setting and hence may be more easily misled by interested parties
- Influenced by the need to secure future contracts
- Insensitive to internal norms and internal relationships

Source: Adapted from Clarke (1999)

Activity 6.4

Using Table 6.4, and applying this to your own organisation (or one you coach/mentor in), take each bullet point and award a score of plus 1 to 10 for the Advantages and minus 1 to 10 for the Disadvantages (with 10 being the most important or relevant for your own organisation). Now add up the scores. Which comes out higher: using an internal or external evaluator?

The timing of evaluation

Evaluation should be built into the planning of the coaching or mentoring process – indeed, it should be specified and described in contracts (whether formal or informal) between beneficiaries and their coach/mentor. Both formative and summative evaluation are essential. Formative evaluation during the course of the coaching/mentoring programme is likely to constitute a process of continual review, a kind of tracking process on progress between the parties. This tracking can take the form of:

- Checking at the end of each coaching/mentoring session – 'How have we done today?' 'Is there anything we have missed?''What would make the process more effective?''What needs to happen to achieve this?'
- Checking at the start of each new session – 'What new behaviours or actions did you try out since we last met?''What went well?''What went less well?''What should we focus on today?' Is more focus, support or encouragement needed on certain areas?

So, formative evaluation is a continuous process of setting targets, tracking achievements and setting new targets.

Summative evaluation takes place at the end of the programme and seeks to bring closure. Hence, summative evaluation is likely to focus on the attainment of final personal goals and checking on the partnership between beneficiaries and the coach/mentor. It is important that both parties discuss these goals and processes honestly and openly. But, above all, summative evaluation is likely to focus on organisational goals and on how and to what extent the coaching has helped to attain them. This may include an attempt to measure the return on investment (ROI) – the financial returns compared to the costs of the coaching programme. This brings us to a theme that is gaining an ever higher focus – measuring the impact of coaching and mentoring.

Quantitative designs in evaluation

Quantitative research relies on the collection of data based on numbers and figures, while qualitative research seeks meanings based on words, sentences and narratives. In many organisational contexts, perhaps due to the rational pragmatic discourse raised in Chapter 1, there is an espoused desire for quantitative measurement since there is a belief that this is accurate, and 'scientific'. However, as we shall see, qualitative evaluation, more closely associated with decision science (recall Chapter 4) is just as valid in many circumstances.

One of the most popular quantitative approaches is the attempt to measure ROI and is an extension of the Kirkpatrick model (see above), in that he argued that the costs and benefits of any training programme should be measured. ROI is calculated as follows:

$$\frac{\text{Estimated coaching benefits} - \text{Costs of coaching}}{\text{Costs of coaching}} \times 100$$

However, as Grant (2012b) points out, the formula has often been modified by, for example, deliberately reducing the financial return figure to produce a 'conservative' estimate or including a rating of the coachee's level of confidence that all or some of the perceived benefits were in fact due to coaching. The result is that the meaning of the ROI metric varies between studies, making it impossible to make reliable comparisons. There are other problems that come from the calculation itself. Say that a coach works with an executive and charges £10,000 for her services. After the coaching, the executive manages to secure a contract for her company worth £1 million. She attributes 50 per cent of this success to the work of her coach. So, using our formula, we would say that the ROI in this coaching was 4900 per cent – quite an impressive figure! However, it is questionable as to the extent to which the successful contract (and hence the financial returns) can be attributed solely to the intervention of the coach. Indeed, pre-specified and precise financial goals are often not the prime focus of coaching contracts and so it becomes difficult to attribute financial outcomes to the coaching. Furthermore, as Grant (2012b) points out, where the coachee's work involves managing others in order to attain organisational goals, the causal chain between coaching and eventual financial outcomes becomes even more tenuous. As an alternative to financial ROI, Grant offers a more holistic well-being and engagement framework (WBEF). The WBEF has two dimensions: a well-being dimension (high–low) and a workplace engagement dimension (high–low) (see Figure 6.1).

In the *area of flourishing*, individuals are highly involved and absorbed in their work, in which they see meaning and purpose. They also enjoy positive relations with their work colleagues. In a coaching evaluation context, this would be a place to achieve. The *area of acquiescence* represents individuals with high levels of well-being but low levels of engagement; so they are physically and emotionally present but not engaged in the goals of the organisation. The *area of distressed but functional* contains individuals who are highly functional but who suffer from high levels of anxiety and stress. Coaching in this quadrant may be particularly challenging since, according to Grant (2011), it is often difficult to identify depression or anxiety, especially if the coach does not have clinical or counselling training. The *distressed and disengaged* quadrant contains individuals who may have high levels of mental illness, including depression, anxiety disorders and chemical dependencies. As an evaluative framework, the WBEF could be used to track coachees' progress over time, assuming that the goal is to move people towards the flourishing quadrant. Of course, this begs the question as to how we measure this progress, which may include both qualitative and quantitative approaches.

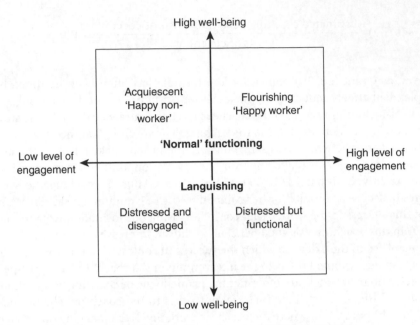

Figure 6.1 The well-being and engagement framework (Grant, 2012b)

Activity 6.5

Take a look at the WBEF. How useful is it as an evaluative framework? How easy is it to assign individuals to one of the quadrants?

Other quantitative approaches to evaluation make use of a simple pre- and post-design – one or more features or elements are measured before the coaching and mentoring intervention, and then measured at some time afterwards. The differences between the pre- and post-scores indicate the success or otherwise of the coaching and mentoring programme. Certainly, being able to quote the post-score gains in a programme lends a certain plausibility. But does it? There are good reasons for calling into question this assumption – indeed, writers on research methods have long queried such an approach. Campbell and Stanley (1963), for example, point out that other factors could have influenced the post-scores.

- *Maturation effects*. If, say, the coaching and mentoring programme takes place over an 18-month period, then participants will be older and more mature at the end of the programme. So, if, for example, we were measuring performance, it is quite possible that many, if not most, participants would be better at performing tasks simply because of their greater maturity.
- *Measurement procedures*. Let us imagine that the coaching and mentoring programme is designed to challenge anti-diversity attitudes in the workforce. The pre-test instrument designed to measure attitudes to diversity might itself make respondents more alert and sensitive to this issue. This itself, independent of the coaching and mentoring intervention, might push up post-test scores.
- *Experimental mortality*. Over a period of time, people leave an organisation. Taking our diversity programme above, if a disproportionate number of people who are hostile to diversity leave the organisation, the average post-test scores may rise compared to the pre-test, irrespective of the coaching and mentoring programme.
- *Extraneous variables*. These might influence the results, particularly if there is a large time gap between the pre- and post-test. By extraneous variables, we mean unwanted variables that influence attempts to measure the outcome of the coaching and mentoring. For example, say a coaching and mentoring programme is introduced to improve job satisfaction in an organisation. Just before the post-test, the organisation grants an across-the-board pay rise for all staff. The post-test finds that job satisfaction is higher than the pre-test. But which intervention caused this – the coaching and mentoring or the pay rise? We don't know (unless, as we shall see below, we can use a research design that controls for the pay rise).

A sounder approach, then, is to make use of a control group – that is, a group that does not receive the coaching and mentoring intervention. A control group helps us to eliminate the potential confounding effect of extraneous variables. As Table 6.5 illustrates, both the coaching and mentoring group and the control group take the pre-test and the post-test. If the post-test scores of the coaching and mentoring group exceed those of the control group, then we can say with some certainty that this is the result of the coaching and mentoring intervention itself, and is not due to chance or extraneous variables (such as the pay rise). If the aim is to 'prove' the effectiveness of a coaching and mentoring programme, then, as we can see in Table 6.5, people would, ideally, be allocated to each group on a random basis. This is because, if people were allocated to the groups (say, by someone in an HR department with an interest in promoting coaching and mentoring), how do we know that they haven't biased this allocation in some way, consciously or unconsciously allocating 'more able' people to the coaching and mentoring group so that their post-test scores will come out best?

Table 6.5   Coaching and mentoring group with a control

Group	Allocation of subjects	Coaching and mentoring programme	Pre-Test	Post-Test
Coaching and mentoring group	Random	Yes	Yes	Yes
Control group	Random	No	Yes	Yes

However, in reality, evaluators may not be in a position to randomly allocate people in this way. Beneficiaries are coached or mentored because they have been identified as the appropriate group for this intervention. In this case, we say that each group is 'intact', a design not as effective as controlling for extraneous variables as random selection of group participants. To improve the validity of the study, then, it is best to improve the *equivalence* between the coaching and mentoring and the control groups. Hence, we need to ensure that both groups are similar against significant variables such as age, sex, seniority, income, etc. If it is not possible to match the groups in this way, then both groups should at least be drawn from similar populations, that is, from similar 'walks of life' (if this is, say, a life-coaching programme), or from the same or similar work environments (for executive or business types of coaching and mentoring) such as the same departments or seniority levels in the organisation.

Table 6.6   Coaching and mentoring group with non-equivalent control

Group	Allocation of subjects	Coaching and mentoring programme	Pre-Test	Post-Test
Coaching and mentoring group	No – intact	Yes	Yes	Yes
Control group	No – intact	No	Yes	Yes

At this point, given that the aim of the exercise is to 'prove' whether coaching and mentoring is effective, the scores of the two groups will be compared. Let us say that there are 20 people in the coaching and mentoring group and 18 in the control, and that the average score of the coaching and mentoring group members rises by 4 points (from 20 to 24) between the pre- and post-test, but the average control group score rises by only 1 point (from 19 to 20). Can we now deduce that coaching and mentoring are effective? Sadly, not. First of all, these scores are averages, with some people in both groups scoring above and below the average. Second, the difference could have occurred merely by chance. So, what is to be done? We need to apply statistical analysis to the data, to see if the differences between the two groups are statistically significant. Here, even if the statistical test tells us the differences are significant, there is still a small probability that chance played a part. But with groups of these sizes, it is unlikely that the statistical test would find significant differences anyway. Normally, we would probably need group sizes of over 50 for the statistical tests to detect significant differences between the two groups.

Finally, let us sound a note of caution. You have probably already been thinking about the ethics of using a control group in the study. The control groups have the drawbacks of the evaluation process (having to complete evaluation forms) with none of the benefits (they don't receive any coaching or mentoring). One way through this dilemma is that the evaluation process remains as it is (the use of the coaching and mentoring group and the control) so that the measurement of the impact of coaching and mentoring can take place. But after this process, the control group does receive the coaching and mentoring intervention. This is sometimes termed a 'waiting-list control'. In practice, many organisations may find it difficult to hold up a coaching and mentoring intervention in this way, once a person's development needs have been identified.

A further issue with this approach is the underpinning philosophy of control group studies. A control group study is a medical model of evaluation and as such is an attempt to apply Newtonian scientific principles to people within a social context. This approach tends to 'objectify' people and detach them from their context as if they were neutral and rootless. Emotional issues also become 'objectified' and this leaves a major question, partly discussed in Chapter 3 and a recurring theme in other chapters – how far can social variables be controlled or taken into account? Additionally, this type of research works on the assumption that human behaviour is predictable – how far is this the case in your experience?

Qualitative designs in evaluation

As we saw earlier, qualitative designs are based on the analysis of words, sentences and narratives – but may also include the analysis of visual media such as photographs and video. In many senses, qualitative approaches lend themselves to the evaluation of coaching and mentoring because both involve the use of words and a focus on processes, attitudes and feelings. In this section, we will explore four kinds of qualitative approaches that lend themselves well to evaluation and particularly the evaluation of coaching and mentoring: Appreciative Inquiry (AI); the World Café; Open Space; and Participant directed feedback.

Appreciative Inquiry (AI)

Appreciate Inquiry (AI) is a process of creative evaluation through constructive dialogue. AI deliberately avoids 'deficit language' ('the problem with this has been …', 'this doesn't work because …') by focusing on what has worked and why. This does not mean that the AI view of the world is naïve and simplistic. 'Fragilities' in the coaching and mentoring relationship are also appreciated and discussed. When applied to coaching, it is likely that AI can be used in a continuous spiral, regularly revisiting themes to uncover what is 'working' for the coachee (and the coach), what needs modifying and what new themes are emerging for discussion. In a sense, AI is a process of continuous evaluation.

AI is based on a new way of engaging people in organisational development and change based around conversational practice. In this sense, it closely mirrors, and indeed compliments, many features of coaching and mentoring themselves. AI focuses on particular ways of asking questions, fostering relationships and increasing an organisation's capacity for change. It therefore stands in stark contrast to traditional approaches to organisational change, dominated by a pervasive metaphor of the organisation-as-machine. Just as machines develop faults or break down, organisations embark on change in order to 'solve a problem'. Indeed, it is almost as if organisations cannot see an issue unless it is framed as a problem (Lewis et al., 2011), so organisations become fixated on finding and naming problems. Implicit in this is the belief that every problem has a logical and right solution, prompting leaders to adopt one new organisational design after another (Lewis et al., ibid.), never realising that the ideal organisational solution is unachievable. You might notice elements of the organisation-as-machine in the quantitative approach to evaluation outlined above.

In contrast to 'naming problems', AI sees organisations as messy, living entities which can be changed by the power of appreciation. When someone is appreciated for what they do, they grow towards that appreciation (Lewis et al., ibid.). The appreciation process is largely engaged through questions (or, in our case, aspects of the coaching and mentoring process). Talking in of itself is not a precursor to action – it *is* action, since the more we talk about the world, the more we see it. Hence, AI can help us to evaluate coaching and mentoring and in doing so, adopts many of the same conversational techniques as coaching and mentoring. For example, like coaching and mentoring, it tends to avoid deficit models of human behaviour and focuses instead on what works for people. According to Webb et al. (2005), AI and evaluation come together to:

- Lessen the fear and scepticism many managers have about evaluation by focusing on success and best experiences
- Engage the whole system in the process of evaluation, ensuring more comprehensive evaluation results

- Create buy-in to the changes recommended which may lead to more resolute decision-making
- Build the organisation's capacity to think about and engage in more evaluative processes

It should not, perhaps, come as much of a surprise to know that AI maps quite closely onto the ubiquitous coaching model, GROW (Goals, Reality, Options and Wrap up). Table 6.7 provides a summary of each model for comparison. So, for example, GROW starts with SMART goals; although AI does not use the SMART formula, it does, nevertheless, seek to define high-level aims.

Table 6.7   A comparison of GROW and AI, showing the mapping between AI and coaching models

GROW		Appreciate Inquiry (AI)	
Goal	The end point the client wants to reach. Usually defined in SMART terms: Specific, measurable, attainable, realistic, timely	Define	Specifying the focus of the inquiry, but as high-level objectives rather than SMART goals
Reality	How far the client is from reaching his/her goals	Discovery	Discovering the organisation's key strengths and appreciating what is best (e.g., leadership, values, success, etc.)
Options/ obstacles	The choice of approaches available for achieving the goal	Dream	Bring out the dream that people have for themselves and the organisation, building on what is best
Wrap up	The steps that need to be taken	Design	Making decisions about the actions to be taken to support the dream
		Destiny	Planning and forming action groups to take the ambitions forward

Case study 6.3

Using Appreciative Inquiry (AI) in evaluation

NodeWire is an international IT networking organisation that designs and manufactures Internet infrastructure and develops software solutions. A year ago, in its UK subsidiary, a decision was taken to introduce executive coaching across the

(Continued)

(Continued)

management grades of its workforce, an operation involving 500 people. The coaching programme, however, has met with mixed success. Some have enjoyed its benefits, but there have been logistical problems, with managers missing or cancelling their coaching appointments at the last minute. Some have only taken up less than half of their allotted coaching hours. An evaluation report has been sent to the head of HR, who has decided to 'investigate the problem' so that it can be 'fixed'.

The coach leading the coaching team, however, offers an alternative approach. Rather than dealing with the issue as a problem, she proposed an Appreciative Inquiry approach, which she explains to the CEO. She proposes that together they select ten coachees some of whom have attended and benefited from their coaching sessions and others who have been more recalcitrant. They will attend a half-day programme based on AI principles, during which they will work through the AI stages, namely:

Discovery. During this stage, participants will reflect on and discuss what have been the positive aspects of the programme. In doing this, participants will be teamed up to act as both interviewers and interviewees, to fully engage everyone in the process. Telling and listening to stories helps to promote engagement and the building of relationships at an early stage.

Dream. During this stage, participants will be asked to imagine the coaching programme at its best, identifying the collective aspirations and hopes of participants and to symbolise these in a graphic form.

Design. Participants will then be asked to develop concrete proposals for achieving the 'dreamed' and improved coaching programme, containing 'possibility' or 'design' statements.

Delivery/Destiny. The outcomes of design will *not* be used to create new targets, fill gaps or generate objectives since this would be counter to the philosophy of AI. Instead, all participants will be invited to take actions that are seen as most congruent with their self-commitment and designs.

The CEO is worried that the AI process does not contain any tangible objectives, solutions or 'fixes'. In the end, he allows the AI workshop to go ahead. Its results are impressive, allowing all participants to talk about coaching within the context of their own stressful work schedules and to design creative solutions as to how they will actively engage with coaching in the future.

Activity 6.6

Case Study 6.3 uses coaches for the process. Who else might contribute?

World Café – conversations that matter

World Café is an ideal method of evaluating a coaching or mentoring programme because it brings together different organisational stakeholders and is based on the principle that people have the capacity to work constructively together, no matter who they are. It helps groups of all sizes to engage in constructive dialogue to foster collaborative learning (Tan and Brown, 2005). Hence, it is a process that has been used in many cultures and with many age groups and in different communities and organisations. At its core then, is the principle of diversity – everyone is needed and is welcome. The World Café is based on the principle of listening (people must be listened to), movement (between tables) and energy. According to Lewis et al. (2011), the World Café is an appropriate technique when the aim is to encourage the sharing of knowledge and when it is important to build mutual ownership of outcomes.

The World Café is a technique which brings people together in groups of anywhere between 12 and several hundred to engage in a series of 20 to 30 minute conversations, gathered around small tables, about subjects that matter to them. Table hosts remain at each table to help to connect the conversations, while participants move between tables after each conversation, bringing with them insights from conversations at previous tables. After two or three rounds, the facilitator may hold a plenary session at which all participants contribute to a general discussion that surfaces key themes and insights. According to Brown and Isaacs (2005), the World Café is based around seven design principles:

1. *Set the context.* The broad purpose of the Café event is set out in the invitation, perhaps with an initial question, or theme, especially one that creates curiosity
2. *Create hospitable space and psychological safety.* Music and room decorations are used to create a relaxed atmosphere. Brown (2002) recommends the use of small, round tables with five people sat around them. On the tables are colourful tablecloths, on which are placed white sheets of paper and marker pens
3. *Explore questions that matter.* Use powerful (open) questions to build a sense of engagement and inquiry. Powerful questions are simple and clear, are thought-provoking, challenge assumptions and evoke more questions
4. *Encourage the contributions of all.* Generate full participation through encouraging careful listening. Consider allowing a moment of silence between each speaker

5. *Connect diverse perspectives.* Invite diverse perspectives into the dialogue to build ideas through cross-pollination. After several rounds (with people moving to new tables after each round), one person stays behind at each table to introduce new group members to the ideas generated by the previous group. These are then built upon, often creating challenging and unique perspectives
6. *Listen together for patterns, insights and deeper questions.* Maintain a balance between the generation of common themes with individual contributions. Get people to listen for new connections in the 'space-in-between' what is being discussed (Brown, 2002)
7. *Harvest and share collective discoveries, making collective knowledge visible and actionable.* Get people to scribble ideas (words and pictures) on the tablecloths or paper. Finish the session with a town-hall style meeting

The World Café fits with coaching and mentoring because they all share similar core values and beliefs: the power of conversations, listening and questioning to initiate understanding and change. Case Study 6.4 offers an example of how the World Café can be used to evaluate a coaching and mentoring programme.

Case study 6.4

Using World Café in evaluation

Twelve months ago, a large, local government department introduced a coaching and mentoring programme for middle managers with the aim of helping them through a difficult process of restructuring and change. Twenty-five managers have been through the programme, with each receiving up to 20 hours of one-to-one mentoring from more senior members of the department. The mentors themselves were all volunteers, some of them new to mentoring. Hence, before the launch of the programme mentors had received two days of training and had been supported by experienced people termed 'mentor-tutors'. It is now time to evaluate the programme. Rather than issue the usual 'happiness sheets' in the form of evaluation forms, the organising team decides that the World Café approach might yield more interesting insights.

A World Café evening is planned at a local hotel, with the evening kicking off with some snacks and soft drinks. Mentees, mentors, mentor-tutors, programme sponsors, four 'table-helpers' and members of the HR team who managed the programme all mingle. At 7 p.m. a whistle is blown to announce the start of the Café session and people are invited to sit at one of the four tables. As people head for the tables, they notice that a 'table host' is sitting at each one and that the tables are covered with paper tablecloths on which there are coloured marker pens. Scribbled on each tablecloth is a question:

Table 1: What has gone well? What factors contributed to the success of the coaching and mentoring programme?

Table 2: Recall a mentoring conversation when you experienced a significant shift in your thinking. What were the qualities that made this a great conversation?

Table 3: If we knew at the start of the programme what we know now, how would we have made the programme different?

Table 4: Imaging we are here in 3 years' time. What will coaching and mentoring look like in the organisation? What did we do to get there?

Over four rounds, people visit each of the tables but not necessarily in the same order – they can choose where they go. At the end of the fourth round, the tablecloths are stuck to a wall and participants are encouraged to stand in front of them to discuss emerging ideas.

The event proves to be a catalyst for change, highlighting both the success of the programme but also the need for:

- More choice when selecting a mentor
- The training of mentors and also rewarding them
- A handbook explaining roles, responsibilities and processes

Activity 6.7

If you were tasked with writing the proposed handbook, what would it contain in terms of main themes?

Open Space

Open Space is a loosely structured method through which people take responsibility for hosting conversations that matter to them. The process begins with everyone in a circle when an invitation is given to consider a specific theme (for example, the evaluation of a coaching and mentoring programme). Open Space works most effectively when issues are complex, the ideas and people involved are diverse, and there are time constraints. It operates according to four guiding principles:

- Whoever comes are the right people
- Whatever happens in the only thing that could have happened

- Whenever it starts is the right time
- When it's over it's over

Open Space also operates according to the Law of Two Feet. If someone finds themselves working in a group but gaining no learning nor contributing, they should use their two feet and go somewhere else. Some of the principles of Open Space are illustrated in Case Study 6.5.

Case study 6.5

Using Open Space in evaluation

Two NHS hospitals introduced a programme for clinical staff, whereby staff at each of the hospitals were paired with someone of a similar occupation for the purpose of peer mentoring. After six months, senior managers are keen to know how the programme is progressing and decide to do this through the Open Space process.

First, they send out a short *invitation*, informing all of those involved of the time and place of the meeting, and stressing the importance of the programme. There is a sense of urgency in the message (a clarion call to action) but also one of inclusivity – people are invited to pass the message onto all those who might be interested. Over 100 people turn up, to be greeted by a large room in which there is an improbably wide circle of chairs, in the middle of which are empty posters and coloured pens. Some people mingle around the room, while some sit on the chairs and engage in conversation. Soon the room is a hubbub of noise. Eventually, someone rings a set of chiming bells, the sound of which brings the room to silence. There is a sense of expectation but no clear idea of what is going to happen next. Someone rises to speak. It is the NHS Trust Chief Executive who originally sponsored the programme. She welcomes everyone and invites them into the circle. She introduces the bell-ringer as the facilitator and then takes her seat in the circle.

The facilitator invites all of those present to look around the circle and to acknowledge those people they know and look at the faces of those who are new to them. While this is done, the facilitator restates the theme of the meeting (the evaluation of the peer-mentoring programme) and tells a short story about how it came about. She also points to the surrounding walls that are empty, apart from some small posters with room numbers and times on them. These, she explains, are our agenda. A number of people giggle. She then explains the four guiding principles of Open Space (see above), and, of course, the Law of Two Feet. Above all, everyone is admonished not to lose time. She invites anyone who wishes to enter the centre of the circle, grab a poster and pen and write their name and their issue. Once they finish, they read out their issues and leave the circle to stick their poster to a wall, beneath one of the room/time posters. Soon there are many posters on all four walls. The meeting now has its agenda!

There is now a sense of excitement in the room and at the invitation of the facilitator, everyone moves to the outside of the room to sign up to sessions/themes indicated by the posters. Soon, spontaneously, some groups are leaving the large room to go, with their poster/theme, to a breakout room. Others are making small circles of chairs in a corner of the room to start their session. People are joining groups, leaving groups, circulating between groups. There is a lot of movement and a lot of energy. In some groups, new posters are being created and stuck around the room, not with questions but with ideas for action. Just before lunch, the facilitator sounds the bells again and calls everyone back to the large circle for a 'news' session, where new sessions can be announced or breakthroughs heralded. Most groups have agreed to write up their ideas and plans, which are later collated and edited into a final document for the whole group of participants. This is an important document for the programme organisers and the basis for future programme development.

Activity 6.8

Taking the Open Space approach outlined in Case Study 6.5, how could you integrate Appreciative Inquiry into the session? What might be the benefits of this?

Participant directed feedback (pdf)

Participant directed feedback (PDF) is a methodology for bringing large groups together to explore a question in which they all have a stake in order to define an approach to researching it and then applying the findings. In participating, members present their experiences but do not represent an organisational position. They commit to bringing their experience but also to being open to the ideas of others. It has been used in a number of studies in organisations, both private and public. It helps to have an experienced facilitator to manage the process but they do not contribute ideas to the pot.

In essence, it starts with a question agreed by participants framed around a theme. For example:

When we are doing our best work (in whatever area is agreed), what factors are present?

Members call out and write down on small cards the factors that they have experienced as important. A large group of cards is usually produced. These are placed on the floor or large table. Members wander around looking at the cards, and where they see items which they think go together, they move the cards into groupings. This is done without discussion, they are individual choices. If a member sees a card which they think belongs somewhere else, they may not move it but can make a copy of it and place it in other grouping.

Gradually the individual decisions coalesce into shared groups. Members then split up into groups, taking responsibility for specific collections of cards. They work in those groups to explore what they think the underlying theme that links them together might be. They use their own experience of those possible themes and name it. They then return to the large group and tell the story of each named theme and an example of it from the collected stories.

The themes are then placed on the table (name at the top, cards underneath) and again members wander around looking for connections between the themes. The process of small groups taking responsibility for themes happens again. When they return, usually a small number of key overarching themes are named and defined.

In the large group, people again share their stories around the overarching themes. They then look, using their experiences, at how they might research those themes across a number of different organisations (it might just be their own but could involve inviting a larger group to participate). The research is then conducted by the members, involving others as needed, and the results are shared with all participants. In collecting the evidence from the research, there is a key emphasis on collecting stories of organisations getting it right that can be shared with others.

Case study 6.6

Using participant directed feedback (PDF) in evaluation

The decade of the 1990s witnessed many changes in the UK workforce, in particular the end of jobs-for-life culture. In its place, the concept of employability emerged (rather than a job for life, we commit to helping you to be more employable and you in return commit to making us, as an organisation, successful). A number of organisations were exploring what this might mean for them. Three organisations, the CIPD, Create and Professional Development Foundation, agreed, supported by the Department for Education and Employment, to bring together a group of organisations to explore this concept. Some 30 organisations agreed to sponsor the process and participate in a three-day participant directed feedback (PDF) Facilitation to define the concept and what it might mean. Out of this process, a number of overarching themes emerged which they agreed to research within their own organisations but inviting others to join. The concept of employability was explored in the research from the employers' and employees' perspectives. More than 900 organisations agreed to take part in the study. The findings, together with more than 50 stories of the practice of organisations and individuals in generating employability, were fed back in a series of presentations.

Activity 6.9

Taking the PDF approach outlined in Case Study 6.6, what key question on evaluation might you be struggling to resolve that could be explored with others in a facilitated group process? What might be the benefits of sharing the approach?

Summary

- Many training and development interventions (including coaching and mentoring) are still evaluated at Level 1 (reaction) of Kirkpatrick's model
- There is growing pressure (especially amongst organisational sponsors of coaching and mentoring) for coaching and mentoring to be measured (often using quantitative data) in terms of its impact on organisational performance and cost–benefit analysis
- Alternative evaluation models to Kirkpatrick include Brinkerhoff, whose two-step approach involves interviewing contrasting groups of most and least successful participants in the intervention
- In quantitative evaluation designs, the use of a control group helps to eliminate the confounding effect of extraneous variables, that is, it helps to identify that it was the coaching and mentoring that had the impact and not other factors
- It would be ethical if the control group did receive the coaching and mentoring intervention once the study has been completed
- Qualitative approaches to evaluation include Appreciative Inquiry, World Café, Open Space and participant directed feedback

Topics for discussion

1. What role, if any, does the Kirkpatrick model offer to the evaluation of coaching and mentoring?
2. Outline some of the challenges in measuring the tangible impact of a coaching and mentoring programme
3. Make out a plausible case for using both quantitative and qualitative methods when evaluating coaching and mentoring
4. How valid is the argument that formative evaluation is more important than summative evaluation?
5. Outline the pros and cons of engaging in Appreciative Inquiry, World Café and Open Space as strategies for evaluating a coaching and mentoring programme. Are there ways of combining these approaches to maximise the effectiveness of evaluation?

Questions that remain

1. How feasible or, indeed, legitimate, is it for the evaluation of coaching and mentoring to be done using a control group?
2. Should measures other than return on investment be found to measure the outcomes of coaching and mentoring?
3. Will organisations that commission coaching make the quantitative measurement of outcomes an integral element of programme design?

Further reading

Brown, J. and Isaacs, D. (2005) *The World Café: Shaping our Futures through Conversations that Matter*. San Francisco, CA: Berrett-Koehler. An excellent introduction to the concepts and processes involved in the World Café approach. It explains the seven design principles of the World Café and provides numerous examples of its workings in practice.

What next?

In Chapter 7, we examine the different discourses found in the different contexts in which coaching and mentoring take place. We invite the reader to engage with a number of case studies and to consider the various discourses which may shape these cases. We suggest that a unifying concept for all these various case studies is 'diversity'. It is the discourse of diversity that may offer a new perspective on coaching and mentoring. By acknowledging difference, rather than seeking differentiation or even unification, we may be able to become tolerant of the variety of practice found in different social settings.

Part III

Coaching and Mentoring in Organisations and Other Contexts

7

Coaching and Mentoring in Specific Contexts

Keywords

Learning, development, power, directive and non-directive, performance

Chapter objectives

After reading this chapter, you will be able to:

- Understand the variety of practice in coaching and mentoring
- Critically understand the influence of context on purpose and practice
- Be able to use a typography of coaching and mentoring to identify and critically evaluate different forms of coaching and mentoring

Introduction

This chapter is slightly different to the other chapters in this book. Whilst it takes a similar structure, this chapter considers a range of specific contexts in which coaching and mentoring take place and explores the variations in practice within these contexts. Its main purpose is to provoke discussion, thought and insight into the different forms of coaching and mentoring, and you, the reader, are asked to draw some meaningful conclusions.

The following case studies serve to highlight the similarities and differences between the various forms of coaching and mentoring. These cases do not represent a definitive collection of coaching and mentoring forms – there are many others! They are drawn from various evaluation studies. This includes:

- The Coaching and Mentoring Research Unit at Sheffield Business School and the interview findings of the PhD work of Tina Salter (2013)
- The research of PhD and Masters candidates for the Professional Development Foundation programme with Middlesex University

We conclude with a discussion and a descriptive typography of coaching and mentoring which was inspired by Salter's (2013) doctoral thesis.

Case study 7.1

Executive coaching

David is the MD of a successful and quite large business. His CEO and HR Director were concerned about his approach to leadership, particularly in Board meetings. They had expectations of him that he was not meeting in terms of his 'change orientation' and 'team building capability'. They decided to offer him a development centre assessment, a 360° review and an executive coach. The coach was briefed by the HR Director and the CEO. His 360° showed that he was rated by seven other colleagues as 9 per cent exceeding the dimensions, 56 per cent fully meeting the dimensions, 29 per cent as partially meeting the dimensions and 3 per cent as not meeting the dimensions. As always with 360° feedback, there were huge discrepancies and contradictions between the assessors. His development centre evaluation was generally strong, with one understated comment that 'he is not clear about his future career progression'.

In coaching session 1, David was able to immediately address all questions linked to this data. He was clear about it all. In session 2, it emerged that David wasn't really interested in any of the areas identified by others for his development. He was generally dismissive of all the data. He was a reluctant coachee! In session 3, the coach changed tack and abandoned the 'data' and the agenda requested by the HR Director and CEO. The coach invited David to say what he really wanted. About 18 months previously, David had applied to join an MBA programme. His CEO's response was to promote him to MD in order to keep him! David had capitulated and agreed to stay as MD. He was 'flattered' and tempted by the package on offer. In session 4, the coach challenged him about the conflict between his ambition and his MD role by saying: 'It sounds like you have been sulking about your wrong decision 18 months ago.' David did not respond well to the challenge, but eventually conceded that to do an MBA was his true ambition. He reapplied, was accepted and resigned his position. He felt fulfilled that he was living his ambition.

Questions

1. What do you notice about this type of executive coaching?
2. What characteristics of this type of coaching can you identify?
3. How many agendas were on the table?
4. Whose needs were being served here and in what ways?
5. What is your view on the developmental needs identified by the CEO and HR Director?
6. What is your view of the other data sets used to identify David's developmental needs?

Case study 7.2

Line manager coaching

Manufacturing Co. invested heavily in coach-training for their line managers. Initially, the line managers coached within their team. This was essentially a one-to-one

(Continued)

(Continued)

arrangement, with the focus being on performance. An evaluation report indicated that the coaches were very happy with the coaching experience and that they felt that the coaching had an impact on their teams. The team members were not so happy. They felt that they couldn't really 'open up' to their line manager and that the line manager often made assumptions about attitudes and behaviours. Basically, team members were compliant but not engaged.

Manufacturing Co. considered this finding and changed the structure of the coaching. Anxious to keep the line involvement, they asked their trained coaches to coach across teams and not within the line, however the line manager was consulted by the coach and supplied the coaching agenda for their team members. A further evaluation reported that, again, coaches really enjoyed the experience but coachees felt that it should be about them and not about their line manager's agenda. Manufacturing Co. now recognised that the managers enjoyed coaching and that it helped them to feel involved and engaged. It improved their skills, which became useful when interacting with their teams. Therefore, they persisted and again changed the structure. Coaches worked across teams as before, but this time the line manager was not involved and the conversations became confidential between the coach and the coachee.

This time the evaluation was very different, for example: 100 per cent of the coaches and 90 per cent of the coachees agreed or strongly agreed that the coaching sessions had been a valuable use of their time; 85 per cent of the coaches and 93 per cent of the coachees agreed or strongly agreed that the coaching relationship had given them the opportunity to reflect on and change some of their ways of thinking and behaving which supported their professional as well as organisational goals; 89 per cent of the coaches agreed or strongly agreed that their coachees proactively set themselves stretching and challenging professional development goals, and 73 per cent of the coachees either agreed or strongly agreed with this statement; 70 per cent of coaches and 67 per cent of coachees reported that they could demonstrate direct benefits in achieving the company's four key goals. A coachee said:

> I'd just like to thank you for giving me this opportunity to be a part of this process. I believe that I have gained a lot of confidence and it has also broken down barriers that were in my way. I think other people would also benefit from coaching and hope that there are more opportunities like this in the future.

Questions

1. What do you notice about Manufacturing Co.'s approach to coaching in the line?
2. What characteristics of this type of coaching can you identify?
3. How many agendas were on the table?
4. How did these change?
5. Whose needs were being served here and in what ways?

Case study 7.3

Coaching psychology

George is a coaching psychologist. He has two degrees in psychology – a BSc and an MSc. He is also a member of the British Psychological Society. He has in addition taken a special course on cognitive behavioural therapy. George believes that it is essential that a coach should have this training. He believes that he brings this deep knowledge of human internal needs and drivers into the coaching room. His approach is normally to listen deeply to what is being said and to probe in order to help the client to reveal and understand his or her deep issue in terms of the main underpinning theories of psychology. For example, the Freudian-based ideas of:

> Dependency, defensiveness, aggression, attitudes towards authority figures and power, fight or flight, escapism, denial, passivity, sense of responsibility and commitment, assumptions, acceptance, control, security and insecurity, conflict, avoidance, confidence, anxiety and stress, projective identification, transference and counter-transference. (Garvey, 2011: 79)

George works with these ideas because he believes that the stresses and strains of modern organisational life create dysfunctional behaviours and destructive emotions, and by exploring, understanding and reframing these, the executive will be able to improve his or her performance at work. He normally works in a non-directive way by using open questions and by probing answers. George also believes that it is important to understand something about organisations to practice as a coach in business-related organisations. His assignments are normally around 6–10 sessions with each client.

(Continued)

(Continued)

Questions

1. What characteristics of this form of coaching can you identify?
2. How many agendas are on the table?
3. Whose needs are being served here and in what ways?
4. How is this approach similar or different from other cases?

Case study 7.4

Sports coaching

Tom is a sports coach. He works with elite athletes. He is a former athlete himself and understands the pressures of high-level competition. Tom also has deep knowledge of the particular sport he coaches in and he believes that, as a former athlete himself, he has picked up the knowledge and skills necessary to coach effectively. He believes that he is able to sense when to be directive and when to take a step back to support the athlete to work through elements that may influence his or her performance. Tom is also very aware of meeting both the needs of the individual and those of the team. He believes that he is adaptable and tries to meet the needs of his coachees by taking into account their age and experience, as well as periods of success and failure. He calls this 'guided discovery' (Salter, 2013).

Tom spends a lot of time observing, diagnosing and giving feedback in what he calls an 'instructive approach'. He readily shares his experience, offers hints and tips and sets goals for his coachees. Above all, he feels that it is vitally important to maintain good, open and long-term relationships with his coachees. Tom focuses primarily on the technical improvement of his coachees. This often involves close observation and the analysis of any problems and then creating targeted small steps and adjustments aimed at making improvements. These, in turn, are observed and feedback is given.

Questions

1. What do you notice about Tom's approach to coaching?
2. What characteristics of this type of coaching can you identify?
3. How is this approach similar or different to the other cases?
4. Whose agenda is being played out here?
5. Whose needs are being served and in what ways?

Case study 7.5

Mentoring in the health sector

A health sector mentoring scheme employed the following definition as a guide: 'Off-line help by one person to another in making significant transitions in knowledge, work or thinking' (Megginson et al., 2006: 5–6). The mentors received substantial training in the use of non-directive mentoring skills and had follow-up learning as a set provision. Mentors were volunteers. Mentees were drawn from those experiencing turbulence in their working lives, in training for their profession or recently qualified (within two years of qualification). The host organisation sought to ensure that mentors were registered with the scheme organisers, were trained, selected, quality assured and supported in their role. For mentees, the host organisation worked to publicise the scheme in order to make sure that it was free at the point of delivery and confidential.

The evaluation reported that mentors demonstrated good listening skills (100 per cent); acted as a sounding board (98 per cent); challenged assumptions (94 per cent); was a confidante (85 per cent); gave encouragement (81 per cent); shared experience (67 per cent); acted as a critical friend (64 per cent); opened up networks (52 per cent); and was an expert adviser (40 per cent).

Topics discussed included: career progression (98 per cent); work–life balance (81 per cent); learning opportunities (81 per cent); mentee's work problems (75 per cent); mentee's continuing professional development (CPD) (67 per cent); time issues (43 per cent); leadership (30 per cent); performance (45 per cent); and personal issues (42 per cent).

The evaluation also produced strong evidence that mentoring developed self-awareness in the mentee, thus making them more able to cope with emotionally charged situations – a relatively high possibility in the health sector.

Compared to 87 per cent of the mentors, 55 per cent of the mentees stated that mentoring helped to develop their leadership abilities and impacted positively on the way they went about their work.

A mentor stated: 'I feel very positively about it and what a fantastic programme it is, what brilliant training it is, and how delighted I am to be involved in it. I would urge them to find resources to keep it going.'

A mentee stated: 'It's an opportunity for people to reflect on my professional career and really personalise as well. … to have support, some direction, some wisdom in reflecting. It's been something I've been wanting for a decade or something, so it's great.'

(Continued)

(Continued)

Questions

1. What do you notice about this approach to mentoring?
2. What characteristics of this type of mentoring can you identify?
3. Whose agenda is being served here?
4. Whose needs were being served here and in what ways?

Case study 7.6

Mentoring for talent development

A large UK-based corporate bank, prior to its collapse in 2008, was implementing a talent-management mentoring programme. The bank was operating in what Grey (2009) called an age of 'fast capitalism'. One of the consequences of this cultural phenomenon was the collapse of the banking system. The traditional ways of doing business and the long-established logic of economics, particularly for the banks, were swept aside in what could be described as a 'social epidemic'. Running up to the banking collapse, management behaviours were shaped to comply with 'fast capitalism' ideals through, for example, very large bonuses and bankers were highly praised as great innovators by the business world and politicians alike (ibid.). This case considers the context in relation to the behaviours of the mentoring participants involved in this scheme.

'Talented' people were identified, first by line-manager nomination and then through development-centre activity. The 'talent' pool participated in various formal development activities and were given a mentor. Its purpose was to accelerate 'talent' development as part of succession planning by using the bank's leadership-competency framework. The framework was meant to be the core topic of discussion.

The mentor was a Board Member. The mentors received a half-day's training and it was felt that this was all that was required as these were experienced people. The mentor and mentee met approximately monthly for about an hour and a half. The problems which led to the collapse started at about the same time as the mentoring scheme.

Topics discussed included:

- Exploring ways to understand and survive the tough climate
- 'Sounding out' the mentor about career options

- Developing political skills to cope and position oneself within the 'new' organisation
- Day-to-day management issues and issues with motivating the team in the current climate and making decisions

Both parties found the discussions useful during the crisis and some extended the relationship beyond the scheme's proposed one year. Some of the relationships ended because the mentors were required to resign. Very few achieved their original objectives but this was not viewed as a problem by either party because they did achieve 'support in difficult transitions'.

Questions

1. What do you notice about this approach to mentoring?
2. What characteristics of the mentoring can you identify?
3. Whose needs were being served here and in what ways?
4. Whose agenda was being played out here?
5. What affect does the context have on the relationships?

Case study 7.7

Mentoring newly qualified teachers (NQTs)

Jane is a very experienced teacher. Due to her substantial experience as a classroom teacher, she was given the role of mentoring newly qualified teachers (NQTs) when they start in her school. This is not only school policy but a requirement of teacher's employment during their probationary year. Jane believes that, because she understands the needs, motivations and expectations of newly qualified teachers, she is well placed to mentor and share her experience. Jane finds that her specialist knowledge and advanced training in classroom management, curriculum and lesson planning comes in very handy when giving her mentees advice. She finds that they learn quickly under her guidance and she hasn't had one drop out yet! Jane also finds that it is important to understand what it means to be a teacher in terms of commitment, motivation and all-round professional behaviour. She recognises that individual schools often have differences in the way they work but her main concern is to help

(Continued)

(Continued)

her mentees to 'hit the ground running' in order to adapt quickly to the culture of her school. Jane finds that, whilst the relationship is a minimum of a year, her mentees often refer to her and seek her out for guidance and advice for two or three years after their probation. Some even become her good friends.

Questions

1. What do you notice about this approach to mentoring?
2. What characteristics of this type of mentoring can you identify?
3. Whose needs were being served here and in what ways?
4. Whose agenda was being played out here?
5. What affect does the context have on the relationships?

Case study 7.8

Community mentoring

Community mentoring is a very wide field but often it revolves around young people who have some sort of difficulty. Addy is a voluntary youth mentor who believes she understands the needs of young people. This she feels is important because it enables her to develop rapport and ultimately a strong long-term relationship. Addy knows that young people need a lot of space and freedom to talk openly and this she feels is best done by intensive listening and open questions. She is not, however, afraid to probe and challenge but knows that this must be done with care and within an established relationship. Addy has been to the 'university of life' and it is this, she believes, that gives her an advantage – she has kind of been there and done many things that these 'troubled' young people are now doing. Addy overcame her difficulties and she believes that she can help others to do the same by sharing her experiences. Her technical training to be a mentor was on boundary-setting and child protection issues. These, Addy feels are important for her own safety because she can get a bit passionate about her work and needs to be careful not to overstep boundaries. Addy makes strong and lasting relationships with her mentees. She feels very proud that she has helped so many young people to get back on the 'straight and narrow'.

Questions

1. What do you notice about this approach to mentoring?
2. What characteristics of this type of mentoring can you identify?
3. Whose needs were being served here and in what ways?
4. Whose agenda is being played out here?

Case study 7.9

Transition from technical to general management

In a study of 12 technical/professional managers who successfully transitioned to general senior management, Durrant (2014) asked them to identify key learning points for them. They came from a wide variety of contexts, yet found common experiences in terms of what they learned in their transitions. Yet, the contexts in which those transitions happened and their own paths of learning resulted in distinctly personal experiences. Thus, although there was common ground, there were specific learning opportunities arising. One core theme was the extent to which they had each found the need to engage in personal sense-making and in building a collection of narratives and insights, which enabled their progress. They reported deep personal changes that coaches as well as organisations need to understand to facilitate such transitions. Some of the insights included:

- Treat people with respect
- Stand on values and principles
- Serve the organisation not yourself
- Teams are the basis of success
- Leaders create solutions
- Seek ideas and knowledge beyond your own

For the executives in this study, the transition from professional to senior leader involved the gradual and continuous evolution of an extensive and integrated set of leadership related beliefs and principles.

(Continued)

(Continued)

Questions

1. What do you notice about their experiences of transitions?
2. What characteristics of these transitions lend themselves to mentoring or coaching activity?
3. What relationship between common themes and specific contexts is being identified in their experiences?
4. What drives the relationship between common themes and personal pathways?

Case study 7.10

Reflections on learning from delivering major policy and practice changes in the investigation and prosecution of fraud

This case study takes the form of a personal reflection on the journey to deliver a major national initiative on the way fraud is tackled in the UK – the Fraud Review of 2006. The project was undertaken by Strickland and formed the basis of his doctorate (2015). While the delivery of the Fraud Review itself was a major undertaking, the reflections on learning that emerge provide significant insights into the contextual nature of leadership and learning. He argues that the process of reflection in examining the work undertaken and the stories behind their creation is a learning journey. By engaging in a deep process of reflection, you learn about not just yourself but also the organisation in which you are embedded:

> However, analysing parts of my life that I had long since forgotten caused me to question my motives and drive to succeed. I trawled through materials, papers and products, which have contributed to make me the person I am. When I consider the process of reflection and the creation of this context statement, I believe that reflection has, for me, been an integral element of the story-telling process – looking back at achievements while providing a vehicle to analyse experiences. This enabled me to understand, not only what happened in the past, but what is happening now and what the future may hold.

This is a powerful statement in support of the reflective process. He continues:

Through these collective Public Works, I have demonstrated how my vision to deliver real change and innovation has inspired others. The works have been transformational in how the police record, analyse and process fraud-related criminality, creating an international model of excellence …

Although delivery of 'Know Fraud' had been a great success, organisationally no one had considered the impact of the system once it was delivered and how it would be managed and used. The system delivered everything, and more, of what had been asked of it. The City of London Police and the National Fraud Intelligence Bureau were then faced with the challenge of how to resource and maximise the potential of what this technology offered.

In many ways, they had become a victim of their own success, this was another example of negative impact of a culture of short-termism and focus on short-term deliverables. This was evidenced when, instead of embracing the new technology, those analysts and researchers who were expected to use the Know Fraud system were reluctant to change and adapt to new methods of working.

System users expected and attempted to make the system work to match how they had always worked. They were unable to appreciate the advanced analytics that the intelligent technology offered. This was not a user problem, but one of re-education and training. System training was not delivered until after the project went live and focused only on technical processes, not on the conceptual changes that users needed to understand to be able to embrace the system.

Questions

1. What do you notice about his approach to reflection?
2. What characteristics of this type of reflection lend themselves to a mentoring process?
3. Whose needs are being served here and in what ways?
4. How is the relationship between vision and implementation being played out here?

Case study 7.11

Reflections from coaching and strategic purpose at the BBC

In an extensive analysis of internal coaching, St John-Brooks (2014) presented many case studies, one of which was from the BBC, as follows.

(Continued)

(Continued)

In the late 1990s, some people from within the Learning and Development (L&D) and HR communities in the BBC became interested in and learned about coaching. At the end of 2000, this led to the formal establishment of an internal coaching service. The purpose was: 'to provide professional, executive leadership and management coaching to support the BBC strategy, equal to or better than that which is available externally. And at a fraction of the cost to the licence payer.'

They identified the following benefits to the organisation:

- The impact of clients being able to address their own leadership performance and effectiveness
- Quicker results from the new appointments coached to maximise impact, influence and effectiveness
- Application of learning from leadership development to organisational life by considering course input to client-specific situations
- Inexpensive means of providing executive coaching accredited coach training, supervision and development to high numbers of staff

Questions

1. What do you notice about this type of executive coaching?
2. What characteristics of this type of coaching can you identify?
3. How many agendas were on the table?
4. Whose needs were being served here and in what ways?

Case study 7.12

Focusing on strengths in team coaching

Following a joint doctorate study of team coaching in the public and private sectors, Peters and Carr (2013) produced a guide (50 tips) to key techniques for team coaching. Intended as a practical tool, one area they considered was a focus on strengths. Here are some of their tips (slightly adapted here).

Wise leaders invest in strengths. If a workplace is only focused on what is not working and how to improve it, the likelihood of employee engagement is low. By finding out what people love to do and helping them to do it more often, you build strengths.

Teams that work like this are engaging for everyone. It includes being compassionate with one another over minor areas that need to improve and selecting members who can complement each other's strengths and weaknesses.

They ask the questions:

- What percentage of the time do you find yourself using your natural strengths at work?
- How frequently are you doing what you love at work?
- How well do you think you leverage other team member's natural strengths?
- How could you do more of what you love and still meet your business needs?

Questions

1. What do you notice about this type of team coaching?
2. What characteristics of this type of coaching can you identify?
3. How many agendas were on the table?
4. Whose needs were being served here and in what ways?

What creates variations in coaching and mentoring practice?

As raised in Chapter 1, across the globe, coaching and mentoring activity are widespread in all sectors and organisations – public, private, large, small and not-for-profit. As can be seen from these limited cases, there are many different versions of coaching and mentoring in many different contexts. These could be examined in various ways by using frameworks found in the literature. For example, Krazmien and Berger (1997: 4) comment that coaching may be shaped and contextualised in relation to the following aspects:

- Organisational change
- The influence of sport
- The guidelines used to coach employees
- The psychosocial

Krazmien and Berger (ibid.) suggest that the emphasis placed on these different elements within organisational contexts will shape the form that the coaching takes and therefore its meaning to the participants. If we take any of the cases outlined above, it is possible to appreciate the influence of both context and purpose on the form that either coaching or mentoring takes.

There are other views. In relation to executive coaching, for example Orenstein (2002: 355) offers four guiding premises:

- The role of the unconscious in individual and group behaviour
- The interaction between the individual and the organisation
- Multilevel organisational forces
- The consultant's use of 'self' as a tool.

Like Krazmien and Berger (1997) above, Orenstein (2002) also suggests that the varying emphasis on these elements will shape the form of executive coaching undertaken.

In relation to mentoring, Anderson and Shannon (1988: 41) offer a schematic in educational settings which serves to highlight the complex dynamic quality of mentoring. These elements include:

- The mentor's disposition, where the mentor may be in a leadership role or serving an 'opening up' function
- The mentoring relationship as either role-modelling, care-giver or nurturing
- The mentoring functions of teaching, sponsoring, encouraging, counselling and befriending
- The mentoring activities of demonstrating, observing, giving feedback and support

In contrast, Garvey (1994) explains mentoring in terms of dimensions – points on a series of five continuums. For example:

- An open/closed dimension which concerns the content of the discussion
- The public/private dimension which highlights the bounded nature of the relationship in terms of confidentiality and what others may know about the relationship
- The formal/informal dimension which relates to the administration and management of the relationship
- The active/passive dimension which is about activity within and outside of the relationship
- The stable/unstable dimension which is about creating and holding to mutually agreed ground rules while being prepared to review them jointly

This description of mentoring relationships emphasises the dynamics of specific and individual relationships within any setting.

In a comprehensive study of the literature of both coaching and mentoring, D'Abate et al. (2003: 367–8) discuss both coaching and mentoring in relation to various descriptions of developmental activity. They identify five main aspects in their taxonomy of developmental constructs in organisational settings:

1. *Participant demographics:* The age, knowledge level or career experience of the participants
2. *Interaction characteristics:* The duration of interaction, regularity of interactions, and the medium used to facilitate interaction, or to span of relationship
3. *Organisational distance/direction:* The hierarchical direction, reporting relationship, or organisational location of participants
4. *Purpose of interaction:* The object of the development, the time frame for the development's purpose, or the beneficiaries of the development
5. *Degree of structure:* The formality of the developmental interaction, including the presence of a development coordinator, the choice to participate, the participant matching process, provision of preparation and support, evaluation of interaction, or formality of interaction termination

In a sense, we return to the problems of definition highlighted in Chapter 1. Recently, working with a group of second-year undergraduates, one of the students, Jess Kirk, said in relation to the definitional difficulties: 'It's well annoying, isn't it?!' It certainly is if we take a cause-and-effect, natural scientific perspective on these variations of meaning.

To return to the question raised at the start of this chapter, 'What creates variations in coaching and mentoring practice?' In sum, these various descriptions of both coaching and mentoring activity have three unifying features, the purpose of the activity, the context in which it happens and the nature of the relationship between the two participants. However, these features do not manifest themselves in the same way. In her doctoral thesis, Salter (2013) adopts a descriptive approach. She took six 'disciplines' found within the coaching and mentoring world:

- Executive coaching
- Sports coaching
- Coaching psychologists
- Mentors of young people
- Leadership mentors
- Mentors of newly qualified teachers

Salter then explored the meanings of coaching and mentoring within these different discipline. The themes identified in her study are presented in Tables 7.1 and 7.2.

It is interesting to note that Salter's (2013) research identified two attitudes towards learning. One is the 'deficit model' (Philip, 2008) and the other is a 'developmental model' of learning. In the deficit model, it is assumed that the learner doesn't 'know' and the coach/mentor does 'know', and therefore the learner needs to be taught or trained. Garvey et al. (2014: 148) refer to this as a 'compliance mindset'. In the developmental model, the coach or mentor may be skilled in facilitating the learner to find

Table 7.1 Summary of emerging themes: Mentor interdisciplinary approaches

	Mentors of young people	Mentors of leaders	Mentors of newly qualified teachers
Philosophy	**Build relationship and offer psychosocial support in order to develop mentee transitioning into adulthood or new role**		
	Relate well to young people	*Relate well to adults*	
	Underpinned by a deficit model	Underpinned by a developmental model	*Underpinned by a deficit model*
	The relationship is important	*The background of the mentor is important*	
	Usually external to the organisation	Usually internal to the organisation	Always internal to the organisation
Practice	**Interpersonal skills needed: Warmth, empathy, active listening, reflective conversation, confidentiality, holistic**		
	Non-directional and flexible	*Directional, career-focused, offering advice and instruction*	
	Help build self-esteem and confidence	*Use observation and feedback to help develop the mentee*	
	Follow child protection and safeguarding policies, and set boundaries with the mentee	*Treat the mentee as autonomous, with some professional boundaries in place*	
	May act as an advocate	May act as a sponsor	May act as a role model

Note: **Bold** denotes an element of mentoring evident in all three disciplines.
   Italics denotes elements of mentoring evident in two disciplines.

Source: Salter (2013: 83, Table 4.2)

Table 7.2 Summary of emerging themes: Coach interdisciplinary approaches

	Executive coaches	Coaching psychologists	Sports coaches
Philosophy	**Need to relate well to others**		
	Help improve the performance of the coachee		
	Balance individual and organisational needs		Athlete-focused
	Underpinned by some therapeutic frameworks	Underpinned by therapeutic frameworks	Underpinned by psychological and physiological frameworks
Practice	**Interpersonal skills needed: Active listening, challenging questions, silence, reflective conversation, holistic**		
	Assess internal and external blocks to identify areas to work on	*Use assessment/diagnostic tools to identify areas to work on*	
	Use a conversational approach to bring about change	Use conversation, drawing on psychotherapeutic framework to bring about change	Use observation, assessment and technological tools to set and monitor goals
	Non-directive: Support the coachee to find their own solutions		Directive: Set strategies to increase performance and enable athlete to win
	Maintain confidentiality		Share information with others able to help increase the athletes' performance

Note: **Bold** denotes an element of coaching evident in all three disciplines.
   Italics denotes elements of coaching evident in two disciplines.

Source: Salter (2013: 86, Table 4.3)

his or her own way forward and this is a 'fairly sophisticated story about autonomy and independence' (ibid.: 122). Salter maps the six disciplines she identifies onto the following heuristic (Figure 7.1).

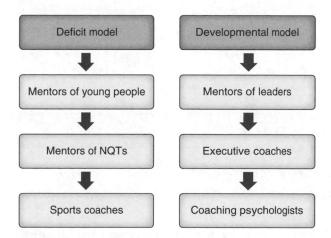

Figure 7.1   Deficit vs development

Note: NQT – Newly Qualified Teacher

Source: Salter (2013: 93, Figure 5.1)

Associated with these attitudes, Salter (2013) also identifies two further elements of coaching and mentoring practice. These are the 'directive' and 'non-directive' approaches. Here, assumptions are made about the coach's or mentor's knowledge and experience and how these might be employed.Salter presents and maps these as shown in Figure 7.2.

This is a very helpful descriptive approach to understanding both coaching and mentoring in different social contexts. Whilst this research has not investigated all possible disciplines in coaching and mentoring, and certainly not all the cases presented here, it does represent an important contribution to both knowledge and practice and offers the potential to be extended into other contexts of both coaching and mentoring. However, when using such categorisations, it is important to keep in mind that they do not define all activities in a sector, only how it emerges in particular contexts. Thus, in educational coaching contexts, you might find, for example, both a deficit and developmental focus and a directive and non-directive approach (van Nieuwerburgh, 2012). The categories do not define the context or activity but they describe what is seen in specific contexts. It is the misuse of categories in this way that leads to interminable debates about what is the difference between consulting, mentoring, coaching, counselling or therapy. Each activity undertaken in a different context might show characteristics of deficit,

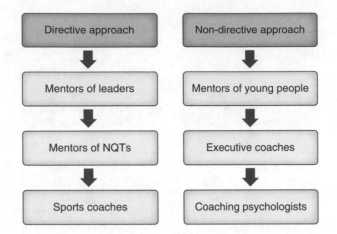

Figure 7.2   Directive vs non-directive

Source: Salter (2013: 95, Figure 5.2)

developmental, non-directive or directive processes. The dissatisfaction with such early attempts to differentiate the boundaries between related activities, for example, coaching and counselling, has been noted by Bachkirova and Cox (2004). The difficulty occurs, they argue, when trying to define some unified notion of counselling or coaching, which is then attributed with assumed features. This is different from the approach adopted here, where we emphasise the importance of the different contexts for specific activities. Ultimately, 'diversity' seems to be the unifying concept and attempts to differentiate or simplify coaching and mentoring activity plays into the hands of the 'managerialist discourse' of the 'rational pragmatic'. This will always be fraught with difficulties.

Summary

This chapter presents 12 case studies of different contexts of coaching and mentoring practice:

- We raise important questions and identify different ways of understanding coaching and mentoring critically in these contexts
- We conclude with an important piece of current research, which has the potential to develop this field further and extend both the theoretical and practical understanding of these social phenomena
- Appreciating and embracing the diversity found in coaching and mentoring seems to be the way forward

Topics for discussion

1. Coaching and mentoring practice has many different roots and therefore many different theoretical underpinnings. How far is the Salter (2013) framework helpful to your understanding of coaching and mentoring in social contexts? Could this be extended?
2. Apply the various influencers on coaching and mentoring disciplines as outlined above in the various contexts you are familiar with in order to gain an insight into coaching and mentoring theory and practice.

Questions that remain

1. How far does power influence theory and practice within the coaching and mentoring worlds?
2. What are the merits of a directive approach? Where might this be helpful?
3. What are the merits of a non-directive approach? Where might this be helpful?
4. What are the implications of a deficit model of learning verses a developmental model?

Further reading

Garvey, B. (2014) *Fundamentals of Coaching and Mentoring* 6 Vols. London: Sage. Vols 1, 2 and 5 are of particular relevance to this chapter.

Jarvis, P. (1992) *Paradoxes of Learning: On Becoming an Individual in Society*. San Francisco, CA: Jossey-Bass Higher Education Series. A full and very interesting account of adult learning theory.

Philip, K. (2008) 'Youth mentoring: A case for treatment?', *Youth and Policy*, 99: 17–31. A critical perspective on youth mentoring with implications for mentoring in other contexts.

What next?

Chapter 8 discusses management and leadership within the managerialist discourse. It takes a critical look at the discourse and highlights some conflicts. We offer an alternative discourse to this dominant discourse of managerialism by highlighting that of the 'coaching and mentoring way' and we ask, are coaching and mentoring positive agents of change in an organisational context, neutral or toxic?

Leadership, Management, Coaching and Mentoring

Chapter outline

- Coaching and mentoring in leadership development
- Leadership and management discourses
- Power in the organisational culture: Monitoring, evaluation, surveillance
- Individual and organisational change

Keywords

Leadership, management, power, change

Chapter objectives

After reading this chapter, you will be able to critically consider:

- The use of coaching and mentoring within leadership and management
- Discourses surrounding leadership, management, coaching and mentoring
- Issues of power in organisational contexts
- Issues of change with the individual and organisational setting
- Provoke thought by offering alternative perspectives

Introduction

Coaching and mentoring are often employed as part of leadership and management development initiatives. It is also often argued that coaching and mentoring contribute to developing self-awareness (Drake 2007; Kram, 1983), flexibility (Byrne et al., 2008; Jones et al., 2006), innovation (Barsh et al., 2008; Dorner and Karpati, 2010), creativity and improvisation – the widely agreed qualities of modern leaders (Bolden and Gosling, 2006; Harris, 2004; Sosik and Megerian, 1999). This chapter discusses these issues and considers how power in the relationship and in the organisational culture may influence and affect coaching and mentoring in their role in one-to-one development.

Not all is rosy in the coaching and mentoring garden and this chapter explores the potential darker sides. However, in this chapter, we offer an alternative discourse to the dominant discourse of managerialism with the notion of the 'coaching and mentoring way' and we ask, are coaching and mentoring positive agents of change in an organisational context, neutral or toxic?

Coaching and mentoring in leadership development

Coaching

In the brief history of coaching section in Chapter 1, we show that coaching was derived from an educational context. However, these early accounts suggest that coaching was about improving academic performance. At about the same time as this educational application, coaching activity was migrating to sporting activity to enhance performance; it was also appearing in newspaper articles on improving specific craft skills as well as developing better 'life' and parenting skills.

In more recent times, the performative element has remained. This can take many forms. For example, one case example found in the *Ridler Report* (2013: 13) is the law firm Freshfields Bruckhaus Dringer LLP. They employ coaching to assist with career progression and developing leadership capabilities and they link coaching to their gender-diversity leadership initiative. In another case (*Ridler Report*, 2013: 15), the financial and business advisory firm Grant Thornton UK, LLP, highlights coaching as having a role in supporting innovation, change and business growth.

The *Ridler Report* of 2011, which asked some different questions to the 2013 survey, found that 89 per cent of respondents reported that executive coaching was an effective method of developing leadership capabilities. It is interesting that in this survey, 18 per cent of respondents said that leaders wanted an ongoing sounding board in the form of a coach and that 60 per cent of respondents employed coaching to assist with the transition and change which came with a new role or promotion. The survey indicates that 76 per cent of respondents rated 'personal chemistry' as a valued quality of an external coach and in 2013 the question of 'chemistry' was analysed in detail to highlight other elements of 'personal chemistry'. These include:

- Sufficient credibility and gravitas in the coach (99 per cent)
- Good listening (97 per cent)
- Interest in sponsor's organisation (88 per cent)
- Sincerity and openness (88 per cent)
- Knowledge of the sponsor's business sector (68 per cent)

These findings and case examples are particularly interesting because the expectations of external coaches are very similar to the qualities, behaviours and outcomes found in mentoring relationships as described by, for example, Clutterbuck (1992), Garvey (2011, 2012), Levinson et al. (1978), Neilson and Eisenbach (2003) and Zey (1989).

Mentoring

In the brief history of mentoring section in Chapter 1, we state that in the eighteenth century, Fénelon, the Archbishop of Cambrai, was the first to present a treatise on mentoring for leadership development. His model of mentoring was essentially experiential learning. For example, he describes how Mentor would take Telemachus (his mentee) to various cities to observe the behaviour of the citizens in the market square. Mentor would ask, 'What kind of leadership produces behaviour like this?' He would then take Telemachus to another city, where people behaved differently and the discussion continued. Fénelon's work was seen by the monarch of the day as a political manifesto which challenged his divine rite. Fénelon lost his pension and was banished: even in those days, leadership development was a challenging business!

In more modern manifestations of mentoring for leadership development we find similar models. From the late 1970s onwards, one discourse on mentoring for leadership in the USA was strongly associated with career sponsorship, where the experiences of an, often, older and more experienced person were shared with the up-and-coming leader of the future (see, for example, Collins, 1978). In the UK, a different discourse of mentoring for leadership emerged in the early 1980s. This emphasised learning and development (see Clutterbuck, 2001). In more recent times in the UK, a hybrid form of mentoring has emerged which is often linked to talent management. Taken with the above discussion on the current uses, qualities and outcomes of coaching in leadership development, it is interesting to note that the term 'coaching' could easily be substituted in Case Study 8.1 as an example for 'mentoring'.

Case study 8.1

The Learning and Development (L&D) function within one of the largest UK banks viewed mentoring as a key element in growing and developing internal leadership capability at the most senior levels in the business. With more than 70,000 employees, their programme focused specifically on the most senior levels within the bank. The mentees were drawn from a pool of senior managers who were identified as being leaders of the future and they were placed in the talent programme. This programme consisted of intensive developmental programmes, using development-centre data to create bespoke development activities. The development of the talent pool was also supported by mentoring. Every member of the bank's Board, including the CEO, participated as mentors.

The mentoring scheme was linked to the bank's leadership competency framework and the L&D manager invited the mentees to participate in the mentoring programme. It was expected that the mentoring would help develop the leadership capability of the mentees and assist them with an accelerated career progression.

The scheme included the following design features:

- Leadership-development focus
- Population drawn from the 'talent' pool
- Training workshop and support for mentors and mentees
- Participants volunteered to participate
- Board-level participation in the mentoring
- Offline, cross-functional mentors and mentees to improve communication, understanding and knowledge sharing across the group
- Matching by agreement
- Scheme-wide agreement on ground rules, regular relationship review, clean closure and a 'graceful exit' by agreement after three sessions
- Ongoing evaluation
- 'Light touch' management of the scheme but with 'draw down' support if required

One mentee said: 'I was absolutely thrilled to be invited to take part.' Another said: 'If you get an opportunity for a one-to-one with a Board Member, you are not going to turn it down are you!' A mentor said: 'I was happy to share my experience.' Another said, 'I was flattered to be asked!'

Of particular interest was the fact that very few of the participants met their original objectives, and yet the evaluation of the programme showed that it had been successful and the majority reported very positive outcomes. One mentee

(Continued)

(Continued)

said: 'The mentoring programme is a good opportunity to develop your skill set in conjunction with a senior member of the organisation.' Another said, 'This was an excellent programme which greatly assisted in my personal and professional development to date.'

The final evaluation question asked the mentees and the mentors: 'Would you participate again?' This received a 100 per cent 'yes'.

Activity 8.1

- What do you notice about the design features of this scheme?
- How might these features influence the operation of the scheme?
- How do you account for participants valuing the experience and gaining much from the mentoring but not achieving their original objectives?
- If the term 'coaching' were substituted for 'mentoring' here, what difference would that make to the case example?

Leadership and management discourses

Johnson and Duberley (2000: 12) argue that the dominant management discourse is rooted in pragmatic positivism, and Garvey and Williamson (2002: 32) operationalise this with the term 'pragmatic, rational manager'. Behind this term sits a discourse which professes that 'good practice' in management is about cause-and-effect decisions, taking action, establishing objectives, individualism and measurement. It is a 'technical' discourse that translates into organisational policies as the manager attempts, but often fails, to control the system (ibid.).

Another discourse associated with the pragmatic, rational is 'change'. Many argue that the pace of change has accelerated and slogans abound in this change discourse – that 'change is the only constant' (a curious oxymoron!), or the more sinister 'change, change or be changed'. Certainly it could be argued that technological advances and political initiatives changed the lives of individuals and organisations. It has brought an increase in competition, for example, and the pressures for people to perform has created the need for people who are able to be innovative and creative, be flexible and adaptive, to learn quickly and apply their knowledge to a range of situations. This has brought both challenge and opportunity.

It could also be argued that the change discourse is simply a way to add pressure on people – to manipulate people and scare them into compliance. The change discourse could be a piece of social engineering aimed at achieving control and giving increased power to the owners of the discourse. Shearing (2001) argues that this discourse is a function of globalisation and has brought us corporatised 'neo-feudalism'. Rather like the barons of medieval times, those who control the discourse create localised 'fiefdoms' in which rules are enforced and power bases established. The barons go for a land grab and we have the new twenty-first-century leadership model – the powerful and greedy model of leadership. Lasch (1995) described these new elites in the global economy as having abdicated fundamental social or political responsibility within the societies they inhabit. They have dubious loyalties and temporarily commit to the highest bidder. These leaders hold the dominant discourse and call for deregulation and freedom at the same time as imposing greater regulation of those they control (Saul, 1997). To accompany this controlling discourse is increased surveillance in the form of appraisal systems, performance management systems, 360° and perhaps coaching (see Nielsen and Nørreklit, 2009) and mentoring (see Carden, 1990), all with the expectation of compliance under the guise of 'risk' reduction or performance improvement.

Normative frameworks or rules are part of the discourse of neo-feudalism as the powerful seek to control and police the ways in which people behave. The 'barons' take the higher moral ground by socially engineering their right to do so, often through techniques and policies based on 'objectivity' and 'rationality'. For example, target-setting, zero hours contracting, hours based workload models performance-related pay and measurement systems. Scientific method applied to organisational life has become a dominant preoccupation of managers.

Further evidence may be found in the ways in which Human Resource functions adopt the pragmatic rational approach in learning and development activities. Here, systematic bodies of generalised knowledge or explicit rules and procedures are created. Specific objectives and learning outcomes are created, often through the 'scientific' approach of Professional Development Reviews, appraisals or 360°s and sometimes development centres and the use of psychometrics. It then, arguably, becomes possible to judge success in learning if these outcomes or objectives are met. This often results in the development of competency frameworks (Ecclestone, 1997; Grugulis, 2000) for learning and development activity (as discussed in Chapter 4).

The merits of this approach include the possibilities of accountability and quality control. However, the emphasis on outcomes often excludes the notion of 'process' and the relational aspects of learning and it creates a 'hegemony of technique' (Habermas, 1974), which simply engineers the achievement of the pre-specified outcomes (Bernstein, 1971). The 'outcome' approach can, of course, get people to where they want to go but it does not promise that travelling to the 'destination' will enrich and develop them. It cannot develop awareness of the different sorts of destination available, nor develop people who are capable of flexibility, innovation, creativity, improvisation and change (Barnett, 1994; Buckingham, 2001) – the widely agreed (Bolden and Gosling, 2006; Sosik and Megerian, 1999) qualities required of the leaders of the future. According to Barnett (1994), there is a genuine risk inherent within the pragmatic rational discourse where one mode of thinking starts to exclude another – 'one best way' takes over. Referring to this discourse as 'strategic reasoning', Barnett (ibid.) states that: 'Society is more rational, but it is a rationality of a limited kind' (p. 37) but that 'genuinely interactive and collaborative forms of reasoning' (p. 32) are being driven out by 'strategic reasoning'.

In Chapter 1, we suggest that both coaching and mentoring offer an alternative discourse to the dominant pragmatic rational discourse of management but are also curiously part of it. It is relatively easy to explain this schizophrenic position. Coaching and mentoring are, arguably at least, 'genuinely interactive and collaborative form[s] of reasoning' (Barnett, 1994: 32). A collaborative form of reasoning suggests at least two people engaging in a learning conversation and we already know that this involves the pair creating a good relationship (Ridler & Co., 2011 and 2013). Here, there is much potential for an alternative discourse to emerge. However, the dominating discourse has the power. To get coaching or mentoring adopted in a school, a voluntary organisation, a private sector business or by government, the advocates of coaching and mentoring need to adopt the dominant discourse of the host sector or business organisation in order to be heard. This means adopting the language of the rational pragmatic, the language of measurement, return on investment (ROI) and performance, and the practitioner who is 'selling' the idea often subscribes to one discourse whilst working with another through their practice.

We argue that both coaching and mentoring do offer real opportunities for changes in performance, thinking and behaviour and can benefit individuals and groups. However, coaching and mentoring, in the main, are rooted in the humanistic discourse of: taking people seriously; involving people; enabling participation and autonomy; listening and sharing; and valuing difference in its many forms. Garvey et al. (2009) describe these values as the 'coaching and mentoring way'. We explore the details of this difference later in this chapter.

Power in the organisational culture: Monitoring, evaluation, surveillance

The following activity is designed to provoke thought about exercise of power in organisational culture.

Activity 8.2

Before reading the quotation, read these questions and keep them in mind, perhaps responding to them as you go along.

Questions

1. In the context of the modern capitalist world, if the word 'managed' were substituted for 'governed', what difference would that make to your thinking?
2. How does this quotation relate to the arguments presented earlier about neo-feudalism?

Consider this quotation:

> To be GOVERNED is to be watched, inspected, spied upon, directed, law-driven, numbered, regulated, enrolled, indoctrinated, preached at, controlled, checked, estimated, valued, censured, commanded, by creatures who have neither the right nor the wisdom nor the virtue to do so. To be GOVERNED is to be at every operation, at every transaction noted, registered, counted, taxed, stamped, measured, numbered, assessed, licensed, authorized, admonished, prevented, forbidden, reformed, corrected, punished. It is, under pretext of public utility, and in the name of the general interest, to be place[d] under contribution, drilled, fleeced, exploited, monopolized, extorted from, squeezed, hoaxed, robbed; then, at the slightest resistance, the first word of complaint, to be repressed, fined, vilified, harassed, hunted down, abused, clubbed, disarmed, bound, choked, imprisoned, judged, condemned, shot, deported, sacrificed, sold, betrayed; and to crown all, mocked, ridiculed, derided, outraged, dishonoured. That is government; that is its justice; that is its morality. (Proudhon, 1923: 293)

The capitalist world, which we inhabit, delivers high standards of living and affluence for millions but it is unsustainable. It has brought us the global financial crisis and is likely to bring another at some point in the future as, indeed, it has precipitated many in the past, back to the collapse of the Vienna Stock Market in 1873 (see Lane and Down, 2010). Despite the restless calls for people to work harder, to become employable, to become more specialised and educated, huge inequalities remain and it is these inequalities and the differentials in power that are a central source of conflict.

Activity 8.3

Consider this …

If we could shrink the earth's population to a village of precisely 100 people, with all the existing human ratios remaining the same, it would look something like the following, there would be:

57 Asians, 21 Europeans, 14 from the Western Hemisphere, both north and south, 8 Africans, 52 would be female, 48 would be male, 70 would be non-white, 30 would be white, 70 would be non-Christian, 30 would be Christian, 89 would be heterosexual, 11 would be homosexual. 6 people would possess 59% of the entire world's wealth and all 6 would be from the United States.

80 would live in substandard housing, 70 would be unable to read, 50 would suffer from malnutrition, 1 would be near death; 1 would be near birth, 1 (yes, only 1) would have a college education, 1 would own a computer. (Anon)

Questions

1. What is your view on the above?
2. How do you account for this situation?
3. How do these data relate to previous comments about neo-feudalism and power?
4. How might coaching and mentoring contribute to changing this situation?

The economist Will Hutton states that: 'Successive British governments have not distinguished between good and bad capitalism in informing how they regulate, tax and procure goods and services … The architecture of British capitalism creates some pretty unwelcome biases' (2011). Hutton argues that the current construction of the deregulated British economy fuels inequalities and rewards the rich and powerful who seek to maximise their own wealth, aided by tax incentives to do so. He argues for 'stakeholder capitalism', where risk is shared and 'good' behaviours are rewarded.

To return to the arguments on discourse and power set out at the start of this book and to quote again:

> language is never 'innocent'; it is not a neutral medium of expression. Discourses are expressions of power relation and reflect the practices and the positions that are tied to them. (Layder, 1994: 97)

Therefore, the discourse of pragmatic rationalism is a power discourse and with a strong performance orientation attached, as is the case with management, there is a heady mix of power bearing down on employees. It is interesting that the words 'manager' and 'employee' represent a power differentiation as does 'coach' and 'coachee', 'mentor' and 'mentee'. Given that a manager is normally also an employee, the absurdity of the nomenclature is even more apparent!

Within the realms of organisations and organisational theory, power is a central concept. Power can help to explain relationships between people, the structures and systems we create for people to work in and concepts of leadership. Concepts of power can also explain how groups, teams, organisations and countries relate, and in coaching and mentoring, concepts of power can shape and influence the dynamics of the relationships.

Jackson and Carter (2000: 76) define power as 'the ability to get someone to do something that they do not particularly want to do'. Influence seems to be a key concept in discourses surrounding power and what seems crucial is the extent of that influence. If, for example, influence is viewed as a continuum, then influence may range from mild to strong, where very strong influence may be seen as coercion, manipulation or in the language of Proudhon (1923) presented above – indoctrinated, controlled, etc. Therefore, power has a moral dimension.

So what is power? French and Raven (1962) suggested that there are five types of power at play in social settings, with Raven adding a sixth at a later date (Forsyth, 2013):

- *Coercive power* – the ability to force someone to do something by the use of threats, the withdrawal of rewards or the threat of demotion or to simply intimidate those who don't comply with unpleasantness and by making life difficult
- *Reward power* – the ability to reward, often financially or through offering opportunities of promotions or special projects
- *Legitimate power* – this is often linked to a person's designation or title. The structures of an organisation often provide this legitimacy
- *Referent power* – is associated with an individual's personal qualities. It is linked to notions such as admiration, or to charm. Power of this type is easily lost but combined with other forms, for example, legitimate power, it can be a useful and positive form of power
- *Expert power* – comes from being the holder of special knowledge or expertise. A consequence of expert power is often that a leader evokes trust in the followers. Interestingly, expertise does not have to be authentic, sometimes it is perceived expertise. Here, followers make assumptions about the leader's expertise and award him or her with status and power
- *Informational power* – is based on the ability to use information to provide persuasive arguments or manipulating information to create a power base. Informational power is about sharing information, restricting it, withholding it, organising it, increasing it or even falsifying it to create a power base in a social setting

In relation to coaching and mentoring, the dynamics of power as articulated above raise important questions.

Taking the first on the list, 'coercive power', how voluntary are coaching and mentoring in the workplace? What should be the level of voluntarism? Could someone choose not to participate? These questions may be addressed to some extent by the design of the coaching or mentoring system and what its purpose or intent might be. Giglio et al. (1998: 93) note that 'organizations are willing to provide a coach for senior level managers when it is perceived that the executive is in trouble'. Other examples of coercive power may be found in government initiatives focused on mentoring disaffected youth. Here, Colley (2003a: 539) states that: 'Compulsion to participate and controlling models of care are being imposed.' The discourse is simple: in Giglio's case, 'you are not performing, have a coach and get mended or you're out'; in Colley's case, 'you must have a mentor because you are "disaffected" and you need to be enabled to subscribe to the Government's agenda or you get your benefits cut'.

The same could be said about 'reward power'. In business mentoring schemes (Garvey, 2012), you may be rewarded with a mentor who is very senior because you are identified as 'talented'. Or you get an expensive external coach because you are an executive (Ridler & Co., 2013).

In the case of 'legitimate power', we find potential mentees looking for a senior mentor because of their seniority (Megginson et al., 2006), or in Nielsen and Nørreklit (2009: 208) where it is legitimate to assume that the coaching manager by virtue of his or her position can 'strengthen the motivation of the employee by creating learning opportunities' and it implies that the 'the actions of the coach (manager), is automatically supposed to generate internal motivation in the coachee'.

In the case of 'referent power', where personal attributes are often at play, the power distance (see Hofstede, 2001) has the potential to distort understanding and meaning. Habermas (1989) developed this notion by offering an alternative in his 'ideal speech' situation. In the case of expert and 'informational power', the ideal speech situation can be nurtured between people who possess the same information or knowledge on a topic, the same skills to debate it and who agree before they discuss the matter to follow the precepts of logic and reason and to respect one another. In the workplace, this model is rarely enacted but it is inherent in, for example, the notion of 'ground rules' within coaching and mentoring and in the underpinning assumption in the large group activity *Open Space Technology* (Owen, 2008; also see Chapter 6). The ideal speech situation is an aspirational standard to be achieved, and in the absence of these conditions, communication can be one-sided, confused and can breed resentment and suspicion.

Individual and organisational change

What seems clear through the rhetoric of change and the discourses of leadership and management is that it is very unclear what 'good' leadership means! As Likierman

(2009: 44) observes, 'successful leadership – how would you know?' Similarly to the coaching and mentoring literature, there is no unifying definition of leadership, much speculation and many fads. Much depends on the context in which leadership happens as to what it means to people. It is rather like Humpty Dumpty in Carroll's *Alice in Wonderland* stories:

> When I use a word, Humpty Dumpty said, in rather a scornful tone, it means what I choose it to mean – neither more nor less. (Carroll, 1998: 186)

However, Bohm (1996: 6) offers some interesting help when he states that:

> A dialogue can be among any number of people, not just two. Even one person can have a sense of dialogue within himself, if the spirit of the dialogue is present. The picture or image that this derivation suggests is of a stream of meaning flowing among and through us and between us. This will make possible a flow of meaning in the whole group, out of which many emerge some new understanding. It's something new that may not have been in the starting point at all. It's something creative. And this shared meaning is the 'glue' or 'cement' that holds people and societies together.

Coaching and mentoring are dialogic relationships and in their purest sense dynamic meaning is created within the dialogue. Dynamic because meaning changes in different contexts – Humpty Dumpty was right when he talked of choice in meaning. Arguably, humankind lives meaningless lives punctuated by the quest for meaning but if meaning is dynamic, nothing is fixed and all is unknowable.

The pragmatic and rational manager often seeks to simplify this complexity with rules and procedures. Inevitably, some subscribe and comply but others may not and differing positions are established. If compliance is an overriding driver in an organisation, the result is little innovation or creativity, and much stress.

Coaching and mentoring offer an opportunity for shared meanings to develop and thus provide some 'glue' for humankind. The antecedents of both coaching and mentoring are in learning, transition and change. As someone learns, they change, and yet the discourses of change are often linked, as discussed above, to power. Garvey and Williamson (2002: 179–80) offer three propositions as practical ways forward to enable change in organisational contexts:

1. Successful change requires sensitive leadership and organisational development
2. Change needs to be positioned as a strategy for the future development of individuals and groups, rather than as threats, fear and anticipated resistance
3. Change needs to be sensitively negotiated and owned by all who participate in it, and to be based on learning and development opportunities

Garvey and Williamson (ibid.) argue that these three are dependent on each other and are dynamic and influenced by the different contexts.

And so, we come to the notion of the mentoring and coaching way in the workplace. These are values-based discourses in their own right. It is widely agreed (see Bartlett, 2007; Darwin, 2000; Palmer and Whybrow, 2007) that both coaching and mentoring, in some forms at least, are rooted in a humanistic philosophy. Humanism emphasises human 'agency'. It, like many philosophies, has a long and varied background. In the eighteenth century, it was associated with the love of humanity and philanthropic acts. In the nineteenth century, it became associated with a revival of classical texts with learning and scholarliness at its heart but religious leaders criticised the notion as anti-religious and as the deification or idolatry of mankind. Proudhon (referenced above), who was an anarchist, agreed but saw humanism as the future for mankind. The International Humanism and Ethical Union (IHEU) state in bylaw 5.1 that:

> Humanism is a democratic and ethical life stance, which affirms that human beings have the right and responsibility to give meaning and shape to their own lives. It stands for the building of a more humane society through an ethic based on human and other natural values in the spirit of reason and free inquiry through human capabilities. It is not theistic, and it does not accept supernatural views of reality.

A derivative of humanism is the notion of humanistic psychology and person-centredness. In essence, this is about enabling an individual to self-actualise (Maslow, 1954) and to develop his or her innate creativity. Taken collectively, it is our view that these elements of humanism as outlined above provide the underpinning of the concept of the 'coaching and mentoring way'.

If there is to be change in the injustices of our current world, the inequalities and the poverty, coaching and mentoring could be a force for good and could be the basis for change within organisations and the 'coaching and mentoring way' could become a philosophy to underpin the change. However, what is clear is that both coaching and mentoring impact on individuals and there is much evidence of this in many different sectors of society. But their ability to affect organisational change, to create a 'coaching culture' or 'mentoring organisation' may simply be neutral as the power dynamics overwhelm them (see, for example, Garvey, 2006a). There is much rhetoric about this but little research and it may be that, despite the general societal dissatisfaction with our neo-feudalist leaders, there may not be sufficient momentum in the 'coaching and mentoring way' to enable change, or the coaching and mentoring way may need to be supplemented by other forces.

Summary

- There is a long association between coaching, mentoring and leadership
- The global financial collapse has brought the need for alternative perspectives on change and on the nature of leadership

- Power issues are associated with coaching and mentoring
- There are alternative more collaborative discourses around coaching and mentoring
- These are developed in the concept of the 'coaching and mentoring way'
- The coaching and mentoring way is rooted in humanism
- While coaching and mentoring may be beneficial for individuals, they may have a neutral influence on organisational change, particularly within the dominant discourse of the pragmatic rational manager
- Chapter 9 extends some of the issues raised here

Topics for discussion

1. How far does the schizophrenic discourse of coaching and mentoring influence practice?
2. What is your understanding of neo-feudalism? Does it exist in your experience? What is your evidence?
3. How does power influence coaching and mentoring within organisations? How can power differentials be reduced?
4. What might the alternative be to the rational pragmatic discourse in management theory?

Questions that remain

1. Are coaching and mentoring able to change whole cultures, if so how?
2. What might bring a societal change in the way that capitalism works?
3. Can stakeholder capitalism be developed? How might the coaching and mentoring way contribute?

Further reading

Garvey, B. and Williamson, B. (2002) *Beyond Knowledge Management: Dialogue, Creativity and the Corporate Curriculum*. Harlow: Pearson Education. A critical account on learning within organisational contexts.

Hutton, W. (2011) *Them and Us: Changing Britain, Why we Need a Fairer Society*. London: Abacus Publications. The title gives a big clue as to its content!

Hutton, W. and Giddens, A. (2012) *On the Edge: Living with Global Capitalism*. London: Random House. A collection of essays on contemporary capitalism that considers the idea of 'new capitalism'.

What next?

Chapter 9 builds on the discourse of the 'coaching and mentoring way'. We consider the main discourses that surround certain strategic options for businesses and speculate about whether or not these aspirations are possible. The issue of what is said versus what is done in organisations is raised as a challenge for the readership. The chapter considers how a coaching or mentoring culture might be achieved by drawing on current practical consultancy projects, and considers how the management discourse could change in order to accommodate a revolution in management practice through a coaching and mentoring approach.

Towards a Coaching and Mentoring Culture

Keywords

Culture, change, strategic choice

Chapter objectives

After reading this chapter, you will be able to critically consider:

- The notions of the complex and the homogeneous organisation
- The discourses of change
- The notion of the 'new' organisation

Introduction

Chapter 8 finished with the notion of the 'coaching and mentoring way' as a concept for change. This chapter explores the notion of developing a coaching and/or mentoring culture with organisational settings and in the context of the notion of the 'coaching and mentoring way'. First, it considers the main discourses that surround certain strategic options for businesses and considers if these aspirations are possible. The issue of what is said versus what is done in organisations is raised as a challenge for the readership. The chapter considers how a coaching or mentoring culture might be achieved by drawing on current practical consultancy projects and considers how the management discourse could change in order to accommodate a revolution in management practice through a coaching and mentoring approach.

Complexity vs homogeneity in culture

Writing about or researching culture is a minefield! The concept of culture is as elusive as coaching and mentoring! Within an organisation, a manager's or consultant's mantra is often 'culture change', and others in those organisations nod wisely at the very idea in a kind of bewildered agreement! However, within this book we have considered the idea of the social context and its influence on mentoring and coaching and this is strongly allied to the idea of culture.

There are many different ways of thinking about culture. Traditional approaches have focused on descriptive typologies. For example, Handy's (1976) typology of four:

Power culture is illustrated by a web. Here, power is concentrated among a small group or a central character. There is little bureaucracy, there are few rules (apart from those imposed by the powerful group or individual) and there is quick decision-making. An example might be a family business or a consultancy firm where the founder is the CEO.

Role culture is illustrated by a Romanesque building. Here, there are hierarchies, heavy bureaucracy and tight rules. Power comes from the position held within the structure. An example might be a public sector organisation or large private sector business.

Task culture is illustrated by a matrix. This culture is about forming teams for specific tasks, and power is derived from expertise. An example might be a scientific consultancy firm or a software house.

Person culture is illustrated by a group of individuals. Here, they believe that they are superior to the organisation that they work in. People are brought together because they have similar beliefs. Professional partnerships often operate in this way and power is derived from individual expertise. An example might be an accountancy firm or a university.

Another typology is presented by Cooke (1987) as:

Constructive cultures where the actors are encouraged to positively interact with each other to fulfil their higher-order motivational satisfaction needs.

Passive/defensive cultures where the actors believe that they must interact with others so as not to threaten their own security.

Aggressive/defensive cultures where the actors are forceful in order to keep their status or security.

Perhaps the best known descriptive framework for culture is Hofstede's (2001). Here, he describes five dimensions of culture:

Power distance where power, as we have discussed in Chapter 8, is an important aspect of culture dynamics. In Hofstede (2001), a high power distance suggests an expectation that some individuals have larger amounts of power than others. A low power distance is about people believing they have equal rights.

Uncertainty avoidance is about coping with the uncertainties of the future. Some cope by creating rules and laws, others through rituals.

Individualism vs collectivism where some organisations or cultures have a high emotional dependency on others and self-interest is minimised for the collective good. This is referred to as 'collectivism'. Where there is a low dependency on others and individuals make decisions based on self-interest, a more individualistic culture persists. Hofstede argues that individualism is a product of the USA model of capitalism. This is a complex dimension, as an individual may, for example, value their duty to the team or group but at the same time as valuing personal independence.

Masculinity vs femininity is about the values associated with gender roles and power relationships. For example, masculinity, in relation to Hofstede's meaning, is about achievement, heroism, bravery, success measured by material means and competitiveness – arguably, the values enacted and espoused through the managerial discourse. Femininity, in Hofstede's terms, emphasises cooperation, consensus and modesty, caring for others and valuing the quality of life above material possessions.

Long vs short-term orientation where in a short-term oriented society, there is a strong concern about establishing truth through traditions but with a focus on quick results with little orientation towards investing for a future. In a long-term orientated society, truth depends on situation and context. Traditions are adapted and changed and people invest for the future.

Case study 9.1

Engineering Co. is a large market-leading multinational engineering company.

In its UK business, there has been a long history of industrial unrest. Formally, managers talk of: 'learning organisation', 'continuous improvement', 'common approach', 'people are our greatest asset', 'bottom-up change'. Informally, they refer to employees as: 'the animals' who need their 'backsides breaking' and they talk of learning and development as 'soft' and a 'waste of time' – 'I did it the hard way and so should they!' Managers speak of employees having to 'like it or lump it'.

The employees say, 'if we work hard and commission these new machines, we lose our jobs and if we don't lose our jobs, we become de-skilled'. They say, 'we won't take any notice of the changes because they will change again quite soon' and 'you can talk about development as much as you like, but if the product is not out the door on Friday, you get your backside kicked'.

Engineering Co. launched a new mentoring scheme to:

- Provide the 'yeast in the bread for culture change'
- Discuss career opportunities and to help resolve learning difficulties
- Be supportive
- Induct new recruits
- Support people in redundancies discussions
- Improve individual effectiveness
- Create internal cultural change

The mentors were existing managers and were given one-and-a-half days of training on the assumption that, being senior, they would already know how to mentor.

The mentoring scheme ran for six months and problems started to appear. Managers said they were too busy and couldn't afford the time. Managers weren't buying into this new 'nice way of going on'. Mentees were cynical. Within a year, the mentoring scheme was abandoned and the word 'mentoring' was banned!

(Based on Garvey, 2006a.)

Activity 9.1

- Using any one of the three typographies outlined above, where would you place Engineering Co.?
- How do you account for the collapse of the mentoring scheme?
- What might have been an alternative approach to culture change?

Case study 9.2

Manufacturing Co. is a large business with manufacturing sites around the UK and Europe. Manufacturing Co. works within a highly competitive and cut-throat environment, with high pressure on quality and price sensitivity. There are constant price wars, short-term contracting for products and increasing costs. Managers are used to aggressive and bruising negotiations with their suppliers and customers and this behaviour spills into relationships with employees. They were hit particularly badly by the financial collapse in 2008 and recovery has been slow.

In 2007, the UK senior team started to develop a 'coaching culture' with the aim of developing and growing the skills, knowledge and confidence of management with respect to facilitating growth. This had the support of the most senior manager, who created a podcast stating that 'everyone will be touched by coaching in the next five years'. This was distributed throughout the whole organisation, both in the UK and Europe.

Initially, 18 senior managers were trained in coaching skills during an intensive two-day workshop. Over the following six months, there were four half-day action-learning sets with participants in smaller groups. Participants were invited to establish up to four coaching relationships during this period and the action-learning sets provided a support and a focus for practical discussions on their coaching experiences. During this time, the 18 coaches worked across departments and outside of the line relationship with 54 coachees throughout the organisation.

Some coaches complained of the lack of time. Coaches and coachees said that coaching transformed their way of working with people in the business and particularly with often strained relationships within the supply chain. Each cohort has been evaluated and the learning from the evaluations has been fed back into the system. In 2010, they started a mentoring scheme to support longer-term development.

Manufacturing Co. had a coaching/mentoring lead and administrative support. Further cohorts were trained in the same way. Some took further development activities to learn more about coaching. Each activity had a similar format of an intensive workshop, followed by action-learning sets. Seven years on, there have been many more cohorts, each with approximately 18 coaches working with four coachees each. The determination of the coaching lead to continue the work has been exemplary and he works relentlessly to enthuse others. Progress continues.

Activity 9.2

- Using any one of the three typographies outlined above, where would you place Manufacturing Co.?
- How do you account for the seeming success of the scheme?
- What do you notice about this approach to culture change?

The difficulty with the typological approach to culture as presented here by Handy, Cooke and to some extent Hofstede, is that they tend to simplify and reduce culture to a series of dimensions. Despite the worthy attempts of these academics to describe culture, perhaps to present homogeneity for managers, the paradox of such reductions is that, in practice there are many exceptions and the cases presented above serve to illustrate the complexity of culture within an organisational context and beyond into wider society.

Complexity theory, when applied to the culture of organisations, is about three types of systems: stable, unstable and complex (Stacey, 1995). All are non-linear feedback systems, where there are many outcomes to any action. The behaviours of a group are more than the sum of individual behaviours and, therefore, small changes always have the potential to escalate into major outcomes. A complex system is stable and unstable, dynamic and at the edge of instability. Such cultures are characterised by short-term predictability and long-term unpredictability. There are, of course, limits to the unpredictability but these limits are not deterministic. Instead, they are governed by highly localised 'rules' with different rules in other parts of the system. Therefore, following rules does not lead to predictable outcomes, nor is it particularly intelligent behaviour. In the case of Engineering Co. in Case Study 9.1, there were multilayers of rules – rules that employees had among themselves and rules that they reserved for interactions with management, and management had the same. A best course of action was difficult to discern because the final outcome was unpredictable, despite the business having a sense of purpose for mentoring. Consequently, a pre-planned and perfectly rational mentoring scheme did not fit in with the complex discourse rules of the players. In contrast, Manufacturing Co. in Case Study 9.2, took a different perspective on culture change with their coaching scheme. They had modest plans, small beginnings and they persisted with encouraging participants to interact and shape the rules in a dynamic and unpredictable manner. Here, then, decisions were coupled with a capacity and a readiness to deal positively with whatever occurred within the complex interactions of the whole and this included the capability to compromise, to be resilient and accept that there may not be a 'right' answer.

The discourse of the rational pragmatic discourse found in management (see Chapters 1, 5 and 8) finds the concept of the complex organisation difficult, as he or she constantly attempts to simplify the complex and control the system. Small wonder that there were approximately 9.9 million days lost to stress related illness in the UK in 2014 (HSE, 2015).

It is obviously attractive to think of an organisation as homogenous. Such a concept is embedded in discourses such as 'we sing from the same hymn sheet', 'getting our ducks in a row', 'strategic alignment'. Burrell and Morgan (1979: 227) argue that there are two main organising assumptions in relation to social groups. One is the concept of 'orderliness' and the other is 'conflict'. An orderliness assumption suggests that every society is a relatively persistent, stable structure of elements. Each element has a function and every functioning social structure is based on consensus. A conflict assumption implies that every society is subject to constant change accompanied by dissensus, coercion by some over others and that every element in that society contributes to its disintegration and change.

Adding further assumptions to the basic 'orderly/conflict' framework, Burrell and Morgan (1979) consider two types of societal change, 'regulatory' and 'radical'. Arguably, then, a combination of the assumption of 'orderliness' with 'regulatory' change produces the notion of a homogeneous society or organisation. Whilst there may be advantages to having a homogeneous organisation, particularly in terms of control, a diverse and complex organisation is more within an individual's experiences, particularly in large organisations. In a complex context, the discourse of homogeneity is clearly inadequate because most medium to large organisations are international and diverse.

A helpful way of thinking about complex cultures is through the idea of Boolean algebra (Waldrop, 1992). This models a complex system as an array of interconnected light bulbs. These were switched on and off by a set of localised rules. The result was an unpredictable pattern of lights going on and off, where the originator was difficult to identify. Some had strong beams and others weak. If we consider this as a human system, the capability to respond positively to whatever emerges in the course of work has the potential to lead to helpful and emergent innovations. Within the light bulb sequence in a Boolean array, all make a contribution because the system is 'open', well connected and responsive. In the human system, this could translate into human qualities and attributes such as openness, good clear communication, being empathetic and sensitive to others and recognition that there is a broad network of strong and weak connections with others in the system. Cavanagh and Lane (2012) have presented a framework for thinking about complexity in coaching. Their position has been subjected to critical review by a number of authors in a special debate on 'Coaching Psychology Coming of Age'. However, this debate points to a lively and diverse set of perspectives on the field which potentially enrich both coaching and mentoring in seeking to address complexity.

Is such a position achievable? What helps and what hinders?

As has been discussed in Chapter 1, coaching and mentoring activity have become widespread in a range of occupational settings. As also has been discussed in Chapter 5, coaching and mentoring are highly individualised processes for informal and open learning and it may be argued are taking over from more traditional forms of learning and development. As discussed in Chapter 5, coaching and mentoring facilitate a more 'situated' (Lave and Wenger, 1991) approach to learning, where the Vygotskian (1978) idea of the 'zone of proximal development' takes on a new meaning as organisations seek to gain advantage by developing the capabilities of their employees. More traditional approaches to learning at work (i.e. training) simply do not deliver what is required (Broad and Newstom, 1992).

Coaching and mentoring then offer the potential, at least, to involve both the cognitive and meta-cognitive learning which is all-engaging and therefore of a higher mental order. This relates well to Knowles' (1984) concept of andragogic adult learning, where the adult concerned actually needs to know something: that they engage with their experience and the experiences of others to involve each other, share and participate actively. What is learned, according to Knowles (ibid.), needs to be relevant and practically applied and thus problem-centred rather than content-oriented. Ultimately, the learning is driven by the individual's own internal motivations rather than external motivators (after Knowles, ibid.).

So, coaching and mentoring hold promise for good change in organisations, so what is holding them back? We would argue that it is the dominant discourse of management! It is highly contestable whether the management education system creates this or reflects this. As raised in Chapter 8, a similar dualistic debate might ensue within the coaching and mentoring worlds but we do hold out hope that the 'coaching and mentoring way' discussed in Chapter 8 might offer a way forward.

What is known about change? Certainly, imposing change from a power position, as was the case in Engineering Co. (Case Study 9.1) doesn't appear to work but a more social approach, as seen in Manufacturing Co. (Case Study 9.2) offers some promise. It is also clear that leadership plays a role in change, as outlined in Chapter 8, and it is the kind of leadership which is accepted by followers as ethical that seems to offer a good way forward. Drawing on the theory found in solution-focused coaching, it is also, rather like complexity theory, small changes that often lead to the biggest change. A key proposition is that productive change requires an explicit commitment to the values of respect for persons, fairness, freedom to think and truthfulness. However, Argyris and Schön (1974) put forward the 'theory in use and espoused theory' and this is discussed next.

Espoused and lived practice

According to Argyris and Schön (ibid.), an 'espoused theory' has many layers of meaning associated with it. It is about the words that are used to express what an individual believes that he or she actually does. It could also mean, however, what an individual might want others to think he or she actually does. It is the theory that someone may express when asked how they might behave under certain circumstances and by expressing it, this becomes a theory to which an individual may align themselves.

A theory in use comes from what is actually done and it is a theory which governs action. This is often tacit and instinctive and it contains deep assumptions about the environment or context of action, the self and others.

In later research, Argyris (1989, 1990) and Argyris and Schön (1992) noted that the differences between espoused theory and theory in use are often accounted for by a lack of education and therefore a lack of self-awareness. As a lifelong advocate of action learning and reflective practice it is not surprising that in later life Argyris was drawn to coaching where, for example, his 'Ladder of Inference' (Argyris and Schön, 1974) has found its way into coaching practice.

The theories of 'in use' and 'espoused' could be applied to the coaching literature versus coaching practice. Here, there seems to be some inconsistencies between what is written and what is done. For example, the non-directive mantra found in much of the coaching literature (for example, Cox et al., 2010; Thomson, 2013), and yet, Ridler & Co. (2011) found that a degree of experience and knowledge and the willingness to share this within the coaching relationship was important to coachees in their choice of coach.

In the mentoring literature, there are also discourses surrounding the emancipatory nature of mentoring within community schemes, for example definitional statements like:

> Mentoring is a one-to-one, non-judgemental relationship in which an individual voluntarily gives time to support and encourage another. This is typically developed at a time of transition in the mentee's life, and lasts for a significant and sustained period of time. (Carrad, 2002)

However, Colley (2003a) argues that this kind of rhetorical definition is loaded with expectations of compliance as youth mentees become commodified and that 'the greatest contradiction is that this brutal commodification of the self is cloaked in the guise of human relationships commonly assumed to be based on warmth and compassion' (Colley, 2003a: 537). So, is leadership and management stuck in its own discourse?

What do managers and leaders really want?

As raised in Chapter 8, the dominant discourse of management and leadership is the rational pragmatic. This discourse pushes out the humanistic discourse discussed in Chapter 8 and leads to the thought that both coaching and mentoring are not simply a good thing but they have to prove themselves rationally and pragmatically. This has created the measurement culture for coaching and mentoring and a particularly pernicious version of this is found in ROI evaluation. In Chapter 6, we suggested that ROI evaluation is 'elusive' and Porter (1995: 45) sheds light on this when he states that:

> Numbers create and can be compared with norms, which are among the gentlest and yet most pervasive forms of power in modern democracies.

He argues that where there is managerial insistence on objectivity accompanied by a management obsession with numbers, a social environment of a lack of trust, weak leadership and morally suspect individualised private negotiation and destructive political behaviour is created. Put in another, provocative, way, the rational pragmatic discourse is a crutch for poor leadership and management!

To add fuel to this argument, Amabile (1997) argues that an environment driven by measurement and strict control, inhibits innovation and creativity. It becomes, like the neo-feudalism argument presented in Chapter 8, a form of coercion, with leaders and managers ranking people, including and excluding and differentiating between people – a kind of anti-diversity agenda. Of course, an alternative and more positive discourse of measurement is that those who meet the standards are likely to feel valued, unique and perhaps indispensable and thus they join the power base.

Clearly, participants in both coaching and mentoring appreciate the influence of a coaching or mentoring experience on their thinking and behaviour but most attempts to quantify this obvious benefit are a bit like trying to quantify friendship or marriage! So, does friendship work? The answer is both 'yes' and 'no'! Does coaching or mentoring work? The answer is both 'yes' and 'no'! Like any other human relationship you win some and you lose some, but this does not negate their potential to affect positive change.

So, what do mangers and leaders really want? One answer may be found in the employee attributes most commonly required by employers. Completing a simple web search using the term 'employee attributes' generates some interesting and very consistent results, as follows:

- Strong work ethic and reliability
- Positive attitude, creative and strategic thinker
- Leadership skills
- Adaptable and flexible with good communication skills
- Honesty, integrity and a good team-player
- Self-motivated and willing to learn and develop
- Specialised knowledge in a particular area of work
- Confident, professional and loyal
- Able to prioritise and solve problems

A formidable list, indeed! Of course, some employers may expect these to be already present in a potential employee and others may wish to develop these. Here, then, there is a link to coaching and mentoring activity.

Parker-Wilkins (2006), for example, found that coaching-developed leadership behaviour helped to build teams and contributed to general staff development. It also improved staff retention, productivity and client satisfaction and increased diversity. Wabbels and Kahaar (2007) suggest that coaching activity can be associated with developing:

- Vision and passion
- Integrity and trust
- Curiosity and confidence
- Commitment and empathy
- Reliability and openness

Garvey and Garrett-Harris (2005), in a literature review of mentoring across many sectors of economic activity, found that mentoring was often associated with:

- Improved performance and productivity
- Career opportunity and advancement
- Improved knowledge and skills
- Greater confidence and well-being
- Greater satisfaction, loyalty and self-awareness
- Leadership development
- Staff retention and improved communication
- Improved morale, motivation and relationships
- Improved learning

It is clear, then, that both coaching and mentoring activity have the potential to develop the very attributes needed by organisations, however there are conflicting messages. So are managers and leaders stuck in a discourse? The answer is 'yes' and 'no'! Can management break free of its dominant discourse?

Can management break free from its dominant discourse?

It is clear that there are alternative discourses and therefore new social structures in organisations beginning to emerge post the 2008 banking crisis. As raised in Chapter 8, coaching and mentoring offer an alternative discourse, the challenge is: can practitioners hold the line and maintain congruence between their espoused and used theories?

Case study 9.3

Consultancy Learn has a base and an 'umbrella' name. They are a private limited company and do not have shareholders. The business exists for mutual benefit. Underneath the umbrella are 168 committed professionals who share similar values. They do not have job descriptions, vacancies or an HR department. There are no managers, no senior partners and there is no hierarchy or differentials in pay grades – professionals are paid for what they do on a mutually agreed basis. There are no set hours of work. The business grows organically. The professionals who make up Consultancy Learn choose to work together because they take personal responsibility, are passionate about their work and collectively learn and innovate. Learning is at the heart of what they do because without learning there is no growth, no improvement and no innovation. Coaching is a key part of what they do among themselves and with others. Financially, the business is sound and its financial model is based on the 1/3 model – 1/3 to the professional, 1/3 on expenses and 1/3 for the business.

Questions

1. What questions come to you about this business?
2. What is the discourse you are coming from when you ask these questions?
3. What do you think keeps this business growing and developing?

This brief case study was based on information gleaned from a live website. We have changed the name to respect the confidentiality of the organisation. This type of organisation is not unique and represents a new sort of business structure underpinned by a different kind of values-based business philosophy. It is much more of the humanist tradition as discussed in Chapter 8 and, therefore, arguably at least, potentially more able to embrace the notion of a coaching culture or perhaps mentoring organisation.

Getting started on the 'new' organisation?

Sherman and Freas (2004: 90) state:

> When you create a culture of coaching, the result may not be directly measurable in dollars. But we have yet to find a company that can't benefit from more candour, less denial, richer communication, conscious development of talent, and disciplined leaders, who show compassion for people.

There are many ways in which change could be achieved. According to Wilson (2011: 408–9), there are three principles in developing a coaching culture and one guiding piece of advice. The advice is, 'don't rush'! The three principles are:

- Self-belief
- Responsibility
- Blame-free

What seems to be important in 'self-belief' is for mangers and leaders to encourage it in others by attempting to 'catch people doing it right', noticing, acknowledging, thanking and praising. Being confident and taking responsibility are key human attributes and linking this to 'blame-free' seems particularly important. If people feel that they will be punished for mistakes, they will not try new things and the organisation cannot develop. In our view, this is devilishly simple but also devilishly difficult at the same time because it means managers and leaders letting go of their own egos and focusing on other people and their needs.

Clutterbuck and Megginson (2005b: 2) state that achieving a coaching culture 'is an ongoing commitment' which is 'far more difficult to budget for'. They go on to suggest that: 'it is possible to make a strong case for developing a coaching culture – one that recognises both the costs of taking this route and the costs of not doing so' (ibid.: 2). In relation to mentoring, Megginson et al. (2006: 7–8) suggest that there are eight elements to consider when trying to develop a mentoring culture:

1. Clear link to a business issue, where outcome is measured
2. Part of culture change process
3. Senior management involved as mentees and mentors
4. Link to long-term talent management established
5. Mentees in the driving seat
6. Light-touch development of individuals and scheme
7. Clear framework, publicised, with stories
8. Scheme design focused on business issues and change agenda

This approach appears rational and pragmatic. However, it is also clearly adopting the managerialist discourse, perhaps in an attempt to gain the attention of management. This list also contains some interesting elements not associated with the managerial discourse. For example, suggesting that mentoring is a part of change and not the main vehicle for it, that the mentee should be in the driving seat and that the management of the scheme should be 'light-touch'. These are perhaps an attempt to change the power dynamics in subtle ways and, overall, they seem to be based on the idea that it is best to start from where an organisation is rather than where one would like it to be! When it comes to the issue of scheme design, Garvey and Garrett-Harris (2005: 36–7) take a different perspective, which has less of an emphasis on the managerial discourse, with elements such as:

> *Voluntarism* – Mentoring is essentially a voluntary activity. The degree of voluntarism will depend on the situation and the circumstances. In some cases, putting people together and asking them to contract for a specific number of meetings (i.e., three) before they review the relationship can be helpful.
>
> It can also assist the process if both parties agree on a 'no-fault divorce clause' as a safeguard.
>
> *Training* – Both the mentor and the mentee will need some orientation towards the scheme. This may involve a skills training programme for both mentors and mentees. Sometimes this can be done with them together in the same programme.
>
> *Ongoing support* – Mentors often need support. This may take the form of a mentor support group or one-to-one mentoring supervision – a mentor to the mentor. There is also benefit in mentors from different sectors coming together to share practice and experiences. The purpose of bringing mentors together is to discuss mentoring process issues, debrief mentors, develop skills and improve understanding.
>
> *Matching* – It is important to have a clear matching process to which the participants subscribe. It is also important to establish a 'no-fault divorce clause' after, say, the first three meetings.
>
> *Establishing reviewable groundrules* – It is important to clarify the boundaries of the relationship at the start. Garvey's (1994) 'Dimensions Framework' is helpful here.
>
> *Ongoing review* – Recent research from the USA (Neilson and Eisenbach, 2003) concludes that the most important factor in successful outcomes to mentoring is regular feedback and review within the relationship about the relationship.
>
> Establishing ground rules at the start can facilitate this process.
>
> *Whose agenda?* – Mentoring is for the mentee. The research suggests that attempts to impose the agenda within mentoring on the mentee result in manipulation and social engineering. The benefits of mentoring to all stakeholders result from broadly following the mentee's agenda.
>
> *Evaluation and monitoring* – Ongoing evaluation of the scheme is important also. There is little point in evaluating the scheme after say, two years, to unearth problems, which could have been resolved at the time.

This list of attributes is drawn from a different, more humanist, discourse and seems to be central to organisational change where coaching and mentoring may play an important role. The argument is simple: changing the way people talk to each other at work, changes the way they relate. Both coaching and mentoring change the way people talk to each other and therefore the way people relate is altered. Organisational and behavioural change depends on changing the discourse. If the espoused humanist values of coaching and mentoring match the 'in-use' discourse, change really can happen. Clearly, the climate which led to the financial crisis was not based on the 'espoused' humanist values of coaching and mentoring and the 'in-use' discourse based on self-interest and greed which was operationalised through successive government policies. Hutton (2011: 395) states that:

> For the last thirty years, Britain has been told there is no alternative. Electorates, governments and the state itself all had to prepare for the juggernaut of the global market. They could not construct or create institutions or initiatives off their own bat that might represent values of fairness, equity or justice; or, if they did, these could only be notes in the margin.

He goes on to argue that big finance became bigger, tax policy dare not redistribute wealth on the basis that those with talent at the top would go elsewhere and that the rich were the wealth creators and therefore had a bigger say in society. Worse, the argument goes, the poor need to help themselves more and the fact that they are poor means that they have brought it on themselves! Labour laws are too stringent on employers and red tape is an unnecessary evil. This, according to Hutton (ibid.) is the 'Them and Us' argument or the 'bad' capitalism discourse. Garvey and Williamson (2002: 194) state that:

> the old frameworks for thinking about the global order of our lives, its political fracture lines, religious and ideological diversity and its sustainability in environmental terms, are all shown to be inadequate.

It is therefore time for a change of discourse and Hutton (2011) argues that the 'good' capitalism discourse is possible. To develop a point made earlier about management education reflecting or creating the dominant discourse, our argument is that the future will be shaped by those currently undertaking management education and this is a good place to start building a different kind of economic system. Of course, coaching and mentoring activity can become part of this new order of things.

Case study 9.4

A very new and major example of the idea that management education could contribute to a change of discourse can be found in the agenda for business education put forward by the United Nation in the form of the initiative the Principles for Responsible Management Education (PRME). To quote from their website:

> The PRME are inspired by internationally accepted values such as the principles of the United Nations Global Compact. They seek to establish a process of continuous improvement among institutions of management education in

(Continued)

(Continued)

order to develop a new generation of business leaders capable of managing the complex challenges faced by business and society in the 21st century. (UN, 2007)

Purpose: We will develop the capabilities of students to be future generators of sustainable value for business and society at large and to work for an inclusive and sustainable global economy.

Values: We will incorporate into our academic activities and curricula the values of global social responsibility as portrayed in international initiatives such as the United Nations Global Compact.

Method: We will create educational frameworks, materials, processes and environments that enable effective learning experiences for responsible leadership.

Research: We will engage in conceptual and empirical research that advances our understanding about the role, dynamics, and impact of corporations in the creation of sustainable social, environmental and economic value.

Partnership: We will interact with managers of business corporations to extend our knowledge of their challenges in meeting social and environmental responsibilities and to explore jointly effective approaches to meeting these challenges.

Dialogue: We will facilitate and support dialog and debate among educators, students, business, government, consumers, media, civil society organisations and other interested groups and stakeholders on critical issues related to global social responsibility and sustainability. (UN, 2007)

Questions

1. How feasible is this idea?
2. What do you see as the challenges in implementing this idea?
3. How deeply embedded do you think the rational pragmatic discourse is in organisations?

Clearly, operationalising such big concepts can be difficult because it requires a wholesale review of the management education curriculum. A challenge is that many management educators also subscribe to the rational pragmatic discourse of management and this is deeply embedded, to the extent that they may dismiss the above by stating: 'We do this already!' This is also our experience of working with some managers who wish to be coaches or mentors in their workplace. They do believe that they 'do this already', but when asked to engage in practical work, they revert to gratuitous advice-giving and solving other people's problems for them. However, there is some hope. Often, when these managers understand non-directive developmental conversations, they see the real benefit for themselves and for others.

Summary

- This chapter discussed the two contrasting cultural contexts of a complex or homogenous culture
- It concluded that complexity is more the norm despite the management discourse to the opposite
- True open dialogue as advocated by the 'coaching and mentoring way' is rarely possible where there is power, real or perceived present
- The idea of espoused theories and theories in use need to be in line for people to view leadership behaviour as authentic
- Rarely do the 'espoused' and 'in-use' theories align
- Change is possible and, indeed, essential to avoid a repeat of the crash of 2008
- Coaching and mentoring could offer the process of change

Topics for discussion

1. The notion of 'Them and Us' creates a lack of equity and an unfair distribution of global wealth. Discuss
2. Unfairness leads to dissatisfaction, unrest and potential conflict. Could the 'coaching and mentoring way' help to address this issue?

Questions that remain

1. Is there an appetite for organisational change?
2. Can vested interests be challenged?
3. What is the role for coaching and mentoring in contributing to culture change?

Further reading

Clutterbuck, D. and Megginson, D. (2005b) *Making Coaching Work: Creating a Coaching Culture* London: Chartered Institute of Personnel and Development (CIPD). An account of developing coaching and to some extent, mentoring, in an organisational context.

Colley, H. (2003b) *Mentoring for Social Inclusion: A Critical Approach to Nurturing Relationships*. London: RoutledgeFalmer. A critical account of mentoring in the 'social' sector.

What next?

Chapter 10 explores the issues concerned with implementing coaching and mentoring within organisations. The chapter itself is part of a critical management discourse which raises questions and explores alternatives.

10

Introducing Coaching and Mentoring into an Organisation

Keywords

Culture, internal coaches, external coaches, team coaching, coaching culture, quality assurance

Chapter objectives

After reading this chapter, you will be able to:

- Explain the role and purpose of coaching and mentoring in an organisational context
- Plan and organise the recruitment of a faculty, using both external and internal coaches and mentors
- Explain the importance and identify the ways in which a coaching and mentoring culture can be built and sustained
- Identify how team coaching can be used to supplement individual coaching
- Discuss the importance and role of supervision in an organisational context

Introduction

In this chapter, we will explore why coaching and mentoring are now quite accepted and valued supportive interventions in many organisations, particularly, but by no means exclusively, large ones, both public and private. As we will see, some organisations plan coaching and mentoring programmes strategically which they then roll out (the scientific-rationalist pragmatic discourse as discussed in Chapter 9), while for others, they develop in the organisation more gradually and iteratively through what Garvey et al. (2009) call 'creep in'. Either way, organisations are now faced by the challenge of choosing between different 'blends' of either internal or external coaches, whether and how to use team coaching and the important but often challenging issue of supervision.

Why coaching and mentoring in organisations?

Many organisations, worldwide, now see coaching and mentoring as essential parts of their culture (as discussed in Chapter 9) and a vital means of supporting people and change. While in the past, coaches and mentors may have been engaged to assist individual managers (often at senior level), it is increasingly the case that they are used at many levels and across organisations. This has often meant that organisations need to use a growing number of coaches and mentors as part of their 'coaching and mentoring faculty'. Looking specifically at coaching, increasing an organisation's coaching capability has been one reason behind the growth of internal coaches, that is, coaches trained or recruited inside the organisation. Another reason is the growing concern that external coaches are expensive. Many organisations are now coping with a number of questions, including:

- How can a coaching culture be developed and sustained?
- Should an organisation use internal or external coaches?
- How should these coaches be recruited and selected?
- How should coaches and coachees be match?
- What about team coaching?

Many organisations see coaching and mentoring as a direct performance-enhancing intervention which can be implemented, not only at individual but also at team, section, department or organisational level. However, given the relatively high costs of coaching (certainly relative to traditional training programmes), the introduction of a coaching or mentoring programme is often part of a strategic intervention. This means that it is usually sponsored at a senior level in the organisation and is often managed and directed by the organisation's human resource department.

Given the increasing range of interventions taking place within organisations, there have been calls to look carefully at the individual psychology bias of many of those people offering their services as coaches. Many would have been trained within one or more individualised models of practice, often derived from a therapy background such as cognitive behavioural or psychodynamic coaches. Critics such as Chapman (2010) argue that we need a greater emphasis of approaches, which link ideas from adult learning and organisational change. He presents a number of ways to bring concepts such as the Balanced Scorecard, Learning Cycles and Complexity together in a framework, which is focused on coaching in organisations. Kahn (2014), another critic of individualised approaches, looks at the axis between the individual's story and the market, organisational needs and the alternative narrative of strategy, culture and business objectives. The business coach, he argues, needs to help to create a better relationship between those stories. We need to keep this critique in mind as we think about creating a cadre of coaches or mentors.

Recruiting a coaching faculty – external

It is not unheard of for senior or other managers to engage the services of a mentor from outside the organisation, often because such people can offer an outsider's perspective. External mentors, however, are relatively uncommon. This section, then, focuses on external coaching, with many organisations now recruiting coaches from outside, especially where the internal resource of coaches or mentors are limited. However, as we shall see, the balance between using external and internal coaches is now changing, with many organisations putting an emphasis on the latter. Yet, as Table 10.1 shows, external coaches are important because they bring with them some sound benefits for the organisation, including an outsider's perspective and experience of coaching in other organisations. However, many organisations have found, particularly as they expand the coaching 'offer', that external coaches can be expensive. There is also a concern that they do not know as much about the organisation and its culture than, say, an internal coach would do. We noted the importance, but also the complexities, of organisational culture in Chapter 9.

According to the *Ridler Report* (2013), of the 145 organisations surveyed (which included companies such as Asda, Barclays, the BBC, Civil Service Learning, Danone, Fujitsu, HTC and News International), one essential characteristic most valued in a coach is their business experience, particularly in building their initial credibility with the coaching sponsor. While admittedly not always the case, external coaches may often be able to offer such experience. But the *Ridler Report* (ibid.) adds that once this initial credibility is established, it becomes less important, professional expertise taking precedent. For senior leaders at Board level, coaches with experience in coaching at this senior level were desired. So, even if an organisation is beginning to grow its internal coaching capability, it is currently more likely that external coaches will meet these requirements.

Table 10.1   Pros and cons of using an external versus an internal coach

	External	Internal
Pros	Can bring an outsider's perspective	Knows the internal culture and issues
	Does not have vested interests or agendas inside the organization	Usually permanently on hand
	Can provide external benchmarking criteria	Can help to promote a coaching culture in the organization
	Coachees are more likely to be honest about their opinions	Has experience of the problems and obstacles in the organisation
	Easier to maintain confidentiality	
	Has access to external networks	
Cons	• Can be expensive • May lack knowledge of the business • Less known by the organisation, so higher risk • Organisation has more concern about corporate confidentiality	Sometimes lacks extensive training as a coach (e.g., short 'line manager as coach' programmes)
		Potential conflict between role as coach and role as line manager or HR member
		May be too much part of the organisational culture to be objective and innovative
		Confidentiality may be harder to keep
		May be too informal

But how do organisations go about recruiting external coaches? If the organisation is using a 'creep in' approach, coaching and mentoring may grow organically (and probably slowly), largely through individuals independently, engaging the services of a coach or mentor. This is often done through the organisation's HR department, or may be completely 'offline' and commissioned and paid for by the individual. Or the organisation may introduce coaching and mentoring, but only for a specific group of people, for example, a new department or managers at a senior level. If, however, a strategic 'roll out' approach is taken, then change is driven throughout the organisation. Here, it may take what Garvey at el. (2009) call a traditional human resources development (HRD) deficit model of coaching, based on identifying needs, planning for meeting them, and then implementing and evaluating the programme. Figure 10.1 shows an example of such a model, based on three stages: Needs Analysis, Recruitment and Selection, and Matching.

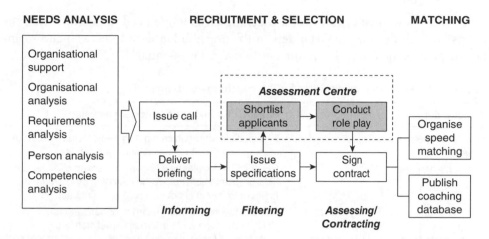

Figure 10.1 Coaching faculty selection process

Needs analysis

A *needs analysis* helps to determine 'what the training needs to achieve' (Arnold, 2005), as well as the level of overall organisational support, including key stakeholders – that is, all those who, for one reason or another, have an interest in the positive outcomes of the programme. Table 10.1 presents some of the potential stakeholders and the reasons why they might be important sources of support and 'buy in' during the needs analysis process. Clearly, if launching a large-scale, high-profile coaching initiative, then top-level management approval (and commitment) is essential. Senior-level commitment will also help to build the support at all levels of the organisation. If the organisation has its own HR department, then this will probably be involved at a strategic level in planning and managing the programme, including getting the 'buy in' of line managers, without whose support no initiative is likely to succeed.

Gray (2010) warns that there are also other important stakeholders who can make or break a coaching and mentoring programme. These include:

- *Opinion leaders* – people who are influential in the organisation because of their position, knowledge or charisma. Their support can be important, especially at an early stage, when the coaching initiative is being actively canvassed
- *Team leaders* – people who manage work areas where the coaching and mentoring might be embedded
- *Blockers* – opinion leaders or those with power or influence who, for whatever reasons, have reservations about the programme and have the ability to disrupt it. These people could exist at any level of the organisation

Table 10.2 shows that planners of a coaching programme need to be aware that the hearts and minds of key stakeholders in the organisation need to be won and maintained. Hence, their inclusion in the needs analysis is essential.

Table 10.2   Potential stakeholders for the coaching needs analysis

Stakeholder	Reasons for inclusion in needs analysis
The CEO, chairperson and executive board	Responsible for organisational strategy, including change management which the coaching might assist
Senior management	Responsible for planning and implementing change. Can help or (often subtly) block the coaching programme if their commitment is not achieved or maintained
The HR department, if the organisation is large enough to have one; if not, those responsible for the HR function	The HR function is best placed to understand the skills, knowledge and performance deficiencies in the organisation (often identified through appraisal processes)
Potential coachees	Their 'buy in' is essential. They must not see coaching as a threat or punishment for low performance
The line managers of potential coachees	May be key suppliers of support – must help to free up space for the coachee to meet their coach and try out new approaches and/or behaviours

Source: Gray (2010)

Needs analysis also includes organisational analysis, which examines systems-wide components of the organisation, including its goals, resources and any internal or external constraints present in the environment (Goldstein and Ford, 2002). Of significance here are the strategic plans and direction of the organisation – how do coaching and mentoring serve to meet these? Questions that arise might include:

- Does the organisation need a coaching and mentoring intervention at this time? What kinds of strategic or operational issues need attention?
- What key behaviours, performance or attitudes require change?
- Have coaching and mentoring been used in the organisation before and, if so, with what effect?
- What do the likely beneficiaries in the organisation know about coaching and mentoring? Do they understand the difference between coaching, mentoring and consultancy? Do those conducting the needs analysis understand the difference?
- What will be the involvement of human resource professionals in the organisation? Will they have overall responsibility for championing, planning, implementing and measuring the impact of the coaching and mentoring programme? If not HR, who will?

Part of needs analysis includes a requirements stage, where the objective is to identify the kinds of jobs, roles or activities that will receive the coaching or mentoring.

A decision might be made that all those within a certain job role will benefit; alternatively, there may follow a person analysis which identifies specific people as beneficiaries within that role. In practice, this process might be too time-consuming and divisive, so all those within the job role are included. The final needs analysis stage, competence analysis, identifies the kinds of new skills or behaviours that are required, linked, of course, to the organisational changes identified above. However, while organisations may set out the broad objectives of a programme, coaches and mentors will usually then need to negotiate an agreement that is focused on performance-level objectives (competencies) at the start of the coaching intervention. But, will these individually negotiated objectives match those set down by the organisation's needs analysis? The extent to which this is not the case will cause tensions at the heart of any coaching or mentoring programme.

Recruitment and selection

The *recruitment and selection* process takes place in three stages – informing, filtering and assessing/contracting – and will be largely the same, whether the organisation is recruiting a faculty of external coaches, internal, or a mixture of the two. The needs analysis will hopefully have provided sufficient information for the writing of a Call document that sets out the following criteria:

- The background to the programme, including a brief history of the organisation, the strategic challenges it faces
- The number of beneficiaries, their positions in the organisation and their location (both nationally, and, if relevant, internationally)
- The kinds of skills, knowledge, experience and qualifications (particularly coaching and mentoring qualifications) that the appointed coaches will need to demonstrate
- Evidence that the coach adheres to a recognised code of ethics for coaching and mentoring
- Evidence of the coaches'/mentors' arrangement for supervision and continuing professional development (CPD)
- The number of hours of coaching and/or mentoring proposed for each coachee
- The duration of the programme, including proposed start and finish dates
- How progress will be evaluated and reported (for example, conference calls or written reports) and the stages at which this evaluation will take place
- The highest price that the organisation is willing to pay per hour for external coaches, or perhaps a band of indicative prices. Details of what costs are excluded – for example, transport costs
- Cancellation arrangements

After the Call, it is resource-efficient to hold a briefing session for prospective applicants that describes the Call document and where questions and comments from coaches can be addressed.

The next part of recruitment and selection is filtering the applicants. This can be conducted effectively through an application form that seeks details of the coaches':

- *Qualifications* – particularly coaching qualifications, and which professional coaching association they have been validated by (if any). It is unlikely that organisations will recruit people whose coaching qualifications do not come with such a stamp
- *Coaching experience* – including total number of hours of coaching, the number of people coached, the sectors they have coached in, the types of organisations (large corporate, small and medium enterprises, public sector, voluntary), and the levels of seniority coached (CEO, Executive Board, middle management, etc.)
- *Experience and the kinds of issues they have addressed* – such as leadership, strategy, work–life balance, stress, performance, motivation, etc.
- *Coaching philosophy* – style and models trained in and used. Training is particularly important, so evidence should be provided of accreditation is areas such as Gestalt, NLP, etc.
- *References* – including people who have been coached by the applicant and who are willing to provide written testaments

Judging the applications can be done through creating a scoring based on weighted criteria from the application form. For example, if the organisation thinks that having a first degree is only moderately important, it could give this a weighting of 2, but if it considered coaching qualifications highly important, then this could have a weighting of, say, 5. A decision needs to be made in advance as to what level of score is acceptable. But whatever system is used, debate about the strengths of individual applications should be encouraged, irrespective of scores. At this stage, the strongest applications are shortlisted.

The final stage of recruitment and selection is assessing between the shortlisted applicants. This could be done through a 'traditional' interview but answering abstract questions would tell us little about how the applicant can actually coach. Much more valid would be to conduct a role-play, as illustrated Case Study 10.1.

Case study 10.1

An Assessment Panel is set up comprising of an organisation's head of HR, two HR members who are qualified coaches, two line managers who support the introduction of coaching, and an independent expert (a member of the Executive Board of one of the professional coaching associations). A member of the organisation who has expressed an interest in experiencing coaching volunteers to play the part of the coachee, and be coached in front of the Panel. For ethical reasons, the volunteer and the Panel agree that the focus of the coaching will be a relatively simple performance issues; the volunteer will not be encouraged to discuss personal or confidential issues in a public forum. The volunteer writes out a short description of their job role, and the kinds of issues, problems or developmental needs they currently face. This is sent to the coach the day before the Assessment Panel session. The coaches are also told that they will have 30 minutes to coach this person.

The members of the Assessment Centre Panel act as observers and use a checklist (see Table 6.3 on p. 122) to score each candidate as well as adding further comments. Observers look out for:

- How the coach initiates the conversation, putting the coachee at ease, setting out (contracting) what they would like from the session
- The quality of the coach's questions and the flow of the conversation
- The coach's ability to offer rapport, warmth, compassion and empathy and, where necessary, challenge

The role-play goes well and is highly effective in differentiating between the coaches. The more effective are able to discuss their coaching model with the coachee, but do not follow it in a restricted or mechanical way – they are eclectic in their approach, drawing on various fields of knowledge as needed. These include humanistic psychology and theories of organisational behaviour. Less effective applicants seem rooted in the GROW model, which they follow somewhat pedantically.

Activity 10.1

Take a look at Table 6.3 on page 122. Are there any competencies that you would not measure? Are there any that you would add?

After the Assessment Panel, the organisation will issue contracts to the successful candidates. Contracts will typically include features such as the general aims of the proposed coaching programme, timescales for preparation and delivery, payment scales, evaluation processes and how confidentiality and intellectual property rights of the organisation are to be protected. Coaches, of course, will also contract with their clients. So, what is the connection between the two contracts? Since the coachee is the primary client, coaches and coachees need to keep the requirements of the programme in mind when agreeing their individual contracts. The extent to which these individual contracts stray from the organisation's aims calls on the coach to make some ethical judgements. For example, the organisational contract might specify that the focus of the coaching programme is change management, helping the beneficiaries to cope with a major organisational restructuring. In addressing this, individual contracts may explore the person's personal experience of organisational change, including the emotional turmoil they have experienced in the past. This would be legitimate. What would be less legitimate would be where the coach asked for help in improving their CV and interviewing skills so that they can escape from the organisation!

Case study 10.2

Contracting for change

A large global oil company has recruited a faculty of 10 executive coaches to help it through a period of organisational change, in which it is placing more emphasis on its retail function (shops on garage forecourts). Retail experts have been recently recruited to expand the knowledge base of the organisation, but at the same time, the head count has been kept in check by making some employees redundant. During the restructuring, all have had to reapply for their jobs. Morale is at rock bottom and even the new recruits are surprised at the shaky atmosphere.

The coaching programme addresses the issue of how staff cope with transition and with what, for most, are new roles (and teams). But it becomes clear to some coaches that what their coachees want help with is in how to quit the organisation. The coaches hold a caucus meeting to discuss progress on the programme and issues arising. They agree to hold a Skype conversation with the head of HR to raise their concerns (while, of course, maintaining confidentiality and not revealing names of individuals). The head of HR is well aware of these morale issues. He instructs the coaches to continue, irrespective of some employees wanting to quit. He rests this decision on the expectation that the department will get through the transition period and stability will ensue.

Activity 10.2

What is your own experience of handling a conflict between organisational objectives and those of a coachee? How can contracting be used to minimise the chances of this conflict?

Matching coachee with coach

Once a cohort of coaches has been selected and contracts signed, the next step is to match them with those in the organisation who have been identified as eligible for coaching. This, however, is not necessarily a simple process. Some organisations make use of psychometric profiling of both coach and coachee in order to identify attributes that in some way support or complement each other. However, there is no conclusive scientific evidence that this works or which psychometric tools are the most appropriate. In other organisations, HR personnel, who may have quite detailed personal knowledge of the coachee, select a coach whom they think is appropriate. This, however, relies heavily on the expertise and subjective opinions of the person responsible for this decision-making. Offered here are two alternative approaches, both of which empower the coachee themselves in making the choice.

Publishing a coach profile database

One way of matching coachees with a member of the coaching faculty, is through the publication of a coach profile database, either as a booklet or as a website. The use of the web allows for profiles to be updated quickly – for example, if a coach leaves the faculty or if a new coach is appointed. Each coach will have their own personal entry based, in part, on the questions that they had answered as part of their application. The entry could also include a photograph. It is polite and prudent to ask all the coaches whether there are any details that they would like to change or add to their entry before it is published.

Once the website (or booklet) is operational, coachees should be provided with clear instructions on the next steps. This might comprise asking them to:

- Browse the database of coach profiles
- Select three potential coaches whom they think they might be able to work with (because an individual coach may not be available or may have a full portfolio of coachees)
- Contact all three and ask to meet up with them or talk over the telephone or on Skype

Once a choice has been made, there should be instructions for what happens next – for example, notifying the HR department, so that the matching can be logged on file, invoices can be generated, etc.

Organising a speed-matching event

The use of a coach profile database can be quite impersonal, so an alternative approach is to use 'speed dating', which allows the coachee to meet all the faculty of coaches and, subject to the amount of time devoted to the event, spend some time getting to know more about them. Face-to-face meetings can be useful for coachees since they may gauge the amount of empathy and trust that might emerge from their relationship with the coach. At the speed-dating event, each coach is given a few minutes to say something (to everyone in the room) about their experience, coaching approach and philosophy. They then sit at their own table and coachees are allowed to ask the coach questions and listen to other peoples' questions (and the coachee's answers). After a period of time (say, 15 minutes), a signal is given for everyone to change tables. The coachees have complete freedom to go to whichever table they choose. The event continues for a pre-planned number of 15-minute time slots or until fatigue becomes obvious.

Recruiting a coaching faculty – internal

We have seen above how an organisation may undertake a planned and systematic approach to developing an external coaching capability. Developing an internal coaching faculty may take a similar route, starting with an analysis of organisational needs, an internal recruitment and selection process and a matching procedure. In practice, however, most organisations seem to grow their internal coaching offer organically and less systematically. Some senior managers, for example, may have engaged the services of an external coach and kept this a confidential arrangement. Hence, there may be coaching taking place that the organisation is unaware of. Increasingly, however, HR departments, particularly in large organisations, have taken a proactive role in promoting and organising coaching (both external and internal). But HRD usually does this within a broader framework. According to Egan and Hamlin (2014), since the 1980s, HRD professionals have increasingly adopted a consultancy approach, adopting roles such as 'training consultant', 'learning consultant' or 'organisational change consultant', and have often seen coaching as similar to 'mentoring', 'training' or 'counselling' – as just one more tool in the HRD learning facilitation toolbox. As Hamlin et al. (2008) point out, much of this coaching intervention is increasingly provided by internal HRD professional, supervisors and managers, by internal mentors and coaches. Coaching can also be provided by line managers, although they may not label it as coaching – but it is coaching, nevertheless. HRD professionals are becoming increasingly sophisticated in their understanding of coaching, realising that for it to be effective, it needs to align with the organisation's core values or business strategies.

So, what about the balance between internal and external coaching? According to the *Ridler Report* (2013), 40 per cent of corporate respondents expect to see a small and 39 per cent a large increase in internal coaching over the next three years. Internal coaching is seen as essential for promoting a coaching culture, particularly by encouraging managers to use a 'coaching style' in leading their teams and influencing others. Internal coaching is more likely to be used when an employee is undertaking a lateral move within the organisation. But in other scenarios, external coaching trumps internal: new appointments from outside the organisation; an under-performing senior executive; eliciting an ongoing sounding board for the CEO or a director. It is not surprising, then, that St John-Brooks (2014) warns that sometimes organisations train up a faculty of internal coaches who then suffer from a dearth of work. Often this can be because of a lack of publicity about the scheme or a 'hands off' approach to matching. She suggests managing coaches more proactively, noticing if a new coach is being under-employed (and their coaching skills degenerating) and pointing clients their way.

In general, then, it seems that internal coaching is increasing through two streams:

- People in the organisation (often, but not exclusively, linked to HR) undertaking coach training and accreditation to become a 'professional' coach
- Managers undertaking 'the manager as coach' or similarly worded internal training so that they are able to hold 'coaching conversations' with their direct reports and others

The latter holds, as yet, unresolved challenges for organisations, since it raises the question – are managers who do some short training, coaches or simply managers who are now better able to manage?

Developing team coaching

Increasingly, the focus in many organisations is one of team coaching, because teams rather than individuals are seen to be the prime unit of performance (Hawkins, 2011a). Here, the coach – or organisational development (OD) consultant – may work with an executive board or top management team, with the focus on how the group as a whole operates as a collective. However, as the *Ridler Report* (2013) acknowledges, there is no clear consensus about the definition of team coaching and how it differs from established interventions such as team building and team facilitation. The kinds of issues addressed typically include:

- Getting agreement and commitment to organisational strategy
- Improving inter-group and intra-group communication
- Resolving conflict
- Managing communication, information and expectations upwards and downwards

While team coaching is currently emerging as a significant theme, it should be remembered that organisational consultants have been facilitating team building and conflict management events for years. Coaches are therefore entering a well-trodden path, the only surprising notion being that some seem to consider it to be new! Another error is to imagine that team coaching is merely individual coaching but on a larger scale since, as a team intervention, it embraces knowledge of organisational development and team development as well as coaching itself. Advocates of team coaching also need to be able to distinguish it from long-standing approaches such as action learning. Or, is team coaching merely action learning by another name?

For coaches, team coaching can create particular challenges. Tensions in a team, for example, may be directed at the coach who may become a lightning rod for conflict. Woods (2014) notes that team coaching is 'not for the faint-hearted' and that coaches can often suffer from anxiety ('can I cope with this or am I out of my depth?'), and that this can sometimes spread to the team. This means that special skills may be required for team coaching that include highly tuned facilitation abilities, systems thinking (understanding the functioning of the team within the wider organisational system) and personal resilience. Understanding group process and decision-making may also be an area that requires greater attention. To the extent that coaches are working to facilitate learning or decision-making in team contexts then, the research on such processes can inform how we work. Many find team working unsatisfactory and, as Hardman (2009) points out, while teams can make effective decisions, very often they fail. In some circumstances, that failure can be catastrophic (Bureau of Air Safety Investigation, 1996; Krackauer, 1998). Lane and Corrie (2012) have listed a number of group processes that can interfere with effective decision-making. In particular, Kayes' (2006) concept of Destructive Goal Pursuit provides an important warning on focusing too closely on the goal to the detriment of the higher value which it is supposed to serve. Its pursuit can become destructive to the organisational purpose.

Having timely access to the supervisor with whom the coach can share anxieties and seek better strategies is essential (see the next section) and can provide a counter to over-narrow decision-making.

Case study 10.3

Team coaching at FastRail

FastRail is a multi-billion pound development project that is working to planned deadlines for its completion. As a highly technical project, it requires a wide range of management skills, including project management, engineering, logistics, operations,

IT, HR and marketing. The top management team comprises 12 highly experienced senior managers, but they need to work together to provide much needed leadership for the project. To help build a cohesive team based on trust, a team coaching programme is put into place. At the first meeting, the coach encourages each member to share their leadership stories, including three significant events in their lives that have helped shape their approach to leadership. Not only does this produce some illuminating stories that all the team can learn from, but it also encourages a level of self-disclosure that helps to build mutual regard and trust. Knowing one another's vulnerabilities, helped the team members bond and gave them a basis for holding honest, challenging conversations in the future.

Activity 10.3

Examining the team-coaching programme in Case Study 10.3, what benefits does the team approach yield over coaching all 12 participants individually? Should individual coaching also comprise part of the programme?

What about supervision?

We are going to look at supervision in detail in Chapter 11, so we will be brief about it here. Let us start with a simple question: Is supervision important in developing coaching within an organisation? In answering this question, it is perhaps best to turn it around and consider what might happen if no supervision took place. As we saw above, one of the main challenges faced by internal coaches is how to maintain boundaries, including confidentiality. Another challenge is that coaching within an organisation often occurs at different levels of time commitment – there may be full-time external and internal coaches working, but also some employees who coach in addition to another role. Then there are line managers who use coaching conversations as part of their everyday job: what kind of support should be offered to these people? Hope (2013) draws on her experience and suggests a blended model of supervision, as illustrated in Table 10.3. Note that this blend of models allows for flexibility and fitting a type of supervision depending on the experience of the coach and the scale of their coaching commitment.

Table 10.3 A blended approach to supervision in an organisation

Supervision model	Role
Highly experienced internal coaches work with a small number of external supervisors	Provide one-to-one supervision
Highly experienced internal coaches are trained as supervisors	Provide support for line managers and those who coach as part of their day job
Group supervision of those who coach as part of their day jobs	Provide opportunity for action learning and peer learning
Internal and external coaches participate in joint group supervision	Provide opportunity for shared learning and a wider community of practice
Internal coaches from different organisations have 'learning dialogues' together	Provide forum for the exploration of practice and learning from outside the immediate organisation
New internal coaches	Provide mentoring by more experienced coaches
Internal coaches in one organisation mentor their counterparts in another	Provide opportunity for sharing experience and perspectives

Source: adapted from Hope (2013)

Putting quality assurance mechanisms in place

Given that coaching and mentoring (but particularly coaching since it is often paid for) are often expensive, organisations will need to ensure that they are getting 'value for money'. Part of this process is putting quality assurance processes in place. Quality assurance aims to ensure that the products or services that an organisation provides or uses are 'fit for purpose'. For a coaching and mentoring programme, creating a quality assurance mechanism will usually be the responsibility of the human resources department, or whoever sponsors the programme. The first step is to set up a Steering Group, the work of which might be to:

- Establish the aims of the programme, ensuring that these are in line with organisational objectives
- Plan for measuring the programme's success and the timing of such evaluation
- Address any problems that may arise, including complaints from coaches, coachees or line managers

Membership of the Steering Group will typically comprise: the senior manager responsible for directing the programme, two or three internal stakeholders such as senior managers from those departments or sections where the programme is focused, a number of coachees and representatives from the coaching faculty (both internal and external).

Quality assurance requires that there is a feedback loop of information about the impact of the coaching programme to ensure that:

- Coaches and coachees are setting goals that fit organisational priorities. For example, the organisation does not want to be paying for 'personal therapy' sessions unless this kind of focus has been agreed in advance
- Coachees are keeping to their appointments and engaging fully with the coaching programme. Coachees (or coaches) who regularly and persistently cancel coaching sessions at the last moment need to be identified
- Coachees are completing any tasks that are designed to try out a new behaviour agreed between them and the coach
- Performance improvements are being achieved

Effective quality assurance relies on feedback from line managers who are in a prime position to recognise whether some of the skills, knowledge or attitudes gained by coachees are being put into practice in the organisation.

Moving towards sustainability

This chapter has sought to highlight the growing importance of coaching, and to demonstrate a strategy for establishing the development needs of the organisation and individuals within it. A model for recruiting and selecting a top-class coaching faculty has also been outlined. This, of course, may be a short-lived initiative unless the programme is successful and coaching becomes part of the cultural landscape of the organisation. Culture here is defined as the values of the organisation, its strategic goals, and the formal and informal systems that guide managers and employees in their every-day working-life (Lindbom, 2007). Strategic goals need to include the development of management skills necessary to achieve the desired organisational results. Coaching can become an important element in the development of these skills, although, as indicated in Chapter 9, it has to be realised that the achievement of a coaching culture is a lengthy and gradual process (Clutterbuck and Megginson, 2005a, 2005b).

For coaching to really take root, it has to occur, not only on a formal but also an informal level. A large proportion of individuals in the organisation should practice coaching behaviours as a means of relating to, supporting and influencing one another (Hart, 2005). One approach to creating this permanent coaching culture is to enlist the services of 'coaching evangelists', people who are willing to act as ambassadors for the coaching programme (Tomlinson, 2008). It also helps if coaching is rewarded and recognised, for example if people are rewarded for knowledge-sharing. Extensive training also has to be provided for coaches at all levels of the organisation, including the top team who should seek to become role models, seeking and using feedback

(Clutterbuck and Megginson, 2005a, 2005b). As we can see, then, the introduction of coaching into an organisation via the recruitment of a coaching faculty is only the first (but important) step in creating a coaching culture in an organisation. The successful recruitment and integration of large-scale coaching faculties may serve to further drive the inexorable rise of coaching and mentoring. Hawkins (2012) offers a seven-stage approach to developing a coaching culture, most of which we have discussed in this chapter:

- Procure external coaches
- Develop internal coaching capability
- Get leaders to support coaching
- Develop team coaching
- Embed coaching into human resource and performance management
- Promote coaching as the dominant style of managing
- Use coaching to do business with stakeholders

We support this list, but would add that supervision is also vital in supporting the whole coaching system.

Summary

- Before developing a coaching capability, an organisation must have a clear understanding of the strategic importance of coaching, why it is needed and by whom
- External coaches are extensively used by organisations, particularly for senior managers
- Internal coaching is growing, partly because it is seen as cheaper than hiring external coaches, but also internal coaches are deemed to know more about the organisation
- In developing a coaching faculty, organisations need to undertake a needs analysis before embarking on recruitment and selection; matching can involve a 'speed-dating' process
- Team coaching is becoming increasingly popular, partly to address and solve tensions and conflicts within teams
- Supervision is essential within organisational coaching, in part to help coaches address the complex issue of maintaining confidentiality
- Quality assurance processes seek to measure whether the aims of the coaching and mentoring programme are being achieved, and is often overseen by a Steering Group
- A coaching culture in an organisation is aided by the promotion of coaching by senior managers (who themselves receive coaching) and if a large proportion of employees practice coaching behaviours

Topics for discussion

1. What criteria should organisations use in determining who receives coaching from an internal or external coach? Should it matter?
2. What should be the role of line managers in the coaching process?
3. Team coaching is just action learning by another name. Discuss.
4. How do the supervision needs of internal and external coaches differ?

Questions that remain

1. Given the costs of coaching, will team coaching soon become the norm? Will this devalue coaching?
2. Should organisations demand that all coaches, irrespective of whether they are internal or external, engage with the services of a supervisor? Should this also apply to mentors?
3. Will holding recognised coach accreditation be the main criterion when organisations recruit external coaches?

Further reading

Forman, D., Joyce, M. and McMahon, G. (2013) *Creating a Coaching Culture for Managers in your Organisation (Essential Coaching Skills and Knowledge)*. Hove: Routledge. A book aimed at managers, leaders and coaches interested in building the practice of coaching and in developing a coaching culture in organisations.

Garvey, R., Stokes, P. and Megginson, D. (2009) *Coaching and Mentoring: Theory and Practice*. London: Sage. See Chapter 10, 'The goal assumption: A mindset issue in organizations', which critically examines the notion that organisations must always set goals for coaching and mentoring, offering alternative perspectives.

What next?

In Chapter 11, we explore the different discourses surrounding coaching and mentoring supervision. We argue that the discourse related to mentoring and supervision vary from coaching and supervision. There is a critical academic discourse throughout.

Part IV

Professional and Personal Development for Coaches: How can I develop my practice?

Towards a Model of Coaching Supervision

Keywords

Supervision, role-modelling, teaching, professional practice, ethics

Chapter objectives

After reading this chapter, you will be able to:

- Describe what is meant by supervision in coaching
- Distinguish between coaching supervision and supervision conducted with other helping professions such as psychotherapy
- Justify the use of supervision in coaching by recognising its benefits
- Critically evaluate the role of the professional coaching associations in promoting supervision

Introduction

When the International Coaching Research Forum (ICRF) met in 2008 to produce 100 coaching research proposals, of the 16 main areas identified by Stern and Stout Rostron (2013) one was on supervision practices. The concepts covered in this subject area consisted of: how supervision is contracted and conducted; the impact of supervision on coach accountability and visible behavioural change; how learning is recognised and coach competence brought into awareness. However, in a review of peer-reviewed journal articles between 2008 and 2012, there were only five articles on supervision practices (twelfth out of the list of 16 themes), while for coaching processes (first out of the 16 themes) there were 88. Supervision, then, is on the agenda – but it is not, some would say regretfully, high up on the agenda. Supervision is mandatory in some helping professions, notably social work, and counselling and psychotherapy (Grant, 2012a). As we shall see, it is growing in coaching but far from mandatory.

As raised in other chapters throughout this book, mentoring, whilst sharing similar skills, is often differently positioned and this leads to a different discourse about supervision. An early reference to supervision is made in Caraccioli's (1760) treatise on mentoring, when he suggests that a mentor needs the support of an experienced mentor in order to improve their mentoring ability. This sets the tone for a developmental approach to mentoring supervision. Barrett (2002: 279) considers supervision as being 'the processes that occur between mentor and mentee during an interaction'. This is a very interesting observation as it suggests that supervision, or the attention to the nature of the dynamics within the mentoring relationship, is crucial to successful outcomes. This view is also supported by Neilson and Eisenbach (2003), who found that within mentoring relationships, 'renewal' through regular feedback about the relationship within the relationship contributed to successful outcomes.

Merrick and Stokes (2003) offer a staged developmental framework for mentors as follows:

- Novice mentor
- Developing mentor
- Reflective mentor
- Reflexive mentor

Similarly, Stoltenberg and McNeill (2010) offer a model of stages of supervisor development. But do coaches and mentors need supervision? Part of the answer to this question depends on what we mean by supervision. Is it a process of control, similar to the way in which a factory supervisor manages and controls the work of an employee? As Carroll (1996) points out, one of the meanings of supervision is to 'oversee'. But if this was the true meaning, then coaches would have nothing to do with it. Or is it a process involving a close relationship between a coach and an experienced (and trained?) other, where the supervisor is engaged in helping the skills and knowledge of the supervisee (and perhaps learning something in return). In the context of psychotherapy, Loganbill et al., for example, describe it as: 'an intensive, interpersonally focused, one-to-one relationship in which one person is designated to facilitate the development of therapeutic competence in the other person' (1982: 4). Page and Wosket (1994) describe supervision as a two-way, interactive process in which the supervisor and supervisee act upon and influence each other, and where the end (re-contracting) mirrors the beginning (the contract). More recently, the CIPD have defined supervision as a: 'structured formal process for coaches, with the help of a coaching supervisor to attend to improving the quality of their coaching, growing their coaching capacity and support themselves and their practice'.

The scale of supervision

While supervision is a compulsory element of professional training (and ongoing professional development) in helping professions such as counselling and psychotherapy, it is not, currently, compulsory for coaches or mentors although some of the bodies in the field have made it so. One reason for this is that training and development is a voluntary activity and not regulated by a single professional body. This is one reason why supervision is not undertaken by all coaches and mentors. There is a paradox here. While some studies suggest that 88 per cent of coaches believe that they should have regular supervision (Hawkins and Schwenk, 2006), others show that only just under half of respondents had a supervisor, whilst a third had some kind of arrangement such as peer supervision (Association for Coaching, 2005). One global study, for example, found that supervision was used in only 15 per cent of the countries surveyed (25 per cent in Western Europe), with most of these being countries with only a small coaching presence. In contrast, in South Africa, which boasts the presence of 1,600 coaches, supervision is hardly used (Bresser, 2009). By comparison, a study by Grant (2012a) found that amongst an experienced sample of 179 coaches, 17 per cent had no supervision, 18 per cent had an informal supervisor, 26 per cent a formal supervisor and 39 per cent used peer supervision. However, it is worth noting that 42 per cent of respondents had been using supervision for less than two years.

Overall, the direction of travel for supervision is encouraging. While Passmore and McGoldrick (2009) comment that coaching supervision is more spoken about than actually practiced, particularly in countries like the UK, the picture is becoming more positive. In the AC's first survey in 2005, only 48 per cent of respondents had supervision in place. In 2008, this had increased to 71 per cent of respondents. As Grant (2012a) points out, there is a growth in the number of UK universities and coach-training organisations now offering theoretically grounded postgraduate programmes in coach supervision. Furthermore, the First International Conference on Coaching Supervision was held at Oxford Brookes University in 2011. Some of this push is coming from coaches themselves. Humphrey and Shepherd (2012) comment:

> According to our study, prestigious coaching providers ... wouldn't represent a coach who wasn't in supervision, believing the latter to be a key support mechanism for any professional and credible coach. This unanimous vote of confidence in supervision is good news for the profession, because it shows that at least some of the major coaching providers are following the standards expected by all the coaching bodies. (Ibid.: 48)

Models of coaching supervision

The world of coaching has not, to date, developed its own distinct model of coaching supervision. Where models of supervision exist, these are ones that have been 'borrowed' from other helping interventions such as nursing, social work, and counselling, where supervision has been common, indeed compulsory, practice for years (Passmore, 2011). In fact, there are more than 30 years of research in the therapy literature on supervisor development (Barker and Hunsley, 2013). Carroll (1996) describes three phases in the development of supervision models within the fields of counselling and psychotherapy. Phase 1 was associated with psychoanalytic models and was largely informal. In 1922, however, the International Psychoanalytic Society formulated a set of standards which included guidelines for supervision but also for the personal analysis of the trainee. Thus began the tension between supervision and therapy that remains unresolved to this day (Carroll, 1996). So, in some models of supervision, the supervisor provides both supervision and personal therapy to the supervisee – a kind of blurring of roles. Phase 2 of supervision, based on counselling models, emerged in the 1950s with an emphasis on skills development and a rather didactic 'teaching' approach by the supervisor, rooted in the supervisor's theoretical orientation and worldview. Phase 3, beginning in the 1970s, was associated with developmental and social role models that emphasised the roles and tasks of the supervisor and the learning stages of the supervisee. Some of these models allow for a more collaborative relationship between supervisor and supervisee.

Developmental models of supervision

Developmental models of supervision have dominated counsellor–psychotherapist supervision, and have focused mainly on a *stages* model of development (Rønnestad and Skovholt, 1993). Such stages models are useful because they allow us to understand changes in a trainee personal constructs. Some models offer three development stages and others four. But all, essentially, demonstrate how the trainee (supervisee) develops from a state of dependency on the supervisor, to more of a peer or equal, as the trainee becomes more skilled, knowledgeable and confident in their own abilities. For example, in the three-stage Integrated Developmental Model (IDM) (Stoltenberg and Delworth, 1987), a trainee progresses in relation to three primary structures – self-awareness and other-awareness, motivation and autonomy:

- *Level 1:* Trainees focus primarily on themselves, especially in terms of fears and uncertainties, often failing to acknowledge the needs of their clients. Although Level 1 trainees tend to be highly motivated, this motivation is characterised by uncertainty and a desire to follow the 'correct' approach to counselling
- *Level 2:* The trainee begins to focus more on the emotional and cognitive needs of the client. However, in doing this, the Level 2 trainee may become pulled into their problems and become as confused and pessimistic as the client themselves
- *Level 3:* Trainees are able to identify the impact that a client's problems has on themselves and can move backwards and forwards between a focus on his/her own emotional responses to the client and what the client is experiencing. Motivation becomes more consistent as the trainee begins to gain greater self-knowledge and understand and accept his/her own strengths and weaknesses

Similar models have been proposed for supervisor development (Heid, 1997; Stoltenberg and McNeill, 2010). However, research by Chagnon and Russell (1995) raises questions about the validity of developmental models. Rather than a sequential process, trainees may 'ebb and flow from one developmental level to the next' (ibid.: 557). In addition, a meta-analysis of numerous empirical studies, finds that differences between levels appear most pronounced largely at a very beginning-level when novice trainees need more support, while interns demonstrate a sense of increasing independence (Holloway, 1987). It is this recognised weaknesses in developmental models that led researchers to explore other alternatives.

Social role supervision models

Social role models emphasise the roles and tasks of the supervisor as well as the stages of development of the supervisee. One of the most influential social role models is the six (now seven) focused model developed by Hawkins and Shohet (2006), which has as its focus the *process* of supervision, but one that is framed within an organisational context, constraints and social norms. In contrast to developmental models and their series of stages, supervision involves operating at multiple levels at all times and involves: a supervisor, a therapist (supervisee), a client and a work context. This is because, while only the supervisor and trainee may be in the room for the supervision session, both the client and work (social) context are present in the supervision session (both consciously and unconsciously). Hence, the supervision process involves two interlocking matrices (see Figure 11.1):

- A coaching system connecting the coach and the client (foci 1 to 3)
- A supervision system connecting the supervisor and coach (foci 4 to 6)

These interlocking matrices are themselves surrounded, and interact with, a broader, organisational context (focus 7).

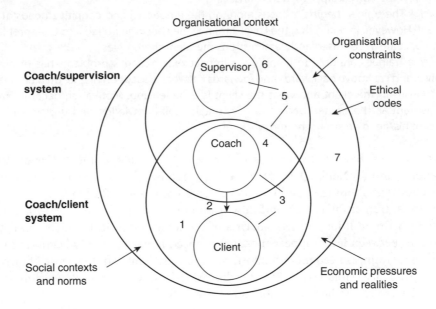

Figure 11.1 The seven foci of supervision

Source: Adapted from Hawkins and Schwenk (2011)

The supervision session pays attention to the coach–client session in two ways:

- Discussing reports, viewing written notes or viewing videotapes of the coaching session
- Discussing how the session is reflected in the here-and-now experiences of the supervision process

The seven foci (as in the name of the model) comprise the following.

Mode 1 The client and their context

Here, the supervisor helps the coach to focus on the client and the choices that the client is making, or as Hawkins and Schwenk term it, 'getting the client(s) into the room' (2011: 30). The first stage here might be to get the coach to describe the client in some detail, including their physical appearance, their verbal and non-verbal behaviours and how they came to engage with coaching.

Mode 2 The coach's interventions

This mode looks at how the coach works with the client. In this mode, the aim is to improve the coach's choices and skills in intervention by exploring the strategies they used and what alternative strategies might be considered. New options are generated through discussion, with the supervisor taking care not to impose their own strategies on the coach.

Mode 3 The relationship between the coach and coachee

The focus here is the relationship that the coach and client are co-creating. Here, the supervisor focuses on what is happening at the conscious but also the unconscious level in the coaching session. It includes looking for clues to the transference that is happening from the client to the coach (and the coach's counter-transference – see the next section).

Mode 4 The coach's awareness

Here, the focus is on the coach's own internal processes and how these are affecting the coaching process. These include the coach's counter-transference, a predominantly unconscious reaction by the coach to the client's transference.

Mode 5 The supervisory relationship (supervision process)

At this level, the processes at work between the coach and client are explored through how they are reflected in the relationship between the coach and the supervisor. So, a coach who is experiencing challenging behaviour from a client, may exhibit challenging behaviour towards the supervisor. The task of the supervisor is to identify this process so that learning can emerge from it.

Mode 6 The supervisor's own process (supervisor's experience/self-reflection)

The emphasis here is on the supervisor's 'here-and-now' experience with the coach, and what can be learned about the coach/coachee from the supervisor's response to the coach, and what they are presenting about the client. For example, does the supervisor feel threatened, challenged or merely bored? In this mode, the supervisor pays attention to his/her own shifting feelings and sensations towards the coach, while at the same time attending to the content and process of the session.

Mode 7 The wider context in which the coaching happens

This focus acknowledges the organisational, social, cultural, ethical and contractual context in which the coaching takes place. This includes a wider group of stakeholders, that includes the client organisation and its stakeholders, the coach's organisation and its stakeholders, and the organisation and professional affiliations of the supervisor. It includes the power and cultural dynamics that underlie these various relationships, 'to understand how the culture of the systemic context might be creating illusions, delusions and collusions in the coach and in oneself' (Hawkins and Schwenk, 2011), and in the relationship between the coach and the supervisor. As Hawkins (2011b) points out, supervisors need to be trained, not only in individual psychology but also to understand the wider organisational context and to see patterns between issues over time.

Thus, the role of the supervisor becomes one of handling the tensions and the sometimes diverse interests between the coach, the coachee and their organisation (Pampallis Paisley, 2006). This often includes coping with the complex dynamics such as maintaining professional boundaries and being aware of the needs and responsibilities of each stakeholder (Carroll, 2006). Hence, while a coach and coachee may negotiate a set of objectives as part of a contracting process, the needs and requirements of the coachee's sponsoring organisation are never far from the surface. Towler calls the organisation the 'invisible client' (2005: 309), which imposes unconscious influences in the supervision room. The supervisors of coaches, therefore, need to be sensitive to and understand the systemic and cultural aspects of organisations. The influences of organisational culture become a significant rather than an incidental factor in the process of supervision (Towler, 2005).

Recognising that the coach has to handle such a complex array of stakeholder needs, Proctor (2008) sees coaching supervision as serving three purposes:

Normative: Ensuring that the supervisee's work is competent, ethical and to a professional standard.

Formative: Building the knowledge, understanding, skills, techniques and behaviours that increase practitioner competence, mastery, maturity and wisdom.

Restorative or supportive: Creating a constructive space away from the coaching relationship for exploring the supervisee's vulnerabilities, confusions, stress, emotions and patterns that impact on their coaching and practice.

Activity 11.1

Taking Proctor's model (2008), identify which of the normative, formative and restorative elements are relevant to the modes in the seven-eyed model. Are some more relevant to certain modes than others?

Modes of supervision

When we talk about supervision, the scenario that springs to mind is of a supervisor and a supervisee (coach or mentor) sitting together in a constructive conversation. Indeed, this is a very common format. However, as this section shows, there are a number of others, some of which are growing in popularity – for example, peer coaching. In selecting a format for supervision, a number of factors may come into play. Grant's (2012a) study of Australian coaches suggests that one reason some coaches choose peer supervision is due to the lack of experienced supervisors. Another factor is cost. But apart from resource issues and costs, these different formats also offer potential benefits. Lane (2011) has argued that as supervision moves from a trainee or early career to a whole career activity, different supervisor roles become valuable, including expert/apprentice, CPD, Peer and Process models.

One-to-one: Supervisor-coach

In this format, a supervisor provides supervision for one other coach in a one-to-one relationship. According to Mead et al. (1999), one-to-one supervision is the classic form, providing a confidential space for undiluted attention and in-depth inquiry, with a typical session lasting between 60 and 90 minutes. Sessions take place between four and six weeks as a minimum, although this can be increased for novice practitioners or where experienced coaches run into trouble. This might be the format favoured by inexperienced coaches, since it is more personal and private, allowing the supervisee to show vulnerability (for example, concern about a lack of skills, whether imagined or real). The Association for Coaching (2005) maintains that inexperienced coaches need to choose a supervisor who has been a practising coach for a number of years.

One-to-One: Peer supervision

Here, two participants provide supervision for each other by taking on the roles of supervisor and coach, alternately. For this to work, both participants need to be experienced as coaches and possess supervision skills. One of the dangers of this approach is where both participants have weaknesses, blind spots or inexperience is the same area. However, one of the strengths is that regular contact can develop deep mutual understanding and promote more insightful feedback and support.

Group supervision: Identified supervisor(s)

Group supervision is a process 'in which supervisors oversee a trainee's professional development in a group of peers' (Holloway and Johnston, 1985: 333). Discussing supervision within the context of counselling, Borders (1991) describes the supervisor as a skilled teacher, and group leader who works with trainees to help them attain their individual goals, as well as the goals of their training programme. She recommends that a group consists of three to six participants plus a supervisor, meeting weekly or biweekly up to 3 hours. There are many ways of organising this. One model is for the supervisor to allocate his or her time amongst the group of coaches they are supervising. Another, is that the coaches allocate supervision time amongst themselves (peer-to-peer coaching) drawing on the supervisor as an expert when and if needed.

Group supervision: Peer group

In peer group supervision, three or more coaches share responsibility for one another's supervision within the group. In this format, there is no supervisor who acts as the expert. Hence, peer group supervision is a form of group supervision, in which it is assumed that the group members have the resources to help themselves and to make sense of their practice (Lakeman and Glasgow, 2009). This works best where all the coaches are of broadly equal experience and training. However, while this format may work well for experience coaches, it is far less suitable for inexperienced coaches who may lack the skills and the perspectives needed to supervise others. When used, it is also essential that there is a clear understanding of where the final responsibility for the clients' welfare rests (Association for Coaching, 2005).

In peer group supervision, members take turns to present themes and issues for the session. The role of facilitator is also shared and rotated each session around the group. The facilitator ensures that group processes are followed, by soliciting comments, feedback and observations in a series of rounds, with participants being allowed to speak without interruption. Processes include sharing positive experiences, seeking advice, reviewing a shared problem, reviewing a critical incident or reviewing an element of coaching practice. In line with the peer group supervision model developed by Heron (1999), participants need to be aware of their supervisory needs, which might be:

- *Restorative* – eliciting validation for doing well with a client or sharing a problem
- *Normative* – seeking advice
- *Developmental* – reflecting on conversations with coaching clients

The success of peer group supervision depends largely on the extent to which facilitation is faithful to the processes described above (Lakeman and Glasgow, 2009). Its potential weakness is that peers may not challenge each other sufficiently or may share each other's blind spots.

A version of peer group supervision is the use of action-learning sets, developed around the ideas of Revans (1982). Here, a group of between five and eight coaches meet on a scheduled basis (typically every four to six weeks for half a day), to learn from and support each other. After 'checking in' and reconnecting with the group, members are given 'air time', to raise problems and concerns. Other members of the group listen without interruption; once the member has told their story, other members ask challenging and supportive questions. The supervisor's role here is to facilitate the processes of the group and to act as an expert (when needed). Childs et al. (2011) recommend the use of action-learning sets for supervision, not in place of traditional approaches but running alongside them.

Case study 11.1

Getting processes right in a supervision action-learning set

A year ago, a group of middle managers completed their training as coaches and so have had 12 months of experience in delivering coaching within the organisation. As managers, they are experienced in making quick, clear decisions, a trait which they have to 'leave at the door' when it comes to asking open questions of their coachees (and avoiding the temptation to give solutions to the coachee's problem). But in their supervision action-learning set, some of these tendencies bubble to the surface. The facilitator reminded them that they needed to avoid coming to sudden judgements and getting side-tracked by telling their own 'war stories'. The facilitator tackled this issue by role-modelling a more appropriate behaviour – slowing down the pace of the questioning, allowing participants time to reflect on their answers, and being relaxed

(Continued)

(Continued)

with silences rather than trying to fill them. As a result, the group began to function more effectively, which led to the facilitator being able to take more of a 'back seat' and allow the group to control its own processes.

Activity 11.2

What else could the facilitator do to move the group processes away from advice-giving? How would you notice that this was working?

Mixing modes

The sections above might suggest a dichotomy between modes, that is, coaches choose one or another. However, a study by Grant (2012a) suggests that some coaches are very flexible, using a combination of modes to serve several purposes. One coach, for example, talked about using three modes of supervision. The first supervisor is a coach of 27-years' standing, who helps deal with challenging clients. The second is a very experienced psychologist (with a PhD) who helps in the psychological relationships with clients, including issues of transference and clients with high levels of stress. Sometimes, clients will be referred to this supervisor for more detailed professional support. The third mode of supervision is informal peer supervision with two executive coaches, with the aim of sharing experiences and broadening knowledge. What is interesting about this example, is how the coach has arranged a network of supervision arrangements that allow for the flexible drawing on specific kinds of support, depending on needs and circumstances. This could include both personal development (skills, competencies and ethical behaviour) and business development.

Media and supervision

Like coaching itself, most participants would, if given the choice, prefer face-to-face contact for supervision sessions. However, due to geographical distance or the logistics of arranging meetings (particularly for group supervision), the use of various communications media can become essential, particularly if they are used as group resources for interactions between live sessions.

Telephone and Skype supervision

Both telephone and Skype conversations offer opportunities for immediate contact (as opposed to having to wait for a meeting) and hence are useful, for example, when a coach faces a crisis and needs rapid reassurance or guidance from a supervisor. However, one of the drawbacks of using communications media is that the intimacy of the one-to-one supervision conversation may be lacking and it is much harder for both parties to observe body language and the subtleties of verbal intonation, both of which may be vital in interpretation of messages and stories. Nevertheless, it could be argued that a telephone or Skype call are better than no conversation. Group calls are also feasible using the telephone's conference calling facility or group calls on Skype.

Email and postal supervision

For those who, due to location, may live in isolated areas, email supervision could prove a useful way of working. However, on its own, typed communication through emails or letters would be entirely lacking in sufficient depth. It is probably best if this method is combined with the telephone and Skype supervision option mentioned above, as it is unlikely that the email and postal option would be sufficient on its own. Emails are probably best for arranging supervisory meetings rather than for supervision itself.

Webinar supervision

A webinar is a web-based seminar, through which online tools and resources allow for real-time interaction between participants. This includes the provision for slideshows and presentations, full motion video (typically of participants or presenters), a whiteboard that participants can add text to, and live text chat. Webinars, however, need to be distinguished from Webcasts, the latter being more didactic in style, with the use of presentations, often using PowerPoint slides, an experience similar to being in a classroom, only here the medium is virtual rather than face-to-face. Webinars are, or should be, much more interactive.

How can webinars be used in a supervision context? Imagine that there is a group of six members, dispersed across the country. Here are just some possible scenarios:

- A supervisor and supervisee undertake a session (video recorded and streamed live via a webcam) in which the supervisee discusses some difficulties with a recent client. Other members of the group observe the session through their computer screens. During this time, they use live chat to send messages to each other (some public, some private), perhaps formulating working hypotheses about what is going on in the session. Once the supervision session is finished, all group members join in an audio discussion
- A group member uses the presentation facility in the webinar to present a new set of theoretical constructs or coaching tools. Group members listen to the presentation and some post observations on the whiteboard

Webinar technology is still in its infancy, and its use in supervision generally and coach supervision specifically, is relatively uncommon. Its use, however, is likely to expand as the technology becomes more mainstreamed and peoples' confidence with it grows.

Activity 11.3

Some claim that supervision must always be a face-to-face activity. What is your view? Can supervision ever be a totally virtual process?

Evaluating the supervision relationship

As we saw in Chapter 6, evaluation involves the systematic collecting of data, so that important modifications and improvements to a programme (in this case, a supervision programme) can be implemented (Gray, 2004). The evaluation of the supervisory relationship can take place at many levels, ranging from ad hoc and informal to highly structured and formal. The difference between these formal and informal approaches is largely around how the evaluation is conducted. With informal evaluation, which is probably by far the most common approach, the supervisor and supervisee may merely discuss the outcomes of their discussions as well as the strength of their relationship, or in de Haan's (2008) term, the 'working alliance'. In contrast, Lincoln and Guba (1994) describe formal evaluation as a kind of disciplined inquiry, where scientific principles of measurement about the content, structure and outcomes of programmes, projects and planned interventions are applied. The question in the supervision relationship then, is what should one evaluate?

 Then there is the question: why evaluate? According to Gray (2004), one result of evaluation is that it allows us a critical window into professional practice. In the case of coaching supervision, it allows both coach and supervisor to develop a greater degree of self-knowledge and the opportunity to learn how interactive processes and outcomes can be improved. This, of course, should not only generate benefits for both supervisor and coach, but most crucially for the coachee and the sponsors of coaching. It is a way of acknowledging the importance of professional practice and of nurturing that practice. However, how we go about evaluation, what is evaluated and how, will depend in large part on the type of evaluation process adopted. Patton (1984) suggests a range of approaches, some of which are listed in Table 11.1. As the table shows, the focus or type of evaluation adopted will help to determine the kind of questions posed or the approaches taken. So, for example, if a supervision programme is evaluated through the scientific-rationalist lens of cost–benefit analysis, we would want to pose questions about the costs of supervision (and the coaching programme) measured against the

Table 11.1 Types of supervision evaluation and their defining question or approach

Focus or type of evaluation	Key questions or approach
Comparative focus	How does the supervision programme compare on specific indicators with the outcomes of those who do not use supervision?
Cost–benefit analysis	What is the relationship between the costs of supervision and the benefits expressed in monetary terms?
Descriptive focus	What occurs in the supervision programme/relationship? What can be observed, both between supervisor and supervisee, and between supervisee (coach) and coachee?
Effectiveness focus	To what extent is the supervision effective in attaining its goals? How can the supervision programme be more effective?
Formative evaluation	How can the supervision programme be improved (during its planning and delivery phase)?
Goal-based focus	To what extent have the goals of the supervision programme been attained?
Impact focus	What are the direct and indirect impacts of the supervision programme on participants and the organisation/community in which coaching takes place?
Process focus	What do participants experience on the supervision programme? How can these processes (the working alliance) be improved?
Quality assurance	Are minimum standards (e.g., as laid down by a professional coaching association) being provided? How can quality be monitored and demonstrated?
Summative evaluation	What is the overall merit or worth of the supervision programme? Should it be modified? Should it continue?

Source: Adapted from Patton (1984)

benefits, calculated (if possible) in monetary terms. To take another example, impact focus, we would want to evaluate the impact that the supervision programme has had on the supervisor/supervisee relationship, on coachees (through better coaching) and on the organisation in which the coaching and supervision is taking place. However, as we noted in Chapter 4, a decision-science approach would welcome 'emergence', which is similar to process evaluation.

In addition to types of evaluation, other commentators have suggested different levels of evaluation. As we saw in Chapter 7, Kirkpatrick (1959) made recommendations for evaluation that have laid the basis for thinking about the subject ever since, particularly in relation to the evaluation of training programme. In the context of coaching supervision, we will apply this to the coach–supervisor process or relationship. Kirkpatrick argues that, in essence, the evaluation of programmes (or as in our case, the supervision programme) should concentrate on four levels: reaction, learning, behaviour and results. At Level 1, for example, the aim of evaluation is simply to gauge participants' reactions and feelings about the supervision – are they satisfied with it? This is the most basic (and some would argue, the least useful) element of evaluation. At Level 2, learning, evaluation seeks to measure or at least gain feedback on, what participants have learned in terms of new supervision skills and attitudes. As we saw earlier, according to some supervision models, there can be a direct teaching element in supervision, with supervisors passing on their knowledge, wisdom and experience. At later stages

Table 11.2 Application of Kirkpatrick's evaluation framework to coaching supervision

Level	Description	Typical questions arising for the coach and supervisor relationship
Level 1: Reaction	Evaluating the reactions of trainees to the programme (often by the use of a questionnaire) How satisfied are they?	How was it for you? As a supervisee, do you think you benefitted? What went well? What should we change for next time?
Level 2: Learning	Measuring the knowledge, skills and attitudes that result from the programme	What have we both learned? What new skills have we acquired? What do we need to improve?
Level 3: Behaviour	Measuring aspects of improved job performance that are related to the training objectives	Am I a better coach? Am I a better supervisor?
Level 4: Results	Relating the results of the training to organisational objectives and other criteria of effectiveness such as better quality, productivity, safety and profits	Are the people that I coach better at their jobs?

in the supervisor–supervisee relationship, as the latter gains in skills and confidence, the learning might become more reciprocal, with the supervisor also learning. At Level 3, behaviour, evaluation seeks to measure actual job performance, or in this case, how effective the supervision is at developing the coaching skills of the coach. But we should not forget that it is also possible and relevant to evaluate the developing skills of the supervisor. Finally, at Level 4, results, does the supervision impact on the skills of the coach in such a way that their coaching produces better results in the coachee? In Table 11.2, we present each of the levels, the kinds of evaluative processes that arise at each level, and how these would apply to coaching supervision.

Internal or external supervision?

An emerging, and important, theme is whether supervisors should be drawn from outside the organisation or internally. Many of the issues within this debate are similar to those around whether to use external or internal coaches, except that, in the case of supervisors, they are handling the interrelationships between a larger group of stakeholders: the seven 'eyes' as in the Hawkins and Schwenk (2011) model. One of the advantages of using internal supervisors (see Table 11.3) is that they are more likely to have an intimate knowledge of the organisation, including its history, organisational culture, ethos, resources (particularly human resources) and 'where the bodies are buried'. This last point is more than flippancy. It raises the notion that within organisations there are unspoken histories, tensions, fears and battlegrounds, most of them created in the exercise of power. In periods of organisation turmoil (for example, restructuring, new leadership or downsizing) supervisors will need to be sensitive to the morale, motivation and feelings of different stakeholders. Another advantage of using internal supervisors is that they are more likely to be accessible, a factor that is particularly important when the supervisee experiences a crisis or critical incident. This, however, should not be exaggerated, as external supervisors are usually very accessible, as we saw earlier through telephone, email or Skype. A further advantage is, particularly if they have initially developed as coaches within the organisation, they are more likely to be familiar with, or even loyal to, the organisation's model or philosophy of coaching – if it adheres to a particular one. However, it may be just as likely that internal coaches (and supervisors) hold to a wide variety of models and methods.

On the negative side, internal supervisors face additional challenges in terms of maintaining confidentiality, largely because they know more internal stakeholders, including not only supervisees, but also their clients and their clients' line managers. In some corporates, as Kahn (2014) argues, it is assumed that all information belongs to the organisation, thus internal supervisors face particular difficulties in maintaining separation and confidences. It might also include senior managers and directors

Table 11.3 Advantages and disadvantages of using internal supervisors

Advantages	Disadvantages
Intimate knowledge of the organisation	Confidentiality harder to maintain
More responsive (on hand – so, quicker?)	Perhaps limited perspectives
Possible sharing of coaching models and philosophy with coaches	Lack of a large enough pool of experienced internal supervisors
	Danger of sharing the assumptions, norms and culture of the coach

of the organisation. Adherence to clear ethical guidelines, then, is essential. Another issue is to do with parallel processing. Dealing with clients who exhibit anxiety, anger, fear, jealousy and perfectionism (to name but a few problems!), coaches may bring these issues into the supervision processes. But being part of the organisation, supervisors may share many of the assumptions, norms and cultural biases of both the coach and their clients! But there are also practical challenges. It is likely that only in large organisations, and ones where coaching has a relatively long history, will there be a sufficiently large enough pool of coaches, some of whom will have trained as supervisors. It can be argued, therefore, that internal supervisors tend to be used where coaching itself is more advanced.

In practice, many organisations make use of both internal and external supervisors. This, however, is probably more a result of serendipity than careful planning.

Activity 11.4

Say you were advising an organisation that is about to implement a supervision system for its 30 internal coaches. Would you advise the use of internal supervisors, external or a mix of both? If both, what would the balance be between internal and external? How would you coordinate their activities for the benefit of: (a) coachees; (b) coaches; (c) the organisation?

Ethics in coaching supervision

The 2008 Dublin Declaration, discussed in Chapter 12, stated that there should be a shared code of ethics amongst the coaching associations. 'The Code underpins the emergence of coaching as a profession, its status, education and development and core competencies' (Dublin Declaration, 2008: 17). However, despite this lofty aim, such a unified code is still to emerge (although we noted the common Code of Conduct in Chapter 12). Most of the professional coaching associations require their members to adhere to the association's own code of ethics. These codes are presented on the association's website and deal with the main principles of ethical practice, which include: respect and dignity for people; competent caring for the well-being of people; integrity; and professional and scientific responsibilities to society. As Lane (2011) points out, most of the main coaching associations possess a code of ethics for supervisors which follow the above principles, including: the Association for Coaching (AC); the Association for Professional Executive Coaching and Supervision (APECS); the Coaches and Mentors of South Africa (COMENSA); the European Mentoring and Coaching Council (EMCC); the International Coach Federation (ICF); and the Worldwide Association of Business Coaches (WABC). In addition to the ethics frameworks developed by many of the coaching associations, a number of groups have come together to collaborate on developing shared guidelines. These groups include the Global Convention on Coaching (GCC) and the International Coaching Research Forum (ICRF). The UK Coaching Round Table consisting of the AC, APECS, EMCC and the UK chapter of the ICF (UK ICF) have produced a statement of shared values (see Table 12.1 in the next chapter). These include that every coach should abide by a code of ethics in their work. However, this presumably means the ethical code of their own organisation – of which, as we have noted, there are many.

At a European level, the Association of National Organisations for Supervision in Europe (ANSE) has developed what it terms a meta-code of ethics for supervisors, to act as a guideline for other coaching associations, should they want to use it. According to ANSE, supervision is inherently an ethical activity. This is, in part, because all supervisors wield power: the power of their knowledge and competence, their power in relation to the supervisee, and the power of their professional experience. Trust is central here, including trust in their own competencies, but above all, ensuring that they are seen as trustworthy by supervisees, colleagues and other stakeholders: 'They will radiate trust in the supervisee, in his or her potential, uniqueness and humanity, and they will actively substantiate it in contact with the supervisee (and others)' (ANSE, 2012: 2). Hence, supervisors will act in a responsible manner, as an integral part of their professionalism, taking responsibility for the maintenance of their skills, and for the learning process of the supervisee. They will also demonstrate integrity, positioning themselves autonomously in relation to stakeholders, clients and colleagues, and adhering strictly to confidentiality. The ethical guidelines presented in the ANSE code of ethics are based on a set of General Principles, as outlined in Table 11.4.

Table 11.4 Statement of ANSE General Principles

1. ANSE agrees to and always acts in accordance with the Universal Declaration of Human Rights (United Nations, UNDHR) and the protocols of the European Convention on Human Rights (ECHR)

2. All people are to be treated with equal respect, in accordance with fundamental human rights, in a just and sensitive manner, and to be valued in their integrity and authenticity

3. ANSE takes supervision as a profession to be exercised autonomously, impartially and methodically

4. ANSE takes supervision as an essentially ethical activity

5. ANSE holds the view that justice and care are essential values of our professional ethics, to be upheld in all supervisory practice

6. ANSE recognises and respects historical, cultural, institutional and supervisory diversity of member organisations, affiliates and individual practitioners

7. ANSE will act according to the principles and requirements set forth herewith, and encourage national organisations to agree to and always act in accordance with the general principles and requirements set forth herewith

Source: ANSE, 2012

Activity 11.5

Examine and compare the ethical guidelines of the following professional coaching and supervision organisations:

International Coach Federation (ICF): www.coachfederation.org/ethics/

European Mentoring and Coaching Association (EMCA): www.emccouncil.org/src/ultimo/models/Download/4.pdf

Association for Professional Executive Coaching and Supervision (APECS): www.apecs.org/ethicalguidelines.aspx

Association of Coaching Supervisors (ACS): www.associationofcoachingsupervisors.com/home/ethical-guidelines/

Worldwide Association of Business Coaches (WABC): www.wabccoaches.com/includes/popups/code_of_ethics_2nd_edition_december_17_2007.html

Association of National Organisations for Supervision in Europe (ANSE): www.anse.eu/tl_files/anse/docs/history/2012%20Code%20of%20Ethics/Code_of_Ethics_2012.pdf

Is there sufficient common ground for a global, unified code of ethics? Should there be?

Supervision and the professional coaching associations

As we saw in the Introduction, in a review of peer-reviewed journal articles between 2008 and 2012, Stern and Stout Rostron (2013) found that there were only five articles on supervision practice. Is supervision a Cinderella subject? Not quite. The professional coaching associations are beginning to take it seriously. The British Psychological Society (BPS), for example, set up a Special Group in Coaching Psychology (SGCP) in 2002 to promote better standards of practice in the coaching profession. In 2006, the SGCP published '*Guidelines on Supervision for Coaching Psychology*', which recommends that all BPS members who provide psychological coaching services should receive regular supervision for their coaching activities. 'While it is not mandatory, it is expected that coaching psychologists will have some form of supervision that best supports their practice' (British Psychological Society, 2006: 5). The guidelines argue that there is no single prescriptive model of supervision, it being left to the supervisor and supervisee to negotiate an appropriate contract.

In an Interim Statement, the EMCC declares that its Code of Ethics requires all its members to have regular supervision. However, it also makes clear that the nature of this supervision (frequency, duration, etc.) is likely to depend on the nature of the coaching/mentoring being undertaken. For example, an executive coach with a strong business focus may have different supervision needs to a coach/mentor whose main focus is with personal/interpersonal skills. The Interim Statement goes on to acknowledge that some EMCC members may engage with supervision because of membership of other professional bodies. It recognises, however, that some members may not, and so the Statement gives some descriptions of supervision based on Proctor's model (normative, formative, supportive) (1986, 2008). Given that this is an Interim Statement, there is an implicit acknowledgement that these guidelines on supervision may change, particularly as formats of coaching and mentoring change across Europe.

The Association for Coaching (AC) aims to encourage its members to undertake supervision as part of a process of continuing professional development (CPD), once they have qualified as coaches. Although not mandatory, coaches are encouraged to join one of the monthly supervision calls. The guide then explains the benefits of supervision, and how a supervisor can be located.

APECS states that supervision for its coaching members is compulsory, laying down that the coach will choose a form of supervision and a supervisor that best fits their learning needs. Supervisors are then required to provide APECS with a short annual report on supervisees, assuring APECS that they are working ethically and to an acceptable standard.

The ICF operates what it calls a Reciprocal Coaching programme, whereby its members are able to buddy up with a fellow coach, as part of each other's ongoing personal and professional development. This is an example of one-to-one peer coaching discussed above in the section on 'Modes of Supervision'. While this is part of the ICF's global offering, the UK ICF chapter is more specific in its supervision offer, stating that: 'The purpose of coach supervision is to support the coach's ("the supervisee's") professional, personal and coaching practice's health and wellbeing'. It is seen as a peer-to-peer relationship, allowing for reflection on the supervisee's skills and competencies (including the ICF Core Competencies and Code of Ethics) and behaviours. Coach supervisors are seen to be generally more experienced than the supervisee, so that they can provide mentoring and training as part of the supervision. The UK ICF chapter also, usefully, provides a list of questions that supervisees can ask of potential supervisors.

In addition to supervision, both the global and UK ICF websites offer access to what are termed mentor coaches, defined as: 'Coaching for the development of one's coaching, rather than coaching for personal development or coaching for business development, although those aspects may happen very incidentally in the coaching for development of one's coaching.' Mentor coaching is provided for ICF members who are preparing for their credentialing examination, something which the mentor coach him/herself must have passed. Given that one of the duties of the mentor coach is to bring the ICF's code of ethics alive and to review and provide oral and written feedback on a series of the mentee's coaching sessions, this does appear to be very like supervision. Indeed, according to a document written by the Association of Coach Training Organizations (ACTO) in collaboration with the ICF, the coach mentor 'is working with the whole coach learner for what is needed, and what they want to accomplish, in relationship to their journey as a coach' (Association of Coach Training Organizations, 2015).

Table 11.5 Summary of positions taken by some of the professional coaching associations to coach supervision

Professional association	Comments
Special Group in Coaching Psychology (BPS)	BPS members are required to undertake supervision as part of their professional practice as psychologists and psychotherapists
EMCC	Requires all members to have regular supervision (although timing and duration are left to members)
Association for Coaching	Encourages members to take supervision
APECS	Compulsory with supervisors being required to provide APECS with a short annual report on supervisees assuring that coaches are working ethically and to an acceptable standard
ICF	The ICF's UK chapter offers guidelines for coach supervision, whereas the ICF's global site does not mention supervision per se
Association of Coaching Supervisors	Seeks to actively promote coaching supervision across the coaching industry, acting as a voice for supervision within the coaching community

This includes help in professional skills competency development, personal development (in terms of seeing themselves in relation to the world), and (if desired) professional and business development. This seems like a confusing picture. The global ICF website offers coach mentoring but does not offer supervision itself; the UK ICF chapter also offers coach mentoring as well as supervision (in its peer-to-peer format). Overall, it seems that mentor coaching is more aimed at initial coach development, while supervision is designed to assist in the reflective practice of more experienced coaches and is thus broader and richer in nature. A summary of the positions of some of the professional coaching associations is provided in Table 11.5.

Activity 11.6

Take a look at the ACTO's document on mentor coaching at: http://icf.files.cms-plus.com/IndCred/Choosing-a-Mentor-Coach.pdf
   What aspects of what is offered might by delivered by supervisors?

International aspects of supervision

So far, we have discussed the supervision relationship assuming that the coach and supervisor usually meet face-to-face. Hence, the relationship is local or regional rather than international. But is this necessarily helpful? As we have seen, coaching is spreading internationally, with coaches operating in both developed and developing countries. However, as we have also noted, supervision is lagging behind coaching, not only in terms of widely accepted theories and models but, critically, in terms of the number of practitioners. If there is a shortage of skilled, experienced and qualified supervisors in the USA, Europe and Australasia, what is the situation in newly emerging coaching countries such as China, India and South Africa? We do not have any data on this, but common sense alone suggests that coaches in these countries may lack access to supervision. Until cohorts of supervisors grow, what can be done? One solution is that supervisors in 'the advanced coaching countries' step in to provide these services. Yet, this is problematic for at least three reasons:

- As noted, there are insufficient numbers of supervisors available in the established countries
- Given geographical distances, supervision would almost certainly have to be entirely virtual, not ideal for the quality of the supervision relationship
- There are no arrangements for professional indemnity insurance in India, China, South Africa or, indeed, many developing countries

The problems highlighted above may effectively bar most supervisors from offering their services in many of these countries, especially where professional indemnity is not in place. Other solutions are needed that, hopefully, will emerge in time.

The darker side of supervision

As we have seen, there has been relatively scant empirical research into supervision, and there has been virtually no research done on the negative experiences of supervision. One exception is the study by Grant (2012a), in which 30 per cent of the 179 respondents reported having some negative experiences of supervision and 26 complained about poor standards of supervision. One coach commented: 'I had a supervisor who did not know how to facilitate/structure good supervision sessions, and did not know how to reflect on practice or demonstrate an understanding where I was at.' Peer-group supervision also came in for some negative comments, with 28 per cent of respondents stating that they had negative experiences, the main problem being with individuals who tended to dominate the group. Some commented on people 'railroading' the agenda. As Grant (2012a) comments, it is important that those who manage peer-group sessions are trained in both supervision and also group-facilitation processes. However, despite these criticisms, it is worth noting that the majority of respondents only had positive experiences of supervision. Given the limited research, we may need to pay attention to the longer history of studies elsewhere on the darker side of supervision and use these as generic warnings. Corrie and Lane (2015) have looked at the misuse of power and issues of resistance and rupture in supervision. This has been explored by Porter and Vasquez (1997), who identified a number of problematic areas including:

- Pathologising supervisees
- Giving therapy, not supervision
- Demanding self-disclosure
- Selectively attending to supervisee limitations
- Verbally attacking supervisees
- Insisting on adherence to the supervisors approach
- Unwanted sexual advances

Murphy and Wright (2005) found that while abuses were rare, more subtle misuses were more common; and Nelson and Friedlanders' Study (2001) found detrimental effects on the supervisees' sense of competence. This was seen as particularly important where dual-role relationships existed (Olk and Friedlander, 1992), and recently Watson and

Lubker (2015) have pointed to contexts (sports coaching) in which such relationships are common.

It is important that, while we encourage the development of supervision, we do not simply assume that it is a good thing. Any activity that is effective can have positive and negative outcomes. We need to recognise and address these.

Summary

- Supervision is not at the very top of the agenda of the coaching associations but is growing rapidly in importance
- Models of supervision include developmental models and social role models, the latter today being more used in coaching supervision models
- Modes of supervision include one-to-one (individual and peer) and group supervision (facilitated by a supervisor or by group members taking turns)
- Most supervision is face-to-face, but communications media can be used, ranging from basic interaction through emails and the telephone, to more interactive media such as Skype and webinars
- Like coaching, supervision should be evaluated to provide a critical window into practice
- A growing issue, particularly in large organisations, is whether to use internal or external supervisors (and coaches)
- Most of the professional coaching associations have their own code of ethics, which they see as both a guide to good practice and as part of professional standards
- Most of the professional coaching associations either recommend supervision or make it mandatory
- While supervision is growing internationally (particularly in Europe, the USA and Australia), in many developing countries this growth will be limited due to the lack of professional indemnity insurance
- Not all coaches find supervision useful, but the majority do, with many finding it essential

Topics for discussion

1. Should supervision for all coaching practitioners be made compulsory by the professional coaching associations?
2. Should supervision be the sole domain of those trained in psychotherapy?
3. Should the outcomes of supervision be measured? If so, how?
4. Is lower cost the only advantage of using peer-group supervision?
5. Is supervision an emerging profession in its own right?

Questions that remain

1. How will supervision develop? How will organisations balance internal and external supervision of their coaching faculty? Will supervision become a sub-profession of coaching?
2. How standardised will supervision become globally? Will it develop in different directions, depending on the national context?
3. Does supervision require its own set of ethical standards?

Further reading

Bachkirova, T., Jackson, P. and Clutterbuck, D. (2011) *Coaching and Mentoring Supervision: Theory and Practice*. Maidenhead: Oxford University Press. A practical and comprehensive book that brings together perspectives from a range of both practitioners and academics.

Hay, J. (2007) *Reflective Practice and Supervision for Coaches*. Maidenhead: Oxford University Press. Helps coaches to review their practice through reflection and through using the services of a supervisor in order to raise self-awareness and improve professional competence.

Passmore, J. (ed.) (2011) *Supervision in Coaching*. London: Kogan Page. A wide-ranging book that provides a variety of supervision models, including reflective practice, Gestalt supervision, and self-supervision using a peer group model. There are also chapters on ethics and on continuing professional development (CPD) for supervisors.

What next?

Chapter 12 explores the discourses surrounding professionalisation, standards, codes of practice, accreditation and ethics. The chapter adopts a critical and balanced stance towards these issues and explores a critical evaluative voice throughout.

12

Professionalisation and Ethics

Keywords

Professionalisation, standards, codes of practice, accreditation, ethics

Chapter objectives

After reading this chapter, you will be able to:

- Describe the term 'professionalisation'
- Critically evaluate the extent to which coaching and mentoring are professional activities
- Explain how codes of ethics are essential elements of professionalisation
- Analyse the steps being taken by the professional coaching and mentoring associations towards professionalising
- Critically evaluate both the advantages and disadvantages of coaching and mentoring moving towards professionalisation

Introduction

What do we mean by 'professionalisation'? The term 'profession' derives from the Latin word 'profiteor', meaning 'to profess'. Professionalisation, then, is the process whereby an employment activity moves from the status of 'occupation' to the status of 'profession' (Gray, 2011). Claims for professional status that are typically associated with the emergence of standards (including ethical standards) and awards through accreditation processes are typical of the efforts that occupations make (or attempt to make) in order to become accepted as a profession. Well-known examples include the legal profession (solicitors and barristers) and those working in medical practice such as doctors and surgeons. However, whether, for example, nurses are members of a profession has been a source of contention for many years across a range of countries.

What is the point of professionalisation? Well, from the perspective of society, citizens and consumers being provided services by people who are professionally trained and accredited has many advantages, not least of which is the potential high level of knowledge, skills and ethical conduct they bring to the service. According someone the accolade of 'professional' is one of the highest forms of compliment (and 'unprofessional' one of the lowest) that one could pay someone. From the perspective of people who seek to join a profession, there are both advantages and disadvantages. On the plus side, those who attain professional qualifications (accountants, doctors, lawyers, etc.) normally expect to achieve much higher than average earnings over their working lifetime. Those who go on to undertake further professional training in a specialism may earn even more. Apart from pecuniary factors, professionals are generally accorded higher levels of trust and status by society. But there is, of course, the negative side, in which becoming a professional requires many years of study, training and demanding examinations to achieve the necessary accreditation and qualifications. Even after qualifying, most professionals will expect to have to undertake ongoing professional training on a regular basis. Yet, clearly, whatever the stress and demands of acquiring professional qualifications, many believe the effort to be worthwhile – demand for higher-education programmes leading to professional accreditation are oversubscribed. According to Grant and Cavanagh (2004), coaching has now reached a level of maturity that it needs to move from a service industry into a genuine profession. But, is it sufficiently coherent as an activity and are individual coaches motivated to do this?

In the area of mentoring, the question of professionalisation is more contentious. Mentoring is often a voluntary activity and the question of remuneration is rarely discussed. The question of professionalisation is perhaps one where those who call themselves 'coaches' and those who call themselves 'mentors' may depart. However, this is not to say that a mentor is some sort of amateur. As discussed in previous chapters, often he or she is a senior and experienced person and acts as a mentor as part of their role. It is also interesting to note that in Chapter 9, we raise the issue of a hybrid role between coaching and mentoring, where the purchasers of coaching services may also require elements of the mentoring approach to learning and development.

In the next sections, we will explore what professionalisation means in more detail and examine the extent to which coaching and mentoring have reached this stage.

What do we mean by professionalisation?

Professionalisation is a contested term since it rests on a *claim* to status (Shirley and Padgett, 2006) and has resulted from a historic struggle between different occupations. If this struggle is successful, the state grants the professional group a degree of autonomy in exchange for self-regulation – a pledge that the profession will set up and enforce a set of standards for professional development and a code of ethics. In the UK, this has meant that professions like medicine and law have been allowed high degrees of self-regulation in terms of education and training, largely because it is assumed that professional practice is aimed at the public good, rather than at narrow self-interest. Of course, the extent to which these professional occupations always act entirely selflessly is a matter of debate.

However, not all occupations make the full transition to professional status. Consultancy, for example, an occupation similar to coaching and mentoring in terms of the close personal service offered to clients by its practitioners, never made it to the status of profession. Rudolph (2003) puts this down to the fact that consultants do not have a monopoly on a specific field of problem-solving, nor do they have recognised quality standards or training regulations. Furthermore, the body of consulting knowledge has not been considered a valid basis for uniform professional training and accreditation (Visscher, 2006). Not making it to full professionalisation status can also mean coming up short of the mark, as what Etzioni (1969) calls a 'semi-profession', examples being nursing, teaching and social work. Semi-professions features include: shorter training, the holding of a less-specialised or coherent body of knowledge and more societal regulation and control.

Activity 12.1

Taking the criteria for a semi-profession, to what extent to do you think that coaching and mentoring meet these criteria? For example, do they have a coherent and widely recognised and accepted body of knowledge that informs practice? How does the length and intensity of coach and mentor training compare, for example, with that for doctors and lawyers?

Of course, we need to ask: who benefits from professionalisation? If occupations self-regulate effectively, then this benefits the state from having to legislate and set up bodies to control their work. Purchasers of coaching and mentoring also benefit because the professionalisation of an occupation raises standards of practice and standardises formal training and accreditation processes. They have a better idea of what they are getting for their money. But the most significant benefits go to those who make the successful journey into the profession. This does mean extensive periods of initial training and examination, followed by continuing professional development (CPD). But apart from the positive element of building up the skills and knowledge of individual practitioners, the training and accreditation processes involved also act as an effective barrier to entry, one reason why professions enjoy relatively high levels of remuneration.

However, in recent years, the fragility of the professions has been noted, while increasingly the traditional pattern of the self-regulated profession has been undermined. The establishment of national standards and competency models mandated by the state and control of the market through regulation and the influence of major insurance companies has led to a loss of autonomy. Some professions have given up self-regulation in order to continue to benefit from monopoly supply but at the cost of state control (see Lane and Corrie, 2006; Lo, 2006).

Pathways towards professionalisation

As we have seen above, the benefits of achieving professional status (even if this were possible) are not clear-cut. Garvey et al. (2009) argue that the development of professional standards for coaching and mentoring may not be feasible since the field is not an occupation with an overall model or theory of practice. They acknowledge the potential benefits: in an ambiguous market, transaction costs are greater where the quality of a product or service is difficult to verify – in other words, purchasers do not know what they are buying and have to set up their own expensive assessment processes for vetting coach applicants. But standards (and the accreditation processes that are often built on them) create an illusion of control. Furthermore, the effectiveness of coaching and mentoring depend on the development of a *process* between coach/mentor and client, not only on what competencies the coach/mentor possesses. It takes two to tango.

We have reached a point, however, where the drivers for the professionalisation of coaching are coming from both coaches and the corporate world (Bluckert, 2004). In 2007, a research study by PwC found that 52 per cent of coaches reported that their corporate clients expected that those coaches they hired should be credentialed and there have been significant moves in this direction. In 2007, the Global Convention on Coaching (GCC) was convened, a group of stakeholders that included purchasers of coaching, coaches and training organisations, and met to discuss the future of coaching.

Meeting in Dublin in 2008, the Convention began with the question: What's possible for coaching? The resulting Dublin Declaration stated that coaching is an emerging profession and that the GCC will seek to:

> Establish a common understanding of the profession through creation of a shared core code of ethics, standards of practice, and educational guidelines that ensure the quality and integrity of the competencies that lie at the heart of our practice.

The Convention, however, also acknowledged some problems. There are no barriers to entry, and anyone can call themselves a coach. Will other professions see a coaching profession as a threat? And a fundamental question arose: Do all parts of the coaching community actually want to see the creation of a coaching profession? Despite these reservations, the GCC made recommendations for the establishment of levels of professional education and training, and called for guidelines for an agreed set of core competencies for coaching and a universal code of ethics. The work of the Convention was followed up by a number of meetings of the UK Coaching Roundtable formed by the International Coach Federation (UK ICF), the Association for Coaching (AC), the European Mentoring and Coaching Council (EMCC) and the Association for Professional and Executive Coaching and Supervision (APECS) and the CIPD (Chartered Institute of Personnel and Development), which agreed on a 'statement of shared professional values'. The work of the Convention highlights the enthusiasm and dedication in some quarters towards the importance of professionalisation. However, according to Bennett (2006), for coaching to be recognised as a profession, much more needs to be done, including:

- Identification of a set of distinct skills, that is skills that are widely accepted as required for performance of skilled coaching
- The development of education and training required to acquire proficiency, that is, both initial and ongoing training to coach, matched to a generally accepted set of competencies
- Recognition of coaching as a profession by those outside it such as other established professions and government agencies
- The provision of a developed, monitored and enforced code of ethics, regulated by a governing body, making the profession self-regulating
- The provision of a public service that is motivated more by altruism than by pure financial gain
- Formalised organisation – for example, a widely accepted professional organisation that represents the profession and those practicing coaching
- The evaluation of standards (credentialing) and accepted requirements for coach competence, systems for monitoring and regulating the delivery of coach services and the means for encouraging a wide array of thought
- The development of an established community of practitioners and publications that support the establishment of a community of practice
- Status or state recognition associated with membership of the profession – for example, recognition of those who have served the profession

- Public recognition from those outside the practicing community that the profession is distinct and actually in existence
- Practice founded in theoretical and empirical research and a defined body of knowledge, including ongoing evidence-based research

---

Activity 12.2

Taking into account Bennett's (2006) list above, on a scale of 1 to 10, with 10 being high, to what extent have coaching and mentoring attained these criteria? Overall, what does this tell you about the challenges of the journey towards professionalisation that coaching has to make? How do these equate to your understanding of mentoring? What does the mentoring community need to do to address these? Should it address these? Who has most to gain and who has most to lose here?

Bennett (2006) argues that there are still substantial gaps in this list if coaching is to become a profession. Currently, there is no widely accepted and coherent theory of coaching, a lack of connection between theory and the development of competency-based education and training and the lack of rigorous and valid means to evaluate and support the monitoring of the practice of coaching. Whilst there may be a slightly more coherent historical base to mentoring (see Chapter 1), the question of relevance to practitioners and the beneficiaries of mentoring remains. Overall, the mentoring world presents different issues. Whilst the coaching world has obsessed itself with professionalisation, the mentoring world grew rapidly through social-mentoring schemes aimed at tackling deeply engrained social problems in both the USA and UK. Garmezy (1982), in the USA, asserts that mentoring was employed to suit both ideological and political reasoning, and Freedman (1999: 21) stated that all too often mentoring was an 'heroic conception of social policy' and became a 'fervor without infrastructure' aimed at, on the one hand, 'saving' disaffected youth but, on the other, controlling them. In the UK, Colley's work derived similar conclusions on social-mentoring programmes. It is in addition important to note that mentoring also grew rapidly in the business context as a means to primarily develop and retain talent. A recent survey (Penna, 2014) suggests that 70 per cent of top Fortune 500 companies have mentoring programmes. The question of professionalisation in both examples is rarely mentioned. That is not to say that those engaging in mentoring do not behave 'professionally'. There is an equal concern about mentor education and training, standards of practice and ethics.

To all this rich mix, we could add that there is a lack of one very important aspect of professional training – supervision. Let us look at some of these gaps in more detail.

The knowledge base of coaching and mentoring

A profession is based on a common body of knowledge that is not generally known to the public, and which is based on scientific research that is unique to the profession (Emener and Cottone, 1989). Hence, claims to professional status depend to a large extent on the claims to these unique forms of expertise that are beyond the reach of others. Some professions draw on quite diverse bodies of knowledge. Accountancy, for example, is based on law, economics, statistics and computing. However, having a broad knowledge base is a necessary but not sufficient basis for claims to professional status. Airline pilots, for example, have considerable skills and knowledge but are not generally regarded as being a profession. However, one would hope that they behave in a professional manner!

So, what about coaching? According to Grant (2005), coaching is a cross-disciplinary occupation that embraces the behavioural sciences, business and economics, adult education (including workplace learning) and philosophy, with the behavioural sciences as probably the most key. Using the GCC (2008) criteria, we could add leadership, management sciences and communication techniques to these. But there are also more specialist domains from which coaching can draw, which include: sports coaching, educational psychology, counselling and clinical psychology, health psychology and organisational psychology (Grant, 2005). For this to become a coherent and integrated body of knowledge, it needs to be tested, based on peer-reviewed empirical research (Grant and Cavanagh, 2004) – not least in the assumptions that underpin what is legitimate research. There is still much to be done here, as we will see in Chapter 14. It may be as Cavanagh and Lane (2012) argue, that coaching may never be a traditional profession but rather emerge as a new type based on a broader range of skills and a diverse knowledge base.

Specialised coach-training programmes

Entry into a profession requires extensive periods of training, normally associated with institutions of higher education that may provide both the training and the assessment processes and accreditation. Goode (1969) argues that occupations that aspire to be a profession need to ensure that their trainees learn as much as those who train in one of the recognised professions. But this is not the end of the matter. Once qualified, professionalisation requires that members engage in learning as part of continuing professional development.

The occupation of coaching is certainly well served (to say the least!) by coaching associations and independent training-provider organisations that offer training and accreditation. The International Coach Federation (ICF), founded in 1995 in the USA, is now a global organisation which claims more than 20,000 members and accredits both individuals and programmes. At an individual level, members (and non-members) can become an Associate Certified Coach, a Professional Certified Coach or a Master Certified Coach through a combination of completing an accredited training programme and providing evidence of coaching experience. Programmes can also be accredited through what the ICF calls its Accredited Coach Training Program (ACTP) and the Approved Coach Specific Training Hours (ACSTH). For the ACTP, participants get instruction on the ICF Core Competencies and Code of Ethics; approved programmes also include observed coaching sessions and a final exam. Those who pass an ACTP programme may apply for individual ICF credentialing. The ACSTH programme is intended for third-party training-providers who want to have their programme approved by the ICF and must be delivered by ICF-approved instructors and observers.

Another large coaching and mentoring association, the EMCC, also offers a comprehensive system of accreditation. Through what the EMCC terms the European Quality Award (EQA), training organisations can attain the accreditation of their programmes at Foundation, Practitioner, Senior Practitioner and Master Practitioner levels. Once a coach/mentor has achieved an award through the EQA, they may then undertake a European Individual Award. Similarly, the AC runs two multilevel schemes – through different levels of accreditation – comprising:

- AC Executive Coach Accreditation Scheme – for coaches working primarily in an organisational context
- AC Coach Accreditation Scheme – for coaches working in all other settings

These programmes are benchmarked against the AC's own competency framework.

The accreditation programmes described above are just examples (although important ones) of the kinds of professional development and accreditation programmes offered by some of the coaching associations. It is clear to see that, as it stands, the coaching industry does not offer a coherent or unified set of programmes or standards to the purchasers of coaching or mentoring, whether these be organisations or individuals. It seems perverse that most of these associations have constructed their own individual competency frameworks (although, in practice, there are similarities and overlaps between them) and codes of ethics. However, it is worth noting that there has been some progress here. In 2013, for example, the EMCC announced that it is offering a shortcut to its individual accreditation award for those of its members who have already been assessed by the ICF on certain criteria, namely: Managing the Contract; Building the Relationship; Enabling Insight and Learning; and Outcome and Action Orientation.

In the field of mentoring, the launch of the Professional Mentor Academy (PMA) in 2014 is the first organisation in the UK and Ireland to focus specifically on professionalising the role of the mentor. The PMA seeks to meet the needs of those coaches who often find themselves moving into a mentoring role, which requires a shift from coaching in terms of skills, perspectives and relationships with the client. A second driver comes from senior leaders and executives who, as they near retirement, wish to develop a nurturing and mentoring role, making use of their vast reservoir of knowledge and experience. In doing this, they do not want to go through the rigorous length and depth of training undertaken by coaches. The PMA is based on the principles that mentors are:

- Non-directive and person-centred – they help other people discover their own wisdom, rather than pass on the mentor's
- Help people with the quality of their thinking, using the mentor's expertise to craft insight-provoking questions
- Have deep knowledge of and insight into human behaviour
- Are able to help mentees think systemically and strategically about the issues they wish to explore
- Combine authenticity, gravitas and humility with an enduring interest in helping other people achieve their potential
- Understand and can manage the boundaries between mentoring and coaching, counselling, psychotherapy, consultancy and other forms of helping

In addressing these principles, the PMA offers a number of accredited and non-accredited programmes (it is currently exploring several possibilities, including a Postgraduate Certificate in Mentoring and Coaching), a database of professional mentors and matching services, and offers expertise in the design of mentoring schemes.

Specialised training – supervision

We discussed supervision in some detail in Chapter 11, so we will not repeat the same content here, but clearly if we seek standards of competence, including ethical standards, then supervision is going to play an important role. As we have seen, supervision is an essential component of those professions that are close to coaching, namely counselling and psychotherapy. The British Association for Counselling and Psychotherapy (BACP), for example, regards supervision as essential for reviewing and monitoring the work of the therapist and an essential part of maintaining good practice. Good practice is an important element of maintaining professional standards. Here, supervision can play a role at two stages: during initial professional training, and then as part of ongoing professional development. However, as we saw in Chapter 11, the engagement of coaches with supervision is, at best, patchy.

The professional development of coaches through supervision raises a host of important (and, as yet, unanswered) questions:

- How formal should the supervision role be? For example, should the professional coaching associations make it a compulsory element of membership? The associations take different stances on this

- What kind of professional development or training should supervisors take? Should the coaching associations agree a set of competencies and standards for the supervisors of coaches and mentors? Should supervisors be accredited?

Independence and autonomy

Another aspect of professionalisation is that individual members of an occupation retain broad authority over the practice of their services, largely unregulated by the state. An occupation must be independent to fulfil its role and be seen to be independent (Schein, 1972). However, in practice, autonomy is rarely absolute, and will only be granted if society believes that the occupation is the sole master of its specialised craft. As argued above, the autonomous professions model is increasingly under threat from the state. Hence, there are bound to be 'turf wars' between an emerging profession and the occupations closest to it in terms of client interest (Goode, 1960). Weight also has to be given to those who receive coaching or mentoring services as to the quality of what they receive. If a profession fails to regulate itself, or if it is shown to be deficient in its self-regulation, then the state may step in to impose its own regulatory framework (Gray, 2011). How concerned a government may be to actually do this remains in doubt.

Some of the coaching associations have been conscious of this perceived threat to their autonomy and have set up processes to track the concerns of individuals and organisational clients on an international basis. In 2002, the ICF established a regulatory committee for this purpose to monitor the actions of government regulatory bodies, mainly in the USA and Canada. Nevertheless, there have been episodes that show how quickly imposed regulation can emerge. The Colorado Mental Health Board is a case in point. Here, a member of the Board argued that coaching, and especially personal coaching, should be regarded as equivalent to psychotherapy. Hence, all coaches should be registered as unlicensed psychotherapists, a direct threat not only to the autonomy of coaches but to their very existence as well. Only after intense lobbying by the ICF and allied coaching associations was there an amendment to the Colorado State legislation, exempting coaching from the state's oversight (Williams, 2010).

Similar issues have emerged in the UK, where the work of practitioner psychologists is now regulated by the Professional Standards Authority for Health and Social Care (PSA) that maintains a register of 200,000 health professionals from 14 professions. Amongst health professions, the group most closely associated with coaching, psychotherapists and counsellors, are regulated by the PSA through their membership of the British Association for Counselling and Psychotherapy (BACP), or other registered bodies. It seems possible, then, that all the various counselling and psychotherapy associations in the UK will soon come under the one state regulator, at least as far as registration is concerned. The perspective of many qualified psychologists is that coaching requires expertise in understanding clients' deep-rooted issues, including mental illness, which many coaches lack (and hence should not be permitted to practice). Will coaching, as represented by non-BACP organisations, seek state regulation? Such an approach is not necessarily viewed negatively by all coaches. A survey amongst 5,000 ICF members (PwC, 2007) found that most agreed that the industry should be regulated in some form in the future. Generally, European coaches were more favourable towards regulation of the industry (73 per cent) than the overall global response (65 per cent). Some of the implications of such regulation are worth noting.

Activity 12.3

1. Mook (2007) cautions that regulation may complicate arrangements for cross-cultural coaching. Say, for example, that the coach resides in a non-regulated country, but the coachee's country of residence is regulated. What might be the implications of this for the coaching relationship? What about coaching ethics?
2. Consider coaching and counselling. To what extent would you say that they compete in a similar market? Are there arguments between the two services in terms of ownership of the coaching and mentoring territory?

A service relationship

A profession provides services via a relationship in which solutions are arrived at based on the client's needs and not the material interests of the professional himself or herself. It is a relationship based on confidentiality, mediated by the boundaries set by an ethical framework (see 'Ethical codes and professionalisation' in the next section). This is because the relationship requires an attitude of professionalism on the part of the coach or mentor, which recognised at all times the potential vulnerability of the client and the implicit inequality in the coach–client interaction. The quality of the service relationship is dependent on the coach or mentor demonstrating unconditional positive regard, accurate empathy, congruence and non-possessive warmth towards the client (Rogers, 1961). It has been argued that all professions draw on a shared set of principles to govern those relationships. These include respect, competence, integrity and responsibility. All codes need to embrace these principles (International Union of Psychological Science, 2008). Lane (2011) has looked at the application of these principles to coaching and supervision. However, a significant issue that arises here is the interface between coaching and therapeutic services, particularly where the coach is a qualified psychotherapist.

Boundaries between coaching and psychotherapeutic interventions have to be clear, articulated and maintained. This is usually done at the contracting stage (and re-contracting if necessary), where the coach/therapist, through discussion with the client, negotiates the kind of service the client wishes to engage with. Of course, the client may begin with, say, coaching to provide them with greater insight into how to manage their team, and then, because the discussion reveals issues to do with confidence and self-efficacy, the conversation may take a therapeutic turn. It is essential at this point that the therapeutic nature of the service is acknowledged through re-contracting. However, a key distinction is that counselling sets out to offer therapy, whereas neither coaching nor mentoring intend that their intervention is therapeutic. However, the very nature of the discussion may, indeed, be therapeutic. But, as Hamlin et al. (2008) make clear, coaching services do not need to be based on psychology – they can be based on human resource management practices that include facilitating cultural and organisational change. Indeed, when coaching or mentoring in a workplace, services are provided both to individuals (recipients) but also to the organisation itself. So, professional practice may include finding ways to report the processes and results of coaching/mentoring to the organisation in a general sense while maintaining confidentiality to the coachee/mentee.

Professional commitment

Another important manifestation of a profession is that its members hold a strong affiliation to it. They identify with the profession and derive pride from the status which membership affords them. Professional training (to attain membership) helps to nurture a psychological amalgamation between the person and their professional role. They also see their professional affiliation as distinguishing them from membership of other professions. For professionals, the nature of their work becomes part of their self-identity.

Do coaching and mentoring meet these standards? One difference is that coaches, for example, tend to offer this service as just one part of their profile. In a global survey of 1,800 coaches, Pennington (2009) found that 41 per cent of respondents spent their time on executive coaching, 25 per cent on other coaching activities, but the rest of the time on other activities which included training facilitation, teaching, consulting, meditation and counselling. The scale of professional commitment to coaching will be partly dependent on the extent to which coaching is the prime activity.

Enforcement of ethical codes

Members of a profession are bound by a code of ethics that defines both ethical and unethical conduct, breaches of which lead to strict enforcement and disciplinary action, which may include expulsion. This position is based on an assumption that ethical codes actually represent a distinction between 'good' and 'bad'. In ethics, this is rarely the case and therefore professions do not just need a code of ethics, they also need professional development on how to implement ethical principles. How far, often punitive, codes allow for subtle interpretations of ethical principles is a matter of debate. What is clear is that implementing ethical principles can only really come out of experience and the ability to reflect on professional practice (Hilton and Slotnick, 2005). In practice, however, the enforcement of ethical codes may be weak and do little to deter transgressions (Mowbray, 1995). In the next section, we look at coaching/mentoring and ethical codes in more detail.

Ethical codes and professionalisation

Let us start with a simple fact: currently, worldwide there are no universal, enforceable ethical codes for coaching practice (Svaleng and Grant, 2010). While most of the coaching associations do have their own code of ethics, these are by no means identical (Gray, 2011). The ICF code stresses the need for coaches to avoid conflicts of interest and to have clear contracts with their clients and sponsors. The EMCC Code of Ethics lays down that coaches should ensure that their level of competence is sufficient to meet the needs of the client and that they understand the context in which the coaching is taking place. Coaches also need to be aware of potential conflicts of interest and boundary issues and they need to maintain confidentiality. The AC stresses that coaches need to recognise when they should refer clients on to more experienced coaches, or to general practitioners, counsellors, psychotherapists or other specialist services.

Ethics, however, is a problematic subject because it deals with moral philosophy, in which complex issues of right and wrong, good and evil, justice and injustice are considered. But while professional bodies lay down normative codes often alongside punitive frameworks, ethics are socially defined within a particular set of social and political conditions. They arise in social interactions and are co-constructed in the particular sites where action happens (Gergen, 2001). It can, therefore, be argued that developing universal codes is itself ethically unsound because ethical issues arise in conditions that are dynamic and changeable. Take, for example, a coach whose client is a senior corporate executive who wants to embark on a high-risk investment strategy for her company. If this coaching conversation was taking place prior to the economic crisis of 2008, when it seemed that economic growth was rapid and perpetual, the coach might remain quite relaxed about this. Post-2008, and given our understanding of what high-risk behaviour might produce, this behaviour should ring alarm bells! In the post-2008 conditions, it might be regarded as unethical for the coach not to at least challenge the assumptions behind the strategy.

Hence, being bound to a code of ethics does not necessarily produce ethical professional practice – coaches need to be professionally trained in *how* to make ethical decisions – to maximise benefit and to enable members to 'do the right thing'. However, our sense of what is ethical or not does not depend on the existence of an external code. Day by day, we make ethical judgements drawing on our own moral compass (Lane and Corrie, 2006) and level of ethical maturity (Carroll and Shaw, 2012). Making ethical judgements, then, needs to be an essential component of all coach-training programmes, whether it be at the initial accreditation stage or as part of on-going professional development. What is also required is an opportunity (for example, workshops) to discuss issues with fellow professionals in a non-judgemental atmosphere (Rossiter et al., 1996). Making ethical decisions should also be one of the conversations that takes place during supervision.

Case study 12.1

Ethical dilemmas

The HR manager of a company employs you to coach 10 of its senior managers, all of whom work long hours in high-stress positions. You sign a confidentiality contract with each of them. At one of your coaching sessions, just after lunch, one of these managers turns up smelling quite strongly of alcohol. You do not raise this issue right away, wanting to get the client 'settled down' into the coaching conversation. You broach the issue towards the end but the client is evasive. At two subsequent meetings, again the smell of alcohol is pervasive. Three of your other coachees in the company make unsolicited comments about this manager, indicating that he is drinking to excess and that this behaviour is making him aggressive towards his subordinates. What should you do?

The confidentiality agreement, signed with the client, suggests that you cannot inform the HR director as to what is happening, since drinking to excess is not itself illegal in most jobs. One approach would be to be very firm with the client, indicating that there would be no more coaching sessions unless he sought professional help for his problem; he should also provide the coach with regular updates on his treatment. However, a 'duty of care' to the client would mean that you would be justified in breaking confidentiality if you felt that there was a risk to the client or those he worked with. Clearly, in certain occupations such as doctor or airline pilot, the coach would be justified in breaking confidentiality in the interests of public safety.

(Adapted from de Haan and Carroll, 2014)

Activity 12.4

Consider a situation where you have come up against an ethical dilemma. How did you seek to deal with it? Did you discuss the matter with other coaches (of course, while observing confidentiality)? Did you discuss the issue with a supervisor? Which of these was helpful?

A critical analysis of coaching and professionalisation

Coaching is an interesting occupation because people become involved in it from such a wide range of working backgrounds. Some come to coaching with an already well-established professional profile as, say, a lawyer, accountant or psychologist. Indeed, many have taken the path from psychology or counselling to coaching because the tasks they undertake have many similarities with coaching. So, some of these people may call themselves a psychologist or a coach, depending on who they are talking to (especially if they are a potential client!). Hence, the professional identity of coaches is often multiple and complex.

Activity 12.5

Coaches and mentors hail from a vast array of occupational backgrounds, and undertake work that is sometimes full-time and often part-time, work as independent coaches or mentors, or work within an organisation and undertake different types of coaching (executive, life, etc.). What implications does this profile have for the professionalisation of this work?

There have, however, been a number of useful initiatives to address this situation that have attempted to provide some clarity for those who seek to purchase or understand this jigsaw of accreditation and standards. As we saw earlier, one of the first was the Coaching Bodies Round Table (CBRT), founded by AC, APECS, EMCC UK and UK ICF, which established in 2008 a Statement of Shared Professional Values, defining the common ground in the Codes of Ethics and Practices used by coaching bodies in the UK (see Table 12.1). The purpose of the Statement was to provide purchasers of coaching with a clear frame of reference for the ethical requirements surrounding good-quality coaching.

Table 12.1 Statement of Shared Professional Values

This statement has been agreed by the coaching professional bodies in the UK who cooperate to enhance the reputation of the coaching industry

In the emerging profession of coaching, we believe that:

- Every coach, whether charging fees for coaching provided to individuals or organisations or both, is best served by being a member of a professional body suiting his/her needs
- Every coach needs to abide by a code of governing ethics and apply acknowledged standards to the performance of their coaching work
- Every coach needs to invest in their ongoing continuing professional development to ensure the quality of their service and their level of skill is enhanced
- Every coach has a duty of care to ensure the good reputation of our emerging profession

The following are fundamental principles by which we expect our members to operate:

Meta-Principle: To continually enhance the competence and reputation of the coaching profession

Principle One – Reputation: Every coach will act positively and in a manner that increases the public's understanding and acceptance of coaching

Principle Two – Continuous Competence Enhancement: Every coach accepts the need to enhance their experience, knowledge, capability and competence on a continuous basis

Principle Three – Client Centred: Every client is creative, resourceful and whole and the coach's role is to keep the development of that client central to his/her work, ensuring all services provided are appropriate to the client's needs

Principle Four – Confidentiality and Standards: Every coach has a professional responsibility (beyond the terms of the contract with the client) to apply high standards in their service provision and behaviour. He/she needs to be open and frank about methods and techniques used in the coaching process, maintain only appropriate records and to respect the confidentiality: (a) of the work with their clients, and (b) or their representative body's members information

Principle Five – Law and Diversity: Every coach will act within the Laws of the jurisdictions within which they practice and will also acknowledge and promote diversity at all times

Principle Six – Boundary Management: Every coach will recognise their own limitations of competence and the need to exercise boundary management. The client's right to terminate the coaching process will be respected at all times, as will the need to acknowledge different approaches to coaching which may be more effective for the client than their own. Every endeavour will be taken to ensure the avoidance of conflicts of interest

Principle Seven – Personal Pledge: Every coach will undertake to abide by the above principles that will complement the principles, codes of ethics and conduct set out by their own representative body to which they adhere and by the breach of which they would be required to undergo due process

About the UK Coaching Bodies Roundtable: The purpose of the Roundtable is to co-labour as representative bodies to maintain the principles on which the various bodies agree and through which the bodies will operate:

- To co-operate to enhance the reputation of the coaching industry
- To issue joint statements on issues of shared concern
- To discuss of the areas where collaboration might be of benefit

Source: Coaching Roundtable March 2008

Activity 12.6

Examine the Principles outlined in Table 12.1. How far do they take us towards the establishment of comprehensive and universal standards for coaching and mentoring?

Up to this point, much of the useful work undertaken on professionalisation has been done by the coaching bodies themselves. However, in 2012, the magazine *Coaching at Work* established the Coaching Sponsors' and Bodies Accreditation Forum, comprised of both the coaching associations that formed the original CBRT and representatives of the purchasers of coaching and mentoring services, namely:

- Coaching associations: UK ICF, APECS, AC, BACP Coaching Division and the EMCC
- Coaching buyers/sponsors: GSK, Asda, News International, Fujitsu and Kent County Council, as well as consultancy organisations KPMG and Ernst and Young

The Accreditation Forum has produced three working documents that summarise and compare the current coach accreditation requirements of four of the coaching bodies involved, so that coaches and those that purchase coaching can:

- Understand the inputs required for each type of coach accreditation, including the different levels and titles from the different bodies
- Explain to the purchasers of coaching services the distinctions between the ICF credentialing and other professional coaching bodies' accreditation requirements
- Note the similarities between the coaching competencies of the main professional coaching bodies, namely the AC, EMCC and ICF

Another, and more controversial, outcome of the Accreditation Forum has been a discussion around creating a Chartered Institute of Coaching. The rationale behind this move is that its supporters claim that such an institute will help create a consistency of standards across the various coaching associations, and give coaching a stronger voice. However, a survey undertaken by *Coaching at Work* in 2014 found that the issue stirred up strong responses on both sides, with broadly 40 per cent of respondents coming out in favour of such a body, 33 per cent against, with 27 per cent undecided. Those who opposed a Chartered Institute argue that there are already too many coaching bodies and that such an institute at this stage will only serve to stamp out creativity in the evolution of the profession and impose a UK-type structure on what is an international movement. However, while many of the respondents are key voices in the coaching industry, including scholars, training providers and corporate purchasers of coaching, the results are based on only 74 responses, too small a sample to be truly representative of the industry.

Nevertheless, on a more positive note, in a joint initiative aimed at self-regulation, some of the larger professional bodies (the ICF, EMCC and AC) have worked together on standards, the result of which has been the development of a common Code of Conduct, setting guidelines the purpose of which is to establish a benchmark for ethics and good practice in coaching and mentoring. The guidelines cover requirements for competencies, training, continuous professional development and ethical standards. The Code was drafted with regard to European law in order to be registered on a dedicated European Union (EU) database that lists self-regulation initiatives in Europe.

The initiative is also designed to inform coaching and mentoring clients, and to promote public confidence in coaching and mentoring as a process for professional and personal development. The Code was filed with the EU in 2011 and has now been signed by more than 15,000 people worldwide.

Activity 12.7

To see the EU database 'Self and Co-Regulation', go to: www.eesc.europa.eu/?i=portal.en.self-and-co-regulation.

Another potentially important development towards coaching industry collaboration has been the founding of the Global Coaching and Mentoring Alliance by the ICF, EMCC and AC. At its launch in November 2013, the Global Alliance declared: 'As a collective of global professional coaching and mentoring bodies, we seek to build alliances, a co-operative spirit, purposes and initiatives where we can partner to make a difference to the emerging profession [sic] and society as a whole.' Like the work undertaken for the common Code of Conduct, the Global Alliance has identified self-regulation as one of its prime commitments.

Activity 12.8

Taking into account the arguments presented in this chapter, would you argue that coaching and mentoring have reached the status of a profession?

Summary

- Professionalisation is the process whereby an employment activity moves from the status of 'occupation' to that of 'profession'
- Claims for professional status are typically associated with the emergence of standards (including ethical standards) and awards through accreditation
- Not all occupations make the full transition to professional status, some remaining as semi- or proto-professions
- Making the transition requires the possession of a defined body of knowledge, frameworks for training and accreditation, standards for ethical practice and self-regulation (autonomy); but an occupation is only a profession if it is regarded as such by those who purchase its services
- Coaching and mentoring are ambiguous occupations which involve a vast array of practice, ranging from executive coaches dealing with senior executives, to life coaches helping people with personal addictions. Coaches and mentors can be full-time or part-time and work independently or within organisations

Topics for discussion

1. Is coaching a profession? Is mentoring a profession? Is yes, what is it that makes them one? If not, what stands in the way?
2. Thinking of coaching or mentoring in your home country, how would you describe the 'offer' compared to coaching or mentoring elsewhere? For example, the scale of coaching or mentoring, the number of professionally trained coaches or mentors and the demand for hiring accredited coaches or mentors
3. Should the professional coaching associations get together to produce one global code of ethics for coaching and mentoring?
4. Professionalisation requires professional behaviour, but professional behaviour does not equal professionalisation. Discuss

Questions that remain

1. Why is coaching attempting to professionalise itself, precisely at a time when the professional status of the traditional professions is under attack?
2. To what extent is the coaching 'industry' united in its attitude towards coaching achieving professional status?
3. Will there be mergers and amalgamations between some of the professional coaching associations to produce, say, one global super-association?

(Continued)

(Continued)

4. Are the differences between how coaching is delivered and understood a foundation for insuperable division? As Garvey et al. (2009) point out, with coaching and mentoring we are dealing with an amorphous cluster of interests and foci: at the client-group level, the differences are vast between executive coaches who deal with the most senior managers in global organisations, while social mentors help some of the most disadvantaged in their communities.

Further reading

Gray, D.E. (2011) 'Journeys towards the professionalisation of coaching: Dilemmas, dialogues and decisions along the global pathway', *Coaching: An International Journal of Theory, Research and Practice*, 4(1): 4–19. This article sets out some of the principles of professionalisation and examines the extent to which coaching meets these criteria.

Hamlin, R.G., Ellinger, A.D. and Beattie, R.S. (2008) 'The emergent "coaching industry": A wake-up call for HRD professionals', *Human Resource Development International*, 11(3): 287–305. An interesting article because it gives an alternative perspective – that coaching is not a profession in its own right but an element of normal human resource development practice.

What next?

Chapter 13 explores the discourses found in research into coaching and mentoring. The discourses of positivism and anti-positivism as well as the discourse of 'quality' in research are raised. We conclude that 'quality' could be improved through adopting a more mixed or interdisciplinary approach to research.

13

Research in Coaching and Mentoring

Keywords

Evidence-based research, conceptual research, empirical research, cross-sectional research, longitudinal research, Mode 2 research

Chapter objectives

After reading this chapter, you will be able to:

- Argue why research is important to coaching and mentoring
- Identify the challenges in coaching and mentoring research
- Describe the landscape of coaching and mentoring research
- Make a case for practitioner-based research
- Speculate on the future of coaching and mentoring research

Introduction

Despite the rapid growth in coaching and mentoring as helping interventions, it is a paradox that both remain relatively unsupported by robust empirical research. As we shall see in this chapter, while research is certainly on the increase, it has lagged behind the practice of coaching and mentoring, to the detriment of both. As we noted in Chapter 1, Grant (2005) points out, the first mention of workplace coaching in peer-reviewed journals was as long ago as 1937. Between then and 2003, a total of 131 coaching-specific papers were published as evidenced in the PsychINFO and Dissertations Abstracts international database. Of these, only 55 were empirical studies, the rest being uncontrolled groups or case studies (recall Chapter 7 for the use of control groups in quantitative research). While Grant (2005) gives some assurance that a figure of 131 articles is not insignificant, he also compares this to the number of papers published in the specialised field of transtheoretical model of change (Prochaska et al., 1992), for which there were over 620 articles. Thus, coaching has a long way to go in terms of both conceptual and empirical studies.

The case in mentoring is different. As mentioned in Chapter 1, the first serious academic mention of mentoring was in Levinson et al.'s (1978) *The Seasons of a Man's Life*. This was followed by Kram's (1985) *Mentoring at Work: Developmental Relationships in Organizational Life*. This is regarded as the seminal text on mentoring and it has certainly been the baseline from which much high-quality research has developed. Savickas (2007: xix) writes: 'At age 21, counting from Kram's 1985 book, mentoring research has reached its majority.' Garvey et al. (2014) argue that, although there is a considerable amount of published mentoring research, the majority is of a particular archetype. This is mainly positivistic large-scale survey research, which, whilst very insightful, rarely considers issues for the practitioner nor does it probe into details.

Why should research into coaching and mentoring concern us? One simple issue is credibility. As Stober and Parry (2005) argue, in the field of psychology, for example, while Freud revolutionised medicine with his theories of psychoanalysis, some argue that it lost ground to cognitive and behavioural approaches because it failed to strengthen its empirical base. If coaching and mentoring remain as under-researched, as they are, will a similar fate await them?

The purpose of this chapter, then, is to explore some of the challenges to researching coaching and mentoring, as well as to outlining the key themes explored in research. We conclude by looking at what might be the next directions for research into coaching and mentoring.

Challenges in coaching and mentoring research

One of the obvious challenges in coaching and mentoring research (and one we will not dwell on here since it has been covered extensively in this book) is distinguishing these helping interventions from one another and from other interventions such as counselling and consultancy. You cannot research what you cannot define, and, as we have seen, some of the debates about what constitutes coaching and mentoring are still with us. Beyond this, coaching and mentoring face practical challenges when it comes to research. At a professional level, as we have seen, coaching and mentoring are served by quite a wide range of professional associations, most of which help their members by providing training and accreditation. Research is, to a large extent, of lesser concern, in part because such associations gain their income (and in a sense, survival) through their accreditation services, not research. However, over the last 10 years some of the professional associations have given research a much higher focus. The International Coach Federation (ICF), for example, has part of its website dedicated to research articles, while the European Mentoring and Coaching Council (EMCC) runs an annual coaching and mentoring research conference as well as a journal that has two sections, a practitioner- and a research-based section. The Association for Coaching (AC) has a research page on its website consisting mainly of non-empirical articles.

Activity 13.1

See the ICF's research pages at: www.coachfederation.org.uk/

See the EMCC's recent annual coaching and mentoring conferences at: www.emccouncil.org/

See the AC's research page at: www.associationforcoaching.com/pages/publications/research

---

As we saw in Chapter 6, there are many challenges in measuring the effectiveness of coaching and mentoring. One weakness in current research is that there are few measures that are aimed specifically at coaching and mentoring. As Stober and Parry (2005) point out, many of the measures we use are borrowed from the social sciences (for example, quality of life assessments) and medical sciences (for example, mental health instruments). So, researchers must either modify these or develop new ones for researching coaching and mentoring. But whatever measures are used, the use of control studies should be at least a part of the coaching and mentoring research landscape. However, many studies conducted in real world settings make it difficult, or even unethical, to randomly assign participants to control groups. Some research designs may also require long timeframes which employer organisations may be reluctant to fund.

As we have seen, many of the studies discussed have been conducted by academics (of which there are a small but growing number in coaching and mentoring research, including the current authors). However, at least in the UK, the practices and policies around research in higher education are not conducive to researching coaching and mentoring. The reasons for this are complex. Exercises such as the Research Excellence Framework (2008–13), for example, grade the output of academics according to the 'quality' or standing of the academic journals they publish in. The ranking of journals is largely dependent on the scale to which the articles they publish are referenced (cited) by articles in other journals. More generalised journals, such as the *British Journal of Management* or *Organization Studies*, tend to be highly cited and therefore ranked. But this means that specialised journals such as those that focus on coaching and mentoring (for example, *Coaching: An International Journal of Theory, Research and Practice* and *International Journal of Evidence Based Coaching and Mentoring*) are generally ranked low. Ironically, this is not to say that they should be regarded as having a diminished value. Indeed, such journals are probably more widely read (especially by practitioners) than the elite journals, and therefore may have a greater impact on professional practice. But they are accorded lower research status, so fewer academics are drawn towards researching for, and publishing in them.

The landscape of coaching and mentoring research

We noted above that coaching and mentoring are relatively under-researched, particularly in terms of robust empirical studies. The purpose of this section is to outline the type of research that has taken place, looking particularly at some of the main themes. The intention is not to attempt to cover all sources, but to provide examples and present a general focus. A professional practice such as coaching and mentoring needs research of all types. However, as we have noted, a professional practice that bases itself only on conceptual research will fail to build the evidence-based foundations that will give it credibility. Empirical studies are needed. These need to include, but also go beyond, the use of individual case studies and of small samples. Ideally, we need at least some longitudinal studies and research that uses large samples and control groups. We will look at coaching research, then mentoring research outputs, before providing a meta-analysis that compares and contrasts the strengths and weaknesses of each.

Coaching research

As noted at the start of this chapter, the number of empirical coaching studies to date has been somewhat limited. In 2001, for example, Kampa-Kokesch and Anderson reported finding only 7 empirically based research studies, while four years later, Feldman and

Lankau (2005) were able to analyse only 20 empirical studies. Joo (2005) identified only 11 research articles out of 78 academic articles on business coaching. Passmore and Gibbes (2007) review 27 empirical articles but tend to focus their arguments on the role of counselling and psychology to business coaching, while De Meuse et al. (2009) reviewed six empirical studies but limited their focus to return on investment (ROI). In this chapter we can point to the growing body of empirically based research (into business coaching) and construct a typology of different research designs as well as coaching themes. In terms of research designs we can distinguish between:

Design 1: Case studies and one-group post-test designs. These are 'pre-experimental' in that, while they can suggest indications of patterns or themes, they cannot provide firm evidence of change due to their weak research designs

Design 2: Quasi-experimental designs. These include either a one-group pre- and post-test design or the use of a non-equivalent control group. This is an improvement on Design 1 in that it uses a control group, but the weakness is that this group is not matched to the features of the experimental group

Design 3: Studies that combine coaching with other development techniques, with coaching not always being the main focus of the study

Within these designs we can also evaluate a large range of evidence-based studies and identify a number of broad themes, namely:

- Benefits or outcomes of coaching. Almost without exception, these studies report the targeted programme as seen by participants as effective in some way. This includes benefits for the sponsoring organisation (such as increased productivity, better communication); benefits for the coachee (improving psychological and social competencies, better self-awareness, assertiveness); and benefits for both the coachee and the organisation (higher levels of motivation, increased loyalty)
- Characteristics and behaviours of effective coaches. These comprise integrity, support for the coachee, communication skills and behaviours and credibility
- Characteristics of the coachee. Compared to the coach, coachees have been given relatively little attention in the coaching research literature
- Features of the coach–coachee relationship, including the effectiveness of the coach-coachee matching process
- Elements of the coaching process, featuring a large number of studies, including a focus on:
  - The impact of goal-setting
  - Maintaining a long-term focus
  - Evaluating progress
- Features of the organisational context, including ways in which sponsoring organisations can share responsibility for the goals and outcomes of coaching programmes

- Conceptual and theoretical approaches that guide coaching research. These are, as discussed elsewhere in this book, highly varied and eclectic and include psychotherapy, cognitive behaviour therapy, approaches designed to improve self-efficacy, concepts related to leadership and action learning

Activity 13.2

Examine the list of evidence-based studies above. Taking the perspective of an organisational sponsor of business coaching, are they addressing valid themes? Are there any themes not here that should be addressed?

Stern and Stout Rostron (2013) report on the progress that has been made since 2008, when a meeting of the International Coaching Research Forum (ICRF) (discussed in Chapter 12) addressed the need for more empirical research into coaching. The ICRF, made up of both practitioners and academics from across the world, initially produced 100 coaching research proposals (Kauffman, 2008), based around 16 themes. The intention was that these could be accessed by stakeholders, with the aspiration that they would stimulate research and hence advance the evidence base of coaching. A summary of these 100 proposals is given in Table 13.1, in which the ICRF participants identify themes such as the coaching relationship, coaching outcomes, coaching processes, supervision and assessment (evaluation) as all worthy of more research.

Table 13.1 Summary of focus areas of coaching research specified by the 100 ICRF proposals

No.	Focus areas	Aspects specified
1.	Coach education and training	Self-directed, classroom, practice and supervision
2.	Coaching relationship	'Chemistry', matching factors, gender same/different style, background, etc.
3.	Coaching outcomes	Relationship with satisfaction, emotional, social, functioning, effectiveness, well-being, sustainable leadership, self-understanding, lifestyle outcomes of health coaching (for different diagnoses, age groups, etc.)
4.	Coaching in organisations	Who, why, outcomes, internal systems of support, impact of coaching on organisations (ethics, productivity)

No.	Focus areas	Aspects specified
5.	Coaches	Competencies, characteristics and practices, compassion, theoretical awareness and application, impact of level of experience on coaching outcomes
6.	Coaching process	Directive vs non-directive, use of questions, feedback, espoused theories vs coaching practices, coaching approaches and impact (strengths-based, gap-based), coaching methods and results for different types (sports, teachers, parents), coaching failures and related factors (process, coachee, coach, organisation, support, etc.)
7.	Research methods and findings in coaching	Random samples, control groups, outcome measures, goal-attainment measures, measurement instruments, baseline of coaching research findings and what coaches want/need from research
8.	Supervision practices	How contracted and conducted, the impact on coach accountability and visible behavioural change and how learning is recognised and coach competence brought to awareness
9.	The business of coaching	Professionalisation of coaching (policy, ethics and governance), intervention processes in organisations and their evaluation
10.	Coaching vs other helping practices	When should coaching be used vs other interventions and what differentiates coaching
11.	How coaching differs by geographic region internationally	Activities, theories, assumptions, processes, impact of language, contracting, goals, models, approaches, interactive efforts – coachee characteristics, readiness, states of mind and emotion, developmental stages, coaching methods and outcomes
12.	Peer coaching	Peer coaching in coach education and development programmes
13.	Contracting	Formal and informal agreements between coaches, coachees, client organisations, guidelines for confidentiality, communication and support, etc.
14.	Coaching readiness by the coachee	Criteria to evaluate, evaluation, decision-making, personal choice or coercion in undertaking coaching?
15.	Use of assessment in coaching	What is done, how does it help, what is the impact, forms of data-gathering and timing?
16.	Impact of coaching on society	How coaching is moving from organisations/institutions out into the broader community. What is its positive impact?

Source: Adapted from Stern and Stout Rostron (2013)

So, what progress has been made towards the realisation of these research themes? Stern and Stout Rostron (2013) examine (English-language) peer-reviewed coaching research articles published since the ICRF conference to explore what progress has been made, as well as the gaps that still exist. In doing this, the authors made use of Grant's (2011) bibliography, selecting only abstracts from peer-reviewed journal articles based only on primary research. In other words, articles based on opinion, comment or self-promotion were excluded. The authors also searched the official listings of the peer-reviewed journals and used a wide range of search engines. The results (in terms of a frequency count of articles published on each of the 16 themes) are presented in Table 13.2, covering the period 2008 to the first half of 2012.

As Stern and Stout Rostron (2013) themselves point out, many of the articles covered in their study, do not correspond exactly to the 16 ICRF focus areas. This is partly because coaching articles are being published in disciplinary fields other than coaching itself. This includes the closely related field of coaching psychology, but also

Table 13.2 Number of peer-reviewed journal articles on coaching research by ICRF focus area by year

Coaching focus area	Year of publication					Total
	2008	2009	2010	2011	2012[a]	
Coaching process	15	26	24	14	9	88
Outcomes	5	11	18	7	5	46
Coaching in organisations	4	7	2	6	3	22
Coaches	4	3	5	2	2	16
Coaching vs other helping practices	3	6	3	1	2	15
Coach education and training	3	3	2	3	1	12
The business of coaching	4	5	3	–	–	12
Coachee readiness in coaching	1	5	4	2	–	12
Coaching relationship	–	1	5	5	–	11
Use of assessment in coaching	–	4	1	1	2	8
Research methods and findings in coaching	–	5	2	–	–	7
Supervision practices	–	4	1	–	–	5
Peer coaching	–	2	1	1	1	5
How coaching differs by geographic region	2	–	–	–	–	2
Impact of coaching on society	–	1	1	–	–	2
Contracting	–	–	–	–	–	–
Total	41	83	72	42	25	263

Note: [a] January to June.

Source: Stern and Stout Rostron (2013)

medicine, business and management, human resources and education and training. As Table 13.2 shows, half of the published articles focus on just two areas: coaching processes (33 per cent of the total), and coaching outcomes (17 per cent). In contrast, there were no articles published on the theme of contracting, and only two on the impact of coaching on society. Table 13.2 also illustrates a worrying trend that, despite a sharp rise in coaching research articles in 2009, since then, the publication rate has been downwards.

In addition to the broader 16 ICRF areas, Stern and Stout Rostron (2013) identify nearly 90 more specific research themes within the 263 peer-reviewed journal articles studied (see Table 13.3). Most of these fall under one or more of the ICRF themes, some addressing several themes. Stern and Stout Rostron (2013) present these as an alphabetical list. However, in Table 13.3, we group them into a number of suggested themes, including the focus of coaching (for example, anxiety, burnout), coaching

Table 13.3   The research landscape of coaching

Theme	Main focus
Research methods in coaching	Appreciative Inquiry (AI)
Focus of coaching	Anxiety
	Burnout
	Coaching cultures
	Conflict
	Effective leader behaviours
	Emotional intelligence
	Happiness
	Health and well-being
	Leadership behaviours/development/competencies/style/transition
	Management development
	Managing change
	Organisational change
	Procrastination
	Turbulence
Coaching models	Attachment theory
	Coaching psychology
	Mindfulness
	Positive psychology
Coaching tools	Metaphor
Coaching media	Audio coaching
	Blended learning
	Distance coaching
	Online coaching

(Continued)

Table 13.3 (Continued)

Theme	Main focus
Types of coaching	Co-active life coaching Co-coaching Executive coaching Group coaching In-house career coaching Interactive active workplace learning Internal executive coaches Life coaching Manager as coach Meta-coaching Narrative Short coaching interventions Strengths-based coaching Team coaching/leadership Writing/narrative coaching Youth coaching
The coach–coachee relationship	Critical incidents Ineffective coaching behaviours Coaching and temperament Meaning-making
Coaching clients	Entrepreneurs Family business Hospital CEO development Leaders (successful) Line managers Managers Non-profit organisations Nurses Nursing management Parents Small and medium enterprises Sports talent Substance abusers (youth)
Coaching evaluation	Feedback process
Issues in coaching	Benefits of coaching Coach regulation Psychological v non-psychological coaching Return on investment (ROI)

media (e.g., audio coaching, online coaching), and coaching clients (e.g., entrepreneurs, family businesses). However, there were also emerging areas not covered by the ICRF themes, including: existential coaching, family business coaching, gender coaching, stress management coaching, team/group coaching and teenage/adolescent/youth coaching. Interestingly, these new themes demonstrate a focus on types of coaching (see Table 13.3). What stands out here, is that many of the published articles are concerned with the kinds of issues that coaching addresses (e.g., anxiety, happiness, etc.) and the markets for coaching (life coaching, team coaching). But how to coach – including theories and models of coaching – seem sadly lacking. Any discussion on the quality or validity of coaching research – the appropriate research methods to be used – is almost totally absent, other than an article on Appreciative Inquiry. As we shall see in the next section, this contrasts with mentoring research where there is a considerable debate on the credibility, or otherwise, of research methods.

Mentoring research

In a meta-analysis of mentoring research, Allen et al. (2008) report on how research in this area has flourished over the last 20 years, with dozens of studies on the benefits of mentoring for the organisation, the mentor and the protégé. However, despite this accumulation of knowledge, research in mentoring in the workplace is relatively new. In stark contrast to coaching research, those involved in the study of mentoring have been committed to a thorough and critical debate on the quality of research designs. Of major concern here has been a focus on what is seen as an over-reliance on cross-sectional designs (snapshots of what is happening at a particular point in time) and self-report data (for example, mentors reporting on their own practice). There has also been a failure to differentiate between different forms of mentoring (formal versus informal), a lack of data on processes within dyad relationships, and the use of questionable psychometric measures. Rather than cross-sectional designs, mentoring research would benefit from longitudinal designs, because mentoring, in contrast to coaching, is often a long-term relationship (Kram, 1985). Mentoring relationships are also inherently dyadic, so research designs need to take into consideration the perspectives of all parties (Allen et al., 2008).

The focus of the Allen et al. (2008) study is on workplace mentoring relationships (excluding studies conducted on youths or students), and involved the analysis of 200 published articles. Given that some articles involved multiple studies, the total number of research studies was 207. As Table 13.4 shows, mentoring research is dominated by quantitative methods, most studies using correlation studies: trying to demonstrate relationships between variables – for example, that a certain style of mentoring will predict successful outcomes. In terms of research settings, 96 per cent of the studies were conducted in field settings rather than in laboratories. Allen et al. (2008), however, argue that this is a limitation. Laboratory research on mentoring would allow researchers to test theories related to subjects such as the attraction process between mentors and protégés, the exchange of tangible and intangible resources within the mentoring relationship, and the development of processes such as trust and disclosure in mentoring. A feature of future research might be to manipulate variables such as the race and gender of mentors to see if the mentoring behaviours are regarded similarly as those offered by non-minority/male mentors.

Table 13.4 Research design features in mentoring research

Category	Frequency	Percentage
Research approach (n = 178)		
Quantitative		
Correlational	149	83.7
Experimental/quasi-experimental	9	5.1
Meta-analysis	2	1.1
Qualitative or combined		
Qualitative	8	4.5
Quantitative and qualitative	10	5.6
Setting (n = 176)		
Field	169	96.0
Lab	7	4.0
Time horizon (n = 176)		
Cross-sectional	160	90.9
Longitudinal	16	9.1

In terms of time horizon, the research found that 90.9 per cent of the studies used cross-sectional designs. As Allen et al. (2008: 349) assert: 'The limited examination of mentoring relationships using longitudinal designs places a theoretical constraint on our understanding of mentoring.' Mentoring research has grown out of a belief that mentoring leads to beneficial outcomes such as career development and favourable job attitudes. However, this causal link between mentoring and such outcomes has yet to be established convincingly. Indeed, some researchers have argued that where a positive relationship exists, this is because protégés are singled out for mentoring because they have high-performance potential (Ragins and Cotton, 1991). Hence, it is hardly surprising that they perform well after mentoring.

Allen et al. (2008) also analyse the sources of data and focus of inquiry of mentoring research. As Table 13.5 illustrates, the overwhelming proportion of studies are based on the use of surveys (94.4 per cent). However, only 6.3 per cent of the studies use multiple data-collection methods, raising concerns about the validity of mentoring research. Triangulation using multiple methods increases construct validity because it provides a more holistic assessment of the construct being measured. As Allen et al. (2008) point out, one of the weaknesses of surveys is that respondents may misunderstand questions, and there is no ability to follow up respondents' answers with clarifying questions. Hence, mentoring research would benefit from a broader use of research methods. Studies also tend to focus on the protégé (80.2 per cent) but many fewer (27 per cent) on the mentor-protégé interaction – which is disappointing, considering that the relationship is such an important and complex one.

Table 13.5   Data sources and focus of mentoring research inquiry

Category	Frequency	Percentage
Data collection methods (n = 178)		
Survey	168	94.4
Focus group	2	1.1
Interview	14	7.9
Observation	1	<1
Case study	0	0
Diary	0	0
Archival	5	2.8
Multiple data collection methods	11	6.3
Multiple sources of data	32	18.2
Primary focus of inquiry (n = 207)		
Protégé	166	80.2
Mentor	64	30.9
Dyad (mentor and protégé interaction)	57	27.5
Organisational	15	7.2

Another theme of the Allen et al. (2008) study is the content areas that have been the focus of mentoring research. As Table 13.6 shows, over 80 per cent of the studies explore the variables that help to predict the success of mentoring, the outcomes of mentoring or the interaction between the two. Less than 10 per cent of mentoring studies concerned themselves with developing the theory of mentoring, a surprising and somewhat disappointing figure.

Table 13.6   General research focus

	Frequency	Percentage
Predictor of mentoring	66	31.9
Outcome of mentoring	60	30.0
Both predictor and outcome	45	21.7
Measurement development	8	3.9
Research review	16	7.7
Theory development	17	8.2
n = 207		

Coaching and mentoring research: bipolar landscapes?

The meta-analysis of coaching and mentoring research presented above contains some 'good news' features. Mentoring research has a track record stretching back over 20 years, while coaching, from a standing start, has begun to develop a credible research platform, with over 250 empirical articles published over the last five years. Although Allen et al. (2008) criticise mentoring research for demonstrating an over-concentration on survey designs, these studies do at least elicit data from large samples, painting a reliable picture of the mentoring landscape. In contrast, coaching appears to lack a coherent base of such studies. The credibility of an intervention will be promoted if it can present a comprehensive range of studies that show both breadth (such as quantitative designs answering 'what' type questions), plus depth (typically, qualitative designs answering 'how' and 'why' type questions).

Why are quantitative studies more prevalent in mentoring rather than coaching research? Any answer here must be tentative. However, one possible factor could lie in the origins of mentoring research in the USA. Pioneering researchers such as Kram, Ragins and others, have conducted their research and published their findings in North American journals, amongst others, where the accepted paradigm is almost overwhelmingly quantitative. The early formative years of mentoring research, therefore, were heavily influenced by the norm of large-scale studies. Although Allen et al. (2008) are probably right in asserting that mentoring research will now benefit from the addition of qualitative designs, there can be little doubt that early quantitative studies have helped to enhance the credibility of mentoring research, particularly in the eyes of organisational sponsors.

One of the strengths of mentoring research is that many studies attempt to identify what works by looking at outcomes of the mentoring process and what features contribute to success. Coaching research largely mirrors this focus, with nearly half of the studies exploring coaching outcomes and processes. For both interventions, a workplace focus is relatively new and much needed, given the rapid growth of both coaching and mentoring in an organisational context.

However, gaps and weaknesses persist. In coaching research, for example, it is surprising that there have been so few empirical studies on supervision, a process identified by Gray and Jackson (2012) as essential for the personal and professional development of coaches. Similarly, coaching research has had little to say about how the outcomes of coaching processes are evaluated. Mentoring research, whilst demonstrating robustness in research methods, lacks some of the nuances of coaching research where studies have looked at the intervention in a wide variety of contexts (e.g., from substance abuse to management and leadership) and types (e.g., career coaching, narrative coaching and co-coaching). Much has been done to push coaching and mentoring towards being evidence-based professions or at least practices. But what can be done to develop this further? The next section explores some approaches.

Towards an evidence-based profession: Mode 2 research

The relationship between theory (usually produced by academics) and practice (the domain, normally of practitioners), has too often been seen in dichotomous terms of theory versus practice, epitomised by human resource development (HRD) activities (including coaching and mentoring) which remain relatively uninformed by sound theory (Swanson, 2001) and are still prone to fads and short-term panaceas. Short et al. (2003: 241) comment that: 'The void is filled by the fads, which falsely offer panacea solutions and lead to the poor reputation of HRD in delivering real long-term benefits.' We face a gap between research and practice which is so significant that it is accorded a variety of names: the research–practice gap; the research–practice divide; the theory–practice void; the implementation gap. Even the terms used to describe key stakeholders are varied; practitioners who contribute to and see a value in research are described in terms such as: researcher–practitioners; scholar–practitioners; practitioner–theorists; and reflective practitioners. In the field of coaching and mentoring, there are already many people who fall into one of these categories. For example, professional coaches who are undertaking a postgraduate qualification in coaching which involves both a taught element and a research project. But apart from formal qualifications, there are many coaches who strive to evaluate (measure) the processes and outcomes of their professional practice.

Some argue that fundamental philosophical differences seem to underpin views on knowledge production and consumption – especially between the academic's search for generalising their results to a wider population and the practitioner's search for specific solutions in their working lives. Some authors argue that this 'rigour–relevance gap' should be bridged (Fincham and Clark, 2009). In contrast, others claim that researchers and researched inhabit separate social systems, leaving an unbridgeable gap, 'not only attributable to different languages and styles in the scientific community, but also to different logics – to differences in defining and tackling problems – that prevail in the systems of science and practice' (Kieser and Leiner, 2009: 517).

Activity 13.3

What is your view on this? Do you regard yourself as a practitioner, a researcher or both? If the latter, what term would you use to describe yourself and why?

In challenging the academic-practitioner divide, Hodgkinson and Rousseau (2009: 538) argue that both groups should come together to produce research that is both rigorous and relevant: 'developing deep partnerships between academics and practitioners, supported by appropriate training in theory and research methods, can yield outcomes that meet the twin imperatives of high quality scholarship and social usefulness'. Starkey et al. (2009) claim that traditional research gives pride of place to 'rigour' (e.g., surveys using large samples), leading to research of interest only to a narrow scholarly community; however, what is also needed is relevance as a necessary condition for rigour, leading to new forms of engagement between theory and practice. While research does not inevitably have to be connected to practice, in an applied field such as HRD (and, of course, coaching and mentoring), there has to be some connection. Stewart (2007: 95) argues that: 'The threat is that academic researchers pay too much attention to their own arguments and debates and too little to the needs and interests of practitioners'; hence, users and funders of coaching and mentoring research need to see more relevance and engagement with the world of practice. It is here that what has been termed 'Mode 2 research' has some potential solutions.

We can understand Mode 2 research better if we first of all look at its dichotomous cousin, Mode 1. Gibbons et al. (1994) describe 'Mode 1 research' as research that closely follows the physical science model. Here, theoretical propositions, resulting largely from an academic agenda, are tested against empirical data, each successive study building on, and in some cases modifying, previous findings. The principle beneficiaries of Mode 1 research are the academic community. Mode 1 researchers strive for the generation of cause-and-effect relationships that can yield generalisations (recall the large-scale survey designs in mentoring research earlier); practitioners such as coaches and mentors, however, need techniques and methods that can be applied immediately, and which may rely on a different evidence base and require an element of trust in the ability of these to deliver robust, practical and valuable outcomes. Anderson et al. (2001: 405) refer to this as short-term 'faith validity', a play on the phrase 'face validity' (it appears valid). The authors argue that this can only be delivered by Mode 2 research.

In Mode 2 research, knowledge is generated in the context of multi-stakeholder teams (e.g., human resource managers, line managers, supervisors, coaches, mentors) that transcend the boundaries of traditional disciplines (it is consciously trans-disciplinary rather than just multi-disciplinary), working on problems to be found in organisational life. The process of knowledge creation involves a continuous interchange between academic theories and the outcomes of various interventions. Hence, frameworks are generated in the context of application itself, often by team members who are potentially users of the new knowledge.

A useful way of exploring Mode 2 research in contrast to other approaches is offered by Anderson et al.'s (2001) typology (see Figure 13.1), which balances practical relevance with methodological rigour. Mode 2 is an approach, then, that requires both academic rigour and practical relevance (see Pragmatic Science, Quadrant 2). Popularist Science (Quadrant 1) has a high practical relevance but the methodological rigour is low (for example, many of the books on emotional intelligence, mentoring and coaching to be found in airport bookshops). Pedantic Science (Quadrant 3) results when research adopts sophisticated and valid designs but produces findings of low practical relevance to organisations or practitioners. This research is usually of interest to only a narrow field of specialist academics. Finally, Quadrant 4, is what Anderson et al. (2001) term 'Puerile Science', where researchers produce studies of very limited practical value, using methods that lack rigour (for example, using small samples and single, non-validated data-gathering instrument – recall some of the arguments in Chapter 6). Coaching and mentoring research which consists of purely personal opinions may fall into this category. While much of this kind of research is screened out by careful journal editors, some of it leaks through into professional and other media to influence the 'organizational Zeitgeist' (Anderson et al., 2001: 396).

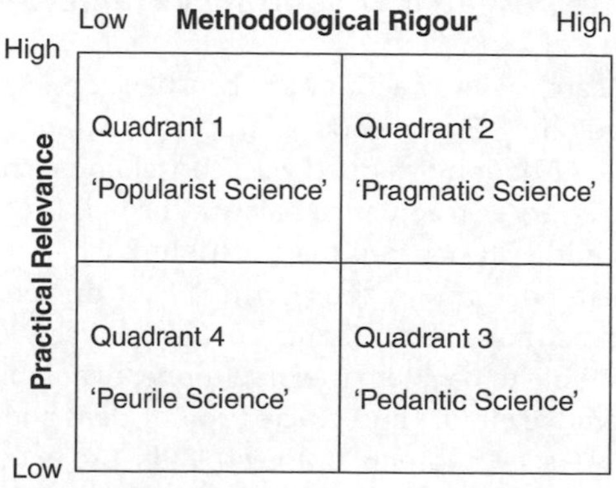

Figure 13.1 Fourfold typology of research

Source: Adapted from Anderson et al. (2001)

Activity 13.4

Take a look at the coaching and mentoring section of your own bookshelves, or online coaching and mentoring articles with which you are familiar. Which of them fall into the four quadrants? Which quadrant has the greatest number of books?

Given the critique of the approaches presented in Figure 13.1, how can the application of Mode 2 be advanced? According to Rynes (2007), this will be helped if researchers make themselves more familiar with practitioners' needs and interests. They could also commit themselves to writing articles for practitioner journals. Academics need to spot trends (while avoiding the latest management fad – see above) and disseminate research findings more quickly (Cascio, 2007). It would help here if research journals, as a requirement, get authors to specify the implications of their findings for practice (Cohen, 2007). Even research methods might have an influence. For example, the use of qualitative methodologies such as grounded theory, case analysis and ethnography, is likely to generate greater interest amongst practitioners, because it tends to generate the kinds of richer stories that they understand and can use (Rynes, 2007). Perhaps this is one area where coaching research is strong and which mentoring research would benefit from developing.

Case study 13.1

The Research Consultancy Framework

An example of 'research with practitioners' can be seen in the development of the Research Consultancy Framework created by Edinburgh Napier University (Francis et al., 2009). Although designed with consultants in mind, the framework is useful because it offers a structure to balance the needs of both academic and practitioner communities. It has four main attributes (see Table 13.7). Actionable knowledge is generated through the partnering of university-based expertise and experienced practitioner-consultants to create 'pracademic' project teams (Francis et al., 2009), able to navigate the practitioner-academic worlds. There is an emphasis on cooperative inquiry and 'co-creation' of ideas and solutions (similar to Appreciative Inquiry – see Chapter 6) both within the project team and in working with clients such as programme sponsors.

Table 13.7 Research Consultancy Framework (adapted for coaching and mentoring)

Attribute	
Actionable knowledge	Actionable knowledge (generated through coaching and mentoring programmes), characterised by high-quality scholarship and high value as perceived by the client
Integration of disciplines/ perspectives	A framework of action is characterised by 'pracademic' project teams able to navigate the practitioner-academic worlds and allow a blend of multiple disciplines and theoretical perspectives
Learning-driven collaboration	Focus on cooperative inquiry and 'co-creation' of ideas and new solutions to problems. It requires a high level of partnership working between coaches/mentors and client, based on transparency, honesty and openness in all exchanges
Sustainability	Focus on sustainable change, based on a complex mix of theory and practice – it requires a leadership orientation that seeks clarification of meaning and purpose, recognition and freedom to express and experiment in ways judged to have sufficient rigour and relevance for the purpose of the project

The effective 'conversion' of complex concepts and ideas into more simple and practical forms is critical to the co-creation process. This rests on the successful development of a balance between the clients' need for convergence of ideas and 'line-of-sight' models (where end goals and direction are clear), and ambiguous situations that call for the opening up of alternate interpretations and questioning (i.e., challenging of 'taken-for-granted' assumptions and current ways of doing things which have been mostly informed by practice-based experience).

Activity 13.5

Examining Case Study 13.1, think of a coaching and/or mentoring programme you have been involved in either as a sponsor, coach/coachee or mentor/mentee. What evidence was there of 'pracademic' teams in the programme? What was the balance between practical outcomes and the generation of new knowledge through research/inquiry? Was this the right balance?

Where next for coaching and mentoring research?

In the sections above, we have explored some of the themes addressed, to date, by those involved in researching coaching and mentoring. As we can see, these are quite broad and diverse, although there are also areas of commonality and focus. But what of the future? Stober and Parry (2005) argue that it is important that the evaluation of coaching, apart from using self-reported measures (e.g., life satisfaction, quality of life) is also tied to the assessment of measurable outcomes (e.g., goal-attainment). In other words, not just measuring what people feel but based on the outcome measures that use information from third parties – for example, peers, partners, supervisors, etc. Apart from the cross-sectional studies discussed in Chapter 6, researchers will increase the credibility of coaching and mentoring if they can undertake more longitudinal studies, documenting the long-term effects of coaching and mentoring. As the body of knowledge grows, we might seek to compare the different approaches and types of coaching and mentoring (e.g., life versus business coaching, and differences between individual and group mentoring, or comparing the impact of internal mentors versus internal coaches). As Passmore and Gibbes (2007) note, there is a need to report coaching research transparently and honestly. This means including those studies that produce null (neutral) or even negative findings as to the effectiveness of coaching and mentoring interventions. Table 13.8 suggests a number of possible research questions for the future. You may have a number of your own.

Table 13.8 Research questions for the future

What are the necessary ingredients for a successful coaching or mentoring relationship that achieves the client's aims?
Do clients experience increased efficacy as a result of coaching or mentoring?
What organisational structures help/inhibit the ability of a coachee to implement coaching goals?
Does mentoring have more impact compared to psychotherapy, peer support or self-help programmes?
What role does social support play in helping a coachee or mentee?
What are the personal characteristics that can predict the success or otherwise of the coachee?
What are the characteristics of the successful coach or mentor?
What concepts or theories seem most compelling for the further development of coaching or mentoring?

Source: Adapted from Stober and Parry (2005)

Activity 13.6

Taking the research questions for the future in Table 13.8, think of some of your own.

Summary

- Despite the rapid growth of coaching and mentoring, both remain under-researched empirically
- The lack of evidence-based research makes the credibility of coaching and mentoring open to challenge, and diminishes their status in the eyes of organisational sponsors
- Workplace research is relatively new in both coaching and mentoring research, but in both cases is now growing
- Coaching research has successfully met many of the aspirations of the International Coaching Research Forum, with evidence-based studies conducted on coaching processes and outcomes
- Mentoring research has primarily used quantitative designs using surveys. Both coaching and mentoring would benefit from presenting a broad landscape of research that includes cross-sectional but also longitudinal studies. This particularly applies to mentoring where relationships can be long term
- Evidence-based coaching and mentoring research would benefit from adopting a Mode 2 approach, in which researchers and practitioners work collectively in identifying the studies worthy of research and designing, and conducting these studies collaboratively

Topics for discussion

1. How important is evidence-based research to the future growth of coaching and mentoring?
2. What kinds of networks or communities can be established which bring together academics and coaching and mentoring practitioners?
3. What are the most significant issues that coaching and mentoring should be addressing?
4. Designs in coaching and mentoring research should always use quantitative designs and large sample sizes. Discuss.
5. What are the pros and cons of using qualitative methods in researching coaching and mentoring?
6. How valid is the argument that longitudinal designs are more valid in mentoring than in coaching research?

Questions that remain

1. What is the role of practitioners in evidence-based research?
2. Should coaching research develop a greater focus on quantitative designs? What form might these take?
3. Should mentoring research develop a greater focus on qualitative designs? To what extent would this change the confidence of mentoring programme sponsors in organisations?
4. What would be the benefit of developing a more integrated approach to coaching and mentoring research, one which regards them as similar and supporting interventions?

Further reading

Grant, A.M. (2005) 'What is evidence-based executive, workplace and life coaching?', in M. Cavanagh, A.M. Grant and T. Kemp (eds), *Evidence-Based Coaching: Theory, Research and Practice from the Behavioural Sciences*. Bowen Hills Qld: Australian Academic Press, pp. 1–12. Tony Grant's journal chapter provides one of the first clarion calls for coaching to be evidence-based.

Stern, L. and Stout Rostron, S. (2013) 'What progress has been made in coaching research in relation to 16 ICRF focus areas from 2008 to 2012?', *Coaching: An International Journal of Theory, Research and Practice*, 6(1): 72–96. A useful overview of what themes in coaching are being addressed.

What next?

In Chapter 14, we engage in a speculative discourse. There is a long tradition of this 'futurist' discourse, which engages in postulation about the possible or probable futures. Obviously, no one can know the future, but the discourse of futurism is often based on an analysis of history and current trends and considers the likelihood of approaching events happening or taking place. This is nicely summed up by the poet Cavafy in the poem 'But Wise Men Perceive Approaching Things':

> People know what is happening.
>
> The gods know about the future,
>
> They are entire and sole possessors of all the lights.
>
> Of the future, things
>
> Wise men see forthcoming events.

(Translated by Bob Garvey)

Coaching and Mentoring and the Future

Keywords

Future, expertise, future threats, GRIN technologies, scenarios

Chapter objectives

After reading this chapter, you will be able to:

- Identify the difference between alternative views of the future
- Distinguish between the implications of those alternatives for our field
- Consider how we might adapt to future scenarios
- Reflect upon the possibility of shaping future scenarios

Introduction: Why consider coaching and the future?

There have been a number of attempts to define or speculate on the future of coaching. As we noted in Chapter 12, the Global Convention on Coaching (GCC) issued the Dublin Declaration in 2008, and in 2012 the International Coach Federation (ICF) sponsored a conference on the 'Future of Coaching'. We will explore these two attempts to set the scene.

We will consider the implications of our critique in this book for possible futures for coaching and mentoring and the extent to which there is a shared agenda that we can take forward.

However, we must look well beyond our professional boundaries if we are to get any sense of where we might be going and the multiple possibilities we can envisage as well as the directions we cannot yet dream of and which will probably come to pass. It is a common feature of the world of commerce that companies are undone not by developments that they foresaw but by those they could not imagine. The same is likely to apply to professional practice, for although their practitioners (through their associations) might seek to control access to the market for services, consumers always find new ways to seek help. Markets also change and we can already see that the hegemony of the West as a source of innovation and the direction of North-to-South trade is likely to be undermined, but we cannot yet grasp the full implications of the move to South-South trade and attempts by China (Asia 2050 report) and others to move from low-cost manufacture to creative industries.

Why speculate if we cannot know where the world is going? This is not because we can say that this will come to pass but, rather, as Watson (2010) points out, it enables us to have conversations about the future – its risks and opportunities. The future is socially constructed out of multiple conversations, it does not just happen to us (Lane and Malkin, 1994). Thus, we need to consider the future and the place of coaching within it, rather than focus on the future of coaching.

We will conclude with a consideration of the implications of our critique in this book for the future and identify what we see are core issues we need to address.

Where have we come from?

There have been two major global attempts to look at the future of coaching and mentoring. In 2008, the Global Convention on Coaching took place in Dublin. This was based on a year of conversations between more than 250 coaches across the world, exploring what they saw as core issues for coaching. Groups considered:

- Professional status
- Knowledge base
- Research
- Core competencies
- Code of ethics
- Education and development
- Mapping the field
- Selection of coaches
- Evaluation of the coaching engagement
- Coaching and society

Following these, 63 participants from 21 countries met for five days of dialogue in Dublin. The experience from some 43 professional bodies, universities, training bodies, clients and buyers of coaching was present in the room but, importantly, the delegates were not there to represent positions from different bodies, rather they were there to explore in an open process to see what emerged. The result was the Dublin Declaration on Coaching. Following the convention, activities on its themes took place in various countries and follow-up meetings have been held in London, Cape Town and Singapore. The GCC was unusual in that it did not try to become a formal organisation but rather saw its role as a neutral system in which dialogue between all those with an interest in coaching could happen unimpeded by sectarian concerns. It concluded with four propositions (the full document, which is available on several websites, contains detailed appendices: www.wabccoaches.com/downloads/gcc/the-dublin-declaration-on-coaching-with-appendices-v1.3.pdf):

> Therefore, we, the delegates of the Global Coaching Convention, hereby declare that the individuals and organizations that comprise the Global Coaching Community need to:
>
> 1. Establish a common understanding of the profession through creation of a shared core code of ethics, standards of practice, and educational guidelines that ensure the quality and integrity of the competencies that lie at the heart of our practice
> 2. Acknowledge and affirm the multidisciplinary roots and nature of coaching as a unique synthesis of a range of disciplines that creates a new and distinctive value to individuals, organizations and society. To accomplish this we need to add to the body of coaching knowledge by conducting rigorous research into the processes,

practices, and outcomes of coaching, in order to strengthen its practical impact and theoretical underpinnings

3. Respond to a world beset by challenges for which there are no predetermined answers by using coaching to create a space wherein new solutions can emerge. In doing so we are stepping into the power of coaching as coaches and inviting our clients to do the same

4. Move beyond self-interest and join with us and other members of the Global Coaching Community in an ongoing dialogue to address the critical issues facing our field, beginning with those that were identified by the ten working groups [see the appendices from the groups appended to this Declaration]

The participants called on themselves and others to take up the issues and continue the dialogue. Several members of this group then joined with other initiatives such as the GCC members' group on research joined with the Institute of Coaching to develop a set of research questions. Australian members went on to join with others to develop standards for work-based coaching.

In 2012, 'The Future of Coaching Summit' (Campone, 2012) adopted a different approach, working on the basis of organisation-to-organisation conversations between professional bodies in the field, and the following all took part: the Association of Coach Training Organizations (ACTO); International Coach Federation (ICF); Graduate School Alliance for Executive Coaching (GSAEC); European Mentoring and Coaching Council (EMCC); and the Australian Psychological Society's Coaching Psychology Special Interest Group (APS). Over a two-day period in July 2012, 29 participants representing 14 professional organisations and five countries engaged in a facilitated process. Among the outcomes was a statement for moving forward:

Directional Statement for Moving Forward: Creating Appropriate Strategic Alliances – Global Forum of Professional Coaching Bodies (Current State) – How to continue the dialogue that would provide clarity on the market for coach education and credentialing amongst professional coaching bodies?

1. Longer Term – Current State Analysis Strategic Priorities of Various Professional Coaching Bodies

2. Shorter Term – Core of Ethical and Professional Standards (Using APS – Code of Ethics using public documents) and Definition of Coaching

3. Identify Stable Core/Commonality

4. What the World Needs from Us – Definition of what we do as coaches

5. Professional Standards, Professional Coach Education and Qualifications – the event produced two key propositions for moving the field forward

Proposition 1: We have a respectful, inclusive process of on-going collaboration and communication amongst professional coaching bodies focused on high-quality coach education and training in the areas of:

a. Code of ethics and professional conduct

b. Credentialing and accreditation schemes and

c. Components of body of knowledge, competencies, process, research, coach supervision

Proposition 2: We propose inviting the bodies attending the '2012 Future of Coaching Summit' (and others who met the criteria for this forum) to continue a collaborative dialogue and develop:

a. A mutually acceptable common definition of coaching and

b. A common core of ethical standards for their members to provide market clarity

Again, there was a call for continued dialogue. There were differences in the purpose and participation in each summit but overlap between the calls is clear.

While we are looking at becoming more of a profession, the professions themselves are becoming increasingly fragile. No longer can they control access to markets, as was once the case. New providers come onto the scene to replace them. There is some stability for those professions prepared to subsume professional autonomy into control by the state, but the state may prove to be a fickle master (Lane and Corrie, 2006; Lo, 2006). All professions, as was discussed in Chapter 12, find themselves increasingly under the direction of competence models defined by state bodies rather than themselves, with major implications for the freedom to practice in a way that is primarily directed to meeting client need. Need, as defined by commissioning bodies, replaces autonomous professional decision-making.

To what extent are we a shared field of endeavour?

Coaching and mentoring exists in many forms. We draw on many disciplines and models of practice. What do the models in common use in coaching and mentoring tell us about how we see the world and our place within it?

For example, there are versions of coaching and mentoring as a model of change, as remediation and transformation. Coaching and mentoring as a model of social control (for example, where the sponsor determines the goals of coaching and the framework to be used, as happens in many organisations) raises questions about when it is in the service of the sponsor and not the client. What do models offer us as coaches and mentors – guidance or the illusion of control? What, if anything, do different contexts for coaching and mentoring have to teach each other?

If we are a shared field of endeavour and can speculate on our future, there needs to be enough commonality to argue for a core profession. Some in the field (Kilberg, 2015) have suggested that only executive coaching has enough in common to consider the possibility of an international body of executive coaches. However, he argues that these encompass existing professions, thus we would not see business executive coaches or psychological executive coaches but rather one field to represent all.

We can consider this argument by looking at three of the fields currently included within coaching – the case of life, sports and business coaching. These three examples ask the question: What do they have in common? Where is the shared purpose that enables us to say that there is a field which we can legitimately call 'coaching and mentoring'? Or are these distinct areas of practice? Perhaps we could as easily argue that life coaching is a form of counselling, sports a form of expert performance and business coaching a form of consultancy and mentoring is a form of education. To be a field, surely there has to be something viable that binds them together. And if these are professions (at least in a traditional sense), there needs to be a codified knowledge base.

We can see this in one field – coaching in education (van Nieuwerburgh, 2012). Peer mentoring by children, tutoring at universities, coaching and mentoring of head teachers, parental coaching and mentoring, all sit in this field yet the contexts for the work while all defined as education, vary dramatically. The *purpose* it is intended to serve holds together as a field only if we call it 'learning' or 'development'. In terms of a traditional concept of a profession it would be difficult to fit coaching and mentoring into a viable structure (Lane et al., 2010) However, as they also argue, it could be that we have to think about coaching and mentoring as a new form of profession, not bound by traditional frameworks – one that is open, flexible and context-led. If our future lies in that direction, then the way we currently are trying within coaching (less so in mentoring, which retains a degree of openness and flexibility) to professionalise will have to be challenged. Our future will look very different between:

> *Scenario 1* – We adopt a traditional professional structure with its externally mandated competence frameworks, codified knowledge and codes of conduct

> *Scenario 2* – We adopt an open flexible approach to meeting client needs and come together as a community of practice rather than a professionalised body

At present, Scenario 1 seems to be favoured, yet the edifice we are creating might not be sustainable in the open market in which we operate. Here sits a problem because of the obvious tensions between the two scenarios.

One way of thinking about it is in terms of 'Big Knowledge' or 'Little Knowledge' (Garvey and Williamson, 2002). 'Big K' evolves by itself and develops in specialist domains. These domains create rules of logic and decide what is 'good' evidence – often through a discourse. Rather like Scenario 1 above, this knowledge is not the property of individual minds.

'Little K' is like Scenario 2. It is the knowledge possessed by individuals. According to Garvey and Williamson (2002: 56): 'It is the knowledge that reflects their experience of work and understanding and of their lifelong attempts to consolidate what they know. … "Little K" is firmly anchored in the realm of individual education and experience.'

Expertise is the product of years of learning within the two domains – 'Big K' and 'Little K' – and there must be interaction between the two for there to be progress in knowledge and practice. For the future of coaching and mentoring, some kind of recognition and integration of both 'Ks' is necessary and not further separation.

What else is happening that might impact on our field?

One area of research that has not much featured in the coaching literature (with sports coaching as the exception) is the study of the development of expertise. In some ways, this is surprising since the evidence suggests that great performance is the product not of innate skills but of years of dedicated practice guided by a coach. Coaching appears to be central to elite performance (Ericsson, 2006), or so coaches themselves tell us!

Expertise refers to the characteristics, skills and knowledge that distinguish experts from novices or lay people. It is assumed that experts can reproduce superior performance in tasks representing the domain – thus, chess grandmasters will out-perform recreational players. However, research in several domains has shown that experts will disagree on what is superior performance and novices may make better decisions (Ericsson, 2006; Lane and Corrie, 2012). Our recognition of the special status of experts has a long history (Ericsson refers back to Socrates), and the Medieval guilds provided long apprenticeships to become journeymen craftspeople followed by eventual acceptance as a master and guild member (Lane and Corrie, 2006). Of course, there is an assumption here that if we know how experts organise their knowledge and performance, we can improve learning to reach those levels, or that we can use that understanding to select those capable of achieving the highest performance.

However, in spite some real problems in this literature over how superior performance can be measured, there is consistent evidence on the development of expert performance where clear measures are possible. In bringing together the work of many researchers in the field, Ericsson (2006) has reviewed the core findings. Drawing on his review we can conclude that:

1. Outstanding performance is not about innate skill but arises from years of practice and coaching
2. The time devoted (around 10,000 hours), but particularly the quality of the practice, were key to the level of expertise achieved

3. It is not easy to develop expertise, it takes: 'struggle, sacrifice, and honest, often painful self-assessment'
4. The time devoted has to be used carefully through 'deliberate' practice – that is focused on tasks that take you beyond the current level of competence and out of your comfort zone
5. The role of the coach is to act as a guide to that deliberate practice but, crucially, to help the performer to learn how to become their own coach

Three core issues arise from this: the nature of the practice; the type of learning; and what it is that coaches do to facilitate superior performance.

The nature of practice

Ericsson contrasts the type of practice most people do with that of expert performers. The former, he argues, focus on the things they already know how to do. The latter involves 'considerable, specific, and sustained efforts to do something you can't do well'. This argument, that experts focus on getting better at the things they cannot do well, perhaps contrasts with work in the field of strengths-based coaching where the emphasis is on enhancing the areas in which you excel. An example used relates to playing a game – you do not get better while playing since you only get one shot. Rather, if you can go back and try alternatives time and again you have the chance to develop expertise. A further example is in the training of radiologists, where students make diagnoses from a battery of old X-rays in which the outcome is known and they can make several attempts. Applied to business, this would include the use of simulations where you can try different scenarios and look at the outcomes, over and over again. This enables experts to think as well as practice deliberately. There is an increasing market for such simulations in fields such as medicine, aviation and business.

The type of learning

Deliberate practice in concerned with improving existing skills and extending your range. This takes considerable concentration, therefore practice is about focus rather than simply hours spent. The enormous concentration required to undertake these twin tasks limits the amount of time you can spend doing them. Two hours a day may be enough, although, as Ericksson points out, this is more than most people in business use to develop their expertise.

Finding the right coaches and mentors

It seems that future experts need to make use of different teachers at various stages of their development. In a study of people across a wide range of organisations, it was found that those who made the most use of learning opportunities at work were those who had a passion for learning originating with parents/carers, focused by a great teacher at school and encouraged by managers, past and present, who took an interest in them (Rajan and Lane, 2000). Garvey (2011: 38) cites an anecdote told by the coach Tome McNab of the twice Olympic decathlon champion Daley Thompson, and comments that elite performance may be serendipitous. However, Ericsson (2006) found that elite performers were often encouraged by parents, found local teachers to take them forward but later found coaches who could take them to more advanced levels. Having an expert coach matters. They accelerate the learning process, are prepared to give difficult feedback and really enjoy working with motivated performers. They identify aspects of performance that need to be improved and push just hard enough to motivate rather than discourage. A key feature of such coaches is that they encourage the creation of the 'inner coach', so the performer can guide their own development. However, it seems that performers who excel also pick coaches who are right for them at the time and choose those who challenge and go beyond the comfort zone. Picking a coach whom you like and who makes you feel comfortable may not be the best route to great performance.

Education as a self-organising system

The educator Sugata Mitra (2005) has been developing over a number of years experiments in self-teaching (known as Hole in the Wall or HiWEL).

Working initially in locations where teachers do not exist or are hard to find he placed computers in holes in walls, allowing children to play with them unaided. He found that they were able to develop a wide range of skills. Taking this further, he started giving children complex tasks and left them to their own devices, and again found that they could solve them. Key elements turned out to be that they collaborated as groups – talking, sharing, exploring without limitations of existing ways of being taught. A later feature which he added was the Granny Cloud – volunteers with no knowledge of the problem-area set acted to encourage children to learn. He concluded that education operates as a self-organising system in which emergence of learning happens. The Grannies as coaches do not need expert knowledge of the topic but rather act to encourage, admire, stand behind and ask coaching questions to prompt further exploration. His view is that we could replace teachers in many areas with computers to aid self-exploration supported by volunteer coaches. He looks to see this as a worldwide phenomenon, bringing education to places that are otherwise inaccessible.

However, there are several criticisms of this work, particularly over its sustainability and the extent to which it seems to exclude teachers rather than find ways to incorporate them. While the HiWEL as an experiment has, according to Arora (2010), shown the capacity of children for self-learning through play and experimentation and that children can become pundits for the digital age, it has considerable challenges. To be sustained, it seems to require significant activity by mediators and the negotiation of relationships with teachers, the content and the school. Mitra's research is showing that self-exploration supported by coaching (non-expert) can generate significant achievements. Nevertheless, the issues raised by Arora and others need to be addressed if this is to be sustainable. What it does raise, is the possibility of new approaches to learning through digital developments supported by coaches or mentors. Where else might this be applied to good effect?

How might the future change?

It is not difficult to imagine a future where, as Hunt (2006) argues, many tasks become automated. The corollary of this is that there will be an increasing need for high levels of skill in occupations of the future. Becker (2002) points to the crucial role of the highly accomplished, thus the role of education and human capital, becomes paramount. To the extent that education can become more of a self-organising system supported by volunteer coaches, this leaves expert coaching to focus on higher levels of performance.

Similarly, there are a number of trends which look to continue. However, we must always be aware that it is events that we do not predict or which, while predicted, emerge in ways that were not considered that fundamentally challenge us.

Predicting future trends is a field of study. Watson (2010), looking at the next 50 years, identified five key areas. We have considered here some of the implications of the trends that he identified.

Ageing

Populations are becoming older: we live longer and want to live more active, healthy lives. With a smaller percentage of young people, the tax take to support the broader range of services that we have come to expect will have to increase substantially. This has implications for social cohesion, attitudes to retirement and the markets that will grow to serve this ageing population. Rajan (1992) has for many years been trying to raise our awareness of the implications of this trend for social and economic policy. On the upside, there is an increasing cadre of people with experience that they wish to share. If examples such as those identified by Mitra can be developed, then we have a ready supply of willing volunteer coaches. Coaching for living in this new demographic is likely to become a vast area of activity.

Power shift eastward

The centre of economic, political and military power is shifting eastwards. Countries like India and China, rather than just being sources of cheap labour, are increasingly global capital hubs and the base for innovation. Those from the East increasingly own Western companies. The consequences to our existing ways of thinking and working, and particularly the demands on the environment, are yet to be fully understood. It is interesting that demand for coaching and mentoring in countries such as China and India is increasing rapidly. A number of UK training groups and universities have set up subsidiaries to take advantage of this trend. However, the role of the mentor (as an older, wiser voice) is already established and so how we think about coaching and mentoring will also have to change. It will look very different than it does now. For example, as countries such as China and India gain economic power and develop their own coaching cadres, will they turn to coach in USA and European businesses?

Global connectivity

Greater connectivity, Watson (2010) argues, is changing how we live, work and think. It has upsides and risks – the latter include the end of privacy, higher banking risk caused by interconnectivity, and information anxiety. The upside includes the potential for greater transparency and the potential for smarter decisions by using the wisdom of crowds through instant polling. Confidentiality is also an issue that will have to face considerable revision. To the extent that coaching and mentoring goes digital, the footprint will become permanent and what the coach does in sessions will be available to share. How will we act when sessions are potentially available to all? Will we become more defensive or standardised in how we coach, rather than take the risks that might be needed to challenge our clients when the sessions are potentially publically available?

Genetics, Robotics, Internet and Nanotechnology (GRIN) technologies

As machines become smarter and capable of operating as experts as well as learning and acting as if they have consciousness, the provision of professional services will change beyond recognition. If we can call up a virtual expert to get advice and that expert has immediately available to it all the expert knowledge necessary to advise me, why would I use a person? The person has less memory power and has to go away to consult another machine to find the information. It is quicker to go directly to the machine itself. When the virtual machine also looks and acts like a person, I can ask for a coach or mentor who fits the ethnic, cultural or any other profile that I prefer. The virtual coach/mentor will look and feel like a person to whom I can relate. They understand my culture and me.

   The argument that a machine can have consciousness is a very lively debate in both neuroscience and physics. The physicist Kaku (2014) has reviewed this. In essence, his argument is that you cannot reverse-engineer the brain because, unlike computers which are deterministic, it is a quantum device and therefore inherently unpredictable. A reverse-engineered system could not be a quantum device, and it therefore can have no consciousness and cannot act like a real brain. It could only approximate some aspects of it.

Perhaps the difference between diagnosis and formulation is an example here. In diagnostics, you compare possibilities against clear criteria that in a standard definition specify a condition. In a formulation, you create with a client a narrative of events, which enables them to find meaning and go on to create a new narrative. It could be that expert devices are very useful for predictable conditions where there is a cause-and-effect relationship. Some areas of diagnostics in medicine, for example, could and already do benefit by a machine capable of comparing multiple instances and concluding on the most likely definition of cause. However, the conversation about how we deal with, respond to or feel about that information is an unpredictable narrative process (Lane and Corrie, 2012).

The environment

This is the biggest threat to the future, and if we fail to act we risk issues of water and food shortages, mass migration and epidemics. We have been talking about the need to address environmental health for a very long time. Since the UN Conference on the Environment in 1972 and calls for action and education on the issue (Lane, 1972), only limited progress has been made. As Ehrlich (1994) has pointed out, the risks that humanity faces are gigantic, bringing starvation to millions, plague and social breakdown. Faced with such a threat, it seems to him that we should take out an insurance policy. That insurance includes efforts to slow the pace of change, plus the flexibility to cope with change that cannot be avoided. Yet, the uncertainty about the course of change has become an excuse for inaction (Lane and Malkin, 1994). We have to grasp the acceptance of a common responsibility for our planet. The GCC (2008) called on coaches to step into their power and 'respond to a world beset by challenges for which there are no predetermined answers'. Many coaches are doing so in projects around the world, yet as a profession our interests seem to be dominated by parochial concerns and self-interest.

Watson (2010) also talks about things that he argues will not change. These include:

- Interest in the future and yearning for the past
- Desire for recognition and respect
- Need for physical objects, actual encounters and live experiences
- Anxiety and fear
- A search for meaning

It is arguable that these have existed as human needs since we became human. They will not change, although how they are manifest will. To the extent that we want to talk about our future and past in a context of recognition and respect within actual physical encounters to deal with our anxieties and fears and to search for new meaning, there will also be a need for live – not virtual – coaches and mentors. In spite of the limitations of real people as memory banks, we may still prefer that type of encounter to an all-knowing machine.

Asia 2050

There is much talk about the Asian future. If (and by no means is this certain) growth continues at current rates, by 2050 Asia will come to gain the dominant economic region a position it held some 300 years ago, before the industrial revolution. There are two aspects of this to note. First, that Asia was the dominant power in the past (probably news to many brought up on an Anglo-centric history curriculum at school); and second, that from a low point in the 1950s, Asia will return to dominance in a relatively short period. Many things could jeopardise this, including climate change, poor governance and poor economic policies, and in particular a failure to match economic development with policies to promote social well-being.

It will require resilient leaders and the harnessing of technology, innovation and entrepreneurship. There is a huge opportunity here for coaching and mentoring to make a contribution. However, we cannot simply import models predicated on a Western mindset and psychological models built largely by white male Anglo-American psychologists (British Psychological Society, 1991). We will need to begin to look at ways of thinking and leading that are more representative of Eastern or transpersonal philosophies.

Predicting the future is ...

> Turbulence is not new but with continued globalisation, increased complexity, accelerating speed of information exchange and market volatility, we are now facing a reality almost unrecognisable to previous generations. (Lane and Down, 2010: 514)

If traditional approaches to leading and managing organisations were based on command and control, they also presumed that the world was predictable. Get the right strategy, apply it, measure the key performance indicators and you are set for success. This, according to Birkenshaw (2010), worked for many large corporations over decades. However, they were ill-prepared for rapid change and many were lost. He raises the increased interest in the concepts of emergence and self-organising systems as a way to think about management models that can cope with complexity in a turbulent world you cannot predict. What happens does so through emergence in self-organising systems. He contrasts different management models. Traditionally, companies sought alignment so that goals assigned to individuals could deliver on the overall strategy. Elaborate systems to funnel alignment down through the organisation existed, with links to payments based on achieved goals. This makes it difficult for individuals to look beyond the goals that determine their pay.

As an alternative he posits the concept of obliquity. He quotes both Wollheim who first proposed the idea, and Kay who applied it to business. Obliquity recognises that the path between our individual beliefs and collective action may be indirect. Overcoming obstacles or meeting targets in business is, according to Kay, often best achieved indirectly. Birkenshaw summarises this as shown in Table 14.1.

Table 14.1   Alignment versus obliquity

	Discourse	Discourse
Management principle	Alignment	Obliquity
Environmental context	Stable	Turbulent
Organisation	Small, simple	Large, complex
Coordination challenge	Relatively easy	Relatively difficult
Consequence of action on others	Predictable, quick feedback	Unpredictable, slow feedback
Types of suitable goals	Direct	Indirect

Let's compare approaches to coaching and mentoring with these alignment and obliquity principles:

1. Coaching or mentoring through goals, and outcome measures …
2. Coaching or mentoring as facilitation of process that will encourage individuals to notice what is happening and choose how they respond to it and learn from that response

Then let's look at how we develop coaches and mentors using these two approaches:

1. In the first, we directly define the competencies needed to assist people to set goals and plan activities to achieve them. We train and measure according to alignment with the competence model. We put students into triads to observe each other using the competencies in accordance with the standards of the professional body. Goals are directly related to a fixed competence model
2. In the second, we get students to self-observe in one-to-one conversation sessions and indirectly see what emerges. We ask them to seek feedback from observers and clients in

terms of what seemed to be happening. We get them to notice what happened inside, outside and over time. Outcomes are indirect and emerge out of the process

If management is to be reinvented to adopt principles such as obliquity so that it is better equipped for rapid change, then coaching and mentoring might need to become an oblique process.

Three elements are perhaps worth further discussion:

- *Goals or skills transfer* – these are assumed to be a core purpose for coaching and mentoring
- *Approved methods defined by standards* – there appear to be relevant methods according to defined standards set by a professional body
- *Ethics as an external process* – ethics are defined externally by the professional body, rather than arising from an internal moral compass or emergent from the interaction between coach or mentor and client

If aligned process needs to be replaced (in appropriate circumstances) with oblique process, Birkenshaw suggests three approaches, as follows.

Pursuing an indirect goal

- The indirect goal has to be something that people can really relate to: it has to be meaningful and measurable
- You need to be able to show how progress towards the indirect goal is leading to progress towards the end goal
- Pay attention to the potential risks of actively pursuing an indirect goal

Pursuing a creative goal

- You need to be able to give your employees the freedom to pursue their own agenda
- You need an effective way of separating out, and investing properly in, the high potential projects

Taking a leap of faith

- You need to truly believe that profits aren't all that important
- Your cause has to be one that consumers want to support
- You need to track your performance on all the dimensions of performance that you care about
- You must take heed of the self-apparent risks of this approach

What might a coach or mentor need to reflect upon when preparing for an assignment in an organisation taking one or other of these three approaches?

Activity 14.1

The EMCC (2015) provides the following definitions of coaching and mentoring. Where might the principles of alignment and obliquity fit within these definitions?

A professional accredited coach is an expert in establishing a relationship with people in a series of conversations with the purpose of:

1.1. serving the clients to improve their performance or enhance their personal development or both, choosing their own goals and ways of doing it;

1.2. interacting with each person or group by applying one or more relevant methods, according to standards and ethical principles set up by a professional association such as EMCC, AC or ICF.

Mentoring is a developmental process, which may in some forms involve a transfer of skill or knowledge from a more experienced person to a less experienced, through learning dialogue and role-modelling; or in other forms may be a partnership for mutual learning between peers or across differences such as age, race or discipline.

4.1 A mentor interacts with each person or group by applying one or more relevant methods according to standards and ethical principles set up by a professional association such as EMCC, AC or ICF.

Case study 14.1

Unlike the other case studies in the book, this one is set in the future.

The Chief Learning Officer (CLO) of a professional body in the health field approaches you in a personal capacity. It has recently started running short courses in coaching and mentoring for its qualified members who work in various health-related professions. Two issues have occurred: one urgent, the other for more long-term reflection. He has been approached by a member who has taken one of their courses and has asked which of the current coaching/mentoring bodies she might usefully join. He has taken the view that he cannot recommend one over another but, rather, could outline the questions she might like to explore in order to make a decision. However, there is a newly appointed CEO who has taken the view that advice cannot be given since they are considering setting up internally their own register of coaches and mentors for the health professions. The CLO (your client) believes that he can still respond to the member and it is right to do so. He would like guidance on how he might outline useful questions for the member on how to choose between professional bodies. How might you help him with this concern?

The second matter raised is that, in the past, he has had considerable freedom to respond to client requests. This is mainly in the form of training providers asking for their short courses to be accredited for CPD. He has taken the view that he can respond to these requests without referral to other committees, as long as they fall within his ambit and fit the regulations.

He has worked this way for a number of years. The clients of the body greatly value his responsiveness and the quality of the advice he gives them in helping to shape their course offers. Organisational members hold him in significant regard for his support, flexibility and responsiveness. Individual members who have sought advice on courses also rate him highly.

The new CEO has stated that this approach fails to take account of broader issues within the professional body, and in future all requests must go to a courses committee which is to meet three times a year. The CEO believes that Professional Bodies are about maintaining and aligning standards. The CLO feels that this replaces client responsiveness with unnecessary beauracracy since the only data on which they can base a decision is his report on the client proposal. He believes that they need to be about responding quickly and often using indirect routes to changing needs. How might you help him with this concern?

Towards a future

If the world of management is going to change, will managers have to spend a lot more effort to become great? Will they, if the expertise research holds, have to practice very much more and thus need great coaches/mentors? If core teams will in future take time to innovate and not pass this off to a separate department, will they need to practice more and be coached?

If the activities in which we engage will become more emergent, will it make sense to maintain separation of the coaching and mentoring field as well as separate professional routes coach, mentor, coaching psychologist, etc.? Might we become one field of coach with different people filling it, whatever their origin?

We have explored these issues in our previous chapters. These give rise to what we see as core agendas for our fields.

Agendas for the future

1. Coaching and mentoring is a contested field – we need to engage with the discourse

This book has highlighted the importance of discourse. The field has a long history, throughout which many discourses have emerged. Most of these are positive but some are not. There is a core discourse around our performative or developmental role, and, in part, coaching is seen as more associated with the former and mentoring the latter. However, the key is that all professional practice is contested – what it is and how it functions for the benefit of some rather than others is part of the debate across many fields. We need to recognise the contested nature of our work and embrace the various discourses so that we may fully understand what it is that we contribute positively and negatively to our clients and society:

- *Agenda for the future* – We need to engage with the contested nature of the field rather than the somewhat cosy dialogue that currently perpetuates an 'all must have prizes' approach to discourse. We challenge the convenient perspectives that our clients use to deceive themselves; we must offer the same rigour to our own deliberations

2. Coaching and mentoring is interdisciplinary in nature – let's embrace it

While psychology is a key influence, other core influences derive from multiple sources such as adult-learning theory. Unlike many professional fields which tend to teach a framework for practice against a core knowledge base, we provide flexibility for our practitioners to develop and build a number of structures within which to practice. This leaves us with an uncomfortable relationship with the idea of evidence-informed practice, which is becoming a core component of many of our sister disciplines:

- *Agenda for the future* – If we are to build a professional field of activity based on models from a number of disciplines as well as those derived from within our field, we need to address the question: 'If we build an interdisciplinary profession from multiple sources, do we need to show that it is coherent and rigorous?' We are as a field very diverse in our practitioner base, our origins and the contexts in which we work. We draw upon a broad and deep range of perspectives. We need to understand the implication of this for us as an increasingly professionalised field

3. Coaching and mentoring is a diverse field – let's build on that creatively

As a diverse field, it behoves each practitioner to be able to state a coherent case for the work they do. Clients need a clear understanding of the offer being made to them when they use our services. Beyond this, we do need to recognise that we come into a context with that self-narrated understanding but that we then have to engage in the reconstruction of it as part of creating a relational narrative for the work between us and relevant stakeholders:

- *Agenda for the future* – Parallel to the issues of us as a developing professional field, there is the question of how individual coaches and mentors work. How they develop a coherent approach to practice has to be addressed in training programmes and be a centrepiece in the work of all practitioners. Each person working as a coach or mentor needs to be able (using whatever model best fits) to state the *purpose* of their work, the *perspectives* that inform it and the *process* they use

4. A narrow focus on skills and competence for coaching and mentoring needs to give way to a concern with excellence

We have fallen into a dominant discourse, that of competence, as a way to define our field. This is a limited framework, which ignores multiple and other more expansive possibilities. It also causes us to treat practice as an uncontested arena, when in practice it is subject to social and political discourse. These need to be fully engaged with so that we do not repeat the failings of others professions who have given up control to the state in the form of regulatory bodies (mandatory or voluntary). There are many different approaches to building competence models, some of which are based on excellence rather than minimum standards. They become aspirations to which we journey rather than fixed points:

- *Agenda for the future* – We need to seriously address the question of the role of competence frameworks for our field. Does our current approach render competence frameworks as necessary or sufficient to reflect our practice? At the very least, we need to engage with this discourse and consider if our approach should be built on models based on excellence rather than on minimum standards. We may need at this point in our development to generate bold, expansive aspirations to which we journey rather than the fixed points of competence

5. Engaging with the role of learning in the coaching and mentoring mix offers a powerful potential for development

Learning theory is a well-developed field and clearly relates to coaching and mentoring practice. Models from experiential learning, typologies of learning and dynamic and situational philosophies are amongst the range of alternatives available. All these elements are present within coaching and mentoring practice and, therefore, these models offer huge potential for authentic, deep and powerful learning:

- *Agenda for the future* – How we learn and the role of learning in the development of our clients has not been to the forefront of our thinking within coaching and mentoring, thereby leaving an incompleteness in our knowledge and practice. Yet, we do talk much about learning as both an individual and situated process. There is considerable research on adult learning in other fields that needs to become centred in our own thinking about the development of our field

6. Evaluation cannot be an afterthought – it needs to drive us forward

Whilst much good work is going on in the evaluation of both mentoring and coaching, evaluation of both lacks evidence-based assessment processes. Too many coaching and mentoring sessions go un-evaluated, while organisations struggle to measure the contribution that we make:

- *Agenda for the future* – We need to move beyond 'happiness sheets' and towards a more creative, exploratory form of evaluation, such as those associated with Appreciative Inquiry, World Café, personal testimony and Open Space. There are many ways we could develop the evaluative base for our field in ways that honour its distinctiveness and breadth

7. Coaching and mentoring operates in widely different contexts – we must appreciate and embrace the diversity found: It seems to be the way forward

We have presented case studies, research, practice and theoretical discourses throughout this book and we raise important questions and identify different ways of understanding our work critically in the contexts in which we practice. We can see that coaching and mentoring practice has many different roots and therefore many different theoretical underpinnings. Rather than seek to eliminate this in pursuit of a codified model of practice as has happened in other professions, we need to embrace it:

- *Agenda for the future* – How we embrace diversity, recognise the different contexts in which we work and yet build coherent (even if diverse) theory, is one of our challenges. Core themes within these include: greater attention to the role of power, understanding the merits of both directive and non-directive approaches and engaging with the implications of both deficit and developmental models. Our agenda has to be to grasp these discourses, not shy away from them

8. We, as coaches and mentors, can step into our power and influence – the dominant discourses in leadership and management: Towards a more stakeholder-led society?

The global financial collapse of 2008 has brought the need for alternative perspectives on change and on the nature of leadership. We have a long association between coaching, mentoring and leadership. We are also rooted in humanism and more collaborative discourses. While we may offer benefit to individuals with whom we work, we may have a neutral influence on the dominant discourse of management. Does this have to be the limit of our influence or can the concept of a 'coaching and mentoring way' contribute to alternative perspectives:

- *Agenda for the future* – Now is the time for us to grasp the influence that coaching and mentoring have within organisations to enter the discourse on stakeholder capitalism. Perhaps we can engage with the alternatives to the rational pragmatic discourse in management theory? Are we here just to serve the agenda of those who pay the bills or should we, as a responsible profession, take seriously our responsibility to a wider society?

9. Let's grasp coaching and mentoring as a way to generate a culture of authentic leadership

Management discourse often espouses the idea of an aligned homogeneous culture. Yet, rarely do the espoused theories align with those in use in the organisation to manage its activities. We can see that complexity is the norm in organisations, in spite of a management discourse, which claims the opposite. If we grasp that complexity, coaching and mentoring can offer a process of change, this means that within our sphere of influence, we need to engage with discourses on equity and an unfair distribution of global wealth. We need to recognise that unfairness leads to dissatisfaction, unrest and potential conflict. Do we need to utilise the 'coaching and mentoring way' to help address this issue?

- *Agenda for the future* – Can we now stimulate the appetite for impacting on organisational change? This does mean that we have to be prepared to challenge vested interests. If we choose to do so, will we need to pay much greater attention to the role of coaching and mentoring in contributing to culture change?

10. Coaching and mentoring is becoming widespread in organisations – let's make sure that all the stakeholders are part of the discourse

Organisations increasingly face a dilemma in achieving an appropriate balance between the use of internal and external coaches. How can the quality of external coaches be assured? How can supervision manage both the individual and speak to the organisational context and politics within which they operate?

- *Agenda for the future* – Currently, with limited exceptions, the voice of the client (individual, organisation and society) is missing from much of the discourse on standards for the field. A significant effort to engage with them as full partners in the debate is needed. Too much of it looks like a discussion for the benefit of those sourcing coaches and mentors and training providers

11. Supervision matters – we need to get on with understanding why and how we can build on it

While supervision is on the increase, it is not used universally by all and there is no widely accepted model of supervision that is being used. The question of who should supervise and what skills and experience they should bring to the role are still unresolved issues:

- *Agenda for the future* – Supervision has to take its place as a key agenda for the field. If, as is increasingly the case, clients demand that coaches and mentors are supervised and professional bodies make it a requirement of membership, we need to know if it adds value, how it adds value and how best to develop it. We cannot with confidence answer those questions at present

12. We are moving towards professionalisation: Let's not do so without consideration of the consequences – it may not be the best route but, if it is, then ethics must be at its core

While there are those who assert that coaching is a profession, or argue that it should become one, coaching still lacks a unified body of knowledge and suffers from fragmented training, assessment and accreditation processes. Mentoring is, on the whole, slightly different in that, apart from in a few places, professionalisation is not such an issue:

- *Agenda for the future* – Whether existing discussions between the professional associations to resolve core issues will make progress remains to be seen. However, this will not be resolved through conversations between a limited number of USA- and European-based organisations when the field is rapidly expanding in many continents. Without the involvement of associations in Africa, Asia and South America, we will end with a very Anglo-centric framework that does not well serve the needs of people, persons and societies

13. Research is the lifeblood of our practice, if it is to be more than a glossy product or fad

Despite the rapid growth in coaching and mentoring as helping interventions, it is a paradox that both remain relatively unsupported by robust empirical research. For coaching, in particular, there is a lack of longitudinal research and too many small-scale case studies:

- *Agenda for the future* – Given the growing amounts of money now devoted to coaching and mentoring, a more robust approach to research must be undertaken if the intervention is to maintain its credibility

So, what does the future look like and what is the role of coaching and mentoring in it?

If we imagine in the future a truly interconnected world with the use of online-based expert/artificial intelligence systems that learn in real time and which provide simulated people, then coaching and mentoring may become commonplace. However, this is likely to be very specific – choose your issue – download the relevant programme. Or it may involve coaches trained in specific techniques to address defined concerns – the coming to terms with cancer coach/mentor, the giving up smoking coach/mentor, the presentational skills coach/mentor. Short, intense training not requiring a 'profession' will become standard. This, of course, will not be restricted to coaching or mentoring. Across all professional fields, we are likely to see competencies broken down into small packages, with people trained in a specific package that can be supported online. Of course, it has happened in the past, thus at one time you saw a solicitor to buy or sell your house – now you may use a conveyancer (with knowledge of that specific activity), in the future you may use an expert system online to complete a sale or purchase. The de-professionalisation of expertise is likely to grow.

Nevertheless, to the extent that people want to connect with other people, this process only goes so far. The Grandmother research (Mitra, 2014) shows that a coach adds value, even where individuals or groups are using online systems to explore ideas and develop skills. It could be that coaching becomes a key part of how education and learning is delivered. As such, understanding the core elements of effective coaching and making these available to all will add real value to the world. Beyond this, for expert development, more will be needed and the role of the professional coach is likely to be further enhanced.

Yet, the need for personal connection and search for meaning may well not be satisfied by virtual learning. If the expertise research is correct, a skilled coach or mentor will always be needed to promote elite performance. So, perhaps coaching or mentoring will divide into that required for elite performance face-to-face, and that required for limited skilled performance provided online. However, it seems that some form of coach/mentor adds value to learning.

If we start to engage with the agenda items raised here and recognise that multiple discourses are in play, we will perhaps summon the courage to face our futures. We recognise that the approach we offer is yet another discourse and is not proffered as a regime of truth. However, we believe – as authors, academics and practitioners with a long-standing commitment to our field – in the power of coaching and mentoring to make a difference to people, persons and societies. We want to see that potential realised. We believe that as a field we are able to grasp the possibilities which this creates.

Thus, the future may be one in which coaching and mentoring are seen as key to performance – we will all seek a coach and become mentors.

References

Agaibi, C.E. and Wilson, J.P. (2005) 'Trauma, PTSD and resilience', *Trauma, Violence & Abuse*, 6(3): 195–216.

Allen, T.D. and Eby, L. (2007) *The Blackwell Handbook of Mentoring: A Multiple Perspectives Approach*. Malden, MA: Blackwell Publishing.

Allen, T.D., Eby, L.T., O'Brien, K.E. and Lentz, E. (2008) 'The state of mentoring research: A qualitative review of current research methods and future research implications', *Journal of Vocational Behavior*, 73(3): 343–57.

Allen, T.D., Eby, L.T., Poteet, M.L., Lentz, E. and Lima, L. (2004) 'Career benefits associated with mentoring for protégés: a meta-analysis', *Journal of Applied Psychology*, 89(4): 127–38.

Alred, G. and Garvey, B. (2010) *The Mentoring Pocketbook* (3rd edn). Alresford: Management Pocketbooks Ltd.

Alred, G., Garvey, B. and Smith, R.D. (1998) 'Pas de deux – Learning in conversations', *Career Development International*, 3(7): 308–14.

Amabile, T. (1997) 'Motivating creativity in organizations: On doing what you love and loving what you do', *California Management Review*, 40(1): 39–58.

American Management Association (AMA) (2008) *Coaching: A Global Study of Successful Practices: Current Trends and Future Possibilities 2008–2018*. Available at: www.amanet.org/training/webcasts/Coaching-A-Global-Survey-of-Successful-Practices.aspx (accessed 27 May 2015).

Anderson, E.M. and Shannon, A.L. (1988) 'Towards a conceptualization of mentoring', *Journal of Teacher Education*, 39(38): 38–42.

Anderson, H. and Goolishian, H. (1992) 'The client is the expert: A not-knowing approach to therapy', in S. McNamee and K.J. Gergen (eds), *Constructing Therapy: Social Construction and the Therapeutic Process*. London: Sage, pp. 25–39.

Anderson, J.A. (1988) 'Cognitive styles and multicultural populations', *Journal of Teacher Education*, 39(1): 2–9.

Anderson, N., Herriot, P. and Hodgkinson, G.P. (2001) 'The practitioner–researcher divide in Industrial, Work and Organizational (IWO) psychology: Where are we now, and where do we go from here?', *Journal of Occupational and Organizational Psychology*, 74(4): 391–411.

Argyris, C. (1982) *Reasoning, Learning, and Action: Individual and Organizational*. San Fransisco, CA: Jossey-Bass.

Argyris, C. (1989) 'Strategy implementation: An experience in learning', *Organizational Dynamics*, 18(2): 5–15.

Argyris, C. (1990) *Overcoming Organizational Defenses: Facilitating Organizational Learning*. Needham, MA: Allyn & Bacon.

Argyris, C. and Schön, D.A. (1974) *Theory in Practice: Increasing Professional Effectiveness*. San Francisco, CA: Jossey-Bass.

Argyris, C. and Schön, D.A. (1992) *Theory in Practice: Increasing Professional Effectiveness* (2nd edn). San Francisco, CA: Jossey-Bass.

Arnold, J. (2005) *Work Psychology: Understanding Human Behaviour in the Workplace* (4th edn). Harlow: Pearson Education Ltd.

Arora, P. (2010) 'Hope-in-the-wall? A digital promise for free learning', *British Journal of Educational Technology*, 41: 689–702. Available at: www.payalarora.com/Publications/Arora-HopeintheWall.pdf (accessed 2 October 2015).

Aryree, S. and Chay, Y.W. (1994) 'An examination of the impact of career-oriented mentoring on work commitment attitudes and career satisfaction among professional and managerial employees', *British Journal of Management*, 5(4): 241–9.

Association for Coaching (AC) (2005) *Association for Coaching Supervision Report*. Available at: www.associationforcoaching.com (accessed 28 April 2013).

Association of Coach Training Organizations (ACTO) (2015) *Choosing a Mentor Coach*. Available at: http://icf.files.cms-plus.com/IndCred/Choosing-a-Mentor-Coach.pdf (accessed 19 October 2015).

Association of National Organisations for Supervision in Europe (ANSE) (2012) Code of Ethics. Available at: www.anse.eu/tl_files/anse/docs/history/2012%20Code%20of%20Ethics/Code_of_Ethics_2012.pdf (accessed 8 November 2013).

Bachkirova, T. and Cox, E. (2004) 'A bridge over troubled water: Bringing together coaching and counselling', *International Journal of Mentoring and Coaching*, 2(1). Available at: www.emccouncil.org/uk/journal.htm (accessed 2 October 2015).

Barker, K.K. and Hunsley, J. (2013) 'The use of theoretical models in psychology supervisor development research from 1994 to 2010: A systemic review', *Canadian Psychology*, 54(3): 176–85.

Barnett, R. (1994) *The Limits of Competence*. London: Open University Press and Society for Research into Higher Education.

Barrett, R. (2002) 'Mentor supervision and development: Exploration of lived experience', *Career Development International*, 7(5): 279–83.

Barsh, J., Capozzi, M. and Davidson, J. (2008) 'Leadership and innovation', *McKinsey Quarterly*, 1: 36–47.

Bartlett, J.E. (2007) 'Advances in coaching practices: A humanistic approach to coach and client roles', *Journal of Business Research*, 60(1): 91–3.

Bates, I. (1997) *The Competence and Outcomes Movement: The Landscape of Research, 1986–1996*. Leeds: School of Education, University of Leeds.

Beck, U. (1992) *Risk Society: Towards a New Modernity*. London: Sage.

Becker, G.S. (2002) 'The age of human capital', in E.P. Lazaer (ed.), *Education in the Twenty-First Century*. Stanford, CA: Hoover Institution Press, pp. 3–8.

Beech, N. and Brockbank, A. (1999) 'Power/knowledge and psychological dynamics in Mentoring', *Management Learning*, 30(1): 7–25.

Bennett, J.L. (2006) 'An agenda for coaching-related research: A challenge for researchers', *Consulting Psychology Journal: Practice and Research*, 58(4): 240–9.

Bennett, N. and Lemoine, G.J. (2014) 'What a difference a word makes: Understanding threats to performance in a VUCA world', *Business Horizons*, 57: 311–17.

Berglas, S. (2002) 'The very real dangers of executive coaching', *Harvard Business Review*, 80(6): 86–92.

Berman, E.M. and West, J.P. (2008) 'Managing emotional intelligence in US cities: A study of social skills among public managers', *Public Administration Review*, July/August: 742–58.

Bernstein, B. (1971) 'On the classification and framing of educational knowledge', in M.F.D. Young (ed.), *Knowledge and Control: New Directions for the Sociology of Education*. London: Collier-MacMillan, Open University, pp. 47–69.

Bieling, P. and Kuyken, W. (2003) 'Is cognitive case formulation science or science fiction?', *Clinical Psychology: Science and Practice*, 10(1): 52–69.

Birkenshaw, J. (2010) *Reinventing Management*. San Francisco, CA: Jossey-Bass.

Bloom, S.L. (2011) 'Trauma-organised systems and parallel process', in N. Tehrani (ed.), *Managing Trauma in the Workplace: Supporting Workers and Organisations*. Hove: Routledge, pp. 139–53.

Bluckert, P. (2004) 'The state of play in corporate coaching: current and future trend', *Industrial and Commercial Training*, 36(2): 53–6.

Bluckert, P. (2006) *Psychological Dimensions of Executive Coaching*. Maidenhead: Open University Press.

Bluckert, P. (2014) 'The gestalt approach to coaching', in E. Cox, T. Bachkirova and D. Clutterbuck (eds), *The Complete Handbook of Coaching* (2nd edn). London: Sage, pp. 80–93.

Bohm, D. (1996) *On Dialogue* (ed. Lee Nichol). Harmondsworth: Penguin.

Boisot, M. (1995) *Information Space: A Framework for Learning in Organizations, Institutions and Culture*. London: Routledge.

Bolden, R. and Gosling, J. (2006) 'Leadership competencies: Time to change the tune', *Leadership*, 2(2): 147–63.

Bono, J.E., Purvanova, R.K., Towler, A.J. and Peterson, D. (2009) 'A survey of executive coaching practices', *Personnel Psychology*, 62(2): 361–404.

Borders, L.D. (1991) 'A systematic approach to peer group supervision', *Journal of Counseling & Development*, 69(3): 248–52.

Boud, D., Keogh, R. and Walker, D. (eds) (1985) *Reflection: Turning Experience into Learning*. London: Kogan Page.

Boyle, M. (1997) 'Clinical psychology theory: Making gender visible in clinical psychology', *Feminism and Psychology*, 7(2): 231–8.

Bramley, P. and Kitson, B. (1994) 'Evaluating training against business criteria', *Journal of European Industrial Training*, 18(1): 10–14.

Bresser, F. (2008) *European Coaching Survey*. Bresser Consulting. Available at: www.bresser-consulting.com (accessed 9 October 2015).

Bresser, F. (2009) *Global Coaching Survey*. Frank Bresser Consulting. Available at: www.frank-bresser-consulting.com (accessed 9 October 2015).

Brinkerhoff, R.O. (2006) *Telling Training's Story: Evaluation Made Simple, Credible, and Effective*. San Francisco, CA: Berrett-Koehler Publishers.

British Psychological Society (BPS) (1991) *The Future of Psychological Science*. Leicester: British Psychological Society.

British Psychological Society (BPS) (2006) *Continuous Supervision*. Leicester: British Psychological Society.

Broad, M.L. and Newstom, J.W. (1992) *Transfer of Training: Action-Packed Strategies to Ensure High Payoff from Training Investments*. Reading, MA: Addison-Wesley.

Brock, V. (2014) *Source Book of Coaching History*. Available at: www.amazon.co.uk/Sourcebook-Coaching-History-Vikki-Brock/dp/1469986655 (accessed 9 October 2015).

Brown, J. (2002) *Resource Guide for Hosting Conversations that Matter at the World Café*. Whole Systems Associates. Prepublication version posted for reader's feedback. Available at: www.inscena.ch/fileadmin/user_upload/inscena/pdf/worldcafe.pdf (accessed 3 October 2015).

Brown, J. and Isaacs, D. (2005) *The World Café: Shaping our Futures through Conversations that Matter*. San Francisco, CA: Berrett-Koehler.

Brundrett, M. (2000) 'The question of competence: The origins, strengths and inadequacies of a leadership training paradigm', *School Leadership and Management*, 20(3): 353–69.

Bruner, J. (1978) *Mind in Society: The Development of Higher Psychological Processes* (ed. M. Cole et al.). Cambridge, MA: Harvard University Press.

Bruner, J. (1985) 'Vygotsky: A historical and conceptual perspective', in J.V. Wertsch (ed.), *Culture, Communication and Cognition: Vygotskian Perspectives*.Cambridge, London and New York: Cambridge University Press, pp. 21–33.

Bruner, J. (1990) *Acts of Meaning*. Cambridge, MA: Harvard University Press.

Bruner, J. (1996) *The Culture of Education*. Cambridge, MA: Harvard University Press.

Brunner, R. (1998) 'Psychoanalysis and coaching', *Journal of Management Psychology*, 13(7): 515–17.

Brunning, H. (2006) 'The six domains of executive coaching', in H. Brunning (ed.), *Executive Coaching: Systems-Psychodynamic Perspective*. London: Karnac Books, pp. 131–51.

Buckingham, M. (2001) 'Don't waste time and money', *Gallup Management Journal*, 3 December. Available at: http://gmj.gallup.com/content/default/asp?ci=259&pg=1 (accessed 3 October 2015).

Bureau of Air Safety Investigation (1996) *Human Factors in Fatal Aircraft Accident*. Available at: www.narcap.org/articles/HumanFactorsinFatalAircraftAccident.pdf (accessed 20 October 2015).

Burrell, G. and Morgan, G. (1979) *Sociological Paradigms and Organizational Analysis*. London: Heinemann.

Byrne, Z.S., Dik, B.J. and Chiauru, D.S. (2008) 'Alternatives to traditional mentoring in fostering career success', *Journal of Vocational Behavior*, 72(3): 429–42.

Cambridge Daily News (1889) 'University Boat Race', *Cambridge Daily News*, 29 January, p. 3.

Campbell, C.P. (1997) 'Training course/program evaluation: Principles and practice', *Journal of European and Industrial Training*, 22(8): 323–44.

Campbell, D.T. and Stanley, J.C. (1963) *Experimental and Quasi-Experimental Designs for Research*. Chicago, IL: Rand McNally.

Campone, F. (ed.) (2012) 'Future of coaching: Building a kaleidoscope: A summit outcomes paper', resulting from the Future of Coaching Summit, Charlotte, NC, 27–28 July.

Caraccioli, L.A. (1760) *The True Mentor, or, An Essay on the Education of Young People in Fashion*. London: J. Coote at the Kings Arms in Paternoster Row.

Carden, A. (1990) 'Mentoring and adult career development', *Counselling Psychologist*, 18(2): 275–99.

Carmin, C.N. (1988) 'Issues in research on mentoring: Definitional and methodological', *International Journal of Mentoring*, 2(2): 9–13.

Carr, M.L. (2011) *The Invisible Teacher: A Self-Mentoring Sustainability Model*. Wilmington, NC: Randall Library, University of North Carolina Wilmington.

Carr, M. (no date) www.selfmentoring.net (accessed 9 October 2015).

Carrad, L. (2002) 'Policy developments in mentoring and volunteering', in A.D. Miller (ed.), *Mentoring, Citizenship and Community: Report of the Third Annual Conference of the London Regional Mentoring Network*. London: London Central Learning & Skills Council.

Carroll, L. (1998) *Alice's Adventure in Wonderland* and *Through the Looking Glass*. England: Penguin Classics.

Carroll, M. (1996) *Counselling Supervision: Theory, Skills and Practice*. London: Cassell.

Carroll, M. (2006) 'Supervising executive coaches', *Therapy Today*, 17(5): 55–7.

Carroll, M. and Shaw, E. (2012) *Ethical Maturity in the Helping Professions*. London: Jessica Kingsley.

Caruso, R.E. (1996) 'Who does mentoring?', Paper presented at 3rd European Mentoring Centre, Conference, London, European Mentoring and Coaching Council (EMCC, emccouncil.org), London, 7–8 November.

Cascio, W.F. (2007) 'Evidence-based management and the market for ideas', *Academy of Management Journal*, 50(5): 1009–12.

Caulkin, S. (1995) 'The measure principal', *The Observer*, 30 July.

Caulkin, S. (1997) 'League tables? A restaurant guide is a lot more use', *The Observer*, 6 April.

Cavanagh, M. and Grant, A. (2006) 'Coaching psychology and the scientist-practitioner model', in D.A. Lane and S. Corrie (eds), *The Modern Scientist-Practitioner: A Guide to Practice in Psychology*. Hove: Routledge.

Cavanagh, M. and Lane, D. (2012) 'Coaching psychology coming of age: The challenges we face in the messy world of complexity', *International Coaching Psychology Review*, 7(1): 75–90.

Cavanagh, M. and O'Conner, S. (2012) *Developmental Coaching in Complex Workspaces*. Sydney: Coaching Psychology Unit Sydney University.

Chagnon, J. and Russell, R.K. (1995) 'Assessment of supervisee developmental level and supervision environment across supervisor experience', *Journal of Counseling & Development*, 73(5): 553–8.

Chapman, L. (2010) *Integrated Experiential Coaching Becoming an Executive Coach*. London: Karnac.

Chappell, C., Rhodes, C., Soloman, N., Tennant, M. and Yates, L. (2003) *Pedagogy and Identity in Individual, Organisational and Social Change*. London and New York: RoutledgeFalmer.

Chartered Institute of Personnel and Development (CIPD) (2012) *Coaching and Mentoring Factsheet*. Wimbledon: Chartered Institute of Personnel and Development.

CIPD (2015a) *Survey Report: Resourcing and Planning*. London: CIPD.

CIPD (2015b) *Survey Report: Learning and Development*. London: CIPD.

Checkland, P. (1989) 'An application of soft systems methodology', in S. Rosenhead (ed.), *Rational Analysis for a Problematic World*. Chichester: Wiley, pp. 101–19.

Childs, R., Woods, M., Willcock, D. and Man, A. (2011) 'Action learning supervision for coaches', in J. Passmore (ed.), *Supervision in Coaching*. London: Kogan Page, pp. 31–44.

Clark, P. (1984) 'The metamorphosis of mentor: Fénelon to Balzac', *Romanic Review*, 75(2): 202–4.

Clarke, A. (1999) *Evaluation Research: An Introduction to Principles, Methods and Practice*. London: Sage.

Clawson, J.G. (1996) 'Mentoring in the information age', *Leadership and Organization Development Journal*, 17(3): 6–15.

Clutterbuck, D. (1985) *Everyone Needs a Mentor* (1st edn). London: Institute of Personnel Management (IPM).

Clutterbuck, D. (1992) *Everyone Needs a Mentor* (2nd edn). London: Institute of Personnel Management (IPM).

Clutterbuck, D. (2001) *Everyone Needs a Mentor* (3rd edn). London: Chartered Institute of Personnel and Development (CIPD).

Clutterbuck, D. and Lane, G. (2004) *The Situational Mentor*. Aldershot: Gower Publishing.

Clutterbuck, D. and Megginson, D. (2005a) 'Creating a coaching culture', *Industrial and Commercial Training*, 38(5): 232–7.

Clutterbuck, D. and Megginson, D. (2005b) *Making Coaching Work: Creating a Coaching Culture*. London: Chartered Institute of Personnel and Development (CIPD).

Cohen, D.J. (2007) 'The very separate worlds of academic and practitioner periodicals in human resource management: Reasons for the divide and concrete solutions for bridging the gap', *Academy of Management Journal*, 50(5): 1013–19.

Colley, H. (2002) 'A "rough guide" to the history of mentoring from a Marxist feminist perspective', *Journal of Education for Teaching*, 28(3): 247–63.

Colley, H. (2003a) 'Engagement mentoring for "disaffected" youth: A new model of mentoring for social inclusion', *British Educational Research Journal*, 29(4): 521–41.

Colley, H. (2003b) *Mentoring for Social Inclusion: A Critical Approach to Nurturing Relationships*. London: RoutledgeFalmer.

Collins, E.G.C. (ed.) (1978) 'Everyone who makes it has a mentor: Interviews with F.J. Lunding, G.L. Clements, D.S. Perkins', *Harvard Business Review*, 56(4): 89–101.

Cooke, R.A. (1987) *The Organizational Culture Inventory*. Plymouth, MI: Human Synergistics, Inc.

Corrie, S. (2010) *The Art of Inspired Living: Coach Yourself with Positive Psychology*. London: Karnac.

Corrie, S. and Lane, D.A. (2010) *Constructing Stories, Telling Tales: A Guide to Formulation in Applied Psychology*. London: Karnac.

Corrie, S. and Lane, D.A. (2015) *CBT Supervision*. London: Sage.

Cox, E., Bachkirova, T. and Clutterbuck, D. (eds) (2010) *The Complete Handbook of Coaching*. London: Sage.

Cox, E., Bachkirova, T. and Clutterbuck, D. (eds) (2014) *The Complete Handbook of Coaching* (2nd edn). London: Sage.

Crotty, M. (1998) *The Foundation of Social Research: Meaning and Perspectives in the Research Process*. London: Sage.

Cullen, E. (1992) 'A vital way to manage change', *Education*, November 13: 3–17.

D'Abate, C.P., Eddy, E.R. and Tannebaum, S.I. (2003) 'What's in a name? A literature-based approach to understanding mentoring, coaching and other constructs that describe development interactions', *Human Resource Development Review*, 2(4): 360–84.

Dalal, F. (2002) *Race, Colour and the Process of Racialization*. London: Routledge.

Daloz, L.A. (1999) *Mentor: Guiding the Journey of Adult Learners*. San Francisco, CA: Jossey-Bass.

Darwin, A. (2000) 'Critical reflections on mentoring in work settings', *Adult Education Quarterly*, 50(3): 197–211.

Darwin, J. (2010) 'Kuhn vs Popper vs. Lakatos vs. Feyerabend: Contested terrain or fruitful collaboration?'. Unpublished Course Notes for the MA in Research Methods, Sheffield Business School, Sheffield Hallam University.

David, S., Clutterbuck, D. and Megginson, D. (2013) *Beyond Goals: Effective Strategies for Coaching and Mentoring*. Farnham: Gower Publishing Ltd.

Dean, M.L. and Meyer, A.A. (2002) 'Executive coaching: In search of a model', *Journal of Leadership Education*, 1: 1–15.

de Bono, E. (2006) *De Bono's Thinking Course: Powerful Tools to Transform Your Thinking*. Harlow: BBC Active, Pearson Education Group.

de Haan, E. (2008) *Relational Coaching: Journeys towards Mastering One-to-One Learning*. Chichester: John Wiley.

de Haan, E. and Carroll, M. (2014) 'Moral lessons', *Coaching at Work*, 9(1): 39–41.

de la Mothe-Fénelon, F. de S. (1808) *The Adventures of Telemachus*, Vols 1 and 2, (trans. J. Hawkesworth). London: Union Printing Office.

De Meuse, K., Dai, G. and Lee, R. (2009) 'Does executive coaching work: A meta-analysis study', *Coaching: An International Journal of Theory, Practice and Research*, 2(2): 117–34.

Dembkowski, S. and Eldrige, F. (2003) 'Beyond GROW: A new coaching model', *International Journal of Mentoring and Coaching*, 1(1). Available at: www.emccouncil.org/uk/journal.htm (accessed 9 October 2015).

Department for Education and Science (DfES) (1986) *Working Together: Education and Training*. Cmnd 9823. London: Her Majesty's Stationery Office (HMSO).

Dewey, J. (1958) *Experience and Nature*. New York: Dover Publications.

Ditzler, J. (1994) *Your Best Year Yet: Ten Questions that Will Change Your Life Forever*. New York: Warner.

Doehrman, M. (1976) 'Parallel processes in supervision and psychotherapy', *Bulletin of the Menninger Clinic*, 40(3): 1–104.

Dorner, H. and Karpati, A. (2010) 'Mentoring for innovation: Key factors affecting participant satisfaction in the process of collaborative knowledge construction in teacher training', *Journal of Asynchronous Learning Networks*, 14(3): 63–77.

Down, M. and Lane, D.A. (2015) 'Leadership for resilient organisations: The changing context of organisational resilience and leadership', in P. Grant, U. Afridi, J. Sternemann and E. Wilson (eds), *Business Psychology in Action: Creating Flourishing Organisations Through Evidence-based and Emerging Practices*. Kibworth Beauchamp: Matador.

Downey, M. (2003) *Effective Coaching: Lessons from the Coach's Coach* (2nd edn). Mason, OH: Texere.

Drake, D.B. (2007) 'The art of thinking narratively: Implications for coaching psychology, and practice', *Australian Psychologist*, 42(4): 283–94.

Drake, D.B. (2008) 'Finding our way home: Coaching's search for identity in a new era', *Coaching: An International Journal of Theory, Research and Practice*, 1(1): 15–26.

Drake, D.B. (2010) 'What story are you in? Four elements of a narrative approach to formulation in coaching', in S. Corrie and D.A. Lane, *Constructing Stories, Telling Tales: A Guide to Formulation in Applied Psychology*. London: Karnac, pp. 239–58.

Drake, D.B. (2014) 'Narrative coaching', in E. Cox, T. Bachkirova and D. Clutterbuck (eds), *The Complete Handbook of Coaching* (2nd edn). London: Sage, pp. 117–30.

Dublin Declaration on Coaching (2008) Available at: www.pdf.net/Files/Dublin%20 Declaration%20on%20Coaching.pdf (accessed 18 November 2013).

Dudley, R. and Kuyken, W. (2014) 'Case formulation in cognitive behavioural therapy: A principle-driven approach', in L. Johnstone and R. Dallos (eds), *Formulation in Psychology and Psychotherapy: Making Sense of Peoples Problems*. Hove: Routledge, pp. 18–44.

Duncan, B. (2002) 'The founder of common factors: A conversation with Saul Rosenzweig', *Journal of Psychotherapy Integration*, 12(1): 10–31.

Dunne, J. (1993) *Back to the Rough Ground: 'Phronesis' and 'Techne' in Modern Philosophy in Aristotle*. Paris: University of Notre Dame Press.

Durrant, D. (2014) *Final Evaluation Report, Creative Economy Coaching Programme*. Available at: www.newleaf.uk.com/wp-content/uploads/Creative-Economy-Coaching-Evaluation-Report-2014.pdf (accessed 9 October 2015).

Dutton, J.E. and Ragins, B.R. (2007) *Exploring Positive Relationships at Work*. Mahwah, NJ: Lawrence Erlbaum Associates.

Eby, L., Rhodes, J.E. and Allen, T.A. (2007) 'Definition and evolution of mentoring', in T.D. Allen and L.T. Eby (eds), *The Blackwell Handbook of Mentoring*. Malden, MA: Blackwell Publishing, pp. 7–20.

Ecclestone, K. (1997) 'Energising or enervating: Implications of National Vocational Qualifications in professional development', *Journal of Vocational Education and Training*, 49(1): 65–79.

Edwards, R. and Usher, R. (2000) 'Research on work, research at work: Postmodern perspectives', in J. Garrick and C. Rhodes (eds), *Research and Knowledge at Work: Perspectives, Case-Studies and Innovative Strategies*. London: Routledge, pp. 32–50.

Egan, G. (1975) *Skilled Helper: Model, Skills, and Methods for Effective Helping*. Belmont, CA: Brooks/Cole Publishing.

Egan, T. and Hamlin, R.G. (2014) 'Coaching, HRD, and relational richness: Putting the pieces together', *Advances in Developing Human Resources*, 16(2): 242–57.

Eggers, J.H. and Clark, D. (2000) 'Executive coaching that wins', *Ivey Business Journal*, 65(1): 66–70.

Ehrlich, P. (1994) 'Uncertainty and insurance', in R. Samuels and D.K. Prasad (eds), *Global Warming and the Built Environment*. London: Spon, pp. xv–xviii.

Ellis, P. (1992) 'Saying it all in standards', *Education and Training Technology International*, 29(3): 198–205.

EMCC (2015) Competence Framework Glossary, September. Available at: www.emccouncil.org/webimages/EU/EIA/emcc-competence-framework-glossary.pdf (accessed 5 December 2015).

Emener, W.G. and Cottone, R.R. (1989) 'Professionalisation, deprofessionalisation, and reprofessionalisation of rehabilitation counseling according to criteria of professions', *Journal of Counseling and Development*, 67(10): 576–81.

Erdem, F. and Aytemur, J.O. (2008) 'Mentoring – A relationship based on trust: Qualitative research', *Public Personnel Management*, 37(1): 55–65.

Ericsson, K.A. (2006) 'An introduction to the *Cambridge Handbook of Expertise and Expert Performance*: Its development, organization and content', in K.A. Ericsson, N. Charness, P.J Feltovich and R.R. Hoffman (eds), *The Cambridge Handbook of Expertise and Expert Performance*. New York: Cambridge University Press.

Ericsson, K.A., Charness, N., Feltovich, P.J. and Hoffman, R.R. (2006) *The Cambridge Handbook of Expertise and Expert Performance*. New York: Cambridge University Press.

Ericsson, K.A., Prietula, M.J. and Cokely, E. (2007) 'The making of an expert', *Harvard Business Review*, July–August, 85(7–8): 114–21.

Erikson, E. (1978) *Childhood and Society*. Harmondsworth: Penguin.

Etzioni, A. (ed.) (1969) *The Semi-Professions and their Organizations*. New York: Free Press.

Fairclough, N. (1992) *Language and Power*. London: Longman.

Feldman, D.C. and Lankau, M.J. (2005) 'Executive coaching: A review and agenda for future research', *Journal of Management*, 31(6): 829–48.

Fernando, S. (2010) *Mental Health, Race and Culture*. London: Routledge.

Filipczak, B. (1998) 'The executive coach: Helper or healer?', *Training Magazine*, 35(3): 30–6.

Fincham, R. and Clark, T. (2009) 'Introduction: Can we bridge the rigour-relevance gap?', *Journal of Management Studies*, 46(3): 510–15.

Forsyth, D.R. (2013) *Group Dynamics* (5th edn). Wadsworth, OH: Cengage Learning.

Francis, H., Reddington, M. and Amati, C. (2009) 'Research consultancy and HRM transformation in action', Paper presented at Knowledge into Practice Conference, Chartered Institute of Personnel and Development (CIPD), November, Edinburgh Napier University, Edinburgh.

Freedman, M. (1999) *The Kindness of Strangers: Adult Mentors, Urban Youth and the New Voluntarism*. Cambridge: Cambridge University Press.

Freire, P. (1972a) *Cultural Action for Freedom*. Harmondsworth: Penguin.

Freire, P. (1972b) *The Pedagogy of the Oppressed*. Harmondsworth: Penguin.

French, Jr, J.R.P. and Raven, B. (1962) 'The bases of social power', in C. Dorwin (ed.), *Group Dynamics: Research and Theory*. Evanston, IL: Peterson, pp. 607–23.

Gabriel, Y. (2004) *Myths, Stories and Organizations: Premodern Narratives for Our Times*. Oxford: Oxford University Press.

Gallwey, T. (1974) *The Inner Game of Tennis*. London: Jonathan Cape.

Garmezy, N. (1982) 'Foreword', in E.E. Werner and R.S. Smith, *Vulnerable but Invincible: A Study of Resilient Children*. New York: McGraw-Hill, pp. xiii–xix.

Garvey, B. (1994) 'A dose of mentoring', *Education and Training*, 36(4): 18–26.

Garvey, B. (1995) 'Healthy signs for mentoring', *Education and Training*, 37(5): 12–19.

Garvey, B. (2006a) 'A case of culture: A mentoring case study based on discussions with the UK Training and Development Manager, Engineering Co', in D. Megginson, D. Clutterbuck, B. Garvey, P. Stokes and R. Garrett-Harris (eds), *Mentoring in Action: A Practical Guide* (2nd edn). London: Kogan Page, pp. 124–33.

Garvey, B. (2006b) 'Let me tell you a story', *International Journal of Mentoring and Coaching*, 4(1). Available at: www.emccouncil.org/uk/journal.htm (accessed 9 October 2015).

Garvey, B. (2011) *A Very Short, Slightly Interesting and Reasonably Cheap Book on Coaching and Mentoring*. London: Sage.

Garvey, B. (2012) 'Mentoring for leadership development: A case study of executive mentoring during the banking crisis', *International Journal of Mentoring and Coaching*, 10(1): 56–76. Available at: www.emccouncil.org/uk/journal.htm (accessed 9 October 2015).

Garvey, B. (2013) 'Ethical frameworks: If only life were that simple', *Coaching at Work*, 8(2): 8–9.

Garvey, B. (2014) 'Neofeudalism and surveillance in coaching supervision and mentoring?', *e-Organisations & People*, 21(4): 41–7.

Garvey, B. and Alred. G. (2000) 'Educating mentors', *Mentoring and Tutoring*, 8(2): 113–26.

Garvey, B. and Garrett-Harris, R. (2005) *The Benefits of Mentoring: A Literature Review*. Hallam University, Sheffield, Report for East Mentors Forum. Sheffield: Mentoring and Coaching Research Unit.

Garvey, B. and Langridge, K. (2006) *The Pupil Mentoring Pocketbook*. Alresford: Teachers' Pocketbooks.

Garvey, B. and Westlander, G. (2012) 'Training mentors: Behaviours which bring about positive outcomes for mentoring', in J. Passmore, D. Peterson and T. Freire (eds), *Wiley-Blackwell Handbook of the Psychology of Coaching and Mentoring*. London: Wiley-Blackwell, pp. 243–65.

Garvey, B. and Williamson, B. (2002) *Beyond Knowledge Management: Dialogue, Creativity and the Corporate Curriculum*. Harlow: Pearson Education.

Garvey, B., Stokes, P. and Megginson, D. (2009) *Coaching and Mentoring: Theory and Practice*. London: Sage.

Garvey, B., Stokes, P. and Megginson, D. (2014) *Coaching and Mentoring: Theory and Practice* (2nd edn). London: Sage.

Gergen, K.J. (2001) 'Relational process for ethical outcomes', *Journal of Systemic Therapies*, 20(4): 7–10.

Gergen, K.J. and Gergen, M.M. (1988) 'Narrative and the self as relationship', in L. Berkowitz (ed.), *Advances in Experimental Social Psychology*, Vol. 21. New York: Academic Press, pp. 17–56.

Gergen, K.J. and Gergen, M. (2004) *Social Construction: Entering the Dialogue*. Chagrin Falls, OH: Taos Institute.

Gibb, S. and Megginson, D. (1993) 'Inside corporate mentoring schemes: A new agenda of concerns', *Personnel Review*, 22(1): 40–54.

Gibbons, M.L., Limoges, C., Nowotney, S., Schwartman, S., Scott, P. and Trow, M. (1994) *The New Production of Knowledge: The Dynamics of Science and Research in Contemporary Societies*. London: Sage.

Giebelhaus, C.R. and Bowman, C.L. (2002) 'Teaching mentors: Is it worth the effort?', *Journal of Educational Research*, 95(4): 246–54.

Giglio, L., Diamante, T. and Urban, J.M. (1998) 'Coaching a leader: Leveraging change at the top', *Journal of Management Development*, 17(2): 93–105.

Gillis, S., Howie, G. and Munford, R. (2007) *Third Wave Feminism: A Critical Exploration* (2nd edn). London: Palgrave Macmillan.

Global Convention on Coaching (GCC) (2008) *The Dublin Declaration on Coaching*. Available at: http://gccweb.ning.com/forum/topics/2328492:Topic:47 (accessed 20 March 2015).

Gold, J., Thorpe, R. and Mumford, A. (2010) *Leadership and Management Development* (5th edn). Wimbledon: Chartered Institute of Personnel and Development (CIPD).

Goldman, L. (1984) 'Warning: The Socratic Method can be dangerous', *Educational Leadership*, 42(1): 57–62.

Goldsmith, M. (2014) *Coaching for Behavioral Change*. Available at: www.marshall-goldsmithlibrary.com/html/marshall/resources.html (accessed 14 October 2015).

Goldsmith, M., Lyons, L. and Freas, A. (eds) (2000) *Coaching for Leadership*. San Francisco, CA: JosseyBass/Pfeiffer.

Goldstein, I.L. and Ford, J.K. (2002) *Training in Organizations: Needs Assessment, Development and Evaluation* (4th edn). Belmont, CA: Wadsworth Thomson Learning.

Goode, W.J. (1960) 'Encroachment, charlatanism and the emerging profession: Psychology, sociology and medicine', *American Sociological Review*, 25: 902–14.

Goode, W.J. (1969) 'The theoretical limits of professionalization', in A. Etzioni (ed.), *The Semi-Professions and their Organizations*. New York: Free Press, pp. 266–313.

Gopee, N. (2011) *Mentoring and Supervision in Healthcare*. London: Sage.

Gould, J. (1981) *The Mismeasure of Man*. Harmondsworth: Penguin.

Grant, A.M. (2005) 'What is evidence-based executive, workplace and life coaching?', in M. Cavanagh, A.M. Grant and T. Kemp (eds), *Evidence-Based Coaching: Theory, Research and Practice from the Behavioural Sciences* Bowen Hills Old: Australian Academic Press, pp. 1–12.

Grant, A.M. (2011) *Workplace, Executive and Life Coaching: An Annotated Bibliography from the Behavioural Science and Business Literature*. Sydney: Coaching Psychology Unit, University of Sydney. Available at: www.instituteofcoaching.org/images/pdfs/CoachingResearchStudiesList.pdf (accessed 9 September 2015).

Grant, A.M. (2012a) 'Australian coaches views on coaching supervision: A study with implications for Australian coach education, training and practice', *International Journal of Evidence-Based Coaching and Mentoring*, 10(2): 17–33.

Grant, A.M. (2012b) 'ROI is a poor measure of coaching success: Towards a more holistic approach using a well-being and engagement framework', *Coaching: An International Journal of Theory, Research and Practice*, 5(2): 74–85.

Grant, A. and Cavanagh, M. (2004) 'Toward a profession of coaching: Sixty-five years of progress and challenges for the future', *International Journal of Evidence Based Coaching and Mentoring*, 2(1): 1–16.

Grant, A. and O'Hara, B. (2006) *The Self-Presentation of Commercial Australian Life Coaching Schools: Cause for Concern?* Sydbet, NSW: Coaching Psychology Unit, School of Psychology, University of Sydney.

Grant, A., Townend, M., Mills, J. and Cockx, A. (2008) *Assessment and Case Formulation in Cognitive Behavioural Therapy*. London: Sage.

Grant, G. (1979) *On Competence: A Critical Analysis of Competence-Based Reforms in Higher Education*. San Francisco, CA: Jossey-Bass.

Grantham Journal (1885) 'Grantham Football Club', *Grantham Journal*, 28 March, p. 8.

Gray, D.E. (2004) 'Principles and processes in coaching evaluation', *International Journal of Mentoring and Coaching*, 2(2). Available at: www.emccouncil.org/uk/journal.htm (accessed 12 October 2015).

Gray. D.E. (2007) 'Facilitating management learning: Developing critical reflection through reflective tools', *Management Learning*, 38(5): 495–513.

Gray, D.E. (2010) *Business Coaching for Managers and Organizations: Working with Coaches that Make the Difference*. Amherst, MA: Human Resource Development HRD Press.

Gray, D.E. (2011) 'Journeys towards the professionalisation of coaching: Dilemmas, dialogues and decisions along the global pathway', *Coaching: An International Journal of Theory, Research and Practice*, 4(1): 4–19.

Gray, D.E. (2014) *Doing Research in the Real World* (3rd edn). London: Sage.

Gray, D.E. and Jackson, P. (2012) 'Coaching supervision in the historical context of psychotherapeutic and counselling models: A meta-model', in T. Bachkirova, P. Jackson and D. Clutterbuck, *Coaching and Mentoring Supervision*. Maidenhead: Oxford University Press McGraw-Hill Education.

Green, L.S., Oades, L.G. and Grant, A.M. (2006) 'Cognitive-behavioural, solution-focussed life coaching: Enhancing goal-striving, well-being, and hope', *Journal of Positive Psychology*, 1(3): 142–9.

Greene, J. and Grant, A.M. (2006) *Solution Focused Coaching: Managing People in a Complex World*. Available at: ftp://89-168-250-248.dynamic.dsl.as9105.com/public/install/pdf/Solution-focused%20coaching.pdf (accessed 14 October 2015).

Grey, C. (2009) *A Very Short, Fairly Interesting and Reasonably Cheap Book about Studying Organisations*. London: Sage.

Griffith, C.R. (1926) *Psychology of Coaching: A Study of Coaching Methods from the Point of View of Psychology*. New York: Charles Scribner's Sons.

Grossman, J.B. and Tierney, J.P. (1998) 'Does mentoring work? An impact study of the Big Brothers Big Sisters program', *Public/Private Ventures Evaluation Review*, 22(3): 403–26.

Grugulis, I. (2000) 'The Management NVQ: A critique of the myth of relevance', *Journal of Vocational Education and Training*, 52(1): 79–99.

Habermas, J. (1974) *Theory and Practice* (first published in 1971 as *Theorie und Praxis*). London: Heinemann.

Habermas, J. (1989) *The Theory of Communicative Competence: The Critique of Functionalist Reason*, Vol. 2. Cambridge: Polity.

Hall, R. (1994) 'A framework for identifying the intangible sources of sustainable competitive advantage', *Strategic Management Journal*, 14(8): 607–18.

Hamel, G. and Prahalad, C.K. (1989) 'Strategic intent', *Harvard Business Review*, 67(3): 1–14.

Hamel, G. and Prahalad, C.K. (1991) 'Corporate imagination and expeditionary marketing', *Harvard Business Review*, 69(4): 81–92.

Hamlin, R.G., Ellinger, A.D. and Beattie, R.S. (2008) 'The emergent "coaching industry": A wake-up call for HRD professionals', *Human Resource Development International*, 11(3): 287–305.

Handy, C.B. (1976) *Understanding Organizations*. London: Oxford University Press.

Handy, C. (1990) *The Age of Unreason*. Reading: Arrow Books.

Hardman, D. (2009) *Judgment and Decision Making: Psychological Perspectives*. Oxford: BPS Blackwell.

Harper, D. and Spellman, D. (2014) 'Formulation and narrative therapy: Telling a different story', in L. Johnstone and R. Dallos (eds), *Formulation in Psychology and Psychotherapy: Making Sense of People's Problems* (2nd edn). Hove: Routledge, pp. 96–120.

Harris, P.R. (2004) 'European leadership in cultural synergy', *European Business Review*, 16(4): 358–80.

Hart, V., Blattner, J. and Leipsic, S. (2007) 'Coaching versus therapy: A perspective', in R.R. Kilburg and R.C. Diedrich (eds), *The Wisdom of Coaching: Essential Papers in Consulting Psychology for a World of Change*. Washington, DC: American Psychological Association, pp. 267–74.

Hart, W. (2005) 'Getting culture: Imbuing your organization with coaching behavior', *Leadership in Action*, 25(4): 7–10.

Hawkins, P. (2011a) *Leadership Team Coaching: Developing Collective Transformational Leadership*. London: Kogan Page.

Hawkins, P. (2011b) 'Systemic approaches to supervision', in T. Bachkirova, P. Jackson and D. Clutterbuck (eds), *Coaching and Mentoring Supervision: Theory and Practice*. Maidenhead: Oxford University Press, pp. 167–81.

Hawkins, P. (2012) *Creating a Coaching Culture*. Maidenhead: Open University Press.

Hawkins, P. and Schwenk, G. (2006) 'Coaching supervision', Paper prepared for the Chartered Institute of Personnel and Development (CIPD) Coaching Conference, London.

Hawkins, P. and Schwenk, G. (2011) 'The seven-eyed model of coaching supervision', in T. Bachkirova, P. Jackson and D. Clutterbuck (eds), *Coaching and Mentoring Supervision: Theory and Practice*. Maidenhead: Oxford University Press, pp. 28–40.

Hawkins, D. and Shohet, R. (2006) *Supervision in the Helping Professions* (3rd edn). Maidenhead: Open University Press.

Hay, J. (1995) *Transformational Mentoring*. London: Sherwood Publishing.

Hayes, W.A. (1991) 'Radical Black psychology', in R.L. Jones (ed.), *Black Psychology* (3rd edn). New York: Harper Row.

Health and Safety Executive (no date) *Tackling Stress: The Management Standard Approach*. Available at: www.hse.gov.uk/pubns/indg406 pdf (accessed 1 February 2014).

Heid, L. (1997) 'Supervisor development across the professional lifespan', *The Clinical Supervisor*, 16: 139–52.

Her Majesty's Stationery Office (HMSO) (1995) *White Paper: Competitiveness: Forging Ahead*, Cm. 2867. London: HMSO.

Heron, J. (1999) *The Complete Facilitator's Handbook*. London: Kogan Page.

Hersted, L. and Gergen, K.J. (2012) *Relational Leading: Practices for Dialogically Based Collaboration*. Chagrin Falls, OH: Taos Institute.

Hillage, J. and Moralee, J. (1996) *The Return on Investors*. Brighton: Institute for Employment Studies, Report 314.

Hilton, S.R. and Slotnick, H.B. (2005) 'Proto-professionalism: How professionalisation occurs across the continuum of medical education', *Medical Education*, 39(1): 58–65.

Hobson, A.J. (2012) 'Fostering face-to-face mentoring and coaching', in S.J. Fletcher and C.A. Mullen (eds), *The SAGE Handbook of Mentoring and Coaching in Eduction*. London: Sage, pp. 59–73.

Hodgkinson, G.P. and Rousseau, D.M. (2009) 'Bridging the research-relevance gap in management research: It's already happening!', *Journal of Management Studies*, 46(3): 534–46.

Hofstede, G. (2001) *Culture's Consequences: Comparing Values, Behaviors, Institutions and Organizations Across Nations* (2nd edn). Thousand Oaks, CA: Sage.

Holloway, E.L. (1987) 'Developmental models of supervision: Is it development?', *Professional Psychology: Research and Practice*, 18(3): 209–16.

Holloway, E.L. and Johnston, R. (1985) 'Group supervision: Widely practiced but poorly understood', *Counselor Education and Supervision*, 24(4): 332–40.

Honoria (1793) *The Female Mentor or Select Conversations*, Vols 1 & 2. London: T. Cadell.

Honoria (1796) *The Female Mentor or Select Conversations*, Vol. 3. London: T. Cadell.

Hook, D. (2011) *A Critical Psychology of the Post-Colonial: The Mind of Apartheid*. London: Routledge.

Hope, S. (2013) 'Eye on the prize', *Coaching at Work*, 9(1): 21.

House, R. and Loewenthal, D. (eds) (2008) *Against and for CBT: Towards a Constructive Dialogue?* Ross-on-Wye: PCCS Books.

HSE (2015) Work Related Stress, *Anxiety and Depression Statistics in Great Britain 2015*. Available at: www.hse.gov.uk/statistics/causdis/stress/stress.pdf (accessed 6 December 2015).

Hughes. J. (2003) 'A reflection on the art and practice of mentorship', *The Journal of Wealth Management*, 5(4): 8–11.

Humphrey, S. and Shepherd, L. (2012) 'Supervised behaviour', *Coaching at Work*, 7(6): 48–50.

Hunt, E.B. (1995) *Will We Be Smart Enough?* New York: Russell Sage Foundation.

Hunt, E. (2006) 'Expertise, talent and social Encouragement', in K.A. Ericsson, N. Charness, P.J. Feltovich and R.R. Hoffman (eds), *The Cambridge Handbook of Expertise and Expert Performance*. New York: Cambridge University Press.

Hunt, J.M. and Weintraub, J.R. (2002) *The Coaching Manager: Developing Top Talent in Business*. London: Sage.

Hutton, W. (2011) 'Good capitalism does exist. And it's more crucial now than ever', *The Observer*, 2 October. Available at: www.theguardian.com/commentisfree/2011/oct/02/will-hutton-ed-miliband-new-capitalism (accessed 10 October 2015).

International Union of Psychological Science (IUPS) (2008) *Universal Declaration of Ethical Principles for Psychologists*. Available at: www.iupsys.net/about/governance/universal-declaration-of-ethical-principles-for-psychologists.html (accessed 20 October 2015).

Jackson, C.G. (1977) 'The emergence of a black perspective in counselling', *Journal of Negro Education*, 46: 230–53.

Jackson, N. and Carter, P. (2000) *Rethinking Organizational Behaviour*. Harlow: Pearson Education.

Jarvis, A. (1997) *Samuel Smiles and the Construction of Victorian Values*. London: Sutton Publishing.

Jarvis, J. (2004) *Coaching and Buying Coaching Services*. London: Chartered Institute of Personnel and Development (CIPD).

Jarvis, J., Lane, D. and Fillery-Travis, A. (2006) *The Case for Coaching: Making Evidence-Based Decisions on Coaching*. London: Chartered Institute of Personnel and Development (CIPD).

Jarvis, P. (1987) *Adult Learning in the Social Context*. London: Croom Helm.

Jarvis, P. (1992) *Paradoxes of Learning: On Becoming an Individual in Society*. San Francisco, CA: Jossey-Bass Higher Education Series.

Jarvis, P. (1995) *Adult and Continuing Education: Theory and Practice*. London: Routledge.

Johnson, H.T. and Bröms, A. (2000) *Profit Beyond Measure*. New York: Free Press.

Johnson, P. and Duberley, J. (2000) *Understanding Management Research*. London: Sage.

Johnson, S.K., Geroy, G.D. and Orlando, V.G. (1999) 'The mentoring model theory: Dimensions in mentoring protocols', *Career Development International*, 4(7): 384–91.

Jones, R.A., Rafferty, A.E. and Griffin, M.A. (2006) 'The executive coaching trend: Towards more flexible executives', *Leadership and Organization Development Journal*, 27(7): 583–95.

Jones, R.L. and Wallace, M. (2005) 'Another bad day at the training ground: Coping with the ambiguity in the coaching context', *Sport, Education and Society*, 10(1): 119–34.

Joo, B. (2005) 'Executive coaching: A conceptual framework from an integrative review of practice and research', *Human Resource Development Review*, 4(4): 462–88.

Joseph, S. (2012) *What Doesn't Kill Us: The New Psychology of Post-Traumatic Growth*. London: Piatkus Little Brown.

Jung, C.J. (1958) *Psyche and Symbol*. New York: Doubleday.

Kagan, C.M. and Duggan, K. (2011) 'Creating community cohesion: The power of using innovative methods to facilitate engagement and genuine partnership', *Social Policy and Society*, 10(3): 393–404.

Kagan, C.M., Burton, M., Duckett, P.S., Lawthom, R. and Siddiquee, A. (2011) *Critical Community Psychology*. Oxford: Wiley-Blackwell.

Kagan, S. (1994) *Cooperative Learning*. San Juan Capistrano, CA: Kagan Cooperative Learning. Available at: www.KaganCoopLearn.com (accessed 9 September 2015).

Kahane, A. (2004) *Solving Tough Problems: An Open Way of Talking, Listening, and Creating New Realities*. San Francisco, CA: Berrett-Koehler.

Kahn, M.S. (2014) *Coaching on the Axis: Working with Complexity in Business and Executive Coaching*. London: Karnac Books.

Kahneman, D.L. (2011) *Thinking Fast and Slow*. New York: Macmillian.

Kaku, M. (2014) *The Future of the Mind*. London: Allen Lane.

Kampa-Kokesch, S. and Anderson, M.Z. (2001) 'Executive coaching: A comprehensive review of the literature', *Consulting Psychology Journal: Practice and Research*, 53(4): 205–28.

Kauffman, C. (2008) *100 Coaching Research Proposal Abstracts*. Available at: https://www.nobco.nl/files/onderzoeken/2008_ICRF_Research_Proposals-2nd_Draft.pdf (accessed 21 October 2015).

Kaufman, R. and Keller, J.M. (1994) 'Levels of evaluation: Beyond Kirkpatrick', *Human Resource Development Quarterly*, 5(4): 371–80.

Kayes, D.C. (2006) *Destructive Goal Pursuit: The Mount Everest Disaster*. Basingstoke: Palgrave Macmillan.

Keise, C., Kelly, E., King, O. and Lane, D.A. (1993) 'Culture and child services', in A. Miller and D.A. Lane (eds), *Silent Conspiracies: Scandals and Successes in the Care and Education of Vulnerable Young People*. Stoke on Trent: Trentham Books, pp. 189–214.

Kelly, S. (2006) 'Cognitive-behavioral therapy with African Americans', in P.A. Hays and G.Y. Iwamasa (eds), *Culturally Responsive Cognitive-Behavioral Therapy: Assessment, Practice, and Supervision*. Washington, DC: American Psychological Association, pp. 97–116.

Kerr, R., McHugh, M. and McCrory, M. (2009) 'HSE Management Standards and stress-related outcomes', *Occupational Medicine*, 59: 574–9. Published online 7 October, doi:10.1093/occmed/kqp146.

Kessels, J.W.M. (1996) *Corporate Education: The Ambivalent Perspective of Knowledge Productivity*. Leiden: Centre for Education and Instruction, Leiden University.

Kieser, A. and Leiner, L. (2009) 'Why the rigour-relevance gap in management research is unbridgeable', *Journal of Management Studies*, 46(3): 516–33.

Kilburg R. (2004a) 'Trudging toward Dodoville: Conceptual approaches and case studies in executive coaching', *Consulting Psychology Journal: Practice and Research*, 56(4): 203–13.

Kilburg, R. (2004b) 'When shadows fall: Using psychodynamic approaches in executive coaching', *Consulting Psychology Journal*, 56(4): 203–13.

Kilberg, R. (2015) 'Personal communication', Paper presented at Excellence Across Borders, Society of Consulting Psychology Mid-Winter Conference, San Diego, CA, 3–5 February.

Kilburg, R. and Diedrich, R.C. (2007) 'Further consideration of executive coaching as an emerging competency', in R. Kilburg and R.C. Diedrich (eds), *The Wisdom of Coaching: Essential Papers in Consulting Psychology for a World of Change*. Washington, DC: American Psychological Association, pp. 267–74.

Kimball, B.A. (1986) *Orators and Philosophers: A History of the Idea of Liberal Education*. New York: Teachers College Press.

Kirkpatrick, D.L. (1959) 'Techniques for evaluating training programmes', *Journal of the American Society of Training Directors*, 13(3–9): 21–6.

Kirkpatrick, D.L. (2005) *Evaluting Training Programs: The Four Levels* (3rd edn). Williston, VT: Berrett-Koehler Publishers, Inc.

Kline, N. (2003) *Time to Think: Listening to Ignite the Human Mind*. London: Cassell.

Knowles, M. (1984) *Andragogy in Action*. San Francisco, CA: Jossey-Bass.

Kolb, D.A. (1984) *Experiential Learning*. Englewood Cliffs, NJ: Prentice Hall.

Kolb, D.A. (2015) *Experiential Learning: Experience as the Source of Learning and Development* (2nd edn). Upper Saddle River, NJ: Pearson Education.

Kolb. D.A. and Fry, R. (1975) 'Toward an applied theory of experiential learning', in C.L. Cooper (ed.), *Theories of Group Processes*. London: John Wiley, pp. 33–58.

Krackauer, J. (1998) *Into Thin Air: A Personal Account of the Mt. Everest Disaster*. New York: Anchor Books.

Kram, K.E. (1983) 'Phases of the mentor relationship', *Academy of Management Journal*, 26(4): 608–25.

Kram, K.E. (1985) *Mentoring at Work: Developmental Relationships in Organizational Life*. Glenview, IL: Scott Foresman.

Kram, K.E. and Chandler, D.E. (2005) 'Applying an adult development perspective to developmental networks', *Career Development International*, 10 (6–7): 548–66.

Krasner, L. and Ullmann, L.P. (1973) *Behavior Influence and Personality: The Social Matrix of Human Action*. New York: Holt, Rinehart and Winston.

Krazmien, M. and Berger, F. (1997) 'The coaching paradox', *Hospitality Management*, 16(1): 3–10.

Lakeman, R. and Glasgow, C. (2009) 'Introducing peer group clinical supervision: An Action Research Project', *International Journal of Mental Health Nursing*, 18(3): 204–10.

Laloux, F. (2014) *Reinventing Organizations: A Guide to Creating Organizations Inspired by the Next Stage of Human Consciousness.* Brussels: Nelson Parker.

Lane, D.A. (1972) 'Education in environmental health', *Community Care*, 4: 149–56.

Lane, D.A. (1990) *The Impossible Child* (2nd edn). Stoke-on-Trent: Trentham Books.

Lane, D.A. (1998) 'Context focused analysis: An experimentally derived model for working with complex problems with children, adolescents and systems', in M. Bruch and F.W. Bond (eds), *Beyond Diagnosis: Case Formulation Approaches in CBT.* Chichester: Wiley, pp. 103–40.

Lane, D.A. (2002) 'The emergent models in coaching', Paper presented at the 4th European Mentoring and Coaching Council Conference (EMCC, emccouncil.org), Cambridge, 12 November.

Lane, D.A. (2011) 'Ethics and professional standards in supervision', in T. Bachkirova, P. Jackson and D. Clutterbuck (eds), *Coaching and Mentoring Supervision Theory and Practice.* Maidenhead: OUP.

Lane, D.A. and Althaus, K. (2011) 'The development of psychotherapy as a specialism for psychologists', *European Psychologist*, 16(2): 132–40.

Lane, D.A. and Corrie, S. (2006) *The Modern Scientist-Practitioner: A Guide to Practice in Psychology.* Hove: Routledge.

Lane, D.A. and Corrie, S. (2012) *Making Successful Decisions in Counselling and Psychotherapy: A Practical Guide.* Maidenhead: Open University Press.

Lane, D.A. and Corrie, S. (2015) 'Cognitive-behavioural formulation and the scientist-practitioner: Working with an adolescent boy', in M. Bruch (ed.), *Beyond Diagnosis: Case Formulation Approaches in Cognitive Behavioural Therapy.* Chichester: Wiley Blackwell, pp. 165–93.

Lane, D.A. and Down, M. (2010) 'The art of managing for the future: Leadership of turbulence', *Management Decision*, 48(4): 512–27.

Lane, D.A. and Malkin, J. (1994) 'Global warming and the built environment: The challenge', in R. Samuels and D.K. Prasad, *Global Warming and the Built Environment.* London: Spon, pp. xxiii–xxxvi.

Lane, D., Kahn, M.S. and Chapman, L. (2016, in press) 'Understanding adult learning as part of an approach to coaching', in S. Palmer and A. Whybrow (eds), *Handbook of Coaching Psychology: A Guide for Practitioners* (2nd edn). Hove: Routledge.

Lane, D.A., Stelter, R. and Stout Rostron, S. (2010) 'The future of coaching as a profession', in E. Cox, T. Bachkirova and D. Clutterbuck (eds), *The Complete Handbook of Coaching.* London: Sage, pp. 357–68.

Lasch, C. (1995) *The Revolt of the Elites and Betrayal of Democracy.* New York: Norton.

Lash, S. and Urry, J. (1987) *The End of Organised Capitalism.* Cambridge: Polity Press.

Lave, J. and Wenger, E. (1991) *Situated Learning: Legitimate Peripheral Participation.* Cambridge: Cambridge University Press.

Law, H. (2007) 'Narrative coaching and psychology of learning from multicultural perspectives', in S. Palmer and A. Whybrow (eds), *Handbook of Coaching Psychology: A Guide for Practitioners*. Hove: Routledge, pp. 174–92.

Lawler, E.E. (1994) 'From job-based to competency-based organizations', *Journal of Organizational Behavior*, 15(1): 3–15.

Layder, D. (1994) *Understanding Social Theory*. London: Sage.

Lee, G. (2003) *Leadership Coaching: From Personal Insight to Organizational Performance*. London: Chartered Institute of Personnel and Development (CIPD).

Lee, G. (2010) 'The psychodynamic approach to coaching', in E. Cox, T. Bachkirova and D. Clutterbuck (eds), *The Complete Handbook of Coaching*. London: Sage, pp. 23–36.

Leiper, R. (2014) 'Psychodynamic formulation: Looking beneath the surface', in L. Johnstone and R. Dallos (eds), *Formulation in Psychology and Psychotherapy: Making Sense of Peoples Problems*. Hove: Routledge, pp. 47–71.

Lesser, M.M. (1983) 'Supervision: Illusions, anxieties, and questions', *Contemporary Psychoanalysis*, 19: 120–9.

Lester, S. (1994) 'Management standards: A critical approach', *Competency*, 2(1): 28–31.

Levinson, D.J., Darrow, C.N., Klein, E.B., Levinson, M.H. and McKee, B. (1978) *The Seasons of a Man's Life*. New York: Knopf.

Lewin, K. (1951) *Field Theory in Social Science: Selected Theoretical Papers* (ed. D. Cartwright). New York: Harper & Row.

Lewis, S., Passmore, J. and Cantore, S. (2011) *Appreciative Inquiry for Change Management*. London: Kogan Page.

Likierman, A. (2009) 'Successful leadership: How would you know?' *Business Strategy Review*, 20(1): 44–9.

Lincoln, Y.S. and Guba, E.G. (1994) *Naturalistic Inquiry* (2nd edn). Newbury Park, CA: Sage.

Lindbom, D. (2007) 'A culture of coaching: The challenge of managing performance for long-term results', *Organization Development Journal*, 25(1): 101–6.

Lo, M.-C. M. (2006) 'The professions: Prodigal daughters of modernity', in J. Adams, E.S. Clemens and A.S. Orloff (eds), *Remaking Modernity: Politics, History, and Sociology*. Durham, NC: Duke University Press, pp. 381–406.

Loganbill, C., Hardy, E. and Delworth, U. (1982) 'Supervision: A conceptual model', *Counseling Psychologist*, 10(1): 3–42.

London Evening Standard (1867) 'University Boat Race', *London Evening Standard*, 14 February, p. 6.

Magnusson, K. and Osborne, J. (1990) 'The rise of competency-based education: A deconstructionist analysis', *Journal of Educational Thought*, 24(1): 5–13.

Marshall, K. (1991) 'NVQs: An assessment of the "Outcomes" approach in education and training', *Journal of Further and Higher Education*, 15(3): 56–64.

Maslow, A. (1954) *Motivation and Personality*. New York: Harper.

McAuley, M.J. (2003) 'Transference, countertransference and mentoring: The ghost in the process', *British Journal of Guidance & Counselling*, 31(1): 11–23.

McClelland, L. (2014) 'Reformulating the impact of social inequalities: Power an social justice', in L. Johnstone and R. Dallos. (eds), *Formulation in Psychology and Psychotherapy: Making Sense of People's Problems*. London: Routledge, pp. 121–44.

McDermott, I. and Jago, W. (2005) *The Coaching Bible: The Essential Handbook*. London: Piatkus Books.

Mead, G., Campbell, J. and Milan, M. (1999) 'Mentor and Athene: Supervising professional coaches and mentors', *Career Development International*, 4(5): 283–90.

Megginson, D. (2007) 'Is goal-setting really essential for coaching success?', *People Management*, October.

Megginson, D. and Boydell, T. (1979) *A Manager's Guide to Coaching*. London: Chartered Institute of Personnel and Development (CIPD).

Megginson, D., Clutterbuck, D., Garvey, B., Stokes, P. and Garrett-Harris, R. (eds) (2006) *Mentoring in Action* (2nd edn). London: Kogan Page.

Meizrow, J. (1998) *Learning as Transformation: Critical Perspectives on a Theory in Progress*. San Francisco, CA: Jossey-Bass.

Merrick, L. and Stokes, P. (2003) 'Mentor development and supervision: A passionate joint enquiry', *International Journal of Mentoring and Coaching*, 1(1). Available at: www.emccouncil.org/uk/journal.htm (accessed 9 October 2015).

Merrick, L. and Stokes, P. (2008) 'Unbreakable? Using mentoring to break the glass ceiling', *International Journal of Mentoring and Coaching*, 6(2). Available at: www.emccouncil.org/uk/journal.htm (accessed 9 October 2015).

Miller, A. and Lane, D.A. (eds) (1993) *Silent Conspiracies: Scandals and Successes in the Care and Education of Vulnerable Young People*. Stoke-on-Trent: Trentham Books.

Mitra, S. (2005) 'Self-organising systems for mass computer literacy: Findings from the "hole in the wall" experiments', *International Journal of Development Issues*, 4(1): 71–81.

Mitra, S. (2014) *TED Talks New Experiments in Self-Teaching*. Available at: www.youtube.com/watch?v=dk60sYrU2RU (accessed 20 March 2015).

Moberg, D.J. and Velasquez, M. (2004) 'The ethics of mentoring', *Business Ethics Quarterly*, 14(1): 95–102.

Mook, M.N. (2007) 'Does coaching need regulation or recognition?', Paper presented at the European Mentoring and Coaching Council Conference, Stockholm, 11–13 October.

Mooney, P. (2008) *The Dublin Declaration on Coaching, Version 1.3*. Dublin: Global Community of Coaches, Dublin. Available at: gccweb.ning.com/forum/topics/2328 492:Topic:47 (accessed 12 October 2015).

Morgan, L.M. and Davidson, M.J. (2008) 'Sexual dynamics in mentoring relationships: A critical review', *British Journal of Management*, 19(1): 120–9.

Mowbray, R. (1995) *The Case against Psychotherapy Registration: A Conservation Issue for the Human Potential Movement*. London: Trans Marginal Press.

Mowbray, R. (1997) 'Too vulnerable to choose', in R. House and N. Totton (eds), *Implausible Professions: Arguments for Pluralism and Autonomy in Psychotherapy and Counselling*. Ross-on-Wye: PCCS Books, pp. 43–54.

Mullen, E. (1994) 'Framing the mentoring relationship as an information exchange', *Human Resource Management Review*, 4(3): 257–81.

Murphy, M.J. and Wright, D.W. (2005) Supervisees' perspectives of power use in supervision, *Journal of Marital and Family Therapy*, 31: 283-295.

Murray, M. (2001) *Beyond the Myths and Magic of Mentoring: How to Facilitate an Effective Mentoring Process*. San Francisco, CA: Jossey-Bass.

Neenan, M. (2009) 'Using Socratic Questioning in coaching', *Journal of Rational-Emotive and Cognitive-Behavior Therapy*, 27(4): 249–64.

Neilson, T. and Eisenbach, R. (2003) 'Not all relationships are created equal: Critical actors of high-quality mentoring relationships', *International Journal of Mentoring and Coaching*, 1(1). Available at: www.emccouncil.org/uk/journal.htm (accessed 9 October 2015).

Nelson, M.L. and Friedlander, M.L. (2001) 'A close look at conflictual supervisory relationships: The trainee's perspective', *Journal of Counselling Psychology*, 48: 384–95.

Nielsen, A.E. and Nørreklit, H. (2009) 'A discourse analysis of the disciplinary power of management coaching', *Denmark Society and Business Review*, 4(3): 202–14.

Nietzsche, F. (1974) *The Gay Science*. London: Vintage Books.

Nonaka, I. (1991) 'The knowledge creating company', *Harvard Business Review*, 69(6): 96–104.

Olk, M. and Friedlander, M.L. (1992) 'Trainee's experiences of role conflict and role ambiguity in supervisory relationships', *Journal of Counseling Psychology*, 39: 389–97.

Orenstein, R.L. (2002) 'Executive coaching: It's not just about the executive', *Journal of Applied Behavioral Science*, 38(3): 355–74.

Orford, J. (2008) *Community Psychology: Challenges, Controversies and Emerging Consensus*. Chichester: Wiley.

Orly, M. (2008) 'Mentoring mentors as a tool for personal and professional empowerment in teacher education', *International Journal of Evidence Based Coaching and Mentoring*, 6(1): 1–18.

Owen, H. (2008) *Open Space Technology: A User's Guide* (2nd edn). San Francisco, CA: Berrett-Koehler Publishers.

Oxtoby, R. (2009) *The 'Deep Structure' Approach to Executive Coaching*. Cape Town: New Voices.

Page, S. and Wosket, V. (1994) *Supervising the Counsellor: A Cyclical Model*. London: Routledge.

Pampallis Paisley, P. (2006) Towards a Theory of Supervision for Coaching: An Integral Approach. D.Prof, Middlesex University.

Palmer, B. (2003) 'Maximizing value from executive coaching', *Strategic HR Review*, 2(6): 26–9.

Palmer, S. and Cavanagh, M. (2006) 'Coaching psychology: Its time has finally come', *International Coaching Psychology Review*, 1(1): 1–3.

Palmer, S. and Szymanska, K. (2007) 'Cognitive behavioural coaching: An integrative approach', in S. Palmer and A. Whybrow (eds), *Handbook of Coaching Psychology: A Guide for Practitioners*. Hove: Routledge, pp. 86–117.

Palmer, S. and Whybrow, A. (2006) 'The coaching psychology movement and its development within the British Psychological Society', *International Coaching Psychology Review*, 1(1): 5–10.

Palmer, S. and Whybrow, A. (2007) *Handbook of Coaching Psychology: A Guide for Practitioners*. Hove: Routledge.

Parker-Wilkins, V. (2006) 'Business impact of executive coaching: Demonstrating monetary value', *Industrial and Commercial Training*, 38(3): 122–7.

Passmore, J. (2011) 'Supervision and continuous professional development in coaching', in J. Passmore (ed.), *Supervision in Coaching*. London: Kogan Page, pp. 3–9.

Passmore, J. (2014) *Mastery in Coaching: A Complete Psychological Toolkit for Advanced Coaching*. London: Kogan Page.

Passmore, J. and Gibbes, C. (2007) 'The state of executive coaching research: What does the current literature tell us and what's next for coaching research?', *International Coaching Psychology Review*, 2(2): 116–28.

Passmore, J. and McGoldrick, S. (2009) 'Super-vision, extra-vision or blind faith? A grounded theory study of the efficacy of coaching supervision', *International Coaching Psychology Review*, 4(2): 143–59.

Passmore, J., Peterson, D. and Freire, T. (eds) (2013) *Wiley-Blackwell Handbook of the Psychology of Coaching and Mentoring*. London: Wiley-Blackwell.

Patton, M.Q. (1984) 'Data collection: Options, strategies and cautions', in L. Rutman (ed.), *Evaluation Research Methods: A Basic Guide* (2nd edn). Newbury Park, CA: Sage, pp. 39–63.

Pedler, M., Burgoyne, J. and Boydel, T. (1991) *The Learning Company: A Strategy for Sustainable Development*. London: McGraw Hill.

Pegg, M. (1999) 'The art of mentoring', *Industrial and Commercial Training*, 31(4): 136–41.

Peltier, B. (2001) *The Psychology of Executive Coaching: Theory And Application*. New York: BrunnerRoutledge.

Penna Survey (2014) *Mentoring: A Valuable Tool in Plugging the Talent Drain*, Summary Report. Available at: www.penna.com (accessed 9 October 2015).

Pennington, W. (2009) *Executive Coaching World: A Global Perspective*. London: Chi Teaching. Available at: www.executivecoachingworld.com/home.htm (accessed 12 October 2015).

Pershing, J.A. and Pershing, J.L. (2001) 'Ineffective reaction evaluation', *Human Resource Development Quarterly*, 12(1): 73–90.

Peters, J. and Carr, C. (2013) '50 tips for terrific teams'. Available at: https://inneractiveleadership.files.wordpress.com/2012/01/50-tips-summary-for-icf.pdf (accessed 9 October 2015)

Pfund, C., Pribbenow, C.M., Branchaw, J., Miller Lauffer, J. and Handelsman, J. (2006) 'The merits of training mentors', *Science*, January, 311: 473–4.

Philip, K. (2008) 'Youth mentoring: A case for treatment?', *Youth and Policy*, 99: 17–31.

Piaget, J. (1970) *Genetic Epistemology*. New York: Columbia University Press.

Porter, T.M. (1995) *Trust in Numbers*. Princeton, NJ: Princeton University Press.

Porter, N. and Vasquez, M. (1997) 'Covision: Feminist supervision, process, and collaboration' in J. Worell and N.G. Johnson (eds), *Shaping the Future of Feminist Psychology*. Washington DC: American Psychological Association, pp. 155–71.

Potrac, P., Jones, R. and Armour, K. (2002) 'It's all about getting respect: The coaching behaviours of an expert English soccer coach', *Sport, Education and Society*, 7(2): 183–202.

Prahalad, C.K. and Hamel, G. (1990) 'The core competence of the corporation', in M.H. Zack (1999) *Knowledge and Strategy*. Woburn, MA: Butterworth-Heinemann, pp. 41–61.

Prasko, J. and Vyskocilova, J. (2010) 'Countertransference during supervision in cognitive behavioral therapy', *Activitas Nervosa Superior Rediviva*, 52(4): 253–62.

PricewaterhouseCoopers (PwC) (2007) *ICF Global Coaching Study*. Lexington, KY: International Coach Federation.

PwC (2013) *ICF Organizational Coaching Study, International Coaching Federation*. Available at: http://coachfederation.org/about/landing.cfm?ItemNumber=827 (accessed 12 October 2015).

Prochaska, J.O., Di Clemente, C.C. and Norcross, J.C. (1992) 'In search of how people change', *American Psychological Association*, 47(9): 1102–14.

Proctor, B. (1986) 'Supervision: A co-operative exercise in accountability', in A. Marken and M. Payne (eds), *Enabling and Ensuring: Supervision in Practice*. Leicester: National Youth Bureau/Council for Education and Training in Youth and Community Work.

Proctor, B. (2008) *Group Supervision: A Guide to Creative Practice* (2nd edn). London: Sage.

Proudhon, P.J. (1923) *General Idea of the Revolution in the Nineteenth Century* (trans. by John Beverly Robinson). London: Freedom Press.

Ragins, B.R. (1989) 'Barriers to mentoring: The female manager's dilemma', *Human Relations*, 42(1): 1–23.

Ragins, B.R. (1994) 'Gender and mentoring: A research agenda', Paper presented at Women and Men in Organizations: Concepts and Applications: the 40th annual meeting of the Southeastern Psychological Association, New Orleans, LA, 30 March – 7 April.

Ragins, B.R. and Cotton, J.L. (1991) 'Easier said than done: Gender differences in perceived barriers to gaining a mentor', *Academy of Management Journal*, 34(4): 939–52.

Ragins, B.R. and Scandura, T.A. (1994) 'Gender differences in expected outcomes of mentoring relationships', *Academy of Management Journal*, 37(4): 957–71.

Ragins, B.R. and Scandura, T.A. (1999) 'Burden or blessing? Expected costs and benefits of being a mentor', *Journal of Organisational Behavior*, 20(4): 493–509.

Rajan, A. (1992) *A Zero Sum Game*. London: Industrial Society.

Rajan, A. and Lane, D.A. (2000) *Employability: Employers and Employees Perspectives*. London: Centre for Research in Employment and Technology in Europe (Create)

Ranson, S. (1992) 'Towards the learning society', *Educational Management and Administration*, 20(2): 68–79.

Revans, R. (1982) 'What is Action Learning?', *Journal of Management Development*, 1(3): 64–75.

Revans, R. (2011) *ABC of Action Learning*. Farnham: Gower.

Ridler & Co. (2011) *The Ridler Report: Trends in the Use of Executive Coaching*. Available at: www.ridlerandco.com/ridler-report/ (accessed 3 October 2013).

Ridler & Co. (2013) *The Ridler Report*. London: European Mentoring and Coaching Council (EMCC) and Ridler & Co. Available at: www.ridlerandco.com/ridler-report/ (accessed 3 October 2013).

Riessman, C.K. (1993) *Narrative Analysis*, Vol. 30. Newbury Park, CA: Sage.

Ringleb, A., Rock, D. and Conser, J. (2010) 'NeuroLeadership in 2010', *NeuroLeadership Journal*, (3): 1–12. Available at: www.davidrock.net/files/NeuroLeadership_in_2010.pdf (accessed 27 February 2015).

Rix, M. and Gold, J. (2000) 'With a little help from my academic friend: Mentoring change agents', *Mentoring and Tutoring*, 8(1): 47–62.

Roberts, A. (1999) *Homer's Mentor: Duties Fulfilled or Misconstrued*. Available at: http://scholar.googleusercontent.com/scholar?q=cache:VE04Pkn3sEgJ:scholar.google.com/+ROBERTS,+A.+(1999)+An+historical+account+to+consider+the+origins+of+the+term+mentor,+History+of&hl=en&as_sdt=0,5 (accessed 9 October 2015).

Roberts, V.Z. and Brunning, H. (2007) 'Psychodynamic and systems psychodynamic coaching', in S. Palmer, and A. Whybrow (eds), *Handbook of Coaching Psychology: A Guide for Practitioners*. Hove: Routledge.

Rock, D. and Page, L.J. (2009) *Coaching with the Brain in Mind*. Hoboken, NJ: Wiley.

Rock, V. (2014) *Source Book of Coaching History*. Available at: www.amazon.co.uk/Sourcebook-Coaching-History-Vikki-Brock/dp/1469986655 (accessed 9 October 2015).

Rodriguez, D., Patel, R., Bright, A., Gregory, D. and Gowing, M.K. (2002) 'Developing competency models to promote integrated human resource practices', *Human Resource Management Special Issue: Human Resources Management in the Public Sector*, 41(3): 309–24.

Rogers, C. (1961) *On Becoming a Person*. Boston, MA: Houghton Mifflin.

Rogers, C. (1969) *Freedom to Learn*. Columbus, OH: Charles E. Merrill Publishing.

Rønnestad, M.H. and Skovholt, T.M. (1993) 'Supervision of beginning and advanced graduate students of counseling and psychotherapy', *Journal of Counselling & Development*, 71(4): 396–405.

Rosinski, P. (2004) *Coaching Across Cultures*. London: Nicholas Brearley.

Ross, L.E, Doctor, F., Dimito, A., Kueli, D. and Armstrong, A.S. (2008) 'Can talking about oppression reduce depression?', *Journal of Gay and Lesbian Social Services*, 19(1): 1–15.

Rossiter, A., Walsh-Bowers, R. and Prilleltensky, I. (1996) 'Learning from broken rules: Individualism, bureaucracy, and ethics', *Ethics and Behavior*, 6(4): 307–20.

Rousseau, J.-J. (1762) *Emile:* or *on Education*, A. Bloom (1979), *Emile* (Introduction, Translation, and Notes by A. Bloom). New York: Basic Books.

Rudd, M.D. and Joiner, T. (1997) 'Countertransference and the therapeutic relationship: A cognitive perspective', *Journal of Cognitive Psychotherapy: An International Quarterly*, 11(4): 231–51.

Rudolph, H. (2003) 'Women in business consultancies: Chances or risks of professionalisation?' Paper presented at 6th European Sociological Association Conference, Research Networks 15, Sociology of Professions, Murcia, 23–26 September.

Rynes, S.L. (2007) 'Let's create a tipping point: What academics and practitioners can do, alone and together', *Academy of Management Journal*, 50(5): 1046–54.

Safran, J.D. and Muran, J.C. (2000) *Negotiating the Therapeutic Alliance: A Relational Treatment Guide*. New York: Guilford Press.

Salter, T. (2013) 'A comparison of mentor and coach approaches across disciplines'. Unpublished PhD, Coaching and Mentoring Programme, Oxford Brookes University.

Saul, J.R. (1997) *The Unconscious Civilization*. Ringwood: Penguin Books.

Savickas, M.L. (2007) 'Foreword', in T.D. Allen and L. Eby (eds), *The Blackwell Handbook of Mentoring: A Multiple Perspectives Approach*. Malden, USA: Blackwell Publishing, pp. xvii–xx.

Schein, E.H. (1972) *Professional Education: Some New Directions*. New York: McGraw-Hill.

Schein, E.H. (1997) *The Concept of Client from a Process Consultation Perspective: A Guide for Change Agents*. Available at: http://dspace.mit.edu/bitstream/handle/1721.1/2647/SWP-3946-36987393.pdf?sequence=1 (accessed 9 September 2015).

Schnell, E.R. (2005) 'A case study of executive coaching as a support mechanism during organizational growth and evolution', *Consulting Psychology Journal: Practice & Research*, 57(1): 41–56.

Schön, D.A. (1983) *The Reflective Practitioner*. New York: Basic Books.

Schön, D.A. (1987) *Educating the Reflective Practitioner: Towards a New Design for Teaching and Learning in the Profession*. San Francisco, CA: Jossey-Bass.

Schutz, A. (1945) 'On multiple realities: Philosophical and phenomenological', in J.V. Wertsch (ed.), *Culture, Communication and Cognition: Vygotskian Perspectives*. New York: Cambridge University Press, pp. 533–76.

Senge, P.M. (1990) *The Fifth Discipline: The Art & Practice of the Learning Organization*. New York: Doubleday/Currency.

Shams, M. and Lane, D.A. (2011) *Coaching in the Family-Owned Business: A Path to Growth*. London: Karnac.

Shearing, C. (2001) 'Punishment and the changing face of the governance', *Punishment & Society*, 3(2): 203–20.

Sheehy, G. (1976) *Passages: Predictable Crises of Adult Life*. New York: Ballantine Books.

Sheehy, G. (1996) *New Passages: Mapping your Life across Time*. London: Harper Collins.

Sherman, S. and Freas, A. (2004) 'The Wild West of executive coaching', *Harvard Business Review*, 82(11): 82–90.

Shirley, J.L. and Padgett, S.M. (2006) 'An analysis of the discourses of professionalism', in D. Wear and J.M. Aultman (eds), *Professionalism in Medicine: Critical Perspectives*. New York: Springer, pp. 25–42.

Shohet, R. (2012) 'Listening to resistance', in D. Owen and R. Shohet (eds), *Clinical Supervision in the Medical Profession*. Maidenhead: Open University Press, pp. 143–56.

Short, D.C., Bing, J.W. and Kehrhahn, M.T. (2003) 'Will human resource development survive?', *Human Resource Development Quarterly*, 14(3): 239–43.

Shotter, J. (1993) *Conversational Realities: An Advanced View of Various Intricacies of Social Construction in Everyday Life*. London: Sage.

Skolimowski, H. (1992) *Living Philosophy: Ecophilosophy as a Tree of Life*. London: Arkana.

Smedley, F. (1866) *Frank Farleigh: Or Scenes from the Life of a Private Pupil*. London: Virtue Brothers and Co.

Smiles, A. (1956) *Samuel Smiles and his Surroundings*. London: Robert Hale.

Smiles, S. (1897) *Self Help: With Illustrations of Conduct and Perseverance*. London: John Murray.

Smith, B. (1990) 'Mutual mentoring on projects', *Journal of Management Development*, 90(1): 51–7.

Smith, R. (1997) 'Practical judgement', The Proceedings of the First Joint Seminar on Knowledge Productivity: Concepts and Issues, Leiden University, Leiden, 20–22 November.

Smither, J.W. and Reilly, S.P. (2001) 'Coaching in organizations: A social psychological perspective', in M. London (ed.), *How People Evaluate Others in Organizations*. Mahwah, NJ: Erlbaum, pp. 221–52.

Smither, J.W., London, M., Flautt, R., Vargas, Y. and Kucrie, I. (2003) 'Can working with an executive coach improve multisource feedback ratings over time? A quasi-experimental field study', *Personnel Psychology*, 56(1): 23–44.

Sosik, J.J. and Megerian, L.E. (1999) 'Understanding leader emotional intelligence and performance: The role of self–other agreement on transformational leadership perceptions', *Group & Organization Management*, 24(3): 367–90.

Special Group in Coaching Psychology (SGCP) (2006) *Guidelines on Supervision for Coaching Psychology*. London: British Psychological Society (BPS).

Spreier, S.W., Fontaine, M.M. and Mallery, R.L. (2006) 'Leadership run amok', *Harvard Business Review*, 84(6): 72–82.

St John-Brooks, K. (2014) *Internal Coaching: The Inside Story*. London: Karnac Books.

Stacey, R.D. (1995) 'The science of complexity: An alternative perspective for strategic change processes', *Strategic Management Journal*, 16(4): 77–95.

Starkey, K., Hatchuel, A. and Tempest, S. (2009) 'Management research and the new logics of discovery and engagement', *Journal of Management Studies*, 46(3): 547–58.

Starr, J. (2002) *The Coaching Manual, The Definitive Guide*. Harlow: Pearson Education.

Stein, I.F. (2009) 'Which hat am I wearing now? An evidence based tool for coaching self-reflection', *Coaching: An International Journal Of Theory, Research and Practice*, 2(2): 163–75.

Stelter, R. (2014) *A Guide to Third Generation Coaching: Narrative-Collaborative Theory and Practice*. Berlin: Springer.

Sterman, J.D. (1994) 'Learning in and about complex systems', *Systems Dynamics Review*, 10(2–3): 291–330.

Stern, L. and Stout Rostron, S. (2013) 'What progress has been made in coaching research in relation to 16 ICRF focus areas from 2008 to 2012?', *Coaching: An International Journal of Theory, Research and Practice*, 6(1): 72–96.

Stewart, J. (2007) 'The future of HRD research: strengths, weaknesses, opportunities, threats, actions', *Human Resource Development International*, 10(1): 93–7.

Stober, D. and Parry, C. (2005) 'Current challenges and future direction of coaching research', in M. Cavanagh, A.M. Grant and T. Kemp (eds), *Evidence-Based Coaching: Theory, Research and Practice from the Behavioural Sciences*. Bowen Hills Old: Australian Academic Press, pp. 13–19.

Stokes, P. (2010) 'What is truth?' Unpublished essay, Sheffield Hallam University Shefield. For access email: r.garvey@yorksj.ac.uk.

Stoltenberg, C.D. and Delworth, U. (1987) *Supervising Counselors and Therapists*. San Fransisco, CA: Jossey-Bass.

Stoltenberg, C.D. and McNeill, B.W. (2010) *IDM Supervision: An Integrated Developmental Model for Supervising Counselors and Therapists*. East Sussex: Routledge, Taylor Francis Group.

Stone, I.F. (1988) *The Trial of Socrates*. Boston, MA: Little, Brown and Co.

Stout Rostron, S. (2009) *Business Coaching: International Transforming Individuals and Organizations*. London: Karnac.

Stout Rostron, S. (2014) *Business Coaching: International Transforming Individuals and Organizations* (2nd edn). London: Karnac.

Strickland, S. (2015) 'Delivering the recommendations of the Fraud Review 2006 and the paradox of police leadership', Doctoral Thesis, University of Middlesex. Available at: http://eprints.mdx.ac.uk/17334/1/SStricklandContextStatement.pdf (accessed 9 October 2015).

Stuart, J. and Hamlyn, B. (1992) 'Competence-based qualifications: The case against change', *Journal of European Industrial Training*, 16(7): 21–32.

Svaleng, I.L.J. and Grant, A.M. (2010) 'Lessons from the Norwegian coaching industry's attempt to develop joint coaching standards: An ACCESS pathway to a mature coaching industry', *Coaching Psychologist*, 6(1): 5–15.

Swanson, R.A. (2001) 'Human resource development and its underlying theory', *Human Resource Development International*, 4(3): 299–312.

Tan, S. and Brown, J. (2005) 'The World Café in Singapore: Creating a learning culture through dialogue', *Journal of Applied Behavioral Science*, 41(1): 83–90.

Tehrani, N. (ed.) (2011) *Managing Trauma in the Workplace: Supporting Workers and Organisations*. Hove: Routledge.

Tehrani, N., Osborne, D. and Lane, D. (2012) 'Restoring meaning and wholeness: The role for coaching after a trauma', *International Coaching Psychology Review*, 7(2): 239–46.

Tennant, M. (1997) *Psychology and Adult Learning*. London: Routledge.

Thomas, L. and Harri-Augstein, S. (1985) *Self-Organised Learning: Foundations of a Conversational Science for Psychology*. London: Routledge & Kegan Paul.

Thomson, B. (2013) *Non-Directive Coaching: Attitudes, Approaches and Applications*. Cheshire: Critical Publishing.

Tomlinson, D. (2008) 'Making coaching part of the culture', *Human Resources*, March: 20.

Towler, J. (2005) 'A grounded theory study of organisational supervision of counsellors: The influence of the invisible client'. PhD thesis, University of Surrey, Guildford.

Tucker, R. (2005) 'Is coaching worth the money? Assessing the ROI of executive coaching', in H. Morgan, P. Hawkins and M. Goldsmith (eds), *The Art And Practice of Leadership Coaching*. Hoboken, NJ: Wiley, pp. 245–54.

Turban, D. and Dougherty, T. (1994) 'Role of protégé personality in receipt of mentoring and career success', *Academy of Management Journal*, 37(3): 688–702.

United Nations (UN) (2007) *Principles for Responsible Management Education (PRME)*. Available at: www.unprme.org/ (accessed 9 October 2015).

UK Gov (2010–2015) *Business Mentors are Ready and Waiting to Support SMEs*. Available at: www.gov.uk/government/news/business-mentors-are-ready-and-waiting-to-support-smes (accessed 16 April 2015).

van Emmerik, I.J.H. (2008) 'It is not only mentoring: The combined influences of individual-level and team-level support on job performance', *Career Development International*, 13(7): 575–93.

van Nieuwerburgh, C. (2012) *Coaching in Education Getting Better Results for Students, Educators and Parents*. London: Karnac.

Visscher, K. (2006) 'Capturing the competence of management consulting work', *Journal of Workplace Learning*, 18(4): 248–60.

Vygotsky, L.S. (1978) *Mind in Society: The Development Of Higher Psychological*. Cambridge, MA: Harvard University Press.

Vygotsky, L.S. (1981) 'The genesis of higher mental functions', in J. Wertsch (ed.), *The Concept Of Activity in Soviet Psychology*. New York: Armonk, pp. 144–88.

Wabbels, H. and Kahaar, I. (2007) *Measuring Coaching: Selling Hot Air or Breaking a Taboo?* Available at: www.kessels-smit.com/files/Artikel_2007_wabbels__kahaar_-_measuring_coching.pdf (accessed 18 February 2014).

Waldegrave, C. (2009) 'Cultural, gender and socio-economic contexts in therapeutic and social policy work', *Family Process*, 48(1): 85–101.

Waldegrave, C. and Tamasese, K. (1993) 'Some central ideas in the "just therapy" approach', *Australian and New Zealand Journal of Family Therapy*, 14(1): 1–8.

Waldrop, M.M. (1992) *Complexity: The Emerging Science at the Edge of Order and Chaos*. London: Viking.

Warr, P., Bird, M. and Rackman, N. (1970) *Evaluation of Management Training*. Aldershot: Gower.

Watkins, M. and Shulman, H. (2008) *Towards Psychologies of Liberation*. London: Palgrave Macmillan.

Watson, J. and Lubker, J. (2015, in press) 'Supervision in applied sport psychology', in D.A. Lane, M. Watts and S. Corrie (eds), *Psychological Supervision*. Maidenhead: Open University Press.

Watson, R. (2010) *Future Files: A Brief History of the Next 59 Years*. London: Nicolas Brealey.

Webb, L., Preskill, H. and Coghlan, A.T. (2005) 'Bridging two disciplines: Applying appreciative inquiry to evaluation practice', *AI Practitioner: The International Journal of AI Best Practice*, February: 1–4.

Webster, F. (1980) *The New Photography: Responsibility in Visual Communication*. London: John Calder.

Western, S. (2012) *Coaching and Mentoring: A Critical Text*. London: Sage.

Wheelahan, L. (2007) 'How competency-based training locks the working class out of powerful knowledge: A modified Bernsteinian analysis', *British Journal of Sociology of Education*, 28(5): 637–51.

Whitmore, J. (2002) *Coaching for Performance: GROWing People, Performance and Purpose* (3rd edn). London: Nicholas Brearley.

Wilber, K. (2000) *Integral Psychology: Consciousness, Spirit, Psychology, Therapy*. Boston, MA: Shambhala Publications.

Wildflower, L. (2013) *The Hidden History of Coaching*. Maidenhead: McGraw-Hill.

Wildflower, L. and Brennan, D. (2011) *The Handbook of Knowledge-Based Coaching: From Theory to Practice*. San Francisco, CA: Jossey-Bass.

Wilkinson, S. (1986) *Feminist Social Psychologies*. Philadelphia, PA: Open University Press.

Williams, D.I. and Irving, J.A. (2001) 'Coaching: An unregulated, unstructured and (potentially) unethical process', *The Occupational Psychologist, British Psychological Society*, 42(April): 3–7.

Williams, H., Palmer, S. and Edgerton, N. (2014) 'Cognitive behavioural coaching', in E. Cox, T. Bachkirova and D. Clutterbuck (eds), *The Complete Handbook of Coaching* (2nd edn). London: Sage, pp. 34–51.

Williams, P. (2006) 'The emergence of academic degrees in personal and professional coaching: What does this mean to the future of coaching?', in P. Williams and S.K. Anderson (eds), *Law and Ethics in Coaching*. New Jersey: John Wiley & Sons, pp. 251–2.

Williams, P. (2010) *The Coaching Profession Grows Up*. Available at: www.life-coachtraining.com/resources/articles/articles/coaching_grows_up.pdf 2 (accessed 2 December 2010).

Williams, P. and Anderson, S.K. (2006) *Law & Ethics in Coaching*. New Jersey: John Wiley & Sons.

Wilson, C. (2007) *Best Practice in Performance Coaching: A Handbook for Leaders, Coaches, HR Professionals and Organizations*. London: Kogan Page.

Wilson, C. (2011) 'Developing a coaching culture', *Industrial and Commercial Training*, 43(7): 407–14.

Woods, D. (2014) 'Fear factor', *Coaching at Work*, 9(5): 28–31.

Yossi, I. (2008) 'What is "coaching"? An exploration of conflicting paradigms', *International Journal of Evidence Based Coaching and Mentoring*, 6(2): 100–13.

Zaleznik, A. (1997) 'Managers and leaders: Are they different?', *Harvard Business Review*, 55(5): 67–78.

Zeus, P. and Skiffington, S. (2000) *The Complete Guide to Coaching at Work*. Sydney: McGraw-Hill.

Zey, M.G. (1984) *The Mentor Connection: Strategic Alliances in Corporate Life*. Homewood, IL: Dow Jones-Irving.

Zey, M.G. (1989) 'Building a successful formal mentor program', *Mentoring International*, 3(1): 48–51.

Index